THE BEST OF
Food&Wine
HOLIDAY COLLECTION

THE BEST OF
Food&Wine
HOLIDAY COLLECTION

American Express
Publishing Corporation
New York

The Best of Food & Wine / HOLIDAY COLLECTION
Designer: Loretta M. Sala
Assistant Editor: Martha Crow
Illustrations: Steven J. Charney

American Express Publishing Corporation
Editor in Chief/Food & Wine: Mary Simons
Art Director/Food & Wine: Elizabeth Woodson
Managing Editor/Books: Kate Slate
Marketing Director: Elizabeth Petrecca
Production Manager: Joanne Maio Canizaro

Published by American Express Publishing Corporation
1120 Avenue of the Americas, New York, New York 10036

Manufactured in the United States of America
ISBN 0-916103-18-8

table of contents

Wine adds a welcome grace note to any dinner table, but never more so than during the holiday season. At this time of year especially, raising a glass with family and friends reminds us that the act of sharing good food and drink rewards us all.

In this practical reference section, you'll find guidance on every aspect of entertaining with wine, from menu planning and matching foods, to selecting proper glassware and pouring. Throughout, there are hints, tips and detailed information on many wine questions that come to mind at holiday time—how to open Champagne safely, decant a bottle of port, find just the right wine to serve with seasonal dishes like roast turkey or glazed ham or to enjoy sipping with fruitcake.

Menu Planning

As every experienced party-giver knows, the right choices are all-important for success, whether you're

sums to serve good wines, it's surprising how many party-givers will lay out a lavish spread of delectable food and then offer an unpalatable, bargain-bin jug wine to accompany it. In other words, don't serve a pizza wine with pâté. Most young simple wines are modestly priced anyway ($10 a bottle or less).

• Offer a red and a white. When you put out an array of dishes, it's likely guests will pick and choose among them, so it makes sense to offer a choice of wines too.

• Choose wines with broad food compatibility. Among reds, choose such wines as Beaujolais, Chianti and California Pinot Noir. Among whites, try Sauvignon Blanc, Bordeaux Blanc sec, Alsace Pinot Blanc and Italian Pinot Grigio. All of these are wines that will go with a wide range of foods. For a celebratory note, you could also offer an attractive California sparkling wine.

entertaining with wine
by Elin McCoy and John Frederick Walker

considering the guest list, the menu—or the wines to pour. Few people have difficulty selecting a bottle to enjoy with a simple family meal, but many find it daunting to choose wines for a crowd, much less decide which wines to serve with a multi-course holiday dinner. But it's not difficult if you first consider the occasion. Will it be casual or formal? Is it a large party with lots of guests or a grand dinner for twelve or an after-dinner get-together for a few close friends.

BUFFET DINNERS
Picking wines for a buffet dinner where a number of dishes are offered together requires a different approach than picking wines to match particular dishes served sequentially. The chief consideration is not whether the wine will be a great match with any particular dish but whether it will be a decent match for almost all of them. Here's what you should keep in mind:

• Pick refreshing wines with straightforward flavors, rather than complex, subtle wines. Young simple wines are likely to bridge the variety of flavors on a buffet table better than a fine old wine.

• Don't skimp on the wine, even if you're having a crowd. Though it isn't necessary to spend extravagant

FORMAL DINNERS
Holidays give many of us the excuse to celebrate with a formal dinner party. What really counts in creating an atmosphere of elegance and sophistication isn't just candlelight and placecards—it's the ease and naturalness with which everything seems to work together, including the wine. That, of course, takes advance planning. When thinking about what wine to serve at a formal dinner, follow these guidelines:

• Offer several different wines. The best way to give maximum sensation with what you pour is to vary it. Since six people at a dinner party may well consume three bottles during a meal, serve three different wines (Champagne, Bordeaux and port, to pick one possible progression) rather than several bottles of the same one.

• Resist the temptation to add a sense of overkill to an already grand table. It's difficult to serve more than four or five courses—and wines to accompany them— without adding confusion and clutter.

• How a succession of courses and wines work together is central to the impression they make. An overly heavy menu—such as a series of richly sauced dishes— doesn't seem half as impressive as a menu that progresses from light to rich. The same applies to the wines served: Start with attractive lighter wines and build to deeper, richer ones.

• The standard advice on serving a sequence of wines is: white before red, young before old, dry before sweet. That's because most white wines seem insubstantial following a red wine and older mature wines usually taste deeper and fuller than young examples. Dry wines stimulate the appetite, while very sweet ones satiate it—which is why they're normally served with dessert. Of course there are exceptions—serving sweet wines as aperitifs, or massively rich whites after very light reds, for example—but most of the time these rules are worth following.

• Remember that the best wine to serve is the wine that goes best with the food (see "Matching Food and Wine," p. 10). A good wine that goes with what's on the plate will always taste better than a grand bottle paired with an inappropriate dish.

Hint: A holiday dinner is often the time when many winelovers pull out a very special wine. If the gastronomic high point of the evening will be the uncorking of, say, a special old Bordeaux, give it a solo bow by pouring it just before serving the course you've paired it with so that it can be appreciated on its own. Be aware that there are risks with any older wine: That Champagne you were given sometime back may have turned flat, that Cabernet that's rested undisturbed in your basement for years may turn out to have a bouquet of old boots. Always have a backup bottle of something similar on hand. . . just in case.

SHOPPING FOR HOLIDAY WINES

How much wine do you need for a party? Use this rule of thumb: You can pour six to eight glasses of wine from a regular bottle (750 ml). Many guests may want only a glass or two, but over the course of a long dinner some guests may consume four or five, from aperitif to dessert wine. Depending on your guests' preferences, not every wine will be equally popular, which means

not every bottle may be finished. To be sure to have enough, plan on a bottle per person overall for a formal dinner and at least a half a bottle per person at a buffet. And when buying wines, remember the following:

• Always try a bottle of wine before buying large quantities. No matter how attractive the price is, no wine is a bargain if you don't like the way it tastes.

• Practice comparison shopping. There are often substantial price differences from store to store, even in the same city; some wine shops hold special sales on items like sparkling wine just before the holidays. If you have a good idea what a wine generally costs, you'll know if a particular offering is a bargain—sale or no sale.

• Shop for quality, not just price. A bargain wine isn't always inexpensive—it's just inexpensive for its quality.

• Plan ahead and buy in advance if possible. This saves money, avoids last minute dashes to the wine store, and lets you pick from the widest possible selection.

Hint: Keep a log of the dinner parties you give, noting the menu, wines, how they worked together and guest preferences. When it comes time to plan another party, it's very useful to have these notes to remind you of possible wine choices and what dishes they complemented. You can also use it to keep track of wines you have on hand at home and to jot down the names of good wines you come across.

What to Buy

APERITIFS/COCKTAIL PARTIES

When you're planning a dinner party it's natural to concentrate on the main event—the dinner and dinner wines. But the time before everyone sits down to eat is equally important. That's the time to set the mood of the evening, start conversations, see to it that everyone is relaxed and comfortable—and to whet your guests' appetites for what's to come. Of course, any advice on what to serve before dinner applies equally well if you're hosting a "cocktail" party where guests will be going on to dinner elsewhere. What's good to drink before a meal-depends in part on what's to follow. If you're planning on pouring fine wine, it makes sense to keep the drinks light.

Sherry is an excellent aperitif choice. Many people think of sherry only as a sweet drink, but in its homeland, Spain, virtually all the sherry that's consumed is bone-dry *fino*. This pale, savory wine is served crackling cold (but not over ice) in small wine glasses as an accompaniment to *tapas*, the famous spicy Spanish appetizers. Fino, in fact, is the ideal choice if you're serving olives, ham or highly seasoned canapés.

Although fino, like all sherries, is a fortified wine and slightly higher in alcohol than table wine, it loses its freshness rapidly. It should be kept in the refrigerator and finished within a few days. Amontillado, another type of aperitif sherry, is slightly browner in color and nuttier in taste than fino, not quite as dry, and especially complements salted nuts. Serve it cool.

The simplest choice for an aperitif is a glass of whatever you'll be drinking with the meal, particularly if it's a crisp white. (see "Light Dry Whites," at right). In fact many people at cocktail parties simply ask for a glass of white wine.

Sparkling wines and Champagnes are always festive aperitifs, never more so than during the holiday season. Those labeled *dry* or *brut* are classic aperitifs that seem to wake up your palate, especially when served with salty or nutty foods, such as roasted almonds, smoked salmon or caviar (see "Guide to Sparkling Wines and Champagne" on the opposite page).

HOLIDAY WHITES

When you scan the crowded shelves of a well-stocked wine store, the choices of white wines seem practically endless. But they're not. Every white wine (other than dessert wines) falls into one of three taste categories: light, dry whites; big, dry whites; and aromatic and fruity whites. What's more, with most white wines, you needn't worry about the vintage, except to buy the youngest, freshest examples.

Light Dry Whites

Light dry whites are what to serve when you want something crisp, clean-flavored and not too heavy—the sort of wine that's ideal to accompany lighter, first-course foods such as shrimp or sole or to have on hand for aperitifs. A light white is generally not aged in bar-

rels (which imparts a richer, deeper taste) and is bottled soon after the vintage to bring out its freshness. It also tastes light because it is low in alcohol—about 11 to 12%. Here are some types to look for:

Wines made from Sauvignon Blanc grapes (or blends of Sauvignon Blanc and Sémillon grapes) are crisp, savory and appetizing, with an attractive herbaceous aroma. These moderately priced wines are particularly good with fish, pasta and tangy goat cheeses. In California, Sauvignon Blanc wines are sometimes labeled Fumé Blanc.

From France, look for Sancerre and Pouilly-Fumé from the Loire Valley, which are also made from the Sauvignon Blanc grape. Other good-value French whites made primarily from Sauvignon Blanc are Entre-deux-Mers and Bordeaux Blanc Sec. Additional attractive light dry French whites made from other grapes include Muscadet from the Loire (a classic accompaniment to shellfish) and the sharp-flavored Aligoté from Burgundy.

Italy has scores of light, dry good-value whites made from various local grapes. Soave, Orvieto, Galestro and Pinot Grigio are among the best choices. Spain has several good blended whites, including white Rioja.

Big Dry Whites

Big dry whites are richer, more mouth-filling, and have more complex flavors than the simpler, lighter whites—just what's wanted for richer fish (such as salmon), chicken in cream sauce or roasted veal. The impression of "bigness" these wines make is partly due to their higher alcohol—12 to 14%—and the fact that many are aged in small oak barrels prior to bottling, which imparts additional flavor and depth.

White Rhônes from France and Sémillon from Australia are among the whites that fall into this category, but the most important "big" white grape by far is Chardonnay.

The white Burgundies of France, such as Meursault, Puligny-Montrachet, Corton Charlemagne and the like are all made from the Chardonnay grape, and are usually expensive. The whites from the Mâcon region of Burgundy (such as Mâcon-Lugny and Mâcon-Viré), although not as full-flavored as their more famous cousins, are moderately priced.

California, Oregon and Washington State produce outstanding Chardonnays that are deep-flavored and round-textured. The complexity and depth of a fine one makes it a wine worth lingering over, and a perfect

continued on page 10

First there's the loud pop, the splash of rising foam in the flute, followed by streams of tiny, racing bubbles sending up a subtle, enticing scent. Then, that matchless taste...dancing, delicate, tartly crisp. It's no wonder a glass of fine sparkling wine is synonymous with celebration.

Champagne, the classic bottling from the French region of the same name, is the most famous sparkling wine, but top-quality examples of the breed are now produced in the U.S. (notably in California), Australia, Spain, Italy and the Loire region of France. The best of these use the traditional Champagne grapes (Chardonnay and Pinot Noir) and follow the time-consuming *méthode champenoise* for production (and often say so on the label). The result is a wine that's superb as an aperitif, remarkably versatile as a dinner wine and almost obligatory for special holiday gatherings.

Serving Sparkling Wine

The palate-tickling effervescence and bracing natural acidity of dry sparkling wines and Champagnes labeled brut is what makes these wines so appetite-enhancing, particularly in combination with salty or nutty hors d'oeuvres. Lighter blanc de blanc bottlings, which emphasize the elegance of Chardonnay and other white grapes, are particularly good as aperitifs. For a large holiday crowd, consider serving a variant of the classic Champagne cocktail. Simply add a dash of cassis to a good sparkling wine, just enough to turn it an attractive rose color and to add an attractive fruity flavor. French Champagne is unnecessarily subtle and expensive for this; instead, buy a dry Spanish *cava* or French sparkling wine from the Loire Valley, which are priced so you can fill a punch bowl for holiday parties. (Add strawberries for a festive garnish.)

Sparkling Wine at the Table

If there's one time of the year when a Champagne dinner doesn't seem an extravagance, it's at holiday time. It's a natural for New Year's Eve. Because its effervescence provides a textural contrast to whatever is being served, Champagne is the one wine traditionally recommended for serving throughout a meal. In truth there are any number of dishes for which this tart, tingling wine would be a poor choice, but there's something about the bubbles and crisp acidity that stands up to a wide variety of foods, from briny shellfish to lighter meat dishes and delicate, nonsugary desserts.

Although it's possible to serve one type of sparkling wine throughout a dinner, it's much more fun to pour a variety. Most of the well-known Champagne firms—and the best sparkling wine producers—offer a range of different styles. If you've started with a crisp blanc de blancs, choose a deeper flavored brut for the first course. Serving a dry, distinguished rosé bottling with the main course is a marvelous touch. With dessert, serve a sweeter demi-sec bottling for a delightful finale.

Buying Sparkling Wine

As every winelover knows, there are sparkling wines to fit every budget, from $3 bubblies to $100 deluxe Champagnes. It's certainly not necessary to pay extravagant sums to get good sparkling wine, but the most inexpensive examples are rarely good buys. To produce such "bargain" bubbly, a winery has to use low-end grapes and rapid bulk processes. It's not surprising, therefore, that the best values in sparkling wines fall into the $10 to $25 per bottle range. (French Champagne starts at about $20 and goes up from there.) Savvy shoppers should watch for sales and other discounts on sparkling wine and Champagnes before and during the holidays.

How to Open Sparkling Wine

Opening a bottle of sparkling wine so that it makes a bang certainly sounds festive, but it often results in a rocketing cork and a wasteful, if spectacular, gush. Because the contents of any sparkling wine are under significant pressure, it's much safer to ease the cork out slowly to avoid injuring yourself or guests. The secret is to never take your hand off the cork. Here's how to do it:

Without shaking the bottle, stand it up on a solid surface and remove the top half of the neck foil. Keeping one hand over the cork, loosen the wire cage with the other. Don't remove it—simply grip the cork and cage firmly, and holding the bottle at a 45° angle, gently twist the bottle off the cork (not the cork out of the bottle, which may break it). Hold the open bottle at the same angle for a few seconds to allow the pressure to equalize, then pour—just a splash. When the foam subsides, slowly top up the glass. Remember that tall flutes look prettier and are easier to handle than saucer-shaped glasses, and they show off the wine better.

Hint: In the unlikely event you have any sparkling wine left over, cap the opened bottle with a Champagne stopper, which will keep the fizz from going flat for a day or two if refrigerated.

continued from page 8
accompaniment to rich dishes such as fish terrines.

Aromatic and Fruity Whites

Wines in this group range from dry to fruity-sweet and light and delicate to intense and striking. What they all share, however, are scents and flavors that suggest perfume, flowers or spice. These wines are extremely versatile on the table, complementing foods for which it can be difficult to find a suitable wine match.

Take baked ham. The saltiness of the meat and the sweetness imparted by honey, sugar or fruit glazes make many dry whites and reds seemed stripped of flavor. While a fruity red is one possible choice, even better is a not-quite-dry white, which will balance the intensity of the ham and the sweetness of the accompanying flavors surprisingly well.

Among the wines to look for in this category are the fragrant and ripely sweet Chenin Blancs, Johannisberg Rieslings and Gewürztraminers from California and the Northwest. In France, Chenin Blanc is widely grown in the Loire Valley region where it is used in the fruity-tart wines of Vouvray.

Johannisberg Riesling is the same grape as the classic Riesling of Germany. At their best, German wines have an enticing floral scent and a ripely sweet flavor balanced by refreshing acidity. Although low in alcohol (9 to 10%) and therefore light in body, their crispness allows them to stand up well to rich foods.

France's Alsace region offers a range of wines with a very distinctive style: bone-dry and aromatic. They're all labeled by the grape used to make the wine—Pinot Blanc, Sylvaner and Pinot Gris as well as Riesling and Gewürztraminer, which has a distinctly spicy scent reminiscent of cloves or allspice and a rich, pungent flavor. Alsace Gewürztraminer is the white to pick if you're looking for one that can stand up to foods normally paired with red wine: duck, pork roast, sausages, quiche.

There's one last category of wines that's best discussed with white wines, because they're also served chilled: rosés. White Zinfandel and other California blush wines are just barely pink, slightly sweet and simple in taste. True rosés are darker pink and the best are fine, dry to off-dry, and characterful. Look for Grenache Rosés and rosés of Cabernet Sauvignon from California and French rosés from Provence and Tavel. These better rosés are excellent with ham, turkey, fish soups and stews, and look particularly attractive on a holiday table.

HOLIDAY REDS

Like white wines, reds can be grouped into three broad taste categories—in this case, light reds, medium-bodied reds and big reds. Light reds are simpler and usually more obviously fruity, while medium and big ones are more complex, with layers of flavor.

All wines change as they age, but few white wines or light reds change for the better. On the other hand, some of the best medium-bodied and big reds do improve if stored under good conditions for several years (or more) before being opened— they become softer and more mellow, gaining additional nuances of flavor in the process.

Light Reds

For informal holiday dining or large crowds, a light, fruity, unfussy red that doesn't require aging, goes with a wide variety

---

MATCHING FOOD AND WINE

The easiest way to find a wine match for a particular meal is to start by thinking of the wine as a special kind of side dish, one that can either complement the food or contrast pleasantly with it—and sometimes both.

To complement the food, a wine should have some similarities with what's being served, such as flavor, intensity or richness. For example:

• Is the dish heavy or light? Substantial food calls for substantial wines; delicate food calls for delicate wines.

• Sophisticated, subtle wines show best with sophisticated subtle food; simple, hearty wines are the best choice with simple, hearty food.

A wine can also contrast attractively with food by its astringency, acidity or flavor. Here are some examples:

• A light, delicate white is appropriate in size and intensity to a dish such as sole stuffed with shrimp. A light white with tart acidity, however, adds a welcoming contrasting note as well—almost like a squeeze of lemon.

• Many rich dishes are nicely balanced by reds with some cutting astringency. A Cabernet Sauvignon has the meaty full flavor to match roast lamb, but also a dry, tannic quality that cuts across the fattiness.

• Similarly, a mildly sweet wine can balance salty flavors (as in ham) as well as a certain amount of spiciness and heat, and a wine with ripe, fruity flavors can add interest to mild dishes such as roast turkey.

of foods, isn't expensive—and tastes good enough to invite a second glass—is ideal.

The quintessential light red is Beaujolais. This French wine is lively, refreshing and zestful and goes with foods as diverse as sausages, chicken, ham, country pâté and just about any cheese. Beaujolais *nouveau* (or *primeur*) is the first Beaujolais available after the harvest, usually in time for Thanksgiving. This superfruity wine is intended for consumption within six months or so, and is at its best during the holiday season. The best Beaujolais come from individual districts, such as Moulin à Vent, Morgon or Brouilly.

The California equivalent to Beaujolais is labeled Gamay (or Gamay Beaujolais) and features much of the same bright grapiness and wide food affinity. Dolcetto is Italy's answer to Beaujolais, an intensely fruity Piemontese red that is similar in style but different in flavor.

Pinot Noir, the classic grape of red Burgundy, yields fruity but subtle wines, with layers of silky-textured, sometimes cherry-like flavors that gain pungency with a few years of bottle age. France's Burgundy region produces a small amount of these famous reds and while simple Bourgogne Rouge or Côte de Beaune Villages can be modestly priced, wines from specific communes such as Nuit-Saint-Georges, Pommard, Volnay or Gevrey-Chambertin can be expensive. These superb, scented wines are splendid with veal, fowl and tender beef dishes such as prime rib.

Excellent Pinot Noirs are also produced in Oregon's Willamette Valley and from several regions in California, notably the Carneros district, and are moderately priced. All of the above are particularly good choices when there's turkey on the table. If it were a matter of finding a wine match for the bird alone, any number of whites and reds would be compatible with its mild-flavored meat. The wine-matching problems come with the strongly flavored side dishes and trimmings—sweet potatoes, cranberry relish, creamed onions and the like. The type of wine most likely to bridge the welter of flavors found in such a spread is a light red whose tart fruitiness echoes the effect of the traditional relishes and trimmings. Alternatively one could serve a rosé or rosé Champagne.

Medium-Bodied Reds

This is the most versatile red wine category on the holiday table because most medium-bodied reds have enough character to stand up to rich entrees like leg of lamb or pork loin but won't overpower delicate dishes such as chicken or veal.

The best-known medium-bodied reds are made from Cabernet Sauvignon. One of the main grapes used for the famous château wines in France's Bordeaux region, it also makes superb wine in California, Australia, Chile and many other wine regions.

Regardless of source, all Cabernet wines have a strong family resemblance: The aroma and flavor often suggests blackcurrant or olives, and the texture is usually quite dry, even mouth-puckering. That's due to the presence of astringent tannins, which can make the wine seem slightly harsh-tasting when young but that soften as the wine ages.

In California, many of the best Cabernet Sauvignons come from the northern counties of Napa and Sonoma. Many of these Cabernets are blended with related grapes such as Merlot, which is increasingly bottled on its own and has the virtue of Cabernet-like flavors but a softer texture.

In Bordeaux, Cabernet Sauvignon is blended with grape varieties that have similar flavors, primarily Merlot and Cabernet Franc. Many Bordeaux wines from well-known districts like the Médoc, Graves, Pomerol and St. Emilion are made by individual estates that market their wines under the château names that appear on the label. A fine, mature Bordeaux is a classic choice to accompany roast goose, duck or game birds.

Italy and Spain also make excellent medium-bodied reds. Chianti, perhaps Italy's most famous wine, is fragrant and piquant in flavor with a dry finish, and Spain's Rioja is smooth and balanced with attractive nuances from long aging in barrels.

Big Reds

The best wine to serve with a holiday dinner isn't always the "best" wine—it depends on the dinner. The nuances of a fine red Burgundy will be lost if you serve it with a hearty cassoulet or venison stew. That sort of full-flavored, savory food is best matched with a big, generous red wine.

In France's Rhône Valley, the northern districts such as Côte Rôtie, St. Joseph and Gigondas make wines primarily from the Syrah grape. They're classic big reds—full-bodied wines with plenty of up-front flavor and spiciness. Similar wines are made in California from the same grape and a related one, Petite Sirah. Another good-value big red from California is Zinfandel—red Zinfandel—which ranges from light and spicy to dark, peppery and powerful.

Barolo and Barbaresco, produced from the Nebbiolo grape, are Italy's big reds. Both have striking, pungent aromas suggesting berries and mushrooms and often have a tarry note or hint of licorice that also comes through in the flavor. Tannic in character with a dry finish, they're excellent with game dishes, garlicky roasts, winter-weight stews and strong cheeses.

DESSERT WINES

If there's one time of the year when opening a dessert wine seems particularly appropriate, it's during the holidays. Although many people think that serving a special wine just to accompany dessert is overkill—especially if they've already offered a red or white with the main course—it's really more a matter of variety than it is of more wine.

The key rule to remember in choosing a wine for a particular dessert is that the dessert shouldn't be sweeter than the wine. Otherwise the wine will seem diminished in flavor, which is why brut Champagne—often recommended with dessert—rarely works well. But if the dessert isn't overrich, a sweeter sparkling wine, such as Italian Asti Spumante, a Muscat such as Beaumes de Venise from France, a late-harvest Riesling from Germany, California or Australia, a Sauternes or port is likely to turn the last course into a grand finale.

In Italy, Muscat wines other than Asti Spumante are labeled Moscato. These are light and delicious, low in alcohol, and often have a very slight sparkle. They're perfect for pairing with berries and cream, cakes and

meringues. Beaumes de Venise is much more intense Muscat, and will stand up to fruit tarts and even homemade ice cream.

Late-harvest Rieslings, with their concentrated, honeyed, apricot-like flavors, are delightful with mild desserts such as Charlotte Russe. Fine Sauternes from the Bordeaux region of France are probably the most famous dessert wines in the world—golden-hued, luscious and lingering. Sauternes are expensive but worth the price for the dramatic impression they make. (Besides, a little goes a long way at that point in the meal.) Sip them alongside lemon soufflé; alternatively, consider a fine Sauternes as dessert in itself, perhaps serving it with a wedge of tangy Roquefort cheese for a striking contrast of flavors.

Port is an increasingly popular fortified wine whose warmth and flavor seem tailor-made for appreciation during the fall and winter months. Four types of port are of interest during the holidays. Ruby port is red and fruity-sweet, and one of the few wines that really goes well with chocolate desserts—provided they aren't too sugary or bitter. Late-bottled vintage port (LBV) is essentially a fine ruby from a particular year. Aged in cask for several years, it does not need decanting. Vintage port is one of the world's great wines, produced only in the best years. It is expensive and requires a decade or more to mature and soften; it also requires decanting. But it is a splendid drink that never fails to impress, especially when showcased with Stilton cheese and some walnuts. Tawny port is aged in cask for many years until it turns golden brown in color and gains a nutty dimension to its warm fruity flavor, which complements nuts or fruitcake.

Hint: During the holidays, tawny ports, as well as nutty, mildly-sweet amontillado and oloroso sherries and smoky, tangy Bual and Malmsey Madeiras are ideal to have on hand to offer guests that drop by. These classic fortified wines are excellent choices for sipping anytime. For one thing, once opened, a bottle will last far longer (weeks, in fact) than any opened table wine will. These wines' concentrated flavor means a small glass is just right, and their balanced sweetness makes the drink complete in itself, although all are fine companions to nuts, mild cakes, cookies, fruitcake and hard cheeses.

Serving

While there's no mystery to wine service—after all, it's basically a matter of opening and pouring—there are some details that are foolish to ignore. The correct serving temperature for reds and whites, scrupulously clean glasses, careful matching of wine and food and the like—all enhance the wine. Use the following as a checklist to be sure that the wine you serve shows at its best.

GLASSWARE

Wineglasses come in all shapes, sizes and colors, but not all are equally flattering to wine. In fact, the impression you have of a wine's smell and taste is directly influenced by the design of the glass. When you're choosing glasses, keep in mind these requirements:

• The glass should be clear, not tinted, and the bowl should be undecorated, so you can appreciate the color of the wine.

• The lip of the glass should curve in to concentrate the wine's bouquet.

• For table wines, the glass should have a capacity of at least 10 ounces. Why this big? To taste and sniff a wine, you need about 4 ounces in the glass, and wine glasses are traditionally filled only half full. That's so the wine can be swirled without spilling and the bouquet can develop.

• The stem of the wineglass should be long enough for the glass to be held by the stem alone. That makes it easier to see the color of the wine and keeps fingermarks off the bowl.

• Almost every European wine district has its own traditional wineglass design, but actually there are only a few basic shapes. The first is the classic tulip-shaped Bordeaux glass. It's the least specialized and consequently the most useful. If you want a single, all-purpose design, this style is the one to buy or to rent from a caterer for a big party.

If your budget and storage space permit, there are three additional types you might want. To showcase fine red wine, especially Pinot Noir, there's nothing better than generous-sized, rounded Burgundy "balloons." For sparkling wine, there's the classic Champagne flute, whose tall, slim profile shows off bubbles best. The tasting glass design, based on a small, chimney-shaped glass professionals often use in analyzing wines, makes an excellent glass for sherry, port and brandy.

Hint: Glasses that are clean to the eye may have traces of unrinsed dishwashing soap, residual kitchen smells, a cardboard aroma from storage in a box or even a water stink, which the alcohol in wine will exaggerate. If you have any doubts about the glassware

you're planning to use, rinse it in warm water and hand-dry it with a clean linen towel.

TABLESETTING

There aren't any complications to serving wine with simple meals: Just pour and enjoy. But when you're having a four-course formal holiday dinner for eight, with two or more wines, questions arise. Do the bottles belong on the table? Do you need a separate glass for each wine? Should guests help themselves? Here are some tips on how to serve several different wines at a dinner:

• Prepare everything ahead. Let's say you're going to serve a white with the first course, a red with the main course, and a sweet wine with dessert. Keep the white waiting in an ice bucket or wine cooler on the table (it makes an inviting centerpiece), the red standing on a nearby sideboard or serving table, and the dessert wine in the refrigerator for later use. In many cases, wines can be opened ahead of time and the corks replaced for easy removal by hand.

• Always use a different glass for each wine. This not only avoids mixing tastes, but putting all the glasses out tells guests how much wine to expect. Most important, it allows them to move on to the next wine without having to finish the one before. Glasses can be the same style. Pour the first wine in the outside glass; the next wine goes in the one to the left of it.

• In most cases, put bottles on the table. Except for very formal dinners, bottles look handsome on dinner tables (but use a wine coaster to protect the tablecloth). On the other hand, decanters are less likely to drip and are necessary when serving an old red that has sediment.

• Let guests serve themselves. Pour out the first glass of white wine just before guests come to the table, but after that the host or hostess can pour a glass for the guest to their left and ask them to pass the wine.

• Always provide water and water glasses for winedrinkers as well as for people who will drink little or no wine; it discourages using wine as a thirst-quencher.

SERVING TEMPERATURES

The reason it's worth serving wines at their appropriate temperatures is because they taste better that way. But you don't need a thermometer if you understand these basic principles:

• White wines are served chilled to underscore their refreshing character; reds are served warmer to maximize bouquet and flavor.

• The ideal temperatures for various wines depends on their character and quality. Fine white wines shouldn't be overchilled because chilling flattens flavor. But for that reason, inexpensive, not-so-subtle jug whites are best served very cold to mask their shortcomings.

• About 45 to 50° F is just right for a fine white (or rosé). That's the temperature that an unchilled bottle will reach after about 90 minutes in the refrigerator.

• The long-standing advice that reds are best at room temperature is sound—if you keep your thermostat at 65° F. That's ideal for tannic reds such as Bordeaux, California Cabernet Sauvignon or Chianti Riserva. But served too warm (over 70° F) these reds taste dull and soupy. Light reds, such as Pinot Noir and Beaujolais, are best when cooler—around 60° F. Don't hesitate to refrigerate a red—half an hour will cool a wine ten degrees.

• The quickest way to cool wine is in ice and water; that's much faster than ice alone. Put the bottle in an ice bucket (which can be anything from a plastic keeper to an antique Georgian silver punch bowl), add one or two trays of ice cubes and fill with cold water. A bottle of white wine will be chilled in half an hour. The problem with most ice buckets, however, is that they are too short for tall bottles. If yours isn't tall enough, turn the bottle upside down for five minutes before opening. If you're chilling wines for a crowd, use a large plastic tub filled with ice and water.

• Once the bottle is chilled it can be kept cold in a wine cooler—a tall, insulated cylinder that retards warming. Some utilize pre-chilled inserts or evaporation to achieve the same end.

OPENING WINE BOTTLES

What stands between you and the wine in a bottle is a cork, which requires a special tool to remove. Invest in a corkscrew that uses leverage, not muscle power, to lift out the cork. The coil (the part that goes into the cork) should look like a stretched-out spring.

Don't forget to remove the foil capsule that covers the top of the cork and the neck of the bottle before inserting the corkscrew. Simply cut the top of the capsule off below the bottle lip. Always take a moment to wipe off the top of the cork with the damp corner of a napkin before uncorking, and wipe again if necessary.

Ease out the cork slowly to prevent it from breaking in half. (If it does, and the remaining part can't be removed, push it into the bottle and decant the contents through a fine wire strainer into another container.)

LETTING WINES "BREATHE"

The notion that wines, particularly reds, taste better if opened some time before serving is widely held but has no basis in fact. Though some winelovers prefer the softer tasting impressions certain fine reds have after modest airing in a decanter, wines actually get all the aeration they need from being poured into a wineglass; it's foolish to think you have to *wait* for them to "breathe" before drinking.

POURING LIKE A PRO

Wine bottles may be just the right shape for aging wine, but their design leaves something to be desired when it comes to pouring out the contents. No matter how carefully it's done, there always seems to be some dribbling. It helps to follow these steps:

• Have a napkin in one hand while you pour with the other.

• Pour slowly, but don't pour hesitantly—that just causes wine to run down the neck of the bottle.

• As you finish pouring the wine, tilt the bottle up. To forestall dripping, give it a slight twist before you pull it away from the glass.

• Dab the mouth of the bottle with the napkin to dry it before pouring the next glass.

DECANTING

Decanting a wine—pouring it into another container for serving—is done for two reasons: Decanters are easier than bottles to pour from at the table. And when a fine old red wine is served, decanting separates the clear wine from the harmless but cloudy sediment that's precipitated after years in the bottle, so that it doesn't end up in the glass.

In practice, this means decanting is really only necessary for substantial reds (Bordeaux, Cabernet Sauvignon, Rhônes, Barolo, vintage port) over a decade old. Since the point is to remove the clear wine from the dregs, it helps to stand the bottle up for an hour (or day) before opening to let the sediment settle.

To decant you'll need a decanter (antiques are nice but a plain carafe works as well), a light source and a corkscrew. Hold the neck of the opened bottle over a lamp, upright flashlight or candle (romantic, but hot) so you can stop pouring when you see the sediment beginning to slide down the shoulder of the bottle toward the neck. Don't omit the light—it eliminates guesswork. Now pour the clear wine in a slow, smooth motion—try not to let it gurgle—into the decanter, and you're ready to serve.

beverages

Colonel Talbott's Bourbon Punch

36 Servings

1 cup sugar
10 whole cloves
2 cinnamon sticks
2 liters bourbon
2 cups apple brandy, such as
  applejack
2 cups orange liqueur,
  preferably Grand Marnier
2 tablespoons aromatic bitters
3 seedless oranges, cut in half
  and then into thin slices
1 lime, thinly sliced
2 apples, cut into 1-inch cubes
1 cup strong freshly brewed
  black tea
1 quart club soda

1. In a small saucepan, combine the sugar with 1 cup of water. Bring to a boil over moderately low heat and cook, stirring to dissolve the sugar, for 5 minutes. Add the cloves and cinnamon sticks, remove the syrup from the heat and let cool.

2. In a large punch bowl, combine the bourbon, apple brandy, orange liqueur, bitters, orange slices, lime slices, apple cubes and tea. Add the syrup and let stand, covered, for 30 minutes, or until cooled to room temperature. Before serving, add ice and pour in the soda.
—*W. Peter Prestcott*

Christmas Melon Ball

This drink from the Inn on the Park in Houston stirs up pleasant memories of more innocent times. Some of us, when we were kids, would collect freshly fallen snow and drizzle fruit syrup over the top. (We also did it with shaved ice during the summer.) If making crushed ice presents a problem or simply isn't to your liking, this recipe is also excellent on the rocks.

1 Serving

1½ ounces Midori (melon
  liqueur)
1½ ounces vodka
6 ounces orange juice
Grenadine
Maraschino cherry, for
  garnish

Mix the Midori, vodka and orange juice together and pour over crushed ice (or ice cubes) in a tall Collins glass. Sprinkle with grenadine. Garnish with a cherry.
—*Warren Picower*

North Woods Apple Sour

4 Servings

½ cup (4 ounces) blended
  whiskey
2 cups apple juice
4 to 6 tablespoons fresh lime
  juice
2 tablespoons maple syrup
⅛ teaspoon cinnamon
⅛ teaspoon ground cloves
Club soda

In a blender, combine the whiskey, apple juice, 4 tablespoons of the lime juice, the maple syrup, cinnamon and cloves. Mix at high speed for 1 minute. Taste and add additional lime juice if desired. Pour into four 8-ounce glasses filled with ice. Top with club soda.
—*W. Peter Prestcott*

Cognac Eggnog

This heady potion will ensure good spirits and holiday cheer. Serve it chilled in a punch bowl or glass pitcher and let your guests indulge themselves. Eggnog will keep in the refrigerator for up to one week.

Makes About 2 Quarts

8 eggs
¾ cup sugar
3 cups milk
2 cups heavy cream
1¼ cups Cognac
1 teaspoon vanilla extract
¾ teaspoon freshly grated
  nutmeg

1. In a large bowl, whisk the eggs and ¼ cup of the sugar until they fall in a ribbon when the whisk is lifted, about 2 minutes.

2. In a heavy medium saucepan, place the milk, cream and remaining ½ cup sugar. Bring to a boil, stirring to dissolve the sugar. Whisk all the hot liquid into the egg mixture.

3. Let the eggnog cool for 5 minutes. Stir in the Cognac, vanilla and nutmeg. Pour the eggnog into two 1-quart bottles, cover and let cool; then refrigerate.
—*Diana Sturgis*

U.N. Plaza Eggnog

For many of us, eggnog is the quintessential holiday season beverage. This rich, coffee-almond flavored cup from the United Nations Plaza Hotel in New York can easily be multiplied to fill your holiday punchbowl.

1 Serving

3 ounces eggnog, chilled
1 ounce Amaretto
½ ounce Kahlúa
Dark bitter chocolate, shaved,
* for garnish*

Combine the eggnog, Amaretto and Kahlúa in an old-fashioned glass and gently stir. Garnish with shaved dark bitter chocolate.
—*Warren Picower*

Fraunces Tavern's Syllabub

Dictionaries despair of identifying the origins of the word "syllabub." However, all authorities agree that the drink has been around for a very long time. It was popular in Elizabethan England and in the early colonies. If there were a single cardinal rule for making a correct syllabub, it would be "Thou shalt bring forth froth!" Also a key to an authentic syllabub is the snappily flavored curdling of cream or rich milk provoked by the acid in fresh lemon juice, wine or cider. The alcoholic components of a syllabub vary somewhat from era to era and continent to continent, ranging from bourbon to ale.

Whatever its proportions, as a holiday drink, syllabub is considerably lighter than eggnog. When sweetened to the degree suggested by Fraunces Tavern, it could also make an interesting alternative to dessert and liqueur, much like an Irish Coffee, serving as an all-in-one finale.

6 Servings

1¼ cups sugar
6 cups red wine
½ cup sweet sherry
Juice and grated zest of
* 1 lemon*
2 cups heavy cream, chilled
Freshly grated nutmeg
* (optional)*

1. In a bowl, stir ¾ cup of the sugar into the wine and stir to dissolve. Divide the sweetened wine among 6 glasses, filling the glasses only three-fourths full.

2. In a mixing bowl, combine the sherry, lemon juice and zest and the remaining ½ cup sugar. Stir until the sugar has dissolved.

3. Add the cream and slowly whisk until it froths. Spoon the sherry-cream topping into the glasses. Sprinkle lightly with nutmeg, if desired.
—*Fraunces Tavern, New York City*

Mulled Wine

An international panacea for an overdose of winter weather, mulled wine has been around in one form or another from possibly as early as the 13th century. Fundamentally a drink made by heating red wine with spices—usually cinnamon and nutmeg—mulled wine has a number of guises: It is *glögg* in Scandinavia, *Gluhwein* in Germany and *vin chaud* in France. French mountaineers add a dash of vanilla and a pinch of white pepper to their *vin chaud*. The most complicated version, Scandinavian *glögg,* goes on to add, at the very least, cardamom pods, almonds, raisins and, for the very hearty, aquavit or vodka.

Although practically any dry red table wine can be used for mulled wine, most early recipes specified Bordeaux- or Burgundy-type reds. The trick to a successful brew lies in the heating. The wine should be warmed, not boiled. In colonial America, the wine was heated with an instrument called a loggerhead—a pokerlike implement that was held over burning logs and then plunged into the wine. Another method of heating called for placing the container of wine directly in the fire. No advice on how best to remove it is extant.

8 Servings

3 allspice berries
6 whole cloves
5 cinnamon sticks
¼ teaspoon caraway seeds,
* lightly crushed (optional)*
½ cup sugar

2 lemons, thinly sliced
*1 bottle (750 ml) Bordeaux or
  other dry red wine*

1. Tie the allspice, cloves, cinnamon sticks and caraway seeds in a square of cheesecloth.

2. In a large nonreactive saucepan, combine 2 cups of water with the sugar, add the bag of spices and bring the mixture to a boil over hight heat. Lower the heat and simmer for 10 minutes. Remove from the heat.

3. Add the lemon slices and let them stand in the mixture, covered, for 20 minutes.

4. Add the wine and heat over moderate heat until hot but not boiling, about 10 minutes. Remove and discard the bag of spices.

5. To serve, ladle into mugs or punch cups.

NOTE: In the summer, try chilled mulled wine for a refreshing change from sangria.

—F&W

Bischop Wyn

For a special touch, float a pint of brandy on top of the mixture and ignite it with a match.

32 Servings

*1 gallon full-bodied red jug
  wine*
1 teaspoon whole cloves
2 teaspoons cinnamon
½ cup raisins
1 orange, sliced
Sugar

In a large nonreactive stockpot, combine 2 quarts of water with the wine, cloves, cinnamon, raisins, orange slices and sugar to taste. Heat, but do not boil. Serve in coffee mugs or 6-ounce tumblers. (If using a glass tumbler, place a spoon in it and pour the hot wine down the back of the spoon into the tumbler to prevent the glass from cracking.)
—F&W

Gluhwein

2 Servings

Thick slice of lemon
4 whole cloves
2 cinnamon sticks
*2 cups full-bodied red jug
  wine*
Sugar

In a nonreactive saucepan, bring 1 cup of water, the lemon, cloves and cinnamon sticks to a boil and boil for 5 minutes. Remove from the heat. Add the wine and reheat, but do not boil. Add sugar to taste and serve in a coffee mug.
—F&W

Mulled Cider

2 Servings

*2½ cups unfiltered,
  unpasteurized apple cider*
*1 teaspoon finely grated
  lemon zest*
*1 cardamom pod, slightly
  crushed, or a pinch of
  ground cardamom*
*1 large cinnamon stick,
  broken in half*
*3 whole cloves, slightly
  crushed*
*2 allspice berries, slightly
  crushed*
*1 slice of orange, halved, or
  coarsely grated orange zest,
  for garnish*
Cinnamon, for garnish

In a small saucepan, combine the cider, lemon zest, cardamom, cinnamon stick, cloves and allspice. Bring to a boil over high heat. Reduce the heat to very low and simmer for 10 minutes. Strain the cider into two mugs. Float half an orange slice sprinkled with cinnamon in each or stir in the grated zest and sprinkle cinnamon on top. Serve hot.
—Linda Merinoff

Cider Wassail Bowl

12 Servings

*1 large tart baking apple, such
  as Granny Smith or
  Greening—unpeeled, cored
  and cut into ½-inch slices*
1 teaspoon lemon juice
*¼ cup plus 1 tablespoon
  (packed) dark brown sugar*
1 tablespoon unsalted butter
1 quart apple cider
*1 tablespoon grated lemon
  zest*
*1 tablespoon grated orange
  zest*
5 whole cardamom pods
6 allspice berries
*1 cinnamon stick, broken in
  half*
6 whole cloves
½ cup dark rum
*½ cup apple brandy, such as
  Calvados or applejack*
1 can (12 ounces) light ale
*¼ teaspoon freshly grated
  nutmeg*

1. Preheat the oven to 300°. Toss the apple slices in the lemon juice. Arrange them in a shallow baking pan in a single layer; sprinkle with 1 tablespoon of the brown sugar and dot with the butter.

2. Bake for about 20 minutes, or until the apples are tender; let cool slightly.

3. Bring the cider, lemon and orange zests and the remaining ¼ cup brown sugar to a boil over high heat in a large saucepan, stirring to dissolve the sugar. Tie the cardamom, allspice, cinnamon and cloves in cheesecloth and add to the cider mixture. Cover and simmer over low heat for 20 minutes.

4. Add the rum, apple brandy and ale and return to a simmer. Remove from the heat and discard the spice bag.

5. Pour the cider into a punch bowl, garnish with the apple slices and sprinkle with the nutmeg. Serve hot in punch cups or small mugs.
—*Melanie Barnard*

Spirited Citrus Cup

Makes About 1½ Quarts

¼ cup honey
½ teaspoon grated orange zest
2 cups orange juice
*3 tablespoons fresh lemon
  juice*
6 whole cloves
*1¼ cups Cognac or other
  brandy*
*2 tablespoons orange liqueur,
  such as Triple-Sec*

1. Place the honey and orange zest in a medium nonreactive saucepan with 2½ cups of water. Bring to a boil, stirring occasionally, and cook until the honey dissolves completely.

2. Add the orange juice, lemon juice and cloves and return to a boil. Remove from the heat and immediately stir in the Cognac and orange liqueur. Serve in heatproof punch glasses.
—*Warren Picower*

Norman Hot Toddy

4 Servings

1 cup milk
⅓ cup heavy cream
1 cinnamon stick
¾ cup Calvados
⅓ cup apricot brandy
Sugar
*Freshly grated nutmeg, for
  garnish*
4 cinnamon sticks, for garnish

1. In a medium saucepan, combine the milk, cream and cinnamon stick. Bring to a simmer over moderate heat. Reduce the heat to low. Stir in the Calvados and apricot brandy and cook until just warmed through; do not boil.

2. Meanwhile, place a large pinch of sugar in each of four mugs or 8-ounce glasses. Place a spoon in each glass to prevent cracking and pour in the hot toddy. Sprinkle with the nutmeg and garnish with a cinnamon stick.
—*Warren Picower*

Hot Scot

If you are serving this drink as an after dinner drink, stir 1 teaspoon of butter in for a truly comforting effect. But if you are serving this as a nightcap, omit the butter.

4 Servings

4 cups milk
½ cup Scotch whisky
¼ cup Drambuie
*4 teaspoons unsalted butter
  (optional)*
*4 dashes of aromatic bitters,
  such as Angostura*

1. Place the milk in a medium saucepan and heat until warmed through; do not boil.

2. Meanwhile, into each of four large mugs or 10-ounce glasses with a spoon in them to prevent cracking, place 2 tablespoons of the whisky, 1 tablespoon of the Drambuie, 1 teaspoon butter and a dash of bitters.

3. Strain the milk into the mugs. Stir gently until the butter melts.
—*Warren Picower*

Hot Buttered Rum

For this tree-decorating favorite, a "batter" of brown sugar, honey, butter and spices is mixed up ahead of time and then spooned into the individual servings of hot rum.

12 Servings

Batter:
*2 sticks (8 ounces) unsalted
  butter, softened to room
  temperature and cut into
  pieces*
*1⅓ cups (packed) brown
  sugar*
*1 teaspoon freshly grated
  nutmeg*
1 teaspoon ground cinnamon
Tiny pinch of ground cloves
1 cup honey

For Each Serving:
1 to 1¼ ounces rum
Boiling water

1. Prepare the batter: In a large bowl, cream the butter with the brown sugar, nutmeg, cinnamon, cloves and honey. Continue to beat until the mixture is completely blended and somewhat fluffy. *(The batter will keep several days if refrigerated, but allow it to return to room temperature before using.)*

2. For each serving: Pour the rum into an 8-ounce porcelain coffee mug and fill the mug with boiling water to within an inch of the rim. Top with a large spoonful of the "batter" and serve. If you wish, stir the drink before serving; or leave this to the drinker.
—*F&W*

Hot Rum Milk with Cardamom

Be sure to use whole cardamom pods, not the seeds, for this recipe, or the flavor will be too intense.

4 Servings

4 cups milk
*2 heaping tablespoons whole
  cardamom pods (about 40)*
3 tablespoons sugar
½ cup dark rum

1. In a heavy medium saucepan, combine the milk, cardamom and sugar. Heat, stirring to dissolve the sugar, until the milk begins to foam.

2. Meanwhile, divide the rum among four large mugs or 10-ounce glasses with a spoon in them to prevent cracking. Strain the milk into the glasses.
—*Anne Disrude*

Orange-Vanilla Coffee

The choice of orange liqueur used in this recipe will have a distinct effect on the flavor of the drink: Grand Marnier, for instance, gives a strong, rich taste, heady with Cognac, while Cointreau will provide a very pleasant, flowery nuance.

4 Servings

3 cups freshly brewed coffee
¼ cup heavy cream
4 teaspoons sugar
¼ teaspoon vanilla extract
2 tablespoons plus 2
* teaspoons orange liqueur*
Curls of orange zest, for
* garnish*

1. In a medium saucepan, combine the coffee, cream, sugar and vanilla. Heat until simmering.

2. Meanwhile, pour 2 teaspoons of the orange liqueur into each of four 10-ounce glasses. Place a spoon in each glass to prevent cracking and pour the hot coffee mixture over the orange liqueur. Garnish with a curl of orange zest.

—*Warren Picower*

Chocolate-Cherry Demitasse

This rich drink is just right for demitasse sipping. If a tall drink is desired, cut the amount of chocolate to 1 ounce and serve the drink in two tall glasses, topped with whipped cream and shaved chocolate.

4 Servings

1½ ounces semisweet
* chocolate, broken into bits*
½ cup milk
¼ cup heavy cream
¼ cup freshly brewed strong
* coffee*
2 teaspoons sugar
¼ teaspoon vanilla extract
⅓ cup kirschwasser (cherry
* brandy)*

1. In a small heavy saucepan, combine the chocolate, milk and cream. Warm over moderate heat, stirring occasionally, until the chocolate melts. Whisk to blend well.

2. Stir in the coffee, sugar and vanilla and heat until simmering.

3. Remove from the heat and stir in the kirschwasser. Serve in demitasse cups.

—*Cathy Fredman*

appetizers

Pumpkin Seed Puree

Serve this rich, piquant puree as a dip with a variety of cut-up vegetables. It can also be served with fried tortillas, toasted pita triangles or cold shrimp.
Makes About 1½ Cups

1½ cups (8 ounces) hulled,
   unsalted pumpkin seeds
   (pepitas)*
3 tablespoons olive oil
2 cloves garlic, crushed
About ¾ cup chicken broth
¼ cup lime juice
1 to 2 jalapeños—seeded,
   deveined and chopped—or
   hot pepper sauce to taste
1 teaspoon salt
¼ teaspoon freshly ground
   pepper
*Available at health food
   stores

1. In a small ungreased skillet, cook the pumpkin seeds over moderate heat, stirring occasionally, until they begin to pop and turn golden brown, 2 to 3 minutes. Place the seeds in a blender or food processor and puree until finely ground. Reserve the ground seeds in the blender.
2. In the skillet, heat the oil over moderate heat. Add the garlic and sauté for about 30 seconds, or until fragrant. Pour the oil and garlic into the blender. Add ¾ cup of the chicken broth, the lime juice, jalapeños, salt and pepper. Process, stopping occasionally to scrape down the sides, until the mixture is pureed. (If the mixture gets too thick, add a bit more chicken broth, a tablespoon at a time.)
—*Jim Fobel*

Salmon Rillettes

Serve this pâté with toast points or crusty French bread.
8 to 10 Servings

½ cup dry white wine
1 carrot, coarsely chopped
1 celery rib, coarsely
   chopped
½ small onion. coarsely
   chopped
4 sprigs of parsley
Pinch of tarragon
12 peppercorns, lightly
   crushed
¾ pound salmon steak, cut
   1¼ inches thick
¾ pound Scotch smoked
   salmon, diced
2 sticks (8 ounces) unsalted
   butter
Pinch of cayenne pepper
1 jar (4 ounces) salmon caviar

1. In a small saucepan, combine the wine, carrot, celery, onion, parsley, tarragon and peppercorns with 1 cup of water. Bring to a boil, then reduce the heat and simmer for 5 minutes. Strain the court bouillon into a skillet.
2. Bring the court bouillon to a boil over moderately high heat. Reduce the heat to a simmer and add the salmon steak; cover and poach, turning once, until just slightly translucent in the center, about 5 minutes. Remove the salmon to a bowl and let cool. Using your hands, flake the salmon, discarding the skin and bones.
3. In a food processor, blend the diced smoked salmon with the butter and cayenne until smooth, about 1 minute.

4. Transfer to a medium bowl and fold in the salmon caviar. Serve at room temperature.
—*The Four Seasons, New York City*

Potted Crawfish

This savory dish can be served as a spread with melba toast or thin crackers or as a first course, scooped onto lettuce-lined plates. The pâté should be served cold, but not directly from the refrigerator. I like to accompany it with mayonnaise that has been flavored with lemon juice and green peppercorn mustard.
8 Servings

1 pound boiled and shelled
   crawfish tails or 1¼ pounds
   medium shrimp—boiled for
   1 minute, shelled and
   deveined
⅔ cup dry white wine
1 garlic clove, bruised
1 large imported bay leaf
4 drops of hot pepper sauce
2 tablespoons minced onion
2 tablespoons minced scallion
2 teaspoons minced parsley
½ teaspoon celery seed
½ teaspoon freshly ground
   pepper
½ teaspoon salt
⅛ teaspoon thyme
1 tablespoon fresh lemon
   juice
1 egg, lightly beaten
½ cup fresh bread crumbs
4 tablespoons unsalted butter,
   melted

1. Preheat the oven to 350°. Coarsely chop the crawfish in a food processor.
2. In a small nonreactive saucepan, combine the wine, garlic, bay leaf and hot sauce. Simmer over moderate heat for 5 minutes. Let

cool, then discard the garlic and bay leaf.

3. In a large bowl, combine the chopped crawfish, onion, scallion, parsley, celery seed, pepper, salt, thyme and lemon juice. Stir in the seasoned wine, egg and bread crumbs. Add the melted butter and mix well.

4. Pack the crawfish mixture into a buttered 5- to 6-cup heatproof ceramic casserole. Bake until set, about 30 minutes. Let cool, then cover and refrigerate for at least 1 hour, until chilled. *(This recipe can be prepared up to 1 day ahead.)*
—Lee Bailey

Country-Style Pâté

This traditional pâté improves as it stands. It should be refrigerated for up to three days before serving.
10 to 12 Servings

1 pound chicken livers,
  halved and trimmed
½ cup Cognac or other
  brandy
1 pound ground beef chuck
1 pound ground pork
  shoulder
¼ pound fresh pork fat, finely
  diced
½ cup fresh bread crumbs
1 tablespoon salt
2 teaspoons freshly ground
  pepper
½ teaspoon allspice
2 tablespoons unsalted butter
¼ pound mushrooms,
  chopped
2 eggs
1 tablespoon plus 1 teaspoon
  tarragon
1 garlic clove, minced
14 thin slices of bacon (about
  ¼ pound)

1. Pick out half of the chicken livers, choosing the plumpest and most perfect. Soak them in the brandy in a small bowl for 30 minutes. Drain the livers, reserving the brandy.

2. In a large bowl, combine the beef, pork, pork fat, bread crumbs, salt, pepper and allspice. Mix well.

3. In a large skillet, melt 1 tablespoon of the butter over high heat. When the foam subsides, add the marinated chicken livers and sauté, turning once, for about 30 seconds on each side, or until lightly browned around the edges. Transfer to a plate and set aside.

4. Melt the remaining 1 tablespoon butter in the skillet. Add the mushrooms and sauté over high heat until they are browned, about 5 minutes. Scrape them into the bowl of meats.

5. In a blender or food processor, puree the remaining raw chicken livers with the eggs, tarragon, garlic and reserved brandy. Add to the meat mixture and mix until well blended.

6. Preheat the oven to 375°. Line a 9-cup (11½-by-4-inch) terrine with crosswise strips of bacon; line the ends of the terrine with lengthwise strips of bacon, allowing the ends to overhang. Evenly spread half the filling in the mold. Arrange the sautéed chicken livers in a row down the center, and top with the remaining meat mixture. Smooth the top and fold the bacon ends over the mixture. Cover the terrine tightly with foil and place in a large roasting pan in the oven. Add enough warm water to the pan to reach halfway up the sides of the terrine.

7. Bake for 1½ hours. Using a bulb baster, remove any melted fat from the top of the meat loaf. Carefully transfer the terrine to a baking sheet or larger pan. Cut out a piece of cardboard to fit inside the terrine,

cover it with foil and place it on top of the meat. Weight down with about 5 pounds of weights or heavy cans. Let cool, then refrigerate, still weighted, overnight. Unmold the pâté before serving if desired.
—Susan Wyler

Parmesan Christmas Trees

If you do not have tree-shaped cookie cutters, use any other shape of cutter to make these zesty cheese toasts, which are festive for any occasion.
Makes 2 Dozen

¾ cup freshly grated
  Parmesan cheese (3 ounces)
½ cup good-quality
  mayonnaise
2 tablespoons grated onion
¼ teaspoon freshly ground
  white pepper
24 slices firm-textured white
  bread

1. Preheat the oven to 400°. In a small bowl, combine the Parmesan cheese, mayonnaise, onion and white pepper.

2. Lay the bread on a work surface and cut with a tree-shaped cookie cutter. (The scraps can be reserved for another use, such as bread crumbs or stuffing.) Spread about 2 teaspoons of the cheese mixture evenly onto each bread tree. Arrange the trees on a large baking sheet and bake for 5 to 7 minutes, until golden and bubbly. Serve immediately.
—Tracey Seaman

Blueberry Biscuit Sandwiches
with Smoked Ham

*Makes About 36 Cocktail
Sandwiches*

2 cups all-purpose flour
½ teaspoon salt
2 teaspoons baking powder
¼ teaspoon baking soda
4 tablespoons unsalted butter
½ cup buttermilk
1 tablespoon molasses
*1 cup fresh or dry-frozen
  blueberries*
*½ pound high-quality, thinly
  sliced ham*

1. Preheat the oven to 425° and lightly grease a baking sheet. In a large bowl, sift together the flour, salt, baking powder and baking soda. Cut the butter into the dry ingredients with a pastry cutter until the mixture resembles coarse meal. Stir the buttermilk with the molasses and add to flour mixture; stir in the blueberries.

2. Work the mixture gently and quickly with your hands until it holds together when squeezed; the dough should be crumbly.

3. Pat the dough out to a ½-inch thickness on a lightly floured board. With a 3-inch floured biscuit cutter, cut out as many rounds of dough as possible. Pat out the scraps to make as many more rounds as possible. Then, with a sharp knife, cut each round into 4 quarters.

4. Transfer the biscuits to the cookie sheet and bake them in the center of the oven for 8 to 10 minutes, or until they are golden brown and puffed. Watch carefully to prevent overbaking.

5. Cut the ham slices into triangles slightly larger than the biscuits. Using a sharp slicing knife, split the biscuits, place one or two ham triangles on top of each, and top each with another biscuit half to make little sandwiches.
—*Martha Stewart*

Salmon Caviar Toasts

The firm, dense homemade bread included here is marvelous for these toasts, but for convenience you can buy a loaf of brioche or firm-textured white bread.

Makes About 4 Dozen

*½ loaf of Toasting Bread
  (p. 130)*
*2½ tablespoons unsalted
  butter, softened*
4 ounces salmon caviar
Lemon wedges, for serving

1. Preheat the broiler. Cut the bread into ⅜-inch-thick slices; trim off the crusts. Spread the butter evenly over one side of the bread slices and arrange them, buttered-side up, in a single layer on a cookie sheet.

2. Broil the bread about 4 inches from the heat until light golden brown, about 1 minute. Toast only one side. Cut each piece of toast into 4 triangles. Let cool. *(The bread can be toasted and cut up 2½ hours ahead.)*

3. Shortly before serving, spread about 1 teaspoon of the caviar onto the toasted side and serve with lemon wedges.
—*Lydie Marshall*

Italian Herbed Toasts

For a festive holiday hors d'oeuvre, serve these flavorful toasts with an array of cheeses—mild Cheddars and goat cheeses are particularly good matches.

Makes About 4 Dozen

*One 10-ounce loaf Italian
  bread*
Herbed Oil (p. 261)
*¼ cup freshly grated
  Parmesan cheese*

1. Cut the bread crosswise into three 4-inch lengths. Wrap individually and freeze for at least 4 hours or overnight.

2. Defrost the bread for 10 to 15 minutes. Trim off the end pieces and cut the bread into even, ¼-inch-thick slices.

3. Preheat the oven to its lowest setting. Arrange the bread slices in a single layer on a wire rack set in a large baking sheet. Place the bread in the barely warm oven and bake until dry, but not browned, about 30 minutes.

4. Preheat the oven to 250°. Lightly brush one side of the bread with the Herbed Oil. Sprinkle the Parmesan cheese over the oiled side of each toast and bake until golden brown and crisp, about 1 hour.
—*Diana Sturgis*

Button Mushrooms with Dilled Sour Cream on Toast

6 Servings

*1½ sticks (6 ounces) unsalted
  butter
6 slices white or whole wheat
  bread, crusts removed
1 pound small button
  mushrooms
Juice of ½ lemon
1½ cups sour cream
½ cup minced fresh dill or 1
  to 2 teaspoons dried
  dillweed
1 tablespoon onion juice
  (squeezed from grated
  onion)
Salt, freshly ground black
  pepper and cayenne pepper
Paprika, for garnish*

1. Preheat the oven to 350°. Melt 1 stick of the butter. Brush the bread slices on both sides with melted butter, arrange them on a baking sheet and bake them until golden.

2. Preheat the broiler. Cut off and discard the mushroom stems. Toss the caps in the lemon juice.

3. In a skillet, heat the remaining 4 tablespoons of butter until the foam dies down. Sauté the mushrooms for only about 1 minute; they must remain firm and unbrowned. Set aside.

4. In a medium bowl, mix the sour cream, dill and onion juice. Add salt, black pepper and cayenne to taste.

5. To serve, place the toast squares on heatproof serving plates, spoon the mushrooms onto the toast and blanket them with the dilled cream. Dust lightly with paprika. Broil for 1 minute, or until bubbly.
—*Pearl Byrd Foster*

Sausage-Stuffed Mushrooms

Parslied toast points make this an attractive first course, but the mushrooms may also be served alone, as an hors d'oeuvre.

4 Servings

*16 medium mushrooms
Fresh lemon juice
½ pound sweet Italian
  sausage
⅛ teaspoon salt
⅛ teaspoon freshly ground
  pepper
4 slices firm-textured
  white bread
3 tablespoons unsalted butter,
  melted
3 tablespoons minced parsley*

1. Preheat the oven to 375°. Remove the mushroom stems and mince them. Paint the caps with lemon juice to prevent discoloration.

2. Remove the sausage meat from the casings and place the meat in a medium bowl. Add the minced mushroom stems, salt and pepper, and mix lightly to blend.

3. Spoon the sausage stuffing into the mushroom caps, smoothing the tops into a rounded shape. Arrange the stuffed mushrooms in a lightly greased small baking dish. Bake for about 15 minutes, or until the sausage meat is no longer pink.

4. Meanwhile, toast the bread slices and trim off the crusts. Cut each slice into 4 triangles. Dip one edge of each triangle into the melted butter and then into the parsley.
—*F&W*

Prosciutto-Wrapped Hearts of Palm

These tasty, bite-size hors d'oeuvres can be prepared the night before.
8 Servings

*¼ cup white wine vinegar
½ cup extra-virgin olive oil
4 sprigs of fresh thyme or ½
  teaspoon dried
¼ teaspoon freshly ground
  pepper
2 cans (14 ounces each) hearts
  of palm, drained and rinsed
½ pound thinly sliced
  prosciutto, halved
  lengthwise
2 bunches of arugula, large
  stems removed*

1. In a nonreactive bowl, combine the vinegar, oil, thyme and pepper.

2. Cut the hearts of palm in half crosswise. (If some are very thick, halve them lengthwise first. Use only the tender stalks.) Wrap each piece in a slice of prosciutto and secure with a toothpick. Place the hearts of palm in the marinade, cover with plastic wrap and refrigerate for 3 hours or overnight.

3. Remove the prosciutto-wrapped hearts of palm from the marinade. Place the arugula leaves on a serving platter and arrange the wrapped hearts of palm on top. Sprinkle with a grinding of pepper and serve at room temperature.
—*Jim Brown*

Sardines Marinated with Lemons and Onions

12 Servings

6 cans (3¾ ounces each)
  sardines in olive oil, drained
2 lemons, thinly sliced
1 large Spanish onion,
  thinly sliced
1 teaspoon thyme
6 imported bay leaves
¼ teaspoon freshly ground
  pepper
¾ cup olive oil
4 to 5 heads of Bibb lettuce,
  separated into leaves

1. In a deep nonreactive baking dish, carefully arrange one-third of the sardines in a single layer. Top with 6 to 8 slices of the lemon, one-third of the onion, one-third of the thyme and 2 bay leaves. Sprinkle with one-third of the pepper. Repeat the layering 2 more times.

2. Pour the olive oil over the sardines. Cover with plastic wrap and refrigerate for at least 12 hours, or up to several days. Use a bulb baster to remoisten the top layer with the olive oil once a day.

3. Before serving, remove the onion slices and chop coarsely. Squeeze the juice from the lemon slices through a sieve into a small bowl. Transfer the sardines to a platter, arranging them, overlapping slightly, in a fish design.

4. Remove and reserve the bay leaves. Whisk the olive oil remaining in the dish into the lemon juice. Drizzle over the sardines. Garnish with 3 or 4 rows of the chopped onion and the bay leaves.

5. Serve with the lettuce leaves in a bowl on the side. To eat, fill a lettuce leaf with a sardine and a sprinkling of chopped onion.
—*Anne Disrude*

Confetti Shrimp

These stir-fried shrimp are a snowball's throw away from shrimp cocktail. You can serve them hot out of the skillet, but the flavors improve when the assembled dish sits at room temperature, making this a great buffet dish.

Makes About 24 Shrimp

1 medium red bell pepper
¼ cup olive oil
1½ pounds (about 24) large
  shrimp, shelled and
  deveined
3 tablespoons minced fresh
  ginger
2 garlic cloves, minced
1½ tablespoons fresh
  lemon juice
1 tablespoon fresh lime juice
¼ teaspoon salt
½ teaspoon Chinese chili oil
¼ cup minced chives or
  scallion greens

1. Roast the pepper directly over a gas flame or under the broiler as close to the heat as possible, turning, until charred all over, about 5 minutes. Place the pepper in a paper bag, fold to close and let steam for 10 minutes. Scrape off the skin with a knife, rinse briefly under cool water, if necessary, to remove burned bits. Remove the stem and seeds. Mince the pepper and set it aside in a small bowl.

2. In a large heavy skillet, heat 2 tablespoons of the oil over high heat. Add the shrimp and cook, turning, until opaque and firm, 2 to 3 minutes. Transfer the shrimp to a medium bowl and set aside to cool.

3. Reduce the heat to moderately low and add the ginger and garlic. Cook, stirring, until fragrant and starting to soften, about 3 minutes. Scrape the ginger mixture into a small bowl and whisk in the lemon juice, lime juice and salt. Whisk in the remaining 2 tablespoons olive oil and the chili oil. Pour the mixture over the cooled shrimp, stir to coat and let sit for at least 1 hour to marry the flavors. *(The recipe can be prepared to this point 1 day ahead; cover tightly and refrigerate overnight. Let sit at room temperature for 1 hour before serving.)* Stir in the chives and minced red pepper and transfer to a serving bowl.
—*Tracey Seaman*

Bacalao Gloria

This recipe stems from my wife Gloria's Caribbean background. Although she was born in New York, her mother is Puerto Rican and her father Cuban. In the Spanish tradition, bacalao (salt cod) cooked with potatoes is served at Christmas, but here I present it in a lighter version over toast.

There are different types of salt cod, and some are drier than others. The drier and saltier the fish, the longer it must be soaked to soften and reduce the saltiness.

12 Servings

1 pound boneless salt cod
  (bacalao)
¼ cup plus 2 tablespoons
  extra-virgin olive oil
2 medium onions, thinly
  sliced
4 large garlic cloves, thinly
  sliced
1 large baking potato, peeled
  and cut into ½-inch dice

12 slices of whole wheat
bread, crusts removed
1 can (35 ounces) Italian
peeled tomatoes, drained
and chopped
1 large yellow bell pepper,
peeled with a swivel-bladed
vegetable peeler and cut into
½-inch strips
½ teaspoon freshly ground
black pepper
⅛ teaspoon cayenne pepper
18 oil-cured olives, pitted
and sliced
¾ cup cilantro (fresh
coriander) leaves, for
garnish

1. Rinse the salt cod under cold running water to remove the salt from the surface, then place in a bowl with 8 to 10 cups of cold water. Let soak for 24 to 48 hours, changing the water twice a day, until the cod is just mildly salty. Drain and rinse under cold running water.

2. Put the cod in a large saucepan and add cold water to cover. Bring to a boil over high heat. Drain the fish in a colander and rinse under cold running water to cool; pat dry. Flake the cod, discarding any pieces of sinew or skin.

3. In a large skillet, heat ¼ cup of the oil. Add the onions and sauté over high heat, tossing, for 2 minutes. Add the garlic and sauté until fragrant, about 30 seconds. Add the potato and cod and sauté, tossing, for 1 minute. Reduce the heat to low, cover and cook, stirring occasionally, until the potato is soft, about 20 minutes. *(The recipe can be prepared to this point up to 1 day ahead. Cover and refrigerate.)*

4. Preheat the oven to 400°. Arrange the bread on a baking sheet and toast in the oven, turning once, until crisp, about 6 minutes per side. *(The toast can be prepared up to 3 hours in advance. Set aside at room temperature.)*

5. Just before serving, reheat the ingredients in the skillet over moderate heat. Add the tomatoes, yellow bell pepper and remaining 2 tablespoons olive oil. Season with the black pepper and cayenne and bring to a boil. Cover, reduce the heat to low and cook for 5 minutes. Stir in the olives.

6. Put the toast on individual plates and top with a large spoonful of the bacalao. Garnish with the cilantro (fresh coriander) leaves and serve hot.
—*Jacques Pépin*

Chesapeake Scalloped Oysters

Scalloped oysters should be prepared just before baking; otherwise the crushed crackers will lose their crispness. To save time, drain the oysters, season the cream and toast the bread crumbs. With this procedure, the oysters can be prepared very quickly.

6 to 8 Servings

1 cup crushed saltine crackers
1 pint shucked oysters (about
24 oysters), drained
½ cup heavy cream
½ teaspoon salt
¼ teaspoon cayenne pepper
½ cup fresh bread crumbs,
lightly toasted
4 tablespoons unsalted butter,
cut into small pieces

1. Preheat the oven to 400°. Sprinkle ¾ cup of the crushed saltines into a large shallow baking dish. Add the oysters in a single layer. Season the cream with the salt and cayenne and drizzle the cream evenly over the oysters.

2. Toss the remaining ¼ cup crushed saltines with the toasted bread crumbs and sprinkle them over the entire dish. Dot with the butter. Bake in the middle of the oven until the oysters are plumped and the crumb topping is light golden brown, about 20 minutes.
—*Camille Glenn*

Broiled Crumbed Oysters and
Shallots

If you half fill a baking pan with rock salt you'll find it easy to anchor the oysters on the half shell so that they will not tip as they broil.

6 to 8 Servings

5 tablespoons unsalted butter
½ cup finely diced shallots
(about 5 large)
¾ cup fine dry bread crumbs
¼ cup fresh lemon juice
½ teaspoon Pernod (optional)
¼ cup finely chopped parsley
¼ cup freshly grated
Parmesan cheese
2 dozen oysters, on the
half shell
Rock salt

1. Preheat the broiler. In a heavy medium skillet, melt the butter; add the shallots and sauté until golden, 4 to 5 minutes. Add the crumbs and cook, tossing, until the crumbs have absorbed all the butter, about 1 minute. Off the heat, mix in the lemon juice, Pernod, parsley and Parmesan.

2. Arrange the oysters in a large shallow baking pan filled with rock salt (or crumpled aluminum foil); top each with about 1 tablespoon of the shallot-crumb mixture. Broil the oysters 4 inches from the heat until bubbly and lightly browned, about 3 minutes. Serve at once.

—*Jean Anderson*

Ricotta Pesto Crescents

Makes About 3 Dozen

1 cup (loosely packed) fresh
   basil leaves
¼ cup olive oil, preferably
   extra-virgin
2 tablespoons walnuts
2 tablespoons freshly grated
   Parmesan cheese
2 garlic cloves
½ teaspoon salt
¼ teaspoon freshly ground
   pepper
1 cup whole-milk ricotta
   cheese, drained of excess
   liquid
Cream Cheese Dough (recipe
   follows)
1 egg

1. Put the basil, olive oil, walnuts, Parmesan cheese, garlic, salt and pepper into a food processor. Puree until the pesto is well blended.

2. Scrape the pesto into a bowl and stir in the ricotta cheese. *(The filling can be made up to 3 days ahead. Cover and refrigerate.)*

3. Remove half the Cream Cheese Dough from the refrigerator and let stand for about 10 minutes, until malleable. Divide this piece of dough in half. On a lightly floured work surface, roll out one piece of the dough about ⅛ inch thick. Using a 3- or 3¼-inch round cutter, cut the dough into circles. Collect the scraps, chill them briefly and reroll them; cut out to make about 10 circles in all.

4. Put about 1 heaping teaspoon of filling in the center of each round. Moisten the edges of the dough with water. Fold one side of the circle over the filling to form a crescent and pinch the pastry together. Crimp the edges with the tines of a fork to seal. Refrigerate for at least 30 minutes, or up to 24 hours. Repeat with all the remaining dough and filling. *(The crescents can be made ahead to this point and frozen, tightly wrapped, for up to 1 month. Bake without defrosting.)*

5. Preheat the oven to 400°. Place the crescents on a buttered baking sheet, preferably nonstick. In a small bowl, beat the egg with 1 teaspoon of water to make a glaze. Brush the glaze over the crescents. Slash with a small knife or prick with a fork to make steam vents.

6. Bake for about 15 minutes, or until golden brown. (Frozen crescents will take about 5 minutes longer.)

—*Dorie Greenspan*

Cream Cheese Dough

While this easy dough can be made by hand or with an electric mixer (see Note), it is a perfect job for the food processor. The machine turns out an excellent, very smooth dough in less than a minute.

Makes About 1½ Pounds

1 package (8 ounces) cream
   cheese
2 sticks (8 ounces) unsalted
   butter
2 cups all-purpose flour

1. Cut the cream cheese into 8 pieces and let stand at room temperature for 10 minutes.

2. Cut the butter into tablespoons and let stand at room temperature for 10 minutes.

3. Put the flour into a food processor. Scatter the cream cheese and butter over the flour and process, turning the machine quickly on and off 6 to 8 times. Then let the machine run until the dough resembles large curds, stopping to scrape down the sides of the bowl once, about 15 seconds; do not let the dough form a ball on the blade.

4. Turn the dough out onto a work surface and gather into a ball. Divide the dough in half and shape each piece into a 4-by-5-by-1-inch rectangle. Wrap the dough tightly in plastic wrap and refrigerate for at least 2 hours before using. *(The dough can be refrigerated for up to 3 days or frozen for 1 month.)*

NOTE: To make the dough by hand or with a mixer, first cream together the butter and cream cheese. Then blend in the flour to form a smooth dough.

—*Dorie Greenspan*

Mushroom-Leek Turnovers

A sophisticated savory just right for chilly evenings. The porcini, with their full, rich flavor, are a nice complement to the silky leeks. This is a filling you may want to try in a tartlet or work into a cream cheese pastry quiche.

Makes About 4 Dozen

1 ounce dried mushrooms,
    such as porcini
1 cup boiling water
4 tablespoons unsalted butter
3 medium leeks (white part
    only), finely chopped
½ pound fresh mushrooms,
    finely chopped
1 tablespoon all-purpose flour
2 tablespoons Cognac or
    other brandy
¼ cup heavy cream
½ teaspoon salt
¼ teaspoon freshly ground
    black pepper
Pinch of crushed hot red
    pepper
Pinch of thyme
¼ cup freshly grated
    Parmesan cheese
Cream Cheese Dough (p. 30)
1 egg

1. Put the dried mushrooms in a small bowl. Pour the boiling water over the mushrooms and let them soak until softened, about 20 minutes. Lift out the mushrooms and squeeze as much liquid as possible back into the bowl; reserve the liquid. Chop the reconstituted mushrooms.

2. Strain the soaking liquid through a sieve lined with a double thickness of dampened cheesecloth into a heavy skillet. Add the chopped reconstituted mushrooms and 1 tablespoon of the butter. Bring the liquid to a boil over moderately high heat and cook, stirring occasionally, until the liquid evaporates, about 3 minutes. Scrape the mushrooms into a bowl.

3. Melt the remaining 3 tablespoons butter in the skillet over moderately high heat. Add the leeks and sauté until softened but not browned, about 5 minutes. Add the fresh mushrooms and sauté, tossing frequently, until their juices evaporate, about 5 minutes.

4. Return the cooked dried mushrooms to the pan. Sprinkle on the flour and cook, stirring, for about 1 minute. Stir in the Cognac and cook until it evaporates, about 1 minute. Stir in the cream and remove from the heat.

5. Add the salt, black pepper, hot pepper, thyme and Parmesan cheese. Scrape the filling into a bowl and let cool to room temperature. *(The filling can be prepared to this point up to 3 days ahead. Cover and refrigerate the filling.)*

6. Remove half the Cream Cheese Dough from the refrigerator and let rest for about 10 minutes, until malleable. Divide the dough in half. On a lightly floured surface, roll out one piece of the dough into a 12-by-8-inch rectangle. Cut the dough lengthwise in half and then crosswise at 2-inch intervals to form 12 rectangles 2 by 4 inches each.

7. Place 1 heaping teaspoon of filling in the center of the lower half of each rectangle. Moisten the edges of the pastry lightly with water. Fold the dough over the filling to form squares, and gently squeezing out the air, pinch to close. Trim any edges that are ragged. Crimp the edges of the pastries with the tines of a fork to seal. Repeat with the remaining piece of dough and more filling. Then remove the second half of the dough from the refrigerator and repeat to form all the turnovers. Refrigerate the turnovers for at least 30 minutes, or for up to 24 hours. *(The turnovers can be made ahead to this point and frozen, well wrapped, for up to 1 month. Bake without defrosting.)*

8. Preheat the oven to 400°. In a small bowl, beat the egg with 1 teaspoon of cold water to make a glaze. Brush the glaze over the squares. With a small knife, cut a slit in the top of each turnover.

9. Bake for about 15 minutes, or until golden brown. (Frozen turnovers will take about 5 minutes longer.)
—Dorie Greenspan

Pork and Olive Finger Pies

Italian green olives, which are easy to find in many delicatessens, add a distinctive flavor to these turnovers.

Makes 1 Dozen

1 pound boneless pork
    shoulder, cut into 1-inch
    cubes and chilled
2 tablespoons unsalted butter
1 medium onion, finely
    chopped
2 garlic cloves, minced
¼ cup dry white wine
1 tablespoon fresh lemon
    juice
1½ tablespoons all-purpose
    flour

⅓ cup chicken stock or
  canned broth
⅓ cup beef stock or canned
  broth
½ teaspoon freshly ground
  pepper
8 large green Italian olives,
  pitted and coarsely chopped
¼ cup minced parsley
Salt
Cornmeal Pastry (recipe
  follows)
1 egg
1 tablespoon Dijon mustard

1. Heat a large heavy skillet over moderately high heat until very hot. Meanwhile, in a food processor, chop the pork in two batches at 2-second intervals until coarsely ground, about 10 seconds. Transfer the meat to the hot skillet and cook, stirring to break up the meat, until browned and most of the liquid has evaporated, about 15 minutes.

2. Add the butter to the skillet and reduce the heat to moderate. Add the onion and cook with the meat until the onion is translucent and starting to brown, about 5 minutes. Stir in the garlic and cook for 2 minutes longer. Add the wine and lemon juice and simmer until almost evaporated, about 3 minutes. Sprinkle the flour over the meat and cook, stirring, until the mixture is thick and pasty, about 2 minutes more.

3. Gradually stir in the chicken and beef stocks and ¾ cup of water and bring to a simmer. Season with the pepper. Cover, reduce the heat to low and simmer gently for 30 minutes. Remove from the heat and stir in the olives and parsley. Season to

taste with salt and pepper. Let cool completely before filling the pies. *(The pork mixture can be made 1 day ahead and refrigerated overnight.)*

4. On a lightly floured surface, roll out 1 disk of the Cornmeal Pastry dough into a 6-by-16-inch rectangle. Using a fluted pastry wheel, trim it to 5 by 15 inches, then cut the rectangle into three 5-by-5-inch squares. Moisten the edges of each square. Scoop 2 rounded tablespoons of the pork mixture onto the lower half of each square and spread evenly, leaving a ½-inch border of pastry exposed. Fold the pastry over to enclose the filling, pressing the edges lightly to seal. Trim the edges with the pastry wheel.

5. Continue with the remaining squares, then repeat with the remaining disks of Cornmeal Pastry dough and filling. *(The pies can be made to this point, wrapped well first in plastic and then in foil, and frozen for up to 1 month. If frozen, unwrap the pies and let sit at room temperature for 10 minutes before proceeding and allow 5 extra minutes baking time.)*

6. Preheat the oven to 400°. Place the pies on a large ungreased baking sheet. In a small bowl, beat together the egg and mustard; brush lightly over the top of each pie. With a small sharp knife, cut three small steam vents in the center of each pie. Bake the pies 25 to 30 minutes, until well browned. (Allow an extra 5 minutes if the pies are frozen.) Let cool on a rack about 5 minutes. Serve whole pies in a basket or cut them in half and arrange on a platter.
—*Tracey Seaman*

Cornmeal Pastry

This pastry can easily be prepared in two batches if your processor is not large enough to accommodate the full quantity of ingredients.
Makes Enough for 12 Turnovers

4 cups all-purpose flour
½ cup white cornmeal
1 teaspoon salt
1 stick (4 ounces) plus 2
  tablespoons cold unsalted
  butter, cut into 20 pieces
⅔ cup chilled shortening
⅔ cup ice water

1. In a food processor, combine the flour, cornmeal and salt; pulse briefly to mix. Add the butter and shortening and process until the mixture resembles coarse meal, about 20 seconds.

2. With the machine on, add the ice water and process just until the dough begins to form a ball. Transfer the dough to a lightly floured surface and knead briefly. Cut the dough in quarters and shape into disks. Wrap each disk in wax paper and refrigerate until ready to roll out. *(The dough can be prepared to this point and refrigerated overnight if desired. Let the dough sit at room temperature for about 5 minutes before rolling out.)*
—*Tracey Seaman*

Cauliflower-Oyster Stew (p. 45).

At left: Armadillo Turkey (p. 61), Sweet Potato Sham (p. 99) and Buttered Okra (p. 89). Above: Salad of Winter Greens (p. 101). At right: Pumpkin Custard Pie (p. 218).

Cranberry Pie (p. 208).

Chicken Liver and Apple
Crescents

This liver filling, flecked with apples and hazelnuts, is a favorite recipe of mine, for it works well both hot and cold: baked in a pastry wrapper, as suggested here, or chilled and served as an excellent spreadable pâté.

Makes About 3 Dozen

2 tablespoons hazelnuts
    (filberts)
1 large garlic clove, quartered
1 medium onion, quartered
2 tablespoons unsalted butter
½ medium, tart apple—
    peeled, quartered and cored
½ pound chicken livers,
    trimmed
1 tablespoon Calvados
½ teaspoon salt
¼ teaspoon freshly ground
    pepper
Pinch of allspice
Pinch of ground cloves
Pinch of freshly grated
    nutmeg
½ teaspoon cinnamon
2 tablespoons heavy cream
Cream Cheese Dough (p. 30)
1 egg

1. Finely chop the nuts in a food processor, turning the machine on and off several times. Transfer to a small bowl.

2. Place the garlic and onion in the food processor and chop.

3. In a large heavy skillet, melt 1 tablespoon of the butter over moderately high heat. Add the garlic and onion and sauté until softened but not browned, about 5 minutes.

4. Meanwhile, chop the apple in the food processor. Scrape the apple into the skillet and cook until softened, 3 to 4 minutes longer. Scrape the mixture back into the food processor.

5. Melt the remaining 1 tablespoon butter in the same skillet. Add the chicken livers and sauté, tossing frequently, until browned outside but still pink in the center, about 5 minutes. Add the Calvados and cook for 30 seconds. Add the livers and the pan juices to the processor. Add the salt, pepper, allspice, cloves, nutmeg, cinnamon and cream. Puree until smooth. Add the chopped nuts and turn the machine quickly on and off several times until just incorporated. Let cool to room temperature before using. *(The chicken liver filling can be made up to 3 days ahead. Refrigerate, covered.)*

6. Remove half the Cream Cheese Dough from the refrigerator and let stand for about 10 minutes, until malleable. Divide this piece of dough in half. On a lightly floured work surface, roll out one piece of the dough about ⅛ inch thick. Using a 3- or 3¼-inch round cutter, cut the dough into circles. Collect the scraps, chill them briefly and reroll them; cut out to make about 10 circles in all.

7. Put about 1 heaping teaspoon of filling in the center of each round. Moisten the edges of the dough with water. Fold one side of the circle over the filling to form a crescent and pinch the pastry together. Crimp the edges with the tines of a fork to seal. Refrigerate for at least 30 minutes, or up to 24 hours. Repeat with all the remaining dough and filling. *(The crescents can be made ahead to this point and frozen, tightly wrapped, for up to 1 month. Bake without defrosting.)*

8. Preheat the oven to 400°. Place the crescents on a buttered baking sheet, preferably nonstick. In a small bowl, beat the egg with 1 teaspoon of water to make a glaze. Brush the glaze over the crescents. Slash with a small knife or prick with a fork to make steam vents.

9. Bake for about 15 minutes, or until golden brown. (Frozen crescents will take about 5 minutes longer.)
—Dorie Greenspan

Fennel Tart with Rosemary

The assertive flavors of fennel and rosemary, napped with extra-virgin olive oil, are mellowed by long, slow cooking. Studs of briny black olives set off the sweetness of the filling, and the whole wheat crust with rosemary adds a pleasing, earthy quality.

10 to 12 Servings

1 cup unbleached all-purpose
    flour
½ cup whole wheat flour
3 tablespoons chopped fresh
    rosemary
¼ teaspoon salt
6½ tablespoons cold unsalted
    butter, cut into pieces
4 tablespoons chilled
    shortening, cut into small
    pieces
¼ cup ice water
3¾ pounds fennel bulbs with
    tops (about 7 small)
1 large onion, halved
    lengthwise
¼ cup extra-virgin olive oil
2 teaspoons coarse (kosher)
    salt
½ teaspoon freshly ground
    pepper
1½ teaspoons chopped flat-
    leaf parsley, for garnish

*12 large imported black
olives, such as Calamata or
Gaeta, pitted and halved*

1. Preheat the oven to 350°. In a
food processor, combine the all-purpose and whole wheat flours with
1½ tablespoons of the rosemary and
the salt. Add 4½ tablespoons of the
butter and the shortening; process
until the mixture resembles coarse
meal.

2. With the machine on, gradually
add the ice water and process just
until a dough forms. Flatten the
dough into a 6-inch disk, cover
tightly and refrigerate until chilled,
or for up to 2 days.

3. On a lightly floured surface,
roll the dough into a 13-inch circle,
¼ inch thick. Carefully lay the dough
in an 11-by-1-inch round fluted tart
pan with a removable bottom and
pat the dough into place. Trim the
excess dough from the rim. Prick the
bottom with the tines of a fork. Line
the dough with aluminum foil and
fill with pie weights or dried beans.
Bake in the middle of the preheated
oven for 10 minutes. Remove the foil
and weights and bake the tart shell
for 25 minutes, or until well
browned. Transfer to a rack and let
cool to room temperature.

4. Trim the tops of the fennel
bulbs. Coarsely chop enough of the
greens to yield ¼ cup; set aside.
Halve the bulbs. Cut out the central
cores and slice the fennel crosswise
into ¼-inch strips; set aside in a large
bowl. Slice the onion halves lengthwise into ¼-inch strips and add to
the fennel. Stir in 3 tablespoons each
of the olive oil and reserved fennel
greens, the remaining 1½ tablespoons rosemary and the coarse salt
and pepper.

5. In a large heavy saucepan, melt
the remaining 2 tablespoons butter
over moderate heat. Stir in the fennel
and onion. Cover and cook, stirring
occasionally, until the vegetables are
very soft and jamlike, about 40 minutes. Uncover, increase the heat to
moderately high and cook until the
mixture caramelizes, about 5 minutes. Season with salt and pepper to
taste and let cool to room temperature. *(The filling can be prepared to
this point up to 2 days ahead. Cover
and refrigerate. Let return to room
temperature before proceeding.)*

6. Spread the fennel filling in the
tart shell. Drizzle the remaining 1 tablespoon olive oil over the tart and
sprinkle the parsley and the remaining 1 tablespoon fennel greens on
top. Decoratively arrange the olive
halves on the tart. Carefully remove
the sides of the pan and transfer the
tart to a platter. Cut into wedges and
serve at room temperature.
—*Sheila Lukins*

soups

Mushroom Consommé

8 Servings

2 pounds opened (see Note)
  button mushrooms, finely
  chopped
1½ ounces dried porcini
  mushrooms
1½ pounds onions, unpeeled
  and cut into eighths
5 medium carrots, cut into
  1-inch pieces
1 can (14 ounces) Italian
  peeled tomatoes, drained
  and coarsely chopped
12 to 15 parsley stems
3 garlic cloves, unpeeled and
  lightly crushed
3 cups chicken stock or
  canned broth
¼ teaspoon thyme
¼ teaspoon freshly ground
  pepper
Salt
Fresh enoki mushrooms or
  thinly sliced button
  mushrooms, for garnish

1. In a large heavy saucepan, place the chopped button mushrooms, dried porcini, onions, carrots, tomatoes, parsley, garlic, stock, thyme and pepper. Add 2 quarts of cold water and slowly bring to a boil over moderate heat. Immediately reduce the heat to low, cover and simmer, skimming occasionally, for 1 hour.

2. Pour the soup through a fine sieve lined with several layers of dampened cheesecloth; discard the solids. Return the liquid to the saucepan, increase the heat to high and boil, uncovered, until the consommé is reduced by about one-fourth. Season with salt to taste. Serve hot, garnished with fresh mushrooms.

NOTE: We recommend using slightly older button mushrooms, with opened caps and exposed dark gills for this recipe. They will contribute a fuller mushroom flavor to the soup. Avoid packaged mushrooms with chemical preservatives.
—Anne Disrude

Baked Silver Onion Soup with White Wine and Toasted Cheese Fingers

If you cannot find silver onions—a special variety of white onions about ¾ inch in diameter—substitute either very small white onions or the smallest yellow onions you can find.

8 Servings

1½ pounds very small silver
  onions
4 tablespoons unsalted butter
¼ cup finely minced celery
7 cups rich chicken stock,
  preferably homemade
2 tablespoons arrowroot (or
  1½ tablespoons cornstarch)
Salt and freshly ground white
  pepper
Small pinch of sugar
¼ to ½ teaspoon ground
  mace
1 cup dry white wine

Toasted Cheese Fingers:
4 slices thin, firm-textured
  white sandwich bread
1 stick (4 ounces) unsalted
  butter, melted
1 generous cup freshly grated
  Parmesan cheese
Paprika, preferably medium-
  hot

1. Preheat the oven to 350°. Peel the onions carefully, leaving them whole. If the onions are larger than bite size, quarter them through the root end.

2. In a large flameproof casserole, melt the butter over moderate heat. Toss the onions and celery in the butter until coated, then cover the casserole tightly. Place it in the center of the oven and bake the vegetables for 30 minutes, removing the cover and stirring them every 10 minutes or so.

3. Meanwhile, in a saucepan, bring 6 cups of the chicken stock to a boil in a saucepan, then lower the heat to a bare simmer. Blend the remaining 1 cup stock with the arrowroot. Add the mixture to the simmering stock and stir over moderate heat until the stock is slightly thickened and smooth. Season to taste with salt, white pepper, the sugar and mace. Set aside.

4. When the vegetables have baked for 30 minutes, add the thickened broth to the casserole in the oven, stirring gently with a wooden spoon. Cover and bake 45 minutes longer or until the onions are tender but not mushy.

5. Meanwhile, make the toasted cheese fingers: Cut each slice of bread into 4 strips. Pour the melted butter into an 11-by-7-inch baking pan. Place the bread strips in the butter, then turn them over once, so that both sides are lightly coated with butter. Sprinkle the cheese onto the bread fingers, then dust them with paprika.

6. Place the pan in the oven and bake the fingers, without turning them, for about 10 to 15 minutes or until golden. Watch carefully to prevent burning.

7. When the onions are done, re

move them from the oven. Place the casserole over moderate heat and stir in the wine. Heat the soup to the simmering point, correct the seasonings and serve, directly from the casserole if possible. Serve with the toasted cheese fingers.
—*Pearl Byrd Foster*

Jerusalem Artichoke Soup

These curious tubers are neither artichokes nor are they from Jerusalem; in fact, they are native to North America and are members of the sunflower family. You will find Jerusalem artichokes—sometimes labeled sunchokes—in specialty produce stores, many supermarkets and some health food shops.

8 Servings

Juice of 2 lemons
3 pounds Jerusalem
  artichokes (sunchokes)
6 tablespoons unsalted butter
2 medium onions, finely
  chopped
2 large carrots, finely chopped
2 large leeks (white part
  only), finely chopped
6 sprigs of flat-leaf parsley
1 teaspoon thyme
5 cups chicken stock or
  canned broth
Salt and freshly ground white
  pepper
6 to 8 tablespoons heavy
  cream
8 sprigs of watercress, for
  garnish

1. Fill a large bowl halfway with cold water and add the lemon juice. Peel the Jerusalem artichokes and drop them into the lemon water to prevent discoloration.

2. In a large saucepan, melt the butter over moderate heat until foaming. Add the onions, carrots, leeks, parsley and thyme. Cover and reduce the heat to moderately low. Cook, stirring occasionally, until the vegetables are tender and lightly colored, about 15 minutes.

3. Add the chicken stock, increase the heat and bring to a boil. Partially cover, reduce the heat to a simmer and cook for 25 minutes. Let cool slightly; then strain, discarding the solids. Return the liquid to the pan.

4. Drain the Jerusalem artichokes and cut them into 1-inch chunks. Add to the liquid in the pan, season lightly with salt and white pepper and bring to a boil. Partially cover, reduce the heat to a simmer and cook, stirring occasionally, until the artichokes are very tender, about 45 minutes.

5. Force the soup through the fine disk of a food mill or puree in batches in a food processor. *(The soup can be prepared to this point several days in advance of serving. Let cool to room temperature; then cover and refrigerate.)*

6. To serve, reheat the soup gently, stirring often. Thin to desired consistency with the cream. Correct the seasoning and serve hot. Garnish each bowl with a sprig of watercress.
—*Michael McLaughlin*

Three-Mushroom Soup

8 to 12 Servings

4 to 6 large dried Polish
  mushrooms, cèpes or porcini
12 large dried shiitake
  mushrooms
3 quarts beef stock or canned
  broth
5 medium carrots, finely diced
5 celery ribs with leaves,
  finely diced
2 large onions, finely chopped
2 tablespoons finely chopped
  parsley
1 pound fresh mushrooms,
  sliced
3 tablespoons chopped
  fresh dill or 2 teaspoons
  dried dillweed
1 tablespoon coarse (kosher)
  salt (omit if using canned
  broth)
½ teaspoon freshly ground
  pepper
½ cup very small dried pasta,
  such as bows, squares,
  alphabet or orzo
2 tablespoons unsalted butter
2 tablespoons all-purpose
  flour
1 cup sour cream

1. Pour 2 cups of hot water over the Polish and shiitake mushrooms, and let them soak for 1 hour.

2. In a large pot, bring the stock to a simmer. Add the carrots, celery, onions and parsley and cook, uncovered, over low heat for 20 minutes, stirring occasionally.

3. Remove the soaked mushrooms from the water; strain the liquid through a sieve lined with a double thickness of cheesecloth and reserve. Cut the mushrooms into pieces slightly larger than the diced vegetables. Add the mushrooms and reserved liquid to the soup. Simmer for 15 minutes.

4. Add the sliced fresh mushrooms, the dill, salt and pepper. Simmer for 15 minutes.

5. Bring the soup to a boil. Stirring constantly, add the pasta. Reduce the heat slightly and cook, stirring occasionally, until the pasta is tender, 4 to 7 minutes.

6. Meanwhile, in a small heavy saucepan, melt the butter over moderately low heat. Add the flour, blending until smooth. Cook, stirring, for about 2 minutes without browning to make a roux. Whisk in 2 tablespoons of the sour cream until blended. Remove from the heat and stir in the remaining sour cream.

7. When the pasta is tender, add the thickened sour cream to the soup. Adjust the heat to a simmer and cook, stirring constantly, until the sour cream is completely incorporated, about 3 minutes. Serve hot or cold.
—*Martha Stewart*

Fresh Pimiento Bisque

In the South, sweet red peppers are called pimientos, and the word bisque is applied to a rather formal first-course soup for a special dinner. This is one of my family's favorite fancy soups. It is strained, very smooth and creamy and served in the most elegant bouillon cups one can muster. Mother's were white French Havilland with a scalloped gold border. When I was a child, I always judged the importance of our guests by whether the Havilland was brought out or not.

6 to 8 Servings

¼ cup rice
4 large red bell peppers,
  coarsely chopped
1 small onion, chopped
2 cups chicken stock or
  canned broth
2 cups milk
½ cup heavy cream
¼ teaspoon cayenne pepper
¼ teaspoon imported sweet
  paprika
¼ teaspoon freshly ground
  white pepper
Salt

1. Place the rice in a small saucepan with 2 cups of water. Bring to a boil, reduce the heat to low and simmer, uncovered, until the rice is overcooked and mushy and the water has almost boiled away, about 40 minutes.

2. In a medium saucepan, combine the red peppers, onion and 2 cups of water. Boil over moderate heat until the peppers are tender but still bright red, about 10 minutes. Drain at once.

3. Put the rice, red peppers, onion and 1 cup of the chicken stock into a blender or food processor. Puree until smooth.

4. Strain the puree into a medium saucepan, add the milk and the remaining 1 cup chicken stock. Simmer over low heat for 5 minutes to thicken slightly. Stir in the cream, cayenne, paprika and white pepper. Season with salt to taste. Cover the bisque and set aside for 1 hour to blend the flavors. Rewarm over low heat before serving.
—*Camille Glenn*

Parsnip Vichyssoise

This rich, thick soup is the result of taking a little creative license with the classic vichyssoise. Parsnips provide a sweet contrast to the potatoes, leeks and garlic, and the flavors are brightened with a dash of lemon juice. I think this soup is best when served just warmed through.

12 Servings

2 large leeks (white parts
  only), halved lengthwise and
  sliced crosswise ½ inch thick
2½ pounds parsnips, peeled
  and cut into 2-inch chunks
3 medium boiling potatoes (¾
  pound), peeled and cut into
  2-inch chunks
8 large garlic cloves, lightly
  crushed
1 large onion, halved and
  thinly sliced
2 tablespoons (packed) light
  brown sugar
1 teaspoon ground cardamom
6 cups chicken stock or
  canned low-sodium broth
1 stick (4 ounces) unsalted
  butter, cut into small pieces

¼ cup fresh lemon juice
3 cups milk
2 cups heavy cream
Salt and freshly ground
  pepper
12 whole chives plus 2
  tablespoons, snipped

1. Preheat the oven to 350°. In a large shallow roasting pan, combine the leeks, parsnips, potatoes, garlic and onion. Sprinkle with the sugar and cardamom and stir to combine. Pour 2 cups of the stock over the vegetables and dot with the butter. Cover tightly with aluminum foil and bake for 2 hours, until the vegetables are very tender, stirring the vegetables occasionally.

2. Transfer the vegetables and any liquid to a large nonreactive saucepan. Add the remaining 4 cups stock and the lemon juice and bring to a boil over high heat. Reduce the heat to moderately low, cover and simmer for 20 minutes.

3. Working in small batches, transfer the vegetables and liquid to a blender or a food processor and puree until just smooth. *(The soup can be prepared to this point up to 2 days ahead. Let cool, cover and refrigerate. It may be necessary to thin the soup with a little stock or water before reheating.)*

4. To finish the soup, add the milk and cream and cook over moderately low heat, stirring occasionally, until warmed through. Do not boil. Season with salt and pepper to taste. Serve in a tureen or in shallow bowls garnished with the whole chives and a sprinkling of the snipped.
—*Sheila Lukins*

Butternut Squash Soup au Gratin

The temptation in making a winter squash soup is to cream it and spice it in the manner of pumpkin soup. This one couldn't be more different. It's garlicky and gratinéed in the manner of French onion soup, and nourishing enough to serve as a main dish. You'll find that this soup will have richer flavor if you make it a day or two before you serve it.

8 to 10 Servings

¼ cup olive oil
1 large onion, chopped
2 small garlic cloves, minced
¼ teaspoon thyme
¼ teaspoon crumbled
  rosemary
2 pounds butternut or other
  winter squash—peeled,
  seeded and coarsely
  shredded (to yield about 5½
  cups)
7 cups chicken stock or
  canned broth
2 cups beef stock or canned
  broth
1¼ cups fresh whole wheat
  bread crumbs (from about 4
  slices)
Salt and freshly ground
  pepper
1 thin loaf of French bread,
  sliced 1 inch thick
4 tablespoons unsalted butter,
  at room temperature
½ cup freshly grated
  Parmesan cheese

1. In a large heavy saucepan, heat 2 tablespoons of the oil. Add the onion and half of the garlic and sauté over moderately low heat, stirring often, until softened and translucent but not browned, about 10 minutes.

Reduce the heat to low, blend in the thyme and rosemary and cook for 5 minutes.

2. Add the shredded squash and sauté, stirring frequently, until slightly translucent, about 5 minutes. Add the chicken and beef stocks. Cover and simmer gently for 1 hour.

3. Strain the soup, reserving the solids and liquid. In a blender or food processor, puree the soup solids in batches with ½ cup of the liquid until silky smooth. Return the remaining liquid and the puree to the saucepan and set over low heat.

4. In a heavy medium skillet, heat the remaining 2 tablespoons oil. Add the remaining garlic and sauté over low heat until softened but not browned, about 2 minutes. Add the bread crumbs and cook, tossing, until all of the oil is absorbed and the bread is lightly browned, 1 to 2 minutes. Stir the crumb mixture into the soup, then season to taste with salt and pepper. *(The soup can be made ahead to this point and either refrigerated or frozen. Reheat before proceeding.)*

5. To gratinée the soup, preheat the oven to 350°. Lightly spread the slices of French bread with the butter on one side only. Place on a baking sheet, buttered-side up, and bake for 8 to 10 minutes, until lightly toasted. Preheat the broiler with the rack set 6 inches from the heat.

6. For each serving, place 2 slices of toast in the bottom of a flameproof soup plate. Ladle the steaming hot squash soup over the toast and sprinkle with about 1 tablespoon Parmesan cheese. Set the soup plates on a baking sheet. Slide the sheet under the broiler and broil just until the cheese is bubbly and lightly browned, 2 to 3 minutes.
—*Jean Anderson*

Butternut Squash and Leek Soup

8 Servings

4½ pounds butternut squash, halved lengthwise
5 tablespoons unsalted butter
4 large leeks (white and tender green), chopped
7 sprigs of fresh thyme or 1 teaspoon dried
5 cups chicken stock or low-sodium canned broth
1¼ teaspoons salt
½ teaspoon freshly ground pepper
½ cup sour cream
2 to 3 tablespoons chopped chives
8 slices of bacon, fried crisp and crumbled

1. Preheat the oven to 350°. Place the squash, cut-side down, on a baking sheet and bake until tender, about 40 minutes. Let cool slightly. Using a spoon, scoop out and discard the seeds. Scrape the squash from the skin.

2. Meanwhile, in a large, heavy saucepan or flameproof casserole, melt the butter over low heat. Add the leeks and thyme and cook, stirring occasionally, until soft and lightly browned, about 40 minutes. Discard the thyme sprigs.

3. Stir in the stock and the squash. Simmer over moderate heat for 20 minutes. In a blender or food processor, puree the soup in batches until smooth. Pour the soup back into the pan and season with the salt and pepper. *(The recipe can be prepared to this point up to 2 days ahead. Reheat the soup before proceeding.)* To serve, ladle the soup into bowls and garnish each serving with 1 tablespoon sour cream, 1 teaspoon chopped chives and a sprinkling of the crumbled bacon.

—Tina Ujlaki

Cream of Carrot and Lemon Soup

This is my favorite vegetable soup. It has a wonderfully vibrant taste and looks beautiful as well.

6 to 8 Servings

6 tablespoons unsalted butter
1 large onion, chopped
1 large garlic clove, sliced
1½ pounds carrots, sliced
3 tomatoes, chopped
1 baking potato, peeled and sliced
¼ cup shredded fresh basil or flat-leaf parsley
4 cups rich chicken or Goose Stock (p. 50) or 3 cups canned chicken broth diluted with 1 cup water
1½ teaspoons salt
¼ teaspoon freshly ground pepper
1 cup crème fraîche
¼ teaspoon hot pepper sauce
¼ cup fresh lemon juice
Carrot curls, crème fraîche and flat-leaf parsley, for garnish

1. In a large saucepan or flameproof casserole, melt 4 tablespoons of the butter. Add the onion and garlic, cover and cook over low heat until softened but not browned, about 5 minutes.

2. Add the carrots, tomatoes, potato, basil, stock, salt, pepper and remaining 2 tablespoons butter. Bring to a boil over high heat, reduce the heat to moderately low and simmer, covered, for 45 minutes.

3. Strain the soup, reserving the broth and the vegetables. Puree the vegetables in a food processor until smooth. Return the puree and the broth to the pan. Add the crème fraîche and hot sauce. Simmer, uncovered, for 15 minutes. *(The recipe can be made to this point up to 1 day ahead. Cover and refrigerate.)*

4. Before serving, reheat the soup and stir in the lemon juice. Ladle the soup into individual soup bowls. Garnish each serving with a carrot curl, a dollop of crème fraîche and a leaf of parsley.

—Lydie Marshall

Squash Soup Spiked with Apple

12 Servings

1 large butternut squash (2 pounds)—peeled, seeded and cut into 1-inch cubes
5 cups chicken stock or canned broth
2 tart apples—such as Greening or Granny Smith—unpeeled, quartered and cored
2 tablespoons fresh lemon juice
Pinch of ground mace
Salt and freshly ground pepper
1 cup heavy cream
12 freshly cut thin apple wedges, for garnish

1. In a large saucepan, simmer the squash in 4 cups of the stock until the squash is tender, about 10 minutes. Puree, in batches if necessary, in a blender or food processor; pass through a fine sieve. Return to the saucepan.

2. In a blender or food processor, puree the quartered apples with the remaining 1 cup stock. Pass through a fine sieve to remove any bits of peel. Add the apple puree to the squash mixture. Bring to a boil, reduce the heat, add the lemon juice and mace and season with salt and pepper to taste. (The soup can be made ahead to this point, cooled and refrigerated or frozen. Reheat the soup before proceeding.)

3. Beat the cream until soft peaks form. Fold two-thirds of the whipped cream into the soup. Heat through, but do not allow to boil. Serve hot, garnished with the apple wedges and a dollop of the remaining whipped cream.
—Pearl Byrd Foster

Oyster and Spinach Soup

Fresh oysters on the half shell are much better in this dish than shucked oysters in a container, which are usually rinsed and hence less flavorful. Your fish market can shuck the oysters for you, or you can shuck them yourself.

While the aromatic soup base can be prepared ahead, the final cooking of the spinach and oysters, which takes only a few minutes, should be done at the last moment, or the oysters will toughen and the spinach may yellow.

12 Servings

4½ dozen freshly shucked
  oysters, liquor reserved
2 to 2½ cups clam juice,
  mussel juice or fish stock

1½ tablespoons unsalted
  butter
1½ tablespoons extra-virgin
  olive oil
2 leeks (white and tender
  green), thinly sliced
3 garlic cloves, minced
1½ pounds fresh spinach,
  stems removed
3 cups heavy cream
1 teaspoon salt, or to taste
1½ teaspoons freshly ground
  pepper

1. Put the oysters and their liquor in a large pot and "wash" them in their liquor. Lift out the oysters and, if they are very large, cut in half with scissors. Put the oysters in a bowl. Strain and measure the oyster liquor. Add enough clam juice to equal 3 cups of liquid, then add 3 cups of water; set the stock aside.

2. In a large saucepan, melt the butter in the olive oil over moderately high heat. Add the leeks and sauté until softened, about 2 minutes. Add the garlic and cook, stirring, for 30 seconds. Stir in the reserved 6 cups stock and bring to a boil. Remove from the heat and set aside for up to 2 hours. (The recipe can be prepared to this point up to 8 hours in advance. Cover and refrigerate.)

3. At serving time, bring the stock to a boil over high heat. Add the spinach, return to a boil and boil for 1 minute. Add the cream, salt and pepper and return to a boil. Add the oysters and bring just to a simmer. Ladle into soup plates and serve immediately.
—Jacques Pépin

Cauliflower-Oyster Stew

This stew—inspired by ingredients of the Pacific Northwest—is mild, rich, full of satisfying flavor, yet very quick to make. A tip on the oysters—if you don't have freshly shucked, buy the smallest possible top-quality jarred oysters. If you can only find medium or even large ones, don't worry. Cut them into bite-size pieces before adding to the stew.

Though additional turmeric is listed as a garnish, its aroma is an essential part of the stew, so don't pass it by.

6 Servings

1 large head of cauliflower
  (about 2 pounds), separated
  into florets
2½ cups milk
1 cup heavy cream
Salt and freshly ground white
  pepper
¼ teaspoon turmeric plus
  more for garnish
24 oysters and ¼ cup of their
  liquor (see Note)
1 tablespoon each chopped
  fresh chives and chervil, for
  garnish

1. Pour 1 inch of water into a large heavy saucepan or medium flameproof casserole and add the cauliflower florets. Cover and steam over high heat until tender, about 10 minutes.

2. Transfer the cauliflower to a food processor and puree with ½ cup of the milk until very smooth. Transfer the puree to the casserole and whisk in the remaining 2 cups milk and the cream until smooth. Cook over moderate heat, whisking occasionally, until very hot, about 3 minutes; don't let it boil or it may curdle. Season with salt and pepper to taste; whisk in ¼ teaspoon of the turmeric.

3. Add the oysters and their liquor and cook, stirring frequently, until just heated through, about 3 minutes. Do not boil or the oysters will become tough and chewy. Serve the stew in warmed bowls, garnished with the chives, chervil and a sprinkling of turmeric.

NOTE: If you shuck your own oysters, rinse the oysters in their liquor. Set them aside, then strain the liquor through cheesecloth to remove any grit.

—Susan Herrmann Loomis

Connecticut Seafood Chowder

Prepare the chowder base a day or two ahead; add the seafood of your choice and finish the soup shortly before serving.

8 to 10 Servings

Chowder Base:
3 ounces salt pork, cut into
  ¼-inch dice
1 medium leek (white part
  only), finely chopped
1 large onion, finely chopped
½ pound boiling potatoes
  (about 2 medium), peeled
  and cut into ⅜-inch dice
1 small celery rib, cut into
  ¼-inch dice
1 cup fish stock or bottled
  clam juice
2 teaspoons chopped parsley
¼ teaspoon oregano

¼ teaspoon thyme
1 bay leaf, broken
¼ teaspoon freshly ground
  pepper

Seafood:
¼ pound bay or quartered sea
  scallops
¼ pound haddock, scrod or
  other firm-fleshed white fish,
  cut into ½-inch pieces
18 quahogs (chowder clams),
  shucked and chopped, with
  3 cups of their liquor
  reserved
3 cups half-and-half or light
  cream
Dash of hot pepper sauce
1 tablespoon unsalted butter
Salt and freshly ground
  pepper

1. In a large kettle or flameproof casserole, sauté the salt pork over moderate heat until crisp and golden, about 5 minutes. Add the leek and onion and sauté until the onion begins to color, about 4 minutes.

2. Add the potatoes, celery, fish stock, parsley, oregano, thyme, bay leaf, pepper and 1 cup of water. Bring to a boil over moderate heat, reduce the heat to low and simmer the chowder base until the potatoes are barely tender, about 7 minutes. *(The recipe can be prepared ahead to this point. Let cool, then cover and refrigerate.)*

3. Shortly before serving, bring the chowder base to a boil over moderate heat; add the scallops, haddock and clams with their reserved liquor. Simmer until the clams are tender, about 5 minutes.

4. Stir in the half-and-half, hot pepper sauce and butter and heat to simmering over moderately low heat. Season with salt and pepper to taste before serving.

—Melanie Barnard

main courses

Roast Goose with Chestnut and Apple Stuffing

Roasting this succulent bird, aromatic with its stuffing of apples, raisins and chestnuts, is actually quite easy for the cook.

6 to 8 Servings

8- to 10-pound goose, giblets reserved
2 cups chestnuts—cooked, peeled and quartered (see Note)
6 cups tart apples, quartered if small or cut into eighths if large (5 or 6 apples)
½ cup raisins
1 cup pitted prunes (optional)
Coarse (kosher) salt
About ⅔ cup water or chicken stock
Salt and freshly ground pepper

1. Remove excess fat and the giblets from the cavity of the goose. (The fat can be rendered and used in cooking other dishes.) Place the neck, the heart and the gizzard (reserve the liver for another use) in the pan in which you intend to roast the goose.

2. Preheat the oven to 400°. Place the chestnuts in a mixing bowl with the apples, raisins and prunes and toss them well. Spoon the stuffing into the cavity of the goose, packing it loosely—the cavity should be about three-quarters full. If you have stuffing left, place it in a shallow baking dish and bake it alongside the goose for the last hour of roasting time.

3. Close the cavity of the goose, using skewers or poultry lacers or sew it up with coarse thread. Tie the legs of the goose together with kitchen string; then, using a separate length, tie the wings together against the back. Place the bird, breast side up, on a rack in the roasting pan. Rub the goose all over with coarse salt.

4. Roast the goose for 1 hour at 400°, then prick the skin with a fork at ½-inch intervals to release the fat. As the fat accumulates, remove it from the pan with a large spoon or a bulb baster. Reduce the temperature of the oven to 350° and roast the goose for another hour. After 2 hours, check for doneness: an instant-reading thermometer inserted in the thickest part of the thigh should read 180°. If not, lower the oven heat to 325° and continue to roast until the goose tests done.

5. Remove the goose from the oven to a platter and let it rest for 10 to 15 minutes before carving. Meanwhile, remove the rack from the roasting pan and remove excess fat from the juices in the pan, using a spoon or a bulb baster. Add the water to the pan juices and set the pan over a stove burner and heat the sauce, scraping up any browned bits. Season the sauce with salt and pepper to taste. Strain the gravy into a warmed sauceboat and pass it separately when the goose is served.

NOTE: If you're using fresh chestnuts, you'll need about 30 to 35 whole chestnuts. Using a small paring knife, cut an X through the shell on the flat side of each one. Place them in a saucepan, cover with boiling water and simmer for 15 to 25 minutes, until just tender but not mushy and the shell and inner brown skin of a nut can be easily removed with a paring knife. Drain the chestnuts and shell, skin and quarter them.
—*Joan Nathan*

Roast Goose with Sausage, Fruit and Nut Stuffing

The stuffing and goose stock for this recipe can be made a day ahead.
❦ Red Bordeaux, such as Cos d'Estournel, or California Cabernet Sauvignon, such as Stag's Leap Wine Cellars

8 to 10 Servings

10- to 11-pound goose, all excess fat removed, giblets reserved
Sausage, Fruit and Nut Stuffing (p. 125)
1 small lemon, cut in half
1 small onion, quartered
1 small carrot, cut into 1-inch lengths
1 celery rib, cut into 1-inch lengths
Grapes and kumquats, for garnish
½ cup Madeira
Salt and freshly ground pepper
2 tablespoons unsalted butter, at room temperature

1. Preheat the oven to 425°. Rinse the goose inside and out; pat dry. Loosely fill the main cavity with 6 to 7 cups of the stuffing. Using a trussing needle or skewers and kitchen string, sew up the opening; secure the legs and wings. Rub the entire bird with the cut sides of the lemon halves. Using a fork, prick the skin all over. Place the goose, breast-side up, on a rack in a shallow roasting pan.

2. Roast for 15 minutes, then lower the oven temperature to 350°. Continue to roast, basting the goose with 2 tablespoons of hot water every 20 minutes and drawing off the fat from the pan with a bulb baster, for about 2½ hours, or until the internal temperature reaches 160°. In-

crease the oven temperature to 425° and roast for about 15 minutes longer, or until the skin is crisp and the internal temperature reaches 180°.

3. Meanwhile, make a stock with the reserved giblets: Chop the neck into 1-inch pieces and cut the gizzard in half. (Reserve the liver for another use.) Place the giblets in a medium saucepan. Add the onion, carrot, celery and 4 cups of water. Bring to a boil over moderate heat, skimming off any scum from the surface. Reduce the heat to low and simmer until the stock is reduced to 1¾ cups, about 2 hours. Strain and skim off any fat.

4. Transfer the goose to a platter, remove trussing strings and garnish with grapes and kumquats.

5. Skim the fat from the pan juices. Pour in the Madeira and stock and bring to a boil over high heat, scraping up the browned bits clinging to the bottom of the pan. Continue to cook the sauce until reduced to 1½ cups, about 4 minutes. Season to taste with salt and pepper and swirl in the butter, 1 tablespoon at a time, until each piece has been incorporated into the sauce. Serve the sauce along with the goose.
—*Melanie Barnard*

Roast East Hampton Golden Goose

If you can buy a fresh goose, choose one with a soft, pliable bill. This indicates that the bird is young.
6 to 8 Servings

12- to 14-pound fresh young goose, or a frozen goose, defrosted
1 lemon, halved
Salt and freshly ground pepper

Apricot-Walnut Stuffing (p. 117)
1 stick (4 ounces) unsalted butter, melted
1 cup port wine (see Note)
¾ cup chicken stock
2 tablespoons arrowroot or cornstarch mixed with 2 tablespoons cold water or chicken stock

1. Preheat the oven to 550°, or to its highest possible setting.

2. Remove and reserve all excess fat from the goose. Rub the cavity and skin with the cut lemon; dust the bird inside and out with salt and pepper. Pierce the skin around the legs and wings with a fork.

3. Stuff the bird loosely with the Apricot-Walnut Stuffing and sew or skewer the cavity; truss the wings and legs. Brush the skin well with melted butter.

4. Place the bird, breast-side down, on a rack in a shallow roasting pan. Roast for 30 minutes. Reduce the heat to 300° and continue to roast, basting frequently with pan juices and pricking the skin often with a fork to release the fat.

5. After 2 hours, turn the goose breast up. Cover the breast with some of the reserved goose fat, pressing the pieces together into a sheet to cover the breast. Continue to roast until the joints move readily and the meat feels soft. The juices will run clear from a small cut in the thigh when the bird is done; approximate roasting time, 3 hours.

6. Remove the crusty fat pieces from the breast, turn the heat up to 450° and brown the skin to a golden crisp. Remove the bird to a hot serving platter.

7. Skim off and discard all but 3 tablespoons of fat from the juices in the roasting pan.

8. Add the port and stock. Set the pan over the heat and scrape the browned bits from the bottom and sides. Stir in the arrowroot mixture and simmer until thickened. Season with salt and pepper to taste and serve in a sauceboat.

NOTE: If you are making the Apricot-Walnut Stuffing (p. 117), you can reserve the port from Step 1 and use it in place of the port called for here.
—*Pearl Byrd Foster*

Roasted Goose with Chicken Liver Stuffing

If at all possible, buy a goose that has not been frozen. For six people, one goose is ideal if you learn how to carve it properly (see Note, below). Since goose has a lot of fat, render it and use at a later date to make delicious confits or roast potatoes.
♟ Jaboulet Côte Rôtie or Guigal Gigondas
6 Servings

10-pound goose, preferably fresh
1 tablespoon minced garlic
1 tablespoon thyme
1 tablespoon coarse (kosher) salt
Rich Chicken Liver Stuffing (p. 124)
3½ cups Goose Stock (recipe follows)
4 tablespoons unsalted butter
Freshly ground pepper

1. Trim the goose: Remove the wishbone by cutting off the membrane around the wishbone. With your fingers, loosen the bone and with a small sharp knife, pry the bone loose from the breast meat, breaking it off on both sides of the wings. Reserve the wishbone and the neck for the goose stock; reserve the

gizzard and liver for the stuffing. Cut off the wing tip and the second joint of the wings and reserve them for the goose stock. Remove all the loose fat from the cavity of the goose and reserve for rendered fat. Rinse the cavity of the bird and pat dry. *(The goose can be prepared to this point up to 2 days in advance. Wrap in aluminum foil and refrigerate.)*

2. The day before you roast the goose, combine the minced garlic, thyme and salt. Rub this dry marinade all over the breast, thighs and legs of the goose. Wrap and refrigerate until ready to roast. Remove the bird from the refrigerator 1 to 2 hours before roasting to let it come to room temperature.

3. Preheat the oven to 425°. Prick the skin of the goose all over. Spoon the Rich Chicken Liver Stuffing into the cavity of the goose and sew it up. Put the goose, breast-side down, in a gratin dish or a roasting pan just large enough to hold the bird. Pour 1 cup of stock into the pan.

4. Roast the goose for 15 minutes. Baste the goose with the pan drippings. Reduce the oven temperature to 350° and continue to roast, basting every 10 minutes, for 1 hour. Remove the goose from the oven. Carefully loosen the goose from the pan and transfer it to a board. Drain all the fat from the pan into a large heatproof glass bowl. Return the goose to the roasting pan, breast-side up; add another ½ cup of the goose stock to the pan. Continue roasting for 30 minutes, basting with the pan drippings every 10 minutes. Remove the goose from the oven and again drain the fat into the bowl.

5. Return the goose to the oven, still breast-side up. Add another ½ cup of the stock and roast for 30 minutes longer, or until the goose is golden brown and tender. Drain the fat into the bowl. There will be 4 to 6 cups of fat. At the bottom of the fat in the glass bowl, you will see the drippings from the roast. Use a gravy separator or just pour and skim off the fat. If you want to save the flavorful fat for the Rich Chicken Liver Stuffing (p. 124) or a future use, strain it into a container; it freezes well. Reserve the goose drippings in the bottom of the bowl. Transfer the goose to a carving board and let rest, covered loosely with aluminum foil, for about 20 minutes before carving.

6. Meanwhile, pour the reserved drippings into the roasting pan. Add the remaining 1½ cups goose stock to the pan and bring to a boil over high heat, scraping up the browned bits from the bottom of the pan. Boil until the liquid is reduced to 1 cup. Strain into a clean saucepan and whisk in the butter. Season the sauce with additional salt and pepper to taste. Carve the goose (see Note) and pass the sauce in a gravy boat on the side.

NOTE: To carve a goose: Cut through the shoulder joints to separate the first joint of the wings from the body. Then cut the skin between the legs and the body and push down on the legs to expose the thigh joints; cut through the joints. With the skin-side down, cut through the leg to separate into drumstick and thigh. With a long thin carving knife held parallel to the breast (an electric knife is great for this), cut the breast meat into thin slices.
—*Lydie Marshall*

Goose Stock

This recipe will yield more than enough to baste the goose. Either freeze the remainder or use it to make a soup to serve with the goose, such as Cream of Carrot and Lemon (p. 44).

Makes 2 Quarts

Reserved wing tips, second wing joints, wishbone (see Note) and neck of goose, or 1 more pound of chicken parts
2 pounds chicken necks, backs and/or wings
1 pound carrots
1 celery rib
2 medium onions, each stuck with 2 cloves
Bouquet garni: 3 sprigs of parsley, 1 teaspoon thyme and 1 bay leaf tied in cheesecloth
1½ teaspoons salt

1. Using a cleaver, cut up the goose and chicken parts into small pieces.

2. Put the goose and chicken parts in a stockpot. Add at least 4 quarts of cold water to cover. Bring to a boil over moderately low heat, skimming the surface several times.

3. Add the whole carrots, celery, onions, bouquet garni and salt to the stockpot. Simmer, partially covered, for 3 hours; strain through a fine-mesh sieve. If there are more than 8 cups, boil to reduce. *(The stock can be made up to 2 days in advance and refrigerated, covered.)*

NOTE: See Step 1 of the Roasted Goose with Chicken Liver Stuffing for how to remove the wishbone.
—*Lydie Marshall*

Roast Duck with Port-Soaked Prunes

The deep black-purple prunes and the golden brown caramelized onions add an autumnal feel to this dish. The duck is delicious with roast potatoes and sautéed Swiss chard.

4 to 6 Servings

4 or 5 small garlic cloves,
*   minced*
1¼ teaspoons cinnamon
1 tablespoon plus 1 teaspoon
*   fresh lemon juice*
Two 5-pound ducks, trimmed
*   of excess fat*
¾ teaspoon salt
¾ teaspoon freshly ground
*   pepper*
24 pitted prunes (8 ounces)
2¼ cups port
1 pint pearl onions
2 tablespoons unsalted butter
1 teaspoon sugar
1 cup chicken stock or canned
*   low-sodium broth*
3 tablespoons orange juice
1 teaspoon finely grated
*   orange zest*

1. Preheat the oven to 500°. In a small bowl, combine the garlic, 1 teaspoon cinnamon and the lemon juice. Crush with the back of a spoon into a rough paste. Rub the insides of the ducks with the paste and lightly season the outside with ¼ teaspoon of both salt and pepper. Place on a rack in a large roasting pan and roast about 1 hour or until browned and the juices run clear when the thigh is pierced with a knife.

2. Meanwhile, in a small nonreactive saucepan, combine the prunes with 1 cup of the port. Bring to a simmer over moderately high heat. Remove from the heat, cover and set aside for at least 30 minutes and up to 2 hours.

3. Make a cross in the root end of each pearl onion. In a medium saucepan of boiling salted water, cook the onions until tender, 5 to 7 minutes, drain and let cool. Peel and trim.

4. In a small sauté pan, melt the butter over high heat. Add the cooked onions and sprinkle with the sugar. Cook, shaking the pan constantly, until the onions have caramelized to a rich brown, about 3 minutes. Set aside.

5. In a medium nonreactive saucepan, place the remaining 1¼ cups port and the chicken stock. Bring to a boil over high heat and reduce to about 1 cup, about 10 minutes.

6. Add the orange juice, orange zest, the remaining ¼ teaspoon cinnamon, the prunes and their liquid and onions to the sauce. Season with the remaining ½ teaspoon each salt and pepper. Cook to warm through, about 3 minutes.

7. Cut the breasts from the ducks and slice each in half. Remove the legs and separate the drumsticks and thighs. Arrange the duck pieces on a large warmed serving platter. Spoon the prunes, onions and sauce on top. Serve hot.
—*Joyce Goldstein, Square One, San Francisco*

Duck with Sweet and Sour Wild Mushroom Cider Sauce

2 Servings

4½-pound duck, trimmed of
*   excess fat*
Salt and freshly ground white
*   pepper*
1 onion, quartered
2 celery ribs, coarsely
*   chopped*
1 bay leaf, broken in half
8 ounces sliced bacon, cut
*   into 1-inch pieces*

½ pound shiitake mushrooms,
*   stems discarded, caps*
*   coarsely chopped*
2 cups unfiltered,
*   unpasteurized apple cider*
1 tablespoon all-purpose flour
2 tablespoons Cognac or
*   other brandy*
2 tablespoons red wine
*   vinegar*
½ teaspoon thyme

1. Preheat the oven to 400°. Rinse the duck well and pat it dry. Cut off the wing tips. Sprinkle the duck inside and out with ½ teaspoon each of salt and pepper, then truss it with string if desired. Prick the duck all over at 1-inch intervals and place it, breast side down, in a roasting pan just large enough to hold it. Arrange the onion quarters, celery and bay leaf around it.

2. Roast the duck for 15 minutes. Turn the duck breast side up and prick again. Continue to roast, turning every 15 minutes, for 45 to 55 minutes more, until the duck is browned and the juices run clear when a thigh is pierced.

3. While the duck roasts, begin making the sauce. In a large skillet, cook the bacon over moderately high heat until lightly browned but not crisp, about 7 minutes. Using a slotted spoon, transfer the bacon to paper towels to drain.

4. Pour off all but 2 tablespoons of the bacon fat from the skillet. Add the mushrooms and cook, stirring, until their juices evaporate, about 10 minutes. Add ½ cup of the cider to the skillet, bring to a boil and cook until the liquid has been reduced by half, about 4 minutes. Whisk in the flour until thoroughly blended. Remove from the heat and set aside.

5. When the duck is cooked, remove it from the roasting pan and cut it in half lengthwise with poultry

shears. Cut out and discard the backbone. Cover the duck halves with foil and keep them warm in a low oven. Discard the fat and vegetables in the roasting pan.

6. Pour the remaining 1½ cups cider into the roasting pan and bring to a boil, scraping the bottom to release any browned bits. Pour the contents of the roasting pan over the mushrooms in the skillet. Add the Cognac, vinegar and thyme and bring to a boil over moderate heat. Cook, stirring frequently, until the sauce thickens slightly, about 10 minutes. Stir in the reserved bacon and season with additional salt and white pepper to taste. Serve the duck on heated plates with the sauce spooned on top.
—Linda Merinoff

Roast Cranberry-Glazed Ducklings with Cranberry Gravy

6 to 8 Servings

Three 5-pound ducklings
1½ teaspoons salt
½ teaspoon freshly ground
   pepper
3 small sprigs of fresh
   rosemary or ¾ teaspoon
   dried, crumbled
2 medium celery ribs, diced
2 medium onions, diced
2 medium tart apples—
   peeled, cored and diced
½ cup light honey
2 cups fresh or frozen whole
   cranberries
2 cups Savory Duck Stock
   (p. 57)
1 tablespoon red currant jelly
1 tablespoon fresh lemon
   juice

2 tablespoons unsalted butter,
   at room temperature

1. Preheat the oven to 450°. Pull all the fat from the body and neck cavities of the ducklings and discard. Clip off the wing tips and reserve these, the giblets and the necks for the duck stock. Rub the body cavities of the ducklings with the salt and pepper (and, if you have no fresh rosemary, with the dried rosemary as well). If using fresh rosemary, tuck a sprig into each body cavity.

2. In a medium bowl, combine the celery, onions and apples and toss well to mix. Loosely fill the ducklings with the mixture. Close the body cavities with poultry pins and kitchen twine. Skewer the flaps of neck skin to the backs of the ducklings. *(The ducks can be prepared ahead to this point; keep loosely covered on a rack in the refrigerator.)*

3. Prick each duckling well all over with a fork and place breast-side down on a rack in a very large shallow roasting pan. Roast the ducklings, uncovered, for 20 minutes. Lower the oven to 350°. Prick the ducklings well all over, turn onto one side and roast for another 20 minutes. Prick each well again, turn onto the opposite side and roast 20 minutes longer. (Remove the duck fat from the roasting pan as it accumulates.) Once again prick the ducklings well, turn breast-side up and roast for 1 hour, pricking lightly about every 20 minutes and pouring off the fat as it collects.

4. Meanwhile, in a heavy medium saucepan, bring 2 cups of water and the honey to a boil over moderate heat. Add the cranberries and boil until the skins pop, about 5 minutes.

5. With a slotted spoon, remove the cranberries. Set half of them

aside for the cranberry gravy. In a blender or food processor, puree the remaining cranberries with the honey mixture. Return the puree to the pan. Boil until reduced to about 1½ cups (the mixture should be glistening and about the consistency of corn syrup). Remove the glaze from the heat and cover to keep warm. *(The glaze can be prepared ahead to this point and reheated.)*

6. When the ducklings test done (the drumsticks should move easily in the hip joints), remove from the oven but leave the oven on. Remove the poultry pins and twine. Remove and discard the stuffing ingredients. Pour the pan drippings into a small bowl and skim off the fat; reserve the drippings for making the gravy.

7. Using a pastry brush, generously paint each duckling with the cranberry glaze. Return to the oven and roast, uncovered, for 5 to 10 minutes, or until the skin looks shiny and glazed. Remove the ducklings from the oven and brush generously with the glaze (set the remainder aside). Transfer the ducklings to a large heated platter and let rest for about 20 minutes.

8. Meanwhile, set the roasting pan over moderate heat, add ½ cup of water and stir, scraping up the browned bits that cling to the bottom to deglaze the pan.

9. Strain the mixture into a heavy medium saucepan and add the reserved cranberry glaze, the reserved duck drippings and the Savory Duck Stock. Set over high heat and boil, whisking frequently, until reduced by one-third, 15 to 20 minutes.

10. Whisk in the currant jelly, lemon juice and butter. Stir in the reserved whole cranberries. Season with salt and pepper to taste. Pour into a heated sauceboat and pass the gravy separately.
—Jean Anderson

Salmon Caviar Toasts (p. 26).

At left: Candied Quinces (p. 151),
Roasted Goose with Chicken Liver
Stuffing (p. 49) and Flageolets with
Garlic Cloves (p. 101).
Above: Cream of Carrot and
Lemon Soup (p. 44) and
Salad of Watercress, Arugula and
Fennel (p. 103).

Ali Baba (p. 171).

Savory Duck Stock

The quickest way to make a rich duck stock, I've found, is to use equal parts water, beef and chicken broth and to cut the vegetables fairly fine so that their flavors are more easily extracted.

Makes About 4 Cups

Giblets, necks and wing tips
from 3 ducklings
2 cups beef broth
2 cups chicken broth
1 large carrot, thinly sliced
1 large celery rib, thinly sliced
1 large onion, cut into slim
wedges
2 large sprigs of parsley
1 small sprig of fresh sage or
¼ teaspoon dried, crumbled
1 small sprig of fresh thyme
or ¼ teaspoon dried
1-inch strip of orange zest
8 peppercorns

1. Place all of the ingredients in a large heavy saucepan; add 2 cups of cold water. Bring to a simmer and cook over low heat, uncovered, for 1½ hours, skimming occasionally.

2. Strain the duck stock. Measure out 2 cups of stock for the Cranberry Gravy (above); freeze the remainder.
—*Jean Anderson*

Roast Fresh Turkey with Madeira Gravy

Serve this roast turkey with Country Ham and Wild Mushroom Stuffing (p. 122).

8 Servings

10-pound fresh turkey, giblets
reserved, at room
temperature
1 stick (4 ounces) unsalted
butter, softened
Salt and freshly ground
pepper
¼ cup vegetable oil
½ cup chicken stock or
canned broth
Madeira Gravy (recipe
follows)

1. Preheat the oven to 325°. Cut off the first joint of each wing and reserve, along with the neck, heart and gizzard, for use in the gravy. Reserve the liver for another use.

2. Rub the breast with 2 tablespoons of the butter. Season the breast and the main cavity lightly with salt and pepper. Truss the turkey if you wish, although this step is unnecessary if the bird is roasted unstuffed.

3. Set the turkey breast-side up in a shallow roasting pan just large enough to hold it comfortably. Dampen a 10-by-20-inch square of cheesecloth, double it and drape it over the turkey breast. About 3½ hours before you wish to eat, put the turkey in to roast.

4. In a small saucepan, melt the remaining 6 tablespoons butter in the oil and chicken stock over low heat. When the turkey has baked for 30 minutes, baste it liberally through the cheesecloth with half the butter mixture. Baste again with the remaining butter mixture after another 30 minutes. After another 15 minutes, baste the turkey with the accumulated juices from the roasting pan and repeat every 15 minutes until the turkey is done (when an instant-reading thermometer in the thickest part of the breast registers 160°). Begin checking the turkey for doneness after 2 hours and 15 minutes.

5. Wrap the turkey well in foil and set aside until ready to carve. Serve with the Madeira Gravy.
—*Michael McLaughlin*

Madeira Gravy

Makes About 3 Cups

6 tablespoons unsalted butter,
at room temperature
1 tablespoon vegetable oil
Turkey necks, giblets and
wing tips reserved from
Roast Fresh Turkey (at left)
2 medium onions, chopped
2 leeks (white part only),
chopped
3 carrots, chopped
1 teaspoon thyme
1 bay leaf
Stems from 1 bunch of
parsley
1 cup dry (Sercial) Madeira
5 cups chicken stock or
canned broth (see Note)
¼ cup all-purpose flour
Salt and freshly ground
pepper

1. In a medium saucepan, melt 2 tablespoons of the butter in the oil over moderate heat until foaming. Add the turkey giblets, neck and wing tips and cook, stirring often, until browned, about 20 minutes.

2. Add the onions, leeks, carrots, thyme, bay leaf and parsley stems; cover, reduce the heat and cook, stirring occasionally, until the vegetables are tender and lightly colored, about 20 minutes.

3. Add the Madeira and chicken stock to the pan. Bring to a boil, partially cover, reduce the heat and simmer for 30 minutes, skimming as necessary.

4. Let cool slightly; then strain, discarding the solids. You should have about 5 cups of stock.

5. Wipe out the pan and return the liquid to it. Bring to a boil and

cook, uncovered, until reduced to 3 cups, about 30 minutes. *(The gravy can be prepared to this point 24 hours in advance. Let cool to room temperature, cover and refrigerate. Reheat slowly until simmering before proceeding.)*

6. In a small bowl, mash the remaining 4 tablespoons butter with the flour to form a smooth, thick paste (beurre manié). Reduce the heat under the gravy to very low and whisk the beurre manié into it, 1 tablespoon at a time. Increase the heat to moderate and simmer, stirring, for 5 minutes. Season with salt and pepper to taste before serving.

NOTE: If you are making the Country Ham and Wild Mushroom Stuffing (p. 122) to go with the turkey, reserve the mushroom soaking liquid from Step 4 and use in place of some of the chicken stock called for here.
—*Michael McLaughlin*

Thanksgiving Turkey with Two Stuffings

You may want to have the butcher remove the wishbone to facilitate stuffing the turkey and carving it after roasting.

❢ Though turkey goes with a wide variety of wines, the many side dishes typical of Thanksgiving require a simple, fruity light red, such as a Beaujolais Nouveau, Duboeuf Beaujolais-Villages or Beaulieu Vineyard Gamay Beaujolais, which will bridge the different tastes and match the festive mood. A fruity sparkling wine, such as Korbel Brut Rosé, would make a delightful alternative.

6 to 8 Servings

1 fresh turkey (10 to 12 pounds), at room temperature, neck reserved
½ lemon

Corn Bread-Sausage Dressing (p. 126)
Chestnut Dressing (p. 118)
¾ teaspoon salt
¾ teaspoon freshly ground white pepper
1 stick (4 ounces) plus 1½ tablespoons unsalted butter, softened
½ pound mushrooms, sliced
3 tablespoons all-purpose flour
3 cups chicken stock or canned broth
1 tablespoon finely chopped parsley

1. Preheat the oven to 425°. Rub the inside of the bird with the cut lemon.

2. Spoon 7 to 9 cups of the Corn Bread-Sausage Dressing into the large tail cavity of the turkey to stuff it loosely. Stuff the neck cavity loosely with some of the Chestnut Dressing; cover with the skin flap. (Wrap the extra stuffing in a baking dish or aluminum foil and bake during the last 15 minutes the turkey roasts and while it rests.) To truss the turkey, close the tail cavity by securing it with twine. Tie the wings close to the body and tie the legs together.

3. Season the turkey with ¼ teaspoon each of the salt and white pepper. Rub 4 tablespoons of the butter into the skin. Set the turkey on its side in a large roasting pan.

4. Roast the turkey until the top side is brown, about 30 minutes. Turn the turkey onto its other side and roast until brown, about 30 minutes longer. Meanwhile, melt 4 tablespoons of the butter. Dampen and thoroughly wring out a 14-by-24-inch piece of cheesecloth. Put it in a small bowl and pour the melted butter over it, turning to coat the cloth evenly.

5. When both sides of the turkey are brown, turn it on its back. Cover it with the buttered cheesecloth. Add the neck to the pan.

6. Reduce the oven temperature to 325°. Baste the turkey breast thoroughly with the pan drippings, using a large bulb baster. Roast the turkey, basting whenever the cheesecloth dries out, for 1½ hours. Carefully remove the cheesecloth and roast, basting every 15 minutes, until the turkey is browned, the juices in the thickest part of the thigh run clear when pricked and a thermometer thrust into the thick part of the bird's thigh registers between 165° and 170°, 60 to 70 minutes longer. Allow the turkey to rest for 15 to 20 minutes before carving.

7. Meanwhile in a large skillet, melt the remaining 1½ tablespoons butter over high heat. Add the mushrooms and cook, stirring occasionally, until the mushrooms are tender and any liquid evaporates, about 3 minutes. Set aside.

8. Transfer the turkey to a carving board. Discard all but ¼ cup fat from the roasting pan. Place the pan over 2 burners set on moderate heat. Add the flour to the fat. Cook, stirring, for 1 to 2 minutes. Whisk in the chicken stock. Bring to a boil, whisking until the sauce is thickened and smooth, about 4 minutes. Add the sautéed mushrooms, the remaining ½ teaspoon each salt and pepper and the parsley. Cook for 1 to 2 minutes to blend the flavors. Serve in a warm sauceboat with the carved turkey.
—*Camille Glenn*

Roast Turkey with Celery and Lemon Stuffing

Whenever possible, buy fresh turkey (you may have to order it in advance). The moistness and full flavor of the bird will surprise you. Frozen turkeys are more available than fresh ones and are generally quite satisfactory, especially if you can find one that is not self-basting (such birds have been injected with liquid fats and chemicals).

6 to 8 Servings

8- to 10-pound turkey
Salt and freshly ground
  pepper
2½ sticks (10 ounces)
  unsalted butter, at room
  temperature
1 large onion, chopped
2 celery ribs, trimmed and
  chopped
4 cups fresh bread crumbs
⅓ cup fresh lemon juice
3 teaspoons grated lemon zest
2 eggs, lightly beaten
All-purpose flour

1. Season the turkey inside and out with salt and pepper.

2. Preheat the oven to 350°.

3. In a heavy pan, heat 1 stick of the butter. Add the onion and celery and cook, covered, for about 15 minutes, or until meltingly soft.

4. Add the bread crumbs, lemon juice, lemon zest and eggs, and toss lightly to mix. Season with salt and pepper to taste.

5. Stuff the turkey, leaving room for the filling to expand during cooking. If there is enough stuffing, fill the neck cavity as well.

6. Truss the bird with kitchen string and skewer or sew the opening and fasten the neck skin to the turkey back. Rub the bird with 4 tablespoons of the butter. Melt the remaining 1 stick butter and soak a clean kitchen towel (or two layers of cheesecloth) in it. Lay it over the bird to cover the breast and legs.

7. Roast for 3½ hours, basting frequently with the juices after the first 30 minutes. After 3 hours, remove the cloth, dust the turkey lightly with flour, and continue roasting for 30 minutes. (The flour helps crisp the skin.) Let the turkey rest on its platter at room temperature for 20 to 30 minutes before carving it.
—F&W

Stuffed Venetian Turkey

The inspiration for this turkey comes from a traditional Venetian recipe in which turkey is spit-roasted and basted with fresh pomegranate juice and port. The turkey is stuffed with a rich combination of pureed chestnuts, ground pork and veal, prunes and port. And it is topped with thin slices of pancetta (a spicy Italian bacon), which protects and flavors the bird while it roasts. In addition, the turkey is basted with pomegranate juice, which gives added flavor and a beautiful, deep mahogany color.

12 Servings

Stuffed Turkey:
12-pound turkey, thawed if
  frozen
1½ pounds chestnuts
3 cups beef stock or canned
  broth
3 cups cubed (½-inch) firm-
  textured white bread
½ cup milk
6 tablespoons unsalted butter
4 celery ribs, chopped

1 medium onion, chopped
½ pound ground veal
½ pound ground pork
2 tablespoons minced parsley
1 teaspoon thyme
3 tablespoons white or tawny
  port
1 cup quartered prunes
½ cup freshly grated
  Parmesan cheese
4 eggs, lightly beaten
1 tablespoon salt
½ teaspoon freshly ground
  pepper
4 to 6 thin slices pancetta or a
  thin sheet of fatback
1½ cups unsweetened
  pomegranate juice*

Sauce:
12 cups chicken stock
1 cup white or tawny port
4 tablespoons unsalted butter

Garnish:
Fresh pomegranate seeds
  (optional)
*Available at health food
  stores

1. Preheat the oven to 400°. Remove the giblets and neck from the turkey and reserve them for the sauce.

2. Prepare the stuffing: Cut an X in the flat side of each chestnut with the tip of a small knife and place them in an ungreased baking pan. Bake for 20 minutes, or until the shells begin to curl. Let stand until cool enough to handle, then remove the shells.

3. Simmer the chestnuts in the beef stock, uncovered, until all the liquid is absorbed, about 40 minutes. Puree the chestnuts through the medium disc of a food mill.

4. Preheat the oven to 350°. Place the bread in a large bowl. Pour on the milk and let the bread soak for 10 minutes, stirring once or twice.

5. In a large skillet, melt 3 tablespoons of the butter over moderate heat. Add the celery and onion and sauté until softened, about 10 minutes. Add to the bowl with the bread. Add the pureed chestnuts, the veal, pork, parsley, thyme, port, prunes, Parmesan, eggs, salt and pepper and mix well. This should yield about 8 cups of stuffing.

6. Turn the turkey breast-side down. Lightly pack about 1 cup of the stuffing into the neck. Pull the neck skin over to seal and fasten it to the turkey with metal skewers or wooden picks. Turn the turkey breast-side up and lightly fill the main cavity with about 4 cups of the stuffing. Fold the wing tips under and truss the turkey. Rub it with the remaining 3 tablespoons butter and cover the breast with the slices of pancetta, securing them with toothpicks. Place the remaining stuffing in a buttered baking dish and set it aside until 45 minutes before the turkey is done.

7. Roast the turkey in the oven for 1½ hours. At the end of that time, baste it generously with pomegranate juice. Roast the turkey about 2 hours longer, basting every 30 minutes with pomegranate juice and the drippings in the bottom of the pan. The turkey is done when the breast meat registers 160° and the thigh meat 170° and the juices run clear. During the last 45 minutes of cooking, bake the extra stuffing, uncovered.

8. While the turkey is roasting, begin preparing the sauce: Boil the chicken stock with the reserved turkey giblets and neck until the liquid is reduced by half. Strain the stock and discard the giblets and neck. Add the port and set the sauce aside until the turkey is done.

9. Remove the turkey from the roasting pan; remove the toothpicks and peel off the pancetta. Pour the drippings out of the pan. Add the sauce to the roasting pan and heat to boiling, scraping up any browned bits that cling to the pan. Cook until reduced by half, about 15 minutes. Strain into a small saucepan, heat to boiling and whisk in the butter, 1 tablespoon at a time.

10. Serve the turkey and stuffing with the sauce. Garnish each serving with the fresh pomegranate seeds, if you wish.
—Silvio Pinto

Traditional Roast Stuffed
Turkey with Pan Gravy

When roasting turkey, consider the fact that the legs and thighs are tougher than the breast meat and take longer to be tenderized by the heat. Also, drumsticks and wings tend to dry out in the oven if they are not properly secured, so correctly trussing the bird is important. Simple instructions for doing this may be found in almost any good basic cookbook. My father used to wrap slices of bacon around the lower part of each drumstick, a trick you might try.

🍷 Fruity red, such as Zinfandel or Beaujolais

8 to 12 Servings

Skillet Corn Bread (p. 137)
1½ cups cubed white toast
2 sticks (8 ounces) plus 2
  tablespoons unsalted butter
3 medium celery ribs,
  chopped
1 medium green bell pepper,
  chopped

1 medium onion, chopped
1 cup chopped scallions
  (about 1 bunch)
Turkey Stock (recipe follows)
1 cup coarsely chopped
  pecans (about 4 ounces)
¼ cup minced fresh parsley
2 teaspoons salt
1 teaspoon freshly ground
  black pepper
¼ teaspoon cayenne pepper
¼ teaspoon thyme
2 hard-cooked eggs, coarsely
  grated
2 large eggs, lightly beaten
15-pound turkey, neck and
  giblets reserved for the stock
2 tablespoons all-purpose
  flour

1. Preheat the oven to 450°. In a large bowl, crumble the Skillet Corn Bread and toss with the toast cubes.

2. In a large skillet, melt 4 tablespoons of the butter over low heat. Add the celery, green pepper, onion and scallions. Cook over low heat, stirring, until wilted but not browned, about 15 minutes.

3. In a small saucepan, melt 4 tablespoons of the butter in ¾ cup of the Turkey Stock. Set aside.

4. Add the pecans, parsley, salt, black pepper, cayenne and thyme to the corn bread mixture. Stir in the wilted vegetables, the hard-cooked eggs, raw eggs and stock mixture. Toss to blend well.

5. Stuff the cavity and neck of the bird loosely. (If there is any extra stuffing, wrap in a buttered foil packet and bake during the last 30 minutes with the turkey.) Sew the openings of the turkey or skewer them shut; truss the bird. In a medium saucepan, melt 1 stick of the butter and soak a 2-foot-long double layer of cheesecloth in it. Place the turkey on a greased rack in a roasting pan and cover the breast with the

butter-soaked cheesecloth. Set the remaining 2 tablespoons butter out to soften.

6. Put the turkey in the oven. Immediately reduce the heat to 325° and roast, basting with any pan juices every 30 minutes, until an instant-reading thermometer inserted into the inner thigh registers 155°, about 3½ hours; remove the cheesecloth from the breast. Continue to roast, basting, until the thigh temperature reaches 180°, 50 to 60 minutes longer. Transfer the turkey to a carving board and let the turkey rest, loosely covered, for at least 15 and up to 30 minutes before carving.

7. Meanwhile, to make the gravy, mash together the softened 2 tablespoons butter and the flour until blended to a paste. Skim the fat off the juices in the turkey roasting pan. Pour in the remaining stock and bring to a boil, scraping up any browned bits from the bottom of the pan. Gradually whisk in the butter paste and boil, whisking, until thickened. Reduce the heat and simmer for 5 minutes. Season with salt and pepper to taste. Strain into a sauceboat.
—*Lee Bailey*

Turkey Stock

Makes About 3 Cups

Turkey neck and giblets
1 medium onion, chopped
1 large celery rib with leaves,
 chopped
1 large carrot, unpeeled and
 chopped
3 sprigs of parsley

1. Preheat the oven to 350°. Put the neck and giblets and the onion in a small roasting or flameproof baking pan and roast for 1 hour, turning, until browned all over. Transfer the browned ingredients to a medium saucepan.

2. Place the roasting pan over high heat. When the pan drippings start to sizzle, pour in 1 cup of water and boil, scraping up all the browned bits from the bottom of the pan. Pour this liquid into the saucepan and add the celery, carrot, parsley and 3 cups of water. Bring to a boil over high heat. Reduce the heat to low and simmer for 1½ hours. Strain, let cool, then cover and refrigerate. *(The stock can be made up to 1 day in advance. If you buy a turkey neck and giblets separately, you can make the stock weeks, or even months, ahead and freeze it.)*
—*Lee Bailey*

Armadillo Turkey

Here is Floridian Robert Barnum's unusual turkey recipe. Use the leftover pineapple for another use, such as a winter citrus fruit salad. We suggest using pineapple juice in a carton or bottle to avoid the unpleasant metallic taste of the canned variety. Cooking time will vary slightly: a fresh, unfrozen bird will take less time to roast than a frozen one.

❧ The use of pineapple with the mild turkey suggests a fruity, light red, such as California Gamay Beaujolais. Try a Charles Shaw or Beaulieu Vineyard. Alternately, a Beaujolais Nouveau would add a nice seasonal touch.

10 to 12 Servings

1 lime, halved crosswise
15-pound turkey
1 small onion, quartered
Freshly ground pepper
1½ cups unsweetened
 pineapple juice
1 large pineapple (about 2
 pounds)

3 tablespoons unsalted butter
Salt

1. Preheat the oven to 325°. Squeeze the lime into the cavity of the turkey and leave the lime halves inside. Place the onion in the cavity. Sprinkle pepper all over the turkey, inside and out. Truss the bird and place it on a rack in a nonreactive roasting pan large enough to hold it with plenty of room to spare.

2. Pour ½ cup of the pineapple juice over the turkey and roast in the lower part of the oven for 30 minutes. Pour another ½ cup of the pineapple juice on top and roast for another 30 minutes.

3. Meanwhile, using a large stainless steel knife and cutting from top to bottom, remove the skin from the pineapple in 4 equal pieces, leaving ¼ inch of pineapple on the skin; set aside.

4. Pour the remaining ½ cup pineapple juice over the turkey and cover the turkey breast with the 4 pieces of pineapple skin. Secure the pineapple skins in place with small metal skewers. Continue to roast the turkey, basting it over the pineapple skin every 30 minutes, for 2½ to 3 hours longer, until deep golden brown and an instant-reading thermometer inserted into the thickest part of a thigh reads 170° to 180°.

5. Remove the roasting pan from the oven and prop the turkey up with the legs slightly higher than the breast to let the juices run back into the breast meat. Let rest for at least 30 and up to 45 minutes.

6. To serve, place the turkey on a heated platter. Pour the pan juices into a small saucepan, scraping up any browned—but not burned—bits from the bottom of the roasting pan. Skim off all the fat from the surface and bring the juices to a boil over high heat. Cook for 1 minute. Re-

move from the heat and let cool slightly, about 2 minutes. Whisk in the butter and season with salt and pepper. Strain the gravy through a coarse sieve into a sauceboat. Remove the skewers and discard the pineapple skins before carving the turkey.
—*Susan Herrmann Loomis*

Quick Roasted Turkey with Lemon-Cornbread Stuffing

Here, instead of the usual slow-cooking method, we quick-roast turkey at a high temperature. This technique not only cuts down on cooking time but also helps to keep the turkey moist. By roasting the turkey this way, we were able to cook a 16-pound bird to perfection in only three hours.

Another time-saving device we discovered is stuffing the bird while the dressing is still hot. This high-temperature, quick-cooking method does involve a bit more watching and basting than the slow-cooking, low-temperature method, but the trade-off is shorter cooking time and a juicy turkey.

16 Servings

One 16-pound turkey,
  thawed if frozen
Lemon-Corn Bread Stuffing
  (p. 127), still hot
1 tablespoon olive oil
1 large onion, sliced
2 carrots, sliced
2 bay leaves
1 sprig of parsley
2 garlic cloves, sliced
6 peppercorns, cracked
¼ cup all-purpose flour
¾ cup dry white wine,
  chicken broth or water
Salt and freshly ground
  pepper

1. Preheat the oven to 475°. Remove the neck and giblets from the turkey and reserve them.

2. Place the turkey breast-side down. Loosely fill the neck with 1 cup of the hot Lemon-Corn Bread Stuffing. Pull the neck skin over the cavity to seal it and fasten to the back of the turkey with skewers or wooden picks. Turn the turkey breast-side up and fold the wings under the turkey.

3. Lightly pack the remaining 5 cups stuffing into the main cavity. Tie the drumsticks together with kitchen string or, if your turkey has a metal clamp, arrange the drumsticks so that the clamp will hold them in place. Rub the turkey with the oil.

4. Place the turkey, breast-side up, on a rack in a roasting pan and roast in the lower third of the oven for 45 minutes. The initial 45 minutes will begin to brown the turkey very quickly, so be sure your oven temperature is not higher than 475°.

5. Meanwhile, make the stock for the gravy (let it simmer while the turkey roasts): Place the reserved neck and giblets in a medium saucepan. Add the onion, carrots, bay leaves, parsley, garlic, peppercorns and 2 quarts of water. Bring to a boil and reduce the heat to low. If the liquid reduces to less than 2 cups at any time, add additional water. Just before the turkey is done, strain the stock and discard the solids; you should have 2 cups of liquid.

6. Lower the oven temperature to 400° and loosely cover the turkey with an aluminum foil tent. Continue to roast, basting with the pan juices every 30 minutes or so, for about 2¼ hours, or until the internal temperature of the breast registers 160° and the thigh meat 170° (the juices will run clear when pierced with a fork).

7. Remove the turkey from the oven and lift it on the rack from the roasting pan; allow it to rest for 20 minutes before carving.

8. Meanwhile, prepare the gravy: Pour the drippings from the roasting pan into a measuring cup and let the fat rise to the top. Spoon off most of the fat but keep 1 cup drippings. Pour these drippings back into the roasting pan and add the flour. Place the pan over 2 burners adjusted to moderate heat and cook, stirring constantly, until the mixture is bubbling, about 3 minutes. Add the wine and reserved stock and cook, stirring constantly, until the gravy thickens and boils, about 2 minutes. Season with salt and pepper to taste.
—*F&W*

Ken Hom's Boned Stuffed Turkey

As a cooking teacher, Ken Hom is particularly interested in teaching the principles of Chinese cooking, several of which he has applied here in this unusual and delicious Oriental-style turkey. The first step is boning the turkey (ask your butcher to do it for you, but save the carcass for making the stock) and marinating it overnight. Then the turkey is stuffed with a melange of Oriental ingredients: Chinese sausage, fresh water chestnuts, scallions and glutinous rice. To ensure that the turkey meat does not become dry, Hom opts to steam the bird (another classic Chinese touch) before giving it a final roasting. The result: an elegant-looking turkey that is moist and bursting with fresh Oriental flavors.

12 Servings

12-pound turkey, boned but
  in one piece, carcass
  reserved
3 tablespoons coarse (kosher)
  salt

1 teaspoon freshly ground
  pepper
3 tablespoons Oriental
  sesame oil
½ cup fresh lemon juice
4 cups Oriental Stuffing
  (p. 111)
Rich Turkey and Chicken
  Stock (recipe follows)

1. Reserve the carcass for making the Rich Turkey and Chicken Stock.

2. Using a needle and thread, sew the turkey closed from the tail almost to the neck leaving an opening 4 to 5 inches long for stuffing.

3. Rub the boned turkey inside and out with the salt, pepper, sesame oil and 2 tablespoons of the lemon juice. Place the turkey in a bowl, pour on the remaining 6 tablespoons lemon juice, cover and refrigerate overnight.

4. Remove the turkey from the marinade and pat it dry. Fill the turkey with the Oriental Stuffing and sew up the cavity to seal the bird. Tie the body with heavy string at 2-inch intervals and tie the legs together to help the turkey hold its shape.

5. Place the turkey, seam-side down, on a heatproof platter on a rack in a large roasting pan. Add enough water to the pan to come just underneath the rack. Cover the roasting pan tightly and bring to a boil over high heat. Reduce the heat to moderate and steam the turkey for 1½ hours, or until the thigh juices run clear when pricked and the center of the stuffing registers 160°; add additional water to the pan during steaming if necessary. Remove the turkey from the platter, reserving any juices that have collected on the platter. Discard the water in the pan.

6. Preheat the oven to 450°. Place the turkey on the rack in the roasting pan and roast for 15 to 20 minutes, or until golden brown.

7. While the turkey is roasting, make the sauce. Pour the stock and the reserved turkey juices into a medium saucepan and boil over high heat until reduced to 3 cups, about 8 minutes. Strain the sauce and skim off any fat. Season with salt and pepper to taste.
—*Ken Hom*

Rich Turkey and Chicken Stock

This exceptionally rich stock simmers for over 8 hours, so you will probably want to prepare it a day ahead. Although the recipe calls for an extravagant amount of chicken, the depth of flavor is well worth the effort and expense for a special Thanksgiving dinner. If you prefer, however, you may omit the whole chickens and substitute extra bones or chicken parts.

Makes 4 Cups

1 turkey carcass
Three 3-pound chickens
2 pounds chicken necks,
  backs, feet or wings
2½ pounds carrots, halved
4 medium onions, halved
3 leeks, white part only
2 garlic cloves, unpeeled
2 teaspoons peppercorns
6 sprigs of fresh thyme or 2
  teaspoons dried
3 bay leaves

1. In a 12- to 14-quart stockpot, place the turkey carcass, whole chickens, chicken parts and enough water to cover, about 8 quarts. Bring to a boil over moderate heat, skimming the scum that rises to the surface; reduce the heat and simmer another 15 minutes, skimming the surface periodically, until only white foam rises to the top.

2. Add the carrots, onions, leeks, garlic, peppercorns, thyme and bay leaves. Return to a simmer and reduce the heat to low. Simmer the stock, partially covered, for 5 hours, skimming off the fat from time to time. Add water, if necessary, to keep the ingredients covered.

3. Strain the stock through a sieve lined with a double thickness of dampened cheesecloth. Skim the fat off the top. Reserve 3 cups of the stock for the Oriental Stuffing (p. 111). You should have about 7 quarts of stock remaining.

4. Boil the 7 quarts of stock over high heat until it is reduced to 4 cups; this takes about 3 hours. Let it cool, then skim off any fat.
—*Ken Hom*

Roast Turkey with Fruit-and-Nut Stuffing

12 Servings

18- to 20-pound turkey,
  thawed if frozen
2 medium onions, sliced
1 carrot, sliced
3 sprigs of parsley
1 bay leaf
Salt
Fruit-and-Nut Stuffing
  (p. 121)
4 tablespoons unsalted butter,
  melted
2 tablespoons minced fresh
  rosemary or 2 teaspoons
  dried, crumbled
2 tablespoons minced fresh
  thyme or 2 teaspoons dried
1 cup dry vermouth

1. Preheat the oven to 375°. Remove the neck and giblets from the turkey and place them in a medium saucepan with 1 quart of water. Add the onions, carrot, parsley and bay leaf and simmer, partially covered, over very low heat for 3½ to 4 hours,

or the entire time that the turkey is roasting, checking occasionally to make certain that the liquid has not evaporated.

2. Lightly sprinkle the main cavity and neck cavity of the turkey with salt.

3. Turn the turkey breast-side down and loosely stuff the neck cavity with about 2 cups of Fruit-and-Nut Stuffing. Pull the neck skin over the cavity and fasten it to the back of the turkey with skewers or wooden picks. Turn the turkey breast side up and fold the wing tips underneath the turkey so that the tips are almost touching.

4. Lightly stuff the main cavity with about 6 to 7 cups stuffing. Place a double layer of aluminum foil over the exposed stuffing to prevent its charring as the bird roasts. Tie the drumsticks together with kitchen twine or, if your turkey has a metal clamp, arrange the drumsticks so that the clamp will hold them in place. Rub the melted butter over the skin.

5. Place the turkey, breast-side up, on a metal rack over a roasting pan and roast it in the bottom third of the oven for 2½ hours. Then add the herbs and vermouth to the pan drippings. Continue roasting the turkey for 1 to 1½ hours, or until the juices run clear and an instant-read thermometer inserted in the thickest part of the thigh measures 180°. If the turkey begins to brown too much, cover it loosely with aluminum foil. Remove the rack containing the turkey from the pan and allow the turkey to rest on it for 20 minutes.

6. In the meantime, pour off all the pan drippings, including the browned bits that cling to the pan, into a tall, narrow, heatproof container. Let the mixture rest for about 5 minutes to allow the fat to rise to the top and then carefully pour off and discard as much of the fat as possible.

7. Remove the giblet broth from the heat and strain it into the container, discarding the solids; blend the liquids. Taste the sauce for seasoning and serve it hot along with the turkey.
—*Martha Stewart*

Roast Turkey with Three-Bread Stuffing

❣ The medley of flavors on a Thanksgiving table requires an emphatic, fruity wine to complement both the turkey and the traditional sweeter side dishes as well. Try a sparkling wine, such as Domaine Chandon Blanc de Noirs, or a chilled light nouveau red—either a Beaujolais Nouveau, such as Duboeuf, or a California Gamay, such as Robert Pecota.

6 to 8 Servings

6½ tablespoons unsalted butter
14-pound turkey, at room temperature, neck and giblets reserved
Three-Bread Stuffing (p. 124)
½ teaspoon sweet Hungarian paprika
1 small onion, quartered
2 tablespoons all-purpose flour
½ teaspoon salt
¼ teaspoon freshly ground pepper

1. Preheat the oven to 450°. In a small saucepan, melt 4 tablespoons of the butter over low heat; remove from the heat. Dampen four 2-foot-long sheets of cheesecloth and soak them in the melted butter.

2. Shortly before you're ready to roast the turkey, loosely fill the large cavity with about 5 cups of the Three-Bread Stuffing; fill the neck cavity with another 2 cups. Wrap the remaining stuffing in buttered aluminum foil and refrigerate.

3. Skewer the neck cavity shut and truss the turkey with butcher's twine, tying the legs together to seal the large cavity. Set the turkey, breast-side up, on a rack in a large roasting pan. Cover the breast with the butter-soaked cheesecloth and place the turkey in the oven. Immediately reduce the heat to 325° and roast, basting occasionally with a bulb baster, until a meat thermometer inserted in the inner thigh reaches 155°, about 3½ hours. Remove the cheesecloth and add the paprika to the pan. Place the remaining foil-wrapped stuffing in the oven to bake. Return the turkey to the oven and continue to roast, basting frequently, until the temperature in the inner thigh reaches 180°, about 1 hour longer.

4. While the turkey roasts, make the stock. In a medium saucepan, melt ½ tablespoon of the butter over moderately high heat. Add the onion and reserved neck and giblets and cook, turning, until well browned on all sides, about 10 minutes. Add 4 cups of water and bring to a boil. Reduce the heat to low and simmer, skimming occasionally, for 1½ hours. Strain the stock and set aside. You should have about 3 cups. *(The stock can be made up to 2 days ahead and kept in the refrigerator.)*

5. When the turkey is done, transfer it to a large platter and cover

loosely with foil to keep warm. Remove the extra stuffing from the oven. Pour the pan juices into a wide cup or bowl and use a ladle to skim off the fat. Place the roasting pan over high heat and when it starts to sizzle and smoke, stir in the turkey stock scraping up any browned bits from the bottom of the pan. Reduce the heat to moderate, stir in the pan juices and simmer for 5 minutes.

6. In a small bowl, mash the remaining 2 tablespoons butter with the flour until smooth. Whisk this paste into the gravy and bring to a boil, whisking until smooth. Reduce the heat to low and keep warm, stirring occasionally, while you carve the turkey. Season the gravy with the salt and pepper and stir in any accumulated juices from the turkey. Serve the turkey with the stuffing; pass the gravy separately.
—Tina Ujlaki

Roast Wild Turkey with Blue Corn Bread and Chorizo Stuffing

10 to 12 Servings

1 stick (4 ounces) plus 3
   tablespoons unsalted butter
1 pound chorizo sausage,
   coarsely chopped
1 small onion, chopped
¼ cup diced celery
¼ cup diced carrot
4 serrano chiles or 2
   jalapeños—seeded, deribbed
   and minced
6 garlic cloves, minced
¼ cup diced peeled chayote
   (optional)
¼ cup bourbon
1 teaspoon minced fresh
   thyme or ½ teaspoon dried
1 teaspoon minced fresh sage
   or ¾ teaspoon dried
2 teaspoons chopped cilantro
   (fresh coriander)
Serrano Chile Blue Corn
   Bread (p. 137), crumbled
Turkey Stock (p. 61)
1¼ teaspoons salt
10-pound turkey, preferably
   wild, neck and giblets
   reserved for stock
⅛ teaspoon freshly ground
   pepper
2 tablespoons all-purpose
   flour

1. In a large heavy skillet, melt 1 tablespoon of the butter over moderately high heat. Add the chorizo and cook, stirring occasionally, until lightly browned, 4 to 5 minutes. Remove and drain on paper towels. Wipe out the skillet.

2. In the same skillet, melt 4 tablespoons of the butter. Add the onion, celery, carrot, serrano chiles, garlic and chayote and cook over moderately high heat, stirring, until the vegetables soften slightly, about 3 minutes. Add the bourbon and cook until the liquid reduces by half, about 5 minutes. Remove from the heat and stir in the thyme, sage, cilantro, reserved chorizo and Serrano Chile Blue Corn Bread. Moisten with ¼ cup of the Turkey Stock and add 1 teaspoon of the salt; toss well.

3. Preheat the oven to 450°. Season the turkey cavity with the remaining ¼ teaspoon salt and the pepper. Fill the cavity and the neck loosely with the corn bread stuffing. Wrap any extra stuffing in a buttered foil packet. Sew the openings of the turkey or skewer them shut, then truss the bird.

4. In a saucepan, melt 4 tablespoons of the butter. Soak a 2-foot-long double layer of cheesecloth in the butter. Set the turkey on its back on a greased rack in a roasting pan and cover the breast with the butter-soaked cheesecloth.

5. Put the turkey in the oven. Immediately reduce the temperature to 325° and roast, basting with the pan juices every 30 minutes, until an instant-reading thermometer inserted into the thickest part of the thigh registers 155°, about 2 hours. Remove the cheesecloth and continue to roast, basting every 20 minutes, until the internal temperature reaches 180°, about 1 hour longer. Bake the extra packet of stuffing during the last 30 minutes. Transfer the turkey to a carving board, cover loosely with foil and let rest for at least 15 and up to 30 minutes before carving.

6. Meanwhile, make the gravy. Mash the remaining 2 tablespoons butter and the flour together to form a paste. Skim the fat off the juices in the roasting pan. Pour in the remaining 3 cups stock and bring to a boil over moderately high heat, scraping up any browned bits from the bottom of the pan. Gradually whisk in the butter paste and boil, whisking constantly, until thickened. Reduce the heat and simmer for 5 minutes. Season the gravy with salt and pepper to taste.

7. Carve the turkey and serve with the stuffing. Strain the gravy into a sauceboat and pass separately.
—Stephan Pyles, Routh Street Cafe, Dallas

Roast Capon
with Date-Nut Dressing and
Chestnut Sauce

The dressing for the capons, made with little cubes of French bread, onions, garlic, scallions and celery, is flavored well with sage, cumin and cayenne. Pistachio nuts add crunchiness and a nice touch of color, and dates lend a sweetness and mellowness to the dressing that cuts the richness of the capon.

The bread for the dressing can be browned ahead but should not be combined with the other ingredients until just before serving, or it will get soggy. After the capons are cooked, you can use the rendered fat as well as some of the drippings to moisten the dressing as you finish it off at the last moment. If there is any dressing left over, it can be reheated in a skillet with a couple of eggs on top and served for lunch the next day.

Fresh capons are much better than frozen. Notice that the capons are cooked here breast-side down most of the time, so that the juices run into the breasts, creating a self-basting bird that needs moistening only when it is turned over near the end. This yields a very juicy capon. The same cooking technique can be used for small turkeys.

12 Servings

9 ounces French bread, cut
    into ½-inch cubes
3 tablespoons extra-virgin
    olive oil
3 large onions—1 chopped, 2
    cut into eighths
6 garlic cloves, minced

6 large celery ribs, cut into
    ¼-inch dice
10 large scallions, minced
1½ teaspoons crushed dried
    sage leaves
1½ teaspoons cumin
¾ teaspoon freshly ground
    black pepper
¼ teaspoon cayenne pepper
1½ cups chopped pitted dates
    (about ½ pound)
2½ teaspoons salt
1½ pounds fresh chestnuts
6 large carrots, cut into
    1-inch pieces
Two 7-pound capons,
    preferably fresh—fat, necks,
    gizzards and hearts reserved
1 cup shelled, unsalted
    pistachio nuts
¾ cup full-bodied dry red
    wine
2 cups brown stock or
    chicken stock, preferably
    homemade
1 tablespoon arrowroot or
    potato starch

1. Preheat the oven to 400°. Spread out the bread cubes on a baking sheet and bake until nicely browned, 8 to 10 minutes. Remove from the oven, but leave the oven on.

2. In a large saucepan or flameproof casserole, heat the olive oil over moderately high heat. Add the chopped onion and the garlic and cook, stirring, until softened but not browned, about 2 minutes. Add the celery, scallions and ¾ cup of water. Bring to a boil, cover and cook for 2 minutes. Stir in the sage, cumin, ½ teaspoon of the black pepper, the cayenne, dates and 1 teaspoon of the salt. Toss gently to mix. (The mixture will be quite wet.) Cover and set the dressing aside without stirring until 30 minutes before serving time. *(The dressing can be prepared to this point up to 1 day ahead. Refrigerate,*

covered.)

3. Score the chestnuts on their flat side. Place half the chestnuts on a baking sheet and bake in the oven for 12 to 15 minutes, until the chestnuts pop open slightly where slit. While they are still hot, press on the chestnuts to open them, then remove the outer shell and the dark skin beneath it. Meanwhile, bake the remaining chestnuts. (It is better to prepare the chestnuts in 2 batches as they are much harder to peel when cool. It doesn't matter if they are broken, since they will be in pieces in the sauce.)

4. In a saucepan, combine the peeled chestnuts with 3 cups of water and ½ teaspoon of the salt. Bring to a boil over high heat, cover and reduce the heat to low. Simmer until the chestnuts are tender and most of the liquid is absorbed, about 30 minutes. Set aside. *(The chestnuts can be prepared to this point up to 2 days in advance. Cover and refrigerate.)*

5. In a large, shallow roasting pan, combine the carrots and the remaining onions with the reserved capon fat, necks, gizzards and hearts. Sprinkle ¼ teaspoon of the salt inside the cavity of the capons and truss them with string to form a nice shape with a puffed-up breast. Set the capons, breast-side up, on top of the bed of vegetables and trimmings in the roasting pan. *(The capons can be assembled to this point up to 6 hours ahead. Wrap and refrigerate.)*

6. Sprinkle ½ teaspoon of the salt on the outside of the capons. Roast the birds for 20 minutes. Turn the capons over, breast down, and roast for 40 minutes. Turn breast-side up again and continue roasting, basting once, for 30 minutes longer, or until the capons are nicely browned and the temperature reads 175° when a meat thermometer is inserted into the inner thigh. Remove the birds from the oven and set them on a large platter breast-side down (so the juices run into the breasts). Set aside in a warm place.

7. Pour the pan juices into a bowl or degreasing cup. Skim off and remove ¾ cup of the fat. Discard the remaining fat and reserve the rest of the juices; there should be about ½ cup.

8. No more than 30 minutes before serving, reheat the dressing over high heat. Remove from the heat and add the reserved ¾ cup fat, the pistachios and the toasted bread cubes; toss lightly. Spread out the dressing in a large shallow baking dish and warm in the turned-off oven for 10 to 15 minutes while finishing the chestnut sauce.

9. Set the roasting pan with the vegetables and trimmings on 2 burners over high heat. When beginning to sizzle, add the red wine, stock and reserved capon juices. Bring to a boil, scraping up the browned bits from the bottom of the pan. Boil until reduced by one-third, about 4 minutes.

Strain the gravy into a medium saucepan, pressing hard on the solids to extract as much liquid as possible.

10. In a small bowl, combine the arrowroot with 3 tablespoons of water and stir to dissolve. Whisk the arrowroot into the gravy. Bring just to a boil over moderately high heat to thicken slightly. Reduce the heat to low and add the chestnuts. (If there is only a small amount of liquid with the chestnuts, add it also. Otherwise, drain off some of the liquid so that it won't dilute the sauce.) Simmer for 5 minutes while you carve the birds. Add any accumulated juices from the capons to the sauce and season with the remaining ¼ teaspoon each salt and pepper.

11. To serve, spoon the dressing onto individual heated plates and place a little white and a little dark meat on top. Coat with some of the chestnut sauce and pass the remainder separately.
—*Jacques Pépin*

Chutney-Glazed Roast
Chicken with Pecan Stuffing

These sumptuous chickens are ideal for Thanksgiving. (Be sure to order large chickens in advance.) You may even want to double the amount of stuffing—it's impossible to resist— and bake the extra quantity.

8 Servings

*Two 4½-pound roasting
   chickens, giblets reserved
1 lemon, cut in half
Salt and freshly ground black
   pepper
1 stick (4 ounces) unsalted
   butter
Pecan Stuffing (p. 121)
About 2 cups rich chicken
   stock, preferably homemade
Two jars (9 ounces each)
   Major Grey's Chutney (or*

*other mango chutney)
¼ cup all-purpose flour
2 to 3 tablespoons chopped
   parsley (no stems)*

1. Preheat the oven to 450°. Remove any excess fat from the chickens and set it aside. Chop the livers coarsely and reserve for the stuffing. Rub the chickens inside and out with the cut lemon. Sprinkle inside and out with salt and pepper. Set the chickens aside. Cut the butter into about 16 thin pats and reserve these, refrigerated, on a plate.

2. Spoon the Pecan Stuffing into the cavities of the chickens, packing it loosely. (Don't stuff the neck cavities.) If there is leftover stuffing, place it in a shallow baking dish and bake it separately.

3. Beginning with the loose flap of skin at the neck end, gently lift the skin over the breast of each chicken by working your fingers between the skin and the flesh. Lay 8 of the reserved chilled butter pats under the skin of each chicken's breast. Lay the reserved pieces of chicken fat over each breast. Carefully remove the skin from each reserved chicken neck, slitting it open lengthwise. Lay the neck skin flat over the fat on the breast; this will help baste the chicken as it roasts. Skewer closed or sew up, the large cavity and neck cavity of each chicken, then truss the birds.

4. Place the chickens, breast-side up, in a large roasting pan (preferably one with a cover) and scatter the necks, gizzards and hearts around them.

5. Pour the chicken stock into the roaster and cover the pan tightly with heavy aluminum foil. Set the cover, if there is one, in place. Roast in the lower third of the oven for 20 minutes.

6. After 20 minutes, reduce the heat to 325° and roast the birds 45 minutes longer. Remove the cover and foil and check the chickens — they should be tender and almost done when the thigh is pricked, the juices will still run somewhat pink. Raise the heat to 450° and roast uncovered for another 10 minutes, browning the chickens slightly. If no chicken stock remains in the pan, add enough to cover the bottom.

7. While the chickens are roasting, puree the chutney until smooth, in a food processor or blender.

8. When the chickens have browned, remove them to an ovenproof platter (lined with foil, if you like). Pour the pan juices through a strainer into a bowl and set aside.

9. Brush the chutney glaze over the chickens, covering them well. Return the birds to the 450° oven and roast until the glazed skin is golden brown, 5 minutes or more. Remove the chickens from the oven and lower the heat to 375°. Allow the chickens to rest for at least 10 minutes before carving.

10. Pour the reserved fat into a saucepan and stir in the flour. Stir over moderate heat for 2 or 3 minutes, until the roux is smooth, pale and slightly foamy. Pour the degreased pan juices back into the roaster and scrape up the browned bits clinging to the bottom and sides. Whisk these juices into the roux in the saucepan and, continuing to whisk, simmer for 5 or 10 minutes. If the gravy is too thick, whisk in more chicken stock. Correct seasonings and swirl in the parsley.
—*Pearl Byrd Foster*

Baked Ham
with Mustard and Apple Jelly
Glaze

The smoked ham called for below is fully cooked, so allow about 10 minutes a pound just to heat it thoroughly and set the glaze.

❡ The salty nature of the ham calls for a fruity, refreshing wine that can also stand up to the tartness of the glaze. A Riesling, such as Schmitt Söhne Piesporter Michelsberg Spätlese, is one solution; a young Oregon Pinot Noir, such as Ponzi, is another.
8 to 10 Servings

1 jar (10 ounces) apple jelly
¼ cup Dijon mustard
1 skinless, partially boned smoked ham (14 pounds)

1. In a small nonreactive saucepan, combine the apple jelly and mustard and bring to a boil over moderate heat, stirring constantly. Cook until the mixture reduces slightly, about 2 minutes. Set aside half of the glaze to serve with the ham as a condiment. *(The glaze can be made 1 day ahead. Let cool completely, then cover and refrigerate.)*

2. Preheat the oven to 325°. With a sharp knife, trim away any excess fat from the ham, leaving a thin layer. For a decorative effect, score the fat with long shallow cuts at ¼-inch intervals. Set the ham, fat-side up, on a rack in a large roasting pan and bake for 1½ hours. (If you don't have a rack, add 1½ cups of water to the pan.) Remove the ham from the oven and brush all over with the glaze. Continue to bake for about 45 minutes longer, until the ham is heated through to the bone and the glaze is set. Brush the ham again with the glaze 30 minutes before it is done.

3. Transfer the ham to a serving platter. Cover loosely with foil and let rest for 20 to 30 minutes to settle the juices before carving. Slice the ham and pass the reserved apple-mustard glaze separately.
—*Diana Sturgis*

Cider-Glazed Ham
with Sweet-and-Sour Grape
Sauce

14 to 18 Servings

1 smoked ham with bone (about 12 pounds)
2 large garlic cloves, thinly slivered
4 cups unfiltered apple cider or juice
½ cup seedless golden raisins
½ cup dry sherry
3 cups seedless green grapes
2 teaspoons Dijon mustard
3 tablespoons (packed) brown sugar
2 tablespoons sherry wine vinegar
½ cup unsweetened applesauce
1 teaspoon arrowroot
½ cup chicken broth

1. Preheat the oven to 325°. Place the ham fat-side up on a rack in a roasting pan. Score the fat in a diamond pattern cutting at 1-inch intervals. Using the tip of a paring knife, make a slit about ½ inch deep in the center of each diamond. Insert a sliver of garlic into each slit. Bake the ham in the lower third of the oven for 2 hours.

2. Pour 2 cups of the apple cider over the ham and bake for 15 minutes. Baste the ham with some of the pan drippings and bake for 15 minutes. Pour the remaining 2 cups apple cider over the ham and continue baking for an additional 45 minutes (for a total of 3¼ hours), basting the ham with the pan drippings every 10 minutes.

3. Transfer the ham to a serving platter or cutting board and allow it to rest for at least 20 minutes before slicing. Serve hot, at room temperature or cold.

4. Meanwhile, make the sauce: Combine the raisins and sherry in a small saucepan. Over medium heat, bring the mixture to a boil; reduce the heat and simmer until the liquid has almost evaporated. Remove from the heat and set aside.

5. Place 2 cups of the grapes into the container of a food processor or blender and puree (the consistency will be rather watery).

6. Place the grape puree in a saucepan along with the mustard, brown sugar, vinegar and applesauce; bring the mixture to a boil over moderate heat, stirring occasionally. Stir in the reserved raisins.

7. Dissolve the arrowroot in the chicken broth; stir the mixture into the sauce. Cook over moderate heat, stirring constantly, until the mixture thickens, 2 to 3 minutes.

8. Using your fingers or a paring knife, peel the remaining grapes or simply halve them and add them to the sauce. Serve warm or hot over the ham.
—F&W

Crusty Baked Ham

❦ Riesling has a natural affinity for ham and smoked meats. A Hogue Cellars Johannisberg Riesling from Washington State, with its crisp acidity, floral scent and fruity flavor, would be a fine choice.

6 to 8 Servings

5-pound boneless smoked ham
4 cups unsweetened apple cider
½ cup Calvados or applejack
¼ cup Dijon mustard
2 cups fresh bread crumbs
½ cup (packed) light brown sugar
2 teaspoons apple cider vinegar

1. Place the ham in a deep nonreactive pot or casserole a bit wider than the ham. Pour in the cider and Calvados. Cover with plastic wrap and refrigerate for 8 hours or overnight, turning the ham occasionally. Remove the ham from the refrigerator early enough to allow it to come to room temperature before cooking, about 2 hours.

2. Preheat the oven to 350°. Remove the ham from the marinade and pat dry. Reserve the marinade. Spread the ham with 3 tablespoons of the mustard. On a long sheet of wax paper, mix together the bread crumbs and brown sugar. Roll the mustard-coated ham in this mixture to coat evenly.

3. Put the ham in a roasting pan and bake until golden brown and heated through, about 1 hour. Let the ham rest for 15 minutes before slicing.

4. Meanwhile, in a small saucepan, boil the marinade over high heat until it is reduced to ½ cup, about 20 minutes. Whisk in the remaining 1 tablespoon mustard and the vinegar. Serve a small amount of this sauce with each serving of ham.
—Warren Picower

Orange and Bourbon Glazed Country Ham

25 to 30 Servings

1 country-style cured ham, at least 14 pounds
1 quart fresh unpasteurized cider or unsweetened apple juice
30 whole cloves
3 bay leaves
1 cup bourbon
1 cup bitter-orange marmalade
¼ cup Dijon mustard

1. Wash the ham under tepid running water, using a brush to scrub away any surface mold or dust. Place the ham in a large pot and cover with cold water. Set aside in a cool place (do not refrigerate); let soak, changing the water at least twice, for about 48 hours.

2. Remove the ham and discard the soaking water. Place the ham in a large stockpot. Add the cider, 12 of the cloves, the bay leaves and 4 cups of water. Set the pot over moderate heat and bring the water to a boil. Cover, reduce the heat to moderately low and simmer until the shank bone is loose enough to move in its socket, 3 to 4 hours, or about 15 minutes per pound. Remove the ham from the cooking liquid, drain and let cool for about 10 minutes, until it can be handled.

3. Using a large sharp knife, remove the skin and enough fat from the ham so that only a ½-inch coating remains. Score the ham fat with crisscross lines to form a diamond pattern.

4. Preheat the oven to 400°. In a small saucepan, combine the bourbon, marmalade and mustard. Cook over moderate heat, stirring occasionally, until just boiling, about 5 minutes.

5. Garnish the ham with the remaining cloves, inserting one in each corner of the diamonds. Using a small brush, coat the ham evenly with the glaze. Place the ham in a large roasting pan. Bake on the lowest shelf of the oven until nicely browned, 20 to 30 minutes.

6. Remove the ham from the oven and let stand for at least 30 minutes before carving. To carve, make a deep vertical cut at the shank end about 4 inches from the end of the bone. Thinly slice the ham on the diagonal toward the shank end. Serve warm, at room temperature or chilled.

—*Nancy Harmon Jenkins*

Virginia Baked Ham with Madeira

Madeira gives this ham a lovely browned glaze. If you have a poorly insulated oven, bake the ham as directed in the recipe for Orange and Bourbon Glazed Country Ham (p. 69).

25 to 30 Servings

1 country-style cured ham, at least 14 pounds
3½ cups good-quality medium-dry Madeira

1. Wash the ham under tepid running water, using a brush to scrub away any surface mold or dust. Place the ham in a large pot and cover with cold water. Set aside in a cool place (do not refrigerate); let soak, changing the water at least twice, for about 48 hours.

2. Place the ham in a roasting pan, skin-side up. Add 2½ cups of the Madeira and 2½ cups of water. Cover the pan and place the ham in a cold oven. Turn the heat to 500° and bake the ham for 20 minutes. Turn the oven off but do not open the door. Let the ham rest for 3 hours. Turn the oven back to 500° and bake the ham for 20 minutes longer. Turn the oven off and, without opening the oven door, let the ham rest for at least 6 hours or overnight.

3. Remove the ham from the oven and discard the cooking liquid. Using a large sharp knife, remove the skin and enough fat so that only a ½-inch coating remains.

4. Preheat the oven to 425°. Score the fat if desired and place the ham in a roasting pan, fat-side up. Pour ½ cup of the Madeira over the ham. Bake for 5 minutes. Pour the remaining ½ cup Madeira over the ham and bake, basting twice with the pan juices, 15 minutes longer, or until the glaze is golden brown all over.

5. Remove the ham from the oven and let rest for at least 30 minutes before carving. To carve, begin at the shank end with a deep vertical cut, 4 inches from the end of the bone. Thinly slice diagonally toward the shank end. Serve warm, at room temperature or chilled.

—*Nancy Harmon Jenkins*

Virginia Baked Ham with Parsley Crumbs

For this recipe, it is very important that the ham remains undisturbed in a tightly closed oven throughout the entire cooking process. If you have a poorly insulated oven or one with a leaky door, do not try to cook a ham by this method. Instead, use the method described in the recipe for Orange and Bourbon Glazed Country Ham (p. 69).

♟ A wine with high acidity and a touch of sweetness would offer some contrast to the saltiness and intensity of baked ham. Try a Mosel, such as Deinhard Green Label or a Joseph Phelps Johannisberg Riesling from California.

25 to 30 Servings

1 country-style cured ham, at least 14 pounds
1¼ cups finely chopped flat-leaf parsley (1 large bunch)
1¼ cups fine dry bread crumbs
1 tablespoon freshly ground pepper
2 garlic cloves, minced

1. Wash the ham under tepid running water, using a brush to scrub away any surface mold or dust. Place the ham in a large pot and cover with cold water. Set aside in a cool place (do not refrigerate); let soak, changing the water at least twice, for about 48 hours.

2. Remove the ham and discard the soaking liquid. Place the ham in a large roasting pan, skin-side up, and add 5 cups of water. Cover the pan with a lid or heavy-duty aluminum foil, folding the foil well around the pan edges to seal the ham tightly.

3. Place the ham in a cold oven. Turn up the oven temperature to 500° and let the ham bake for 20 minutes. Turn the oven off but do not open the door. Let the ham rest in the oven for 3 hours. Again turn the heat to 500° and bake for 20 minutes. Turn the oven off and, again without opening the oven door, leave the ham in the turned-off oven for at least 6 hours or overnight.

4. Remove the ham from the oven. Reserve 1½ cups of the ham stock. Using a large sharp knife, remove the skin and enough fat so that only a ½-inch coating remains. Score the ham fat with crisscross lines to form a diamond pattern.

5. Preheat the oven to 400°. In a large mixing bowl, combine the parsley, bread crumbs, pepper and garlic. Mix to blend well. Using a spatula, coat the ham with the crumb mixture, pressing gently so the crumbs adhere to the scored fat. Drizzle ½ cup of the reserved stock over the ham. Place in a roasting pan and set on the lowest shelf of the oven.

6. Bake, basting the crumb topping with a little more of the reserved stock every 5 minutes, for 20 to 30 minutes, until the crumbs are nicely browned. (Add 1 cup of water to the pan if any of the drippings begin to burn.)

7. Remove the ham from the oven and let rest for at least 30 minutes before carving. To carve, begin at the shank end with a deep vertical cut, 4 inches from the end of the bone. Thinly slice diagonally toward the shank end. Serve warm, at room temperature or chilled.
—Nancy Harmon Jenkins

Baked Fresh Ham
with Coffee Glaze and
Turnips

Surprising as it may be, this recipe calls for instant coffee. However, the instant is used here to fortify freshly brewed coffee, which allows the brew to stand up to the warm, hot notes of turnips and chiles without diluting the glaze with too much liquid. Serve the ham and turnips on a bed of steamed turnip greens, kale or spinach.

❦ Although ham normally calls for fruity white wines, the glaze in this case begs for added complexity. Try a California Zinfandel, such as Ridge or Phelps.

12 Servings

1 small bone-in shank end of fresh ham (about 7½ pounds)
8 cups strong brewed coffee
4 cups pineapple juice
1 cup dry white wine
½ cup vegetable oil
2 Spanish onions, finely diced
1 head of garlic, peeled and chopped
4 plum tomatoes, chopped
3 small dried red chile peppers, with seeds, chopped
¼ cup white wine vinegar
2 teaspoons cumin
¼ cup instant espresso powder or ¾ cup instant coffee granules
1 cup chicken stock or canned broth
1 tablespoon coarse (kosher) salt
1 tablespoon freshly ground pepper
4 tablespoons unsalted butter
3 pounds turnips, peeled and thinly sliced

1. Trim the ham to remove the heavy skin and fat. Place in a large nonreactive pot and add the brewed coffee, pineapple juice and white wine. Cover and marinate in the refrigerator for 2 days, turning the ham 2 to 3 times daily. Remove the ham from the refrigerator about 2 hours before proceeding.

2. Preheat the oven to 300°. In a large heavy skillet, heat the oil. Add the onions and garlic and cook over moderate heat until softened but not browned, about 8 minutes. Stir in the tomatoes and chile peppers and sauté for 2 minutes longer. Add the vinegar, cumin, instant espresso powder and chicken stock. Boil until reduced by half, about 10 minutes. Remove from the heat and stir in 1 cup of the ham marinade. Puree the mixture in a food processor or blender until smooth.

3. Remove the ham from the remaining marinade and discard the marinade. Season the ham with the salt and pepper and place meatier-side down on a rack in a large roasting pan. Brush the puree on the ham, lightly covering the top and the sides; reserve the remaining puree.

4. Bake the ham for 3½ hours, basting with the reserved puree every 30 minutes and turning every 1½ hours, ending with the meatier side up. Let stand for 15 minutes before thinly slicing.

5. Meanwhile, in a large heavy skillet, melt the butter over moderately high heat. Add the turnips and sauté, turning frequently, until golden and tender, 10 to 12 minutes. Arrange the carved ham and the turnip slices on a large platter and serve hot.
—Gordon, Chicago

Confit of Quail
and Spareribs

This preserved garniture for choucroute owes its inspiration and success to Paula Wolfert, whose book *The Cooking of South-West France* provides wonderfully detailed instructions for making confit.

12 Servings

   3 tablespoons plus 1 teaspoon
      coarse (kosher) salt
   1 tablespoon plus 1 teaspoon
      thyme
   2 teaspoons ground juniper
      berries
   2 teaspoons ground allspice
   1½ teaspoons finely crumbled
      imported bay leaves
   1 teaspoon coarsely cracked
      black pepper
   12 quail (2¾ to 3 pounds
      total)—rinsed and dried,
      necks and gizzards reserved
      for Pork Stock (p. 77)
   2 slabs of pork spareribs (6
      pounds), halved lengthwise
      (ask your butcher to do this)
   8 to 10 cups fresh rendered
      pork and goose fat
      (see Note)
   4 garlic cloves, peeled

1. In a small bowl, combine the salt, thyme, juniper berries, allspice, bay leaves and pepper to make a seasoning mixture. Place the quail in a large baking dish.

2. Trim and discard the fat from the ribs. Trim each strip of ribs into a long, even rectangle; reserve the trimmings (about 2½ pounds) for the Pork Stock (p. 77). Place the strips of ribs in a single layer in another baking dish.

3. Sprinkle half the seasoning mixture over and inside the quail. Sprinkle the remainder over both sides of the ribs. Cover with plastic wrap and refrigerate overnight.

4. Rinse the seasonings from the quail and ribs under cold running water; dry well with paper towels. Truss the quail. Separate the ribs into individual pieces and set aside.

5. In a large heavy pot, melt 8 cups of the fat over low heat until clear, about 15 minutes. Add the garlic and the quail. If they are not completely covered with fat, add some of the remaining 2 cups of fat.

6. Over moderately low heat, slowly heat the fat to 160°. Cook the quail until firm to the touch, about 1 hour.

7. Remove from the heat and let the quail cool in the fat for 1 hour. With a slotted spoon, transfer the birds to a platter. Cover loosely with foil and set aside.

8. Place the ribs in the fat, adding more fat if necessary to cover the ribs. Over moderately low heat, cook the ribs for 2 hours, until the meat can be easily pierced with a fork; do not let the temperature exceed 160°.

9. Remove from the heat and let cool in the fat for 1 hour. With a slotted spoon, transfer the ribs to a platter and cover loosely with foil. Remove the garlic from the fat and discard.

10. Bring the fat to a simmer, skimming frequently, over moderately high heat. Let bubble until the steam from the evaporating moisture stops, about 10 minutes. Remove from the heat and let cool for 15 minutes.

11. Place the ribs and quail in a deep container (large enough to hold all the meat with 2 to 3 inches of head space). Strain the warm fat over the meat. Let cool to room temperature, then cover with plastic wrap

and refrigerate. If the ribs and quail are not completely submerged, let the fat harden overnight, then pour on a layer of vegetable oil to completely cover. Replace the plastic wrap and refrigerate for at least 4 days or up to 1 week.

12. Four or 5 hours before serving, remove the confit from the refrigerator and pour off any vegetable oil, reserving it for another use. Let the confit slowly return to room temperature. Remove the ribs and quail from the fat and place on a baking rack set over a large baking pan. Place in the oven and turn the heat to 250°. Bake until the fat has run off the meat, about 30 minutes. Remove the ribs and quail and set aside. Reserve ¼ cup of the fat in the pan for the potatoes in Step 6 of the choucroute recipe.

13. Place the quail in a large skillet over moderate heat and sauté, turning occasionally, until evenly browned, about 10 minutes. Drain on paper towels and cover loosely with foil until ready to serve. Sauté the ribs in the same manner until evenly browned; cover and keep warm for up to 1 hour until ready to serve.

NOTE: Rendered goose fat is available from some specialty food stores and mail-order sources, especially those that specialize in German or East European cooking. Fresh rendered pork fat is available from most butcher shops. If fresh rendered pork fat is unavailable, do not use commercial lards; use all goose fat instead.

—Anne Disrude

Parsnip Vichyssoise (p. 42).

Glazed Roasted Shallots and Garlic (p. 97) and Spiced Butternut Squash (p. 98).

Fragrant Barley (p. 108) and Pork Loin with Wild Mushroom-Sage Stuffing (p. 78).

Christmas Bread Pudding with Amaretto Sauce (p. 189).

Holiday Choucroute

This is a robust and spectacular wintertime dish. As befits the centerpiece of a festive meal, our recipe calls for a superb and delicious Confit of Quail and Spareribs. However the dish will be equally rewarding with only the sausage garnish. Simply skip Steps 1, 5 and 9; in Step 6, roast the new potatoes in ¼ cup fresh rendered pork or goose fat.

10 to 12 Servings

Confit of Quail and Spareribs (p. 72)
2 tablespoons fresh rendered pork or goose fat
2 large Spanish onions (2½ pounds), thinly sliced
Pork Stock (recipe follows)
6 pounds fresh sauerkraut, rinsed and squeezed dry
1 pound double-smoked slab bacon, cut crosswise into 3 pieces
2 cups dry white wine
6 imported bay leaves
1 teaspoon thyme
10 juniper berries
5 garlic cloves, peeled
8 ounces dried pears, cut into thin strips*
36 small red potatoes (about 4 pounds)
1 pound bratwurst
½ pound Polish sausage
1 pound weisswurst
1 pound knockwurst
½ pound cocktail franks
Kale, for garnish
*Available at health food stores

1. Make the Confit of Quail and Spareribs through Step 11 up to a week before you plan to serve the choucroute.

2. In a large flameproof casserole, melt the fat over moderate heat. Add the onions and cook, stirring frequently, until caramelized to a deep golden brown, about 1 hour.

3. Add the Pork Stock, sauerkraut, bacon, wine, bay leaves, thyme, juniper berries, garlic and pears. Place over moderately low heat and simmer, partially covered, for 3 hours, stirring occasionally. (Add water ½ cup at a time if the sauerkraut begins to stick.)

4. Let cool to room temperature, cover and refrigerate at least overnight or for up to 1 week to let the flavors mellow.

5. Four or 5 hours before the choucroute is to be served, return the confit to room temperature and bake to remove excess fat as directed in Step 12 of the confit recipe.

6. Increase the oven temperature to 375°. Pour off all but ¼ cup of the fat accumulated in the baking pan with the confit, add the potatoes and toss to coat with the fat. Roast the potatoes for about 30 minutes, or until fork tender. (When the potatoes are done, reduce the oven temperature to 150°.)

7. Meanwhile, warm the sauerkraut slowly over moderate heat until simmering. Add the bratwurst and Polish sausage, burying them in the sauerkraut. Simmer until the bratwurst is no longer pink inside, 30 to 35 minutes. Wrap the meats in foil and keep warm in the oven.

8. Bury the weisswurst and knockwurst in the sauerkraut and simmer until plumped, about 20 minutes. During the last 10 minutes of cooking, add the cocktail franks to the sauerkraut. Wrap the weisswurst, knockwurst and cocktail franks in foil and keep warm in the oven until ready to serve.

9. Meanwhile, complete Step 13 of the confit recipe.

10. To serve, garnish the rim of a very large platter with kale. Mound the sauerkraut on the platter. Slice the sausages and arrange them on top, along with the confit of quail and spareribs.
—Anne Disrude

Pork Stock

Makes About 6 Cups

2½ pounds pork rib trimmings and quail necks and gizzards, all reserved from Confit of Quail and Spareribs (p. 72)
5 pounds pork neck bones, cut into 2-inch sections

1. Place a large roasting pan in the oven and preheat the oven to 425°. Place the rib trimmings, quail necks and gizzards and pork bones in the pan and bake. turning occasionally, until deep brown, 1 to 1½ hours.

2. Transfer the meat and bones to a large stockpot. Pour off and discard all fat from the roasting pan; blot up any remaining film of grease with paper towels. Add enough cold water to cover the bottom of the roasting pan and bring to a boil over high heat, scraping up any browned bits that cling to the bottom. Pour this liquid into the stockpot. Add enough cold water to cover the meat and bones by 1 inch.

3. Bring the water slowly to a simmer over moderate heat, skimming occasionally. Reduce the heat to low and simmer, skimming the surface

occasionally, for 4 hours.

4. Drain the stock. Let cool to room temperature, then refrigerate.

5. Strain the chilled stock through a fine sieve lined with several layers of dampened cheesecloth into a large saucepan. Boil the stock, skimming occasionally, until reduced by half, about 1 hour. Let cool to room temperature, then refrigerate for up to 3 days before using.
—Anne Disrude

Pork Loin with Wild Mushroom-Sage Stuffing

Since pork is much leaner these days, it requires shorter cooking times. For a succulent flavor, it is important to baste often while cooking. The internal temperature will rise 5 to 10 degrees as it sits after it is removed from the oven. Ask your butcher to cut a lengthwise pocket in the roasts for stuffing. When preparing the mushrooms for the stuffing, be sure to leave them fairly large and cook them quickly over brisk heat so that they will not release too much liquid. Prepare the mushrooms ahead of time so that they can cool completely before stuffing.

❦ This dish calls for a rather rich red, and the hint of sage points to one with herbaceous notes. Try a fine Bordeaux, such as Château Prieuré-Lichine, or a flavorsome California Cabernet Sauvignon, such as Simi Reserve.

12 Servings

Two 2½-pound boneless center-cut pork loins, about 10 inches long, with a lengthwise pocket for stuffing cut in each
1 garlic clove, halved
Wild Mushroom-Sage Stuffing (p. 119)
1 tablespoon unsalted butter

2 tablespoons olive oil
½ cup Calvados or apple brandy
1½ cups chicken stock or canned low-sodium broth
1 teaspoon red currant jelly
2 tablespoons finely chopped fresh sage plus 1 bunch of fresh sage, for garnish
¾ teaspoon thyme
½ teaspoon freshly ground pepper

1. Preheat the oven to 350°. Rub the surface of the pork loins with the garlic; reserve the garlic. Fill each pocket with half of the Wild Mushroom-Sage Stuffing, pushing the stuffing through with the handle of a wooden spoon if necessary. Tie each loin with 4 crosswise pieces of string. *(The pork loins can be prepared to this point several hours ahead. Cover and refrigerate.)*

2. In a large heavy skillet, melt the butter in the olive oil over moderately high heat. Add the reserved garlic and cook for 1 minute; discard the garlic. Add the stuffed pork loins to the skillet, one at a time, and cook, turning, until well browned all over, about 8 minutes per loin. Transfer to a large roasting pan.

3. Increase the heat to high and add the Calvados to the skillet. Boil until slightly thickened, about 3 minutes. Stir in the chicken stock, red currant jelly, chopped sage, thyme and pepper. Pour this liquid over the meat.

4. Insert a meat thermometer almost through one of the pork loins. Roast in the middle of the oven for about 50 minutes, until the temperature reaches 150°. Transfer the roasts to a large platter, cover loosely with foil; let rest for 15 minutes.

5. Degrease the pan juices and pour into a sauceboat. Carve the roasts into ½-inch slices and arrange on a warmed platter. Garnish with the bunch of sage and pass the sauceboat at the table.
—Sheila Lukins

Roast Fresh Ham with Riesling, Dill and Mustard Sauce

8 Servings

7 leeks, trimmed
7- to 8-pound half of a fresh ham, either the shank or butt half
4 tablespoons finely chopped fresh dill plus 2 tablespoons dried dillweed
3 cups Riesling or good dry white wine
2 teaspoons salt
2 cups heavy cream
2½ tablespoons Dijon mustard

1. Preheat the oven to 325°.

2. Spread the leeks in a roasting pan, arranging them in a layer no larger than the ham, which will be resting on them. (If the leeks are exposed, they will burn.) Sprinkle the leeks with the dried dillweed.

3. Place the ham on top of the leeks, flat-side down, and roast it for 1 hour.

4. Turn the ham over—flat-side up—and roast it for 1 hour.

5. Turn the ham again, flat-side down, and roast for a third hour.

6. Remove the ham from the oven, place it on a cutting surface, and carefully cut off the skin with a very sharp knife; remove only the skin, leaving a layer of fat on the meat. Loosen the leeks in the pan with a spatula if they have stuck to the pan.

7. Return the ham to the pan, flat-side down. Baste it with 1 cup of the Riesling and sprinkle it with 1 teaspoon of the salt. Roast it for 30 minutes.

8. Remove the ham from the oven and increase the oven temperature to 350°.

9. Using a sharp knife, score the fat, making shallow cuts about 1½ inches apart in a diamond pattern; be careful not to cut into the meat. Baste the roast with fat from the roasting pan, pour over it another cup of the Riesling, and sprinkle it with the remaining teaspoon of salt. Return the roast to the oven.

10. Continue to roast the ham, basting it every 10 minutes or so with pan juices, for about 1 hour, or until a meat thermometer inserted into the thickest part registers 170°. Let the meat rest on its serving platter while you prepare the sauce, or for about 20 minutes. Discard the leeks.

11. In a nonreactive skillet, boil the remaining 1 cup Riesling and the cream until it is reduced to 1½ cups. With a whisk, beat the mustard and the fresh dill into the sauce and blend well. Serve the sauce in a heated bowl or sauceboat.
—F&W

Rioja-Style Roast Lamb and Potatoes

An easy dish to prepare, since the oven does practically all of the work. The result: lamb and potatoes given a deliciously different edge by the sharpness of vinegar.

♥ Red Rioja, such as Olarra Reserva
8 to 10 Servings

1 head of garlic, divided into individual cloves and peeled
8-pound leg of lamb, trimmed of excess fat
½ cup plus 3 tablespoons olive oil
5 baking potatoes, peeled and cut into ¼-inch slices
1 tablespoon coarse (kosher) salt
½ teaspoon freshly ground pepper
6 tablespoons chopped parsley
1 cup red wine vinegar

1. Preheat the oven to 350°. Slice 3 cloves of garlic in half lengthwise. Cut 6 slits in the lamb and insert a half-clove in each slit.

2. Grease a shallow roasting pan with 3 tablespoons of the olive oil. Place the lamb in the center of the pan and arrange the potatoes around the edges. Sprinkle the remaining ½ cup oil evenly over the potatoes and the lamb. Sprinkle the lamb with the salt, pepper and 3 tablespoons of the parsley. Roast in the oven for 45 minutes.

3. Meanwhile, in a blender, combine the remaining garlic with the remaining 3 tablespoons parsley to form a paste. Blend in the vinegar.

4. Remove the lamb from the oven and spoon the vinegar mixture over the leg. Turn the potatoes. Return the pan to the oven and continue roasting, turning the potatoes occasionally, for 35 to 45 minutes, until the lamb registers 125° on an instant-reading meat thermometer for rare, or 135° for medium rare. Turn the oven off.

5. Remove the lamb to a carving board and let rest, loosely covered with foil, for 10 to 15 minutes. Cover the roasting pan with foil and leave the potatoes in the oven until ready to serve.
—F&W

Lemon-Herb Veal Roast

The day after you serve this, you can make great sandwiches with the leftovers. Serve thin slices of the veal on hearty bread slathered with Garlic-Oregano Mayonnaise.

12 Servings

1 boneless veal shoulder roast (5 pounds), trimmed and tied
2 large garlic cloves, minced
⅔ cup fresh lemon juice
¼ cup white wine vinegar
2 tablespoons minced fresh oregano or 1 tablespoon dried
1 tablespoon minced fresh thyme or 1½ teaspoons dried
½ teaspoon salt
1½ teaspoons coarsely ground pepper
⅔ cup extra-virgin olive oil
Garlic-Oregano Mayonnaise (recipe follows)

1. Place the veal roast in a large nonreactive bowl. In a medium bowl, whisk together the garlic, lemon juice, vinegar, oregano, thyme, salt and pepper. Add the oil in a slow, steady stream, whisking constantly until incorporated. Pour this marinade over the veal and turn to coat. Cover with plastic wrap and refrigerate overnight, turning once or twice. Remove from the refrigerator and let sit at room temperature for 1 hour before roasting.

2. Preheat the oven to 350°. Remove the veal from the marinade and transfer it to a roasting pan. Roast the veal for 1 hour and 45 minutes, or until the internal temperature reaches 160° on an instant-reading thermometer. Remove from the oven and let rest for at least 10 minutes before carving. Thinly slice and ar-

range on a platter. Before serving, pour any cooking juices over the meat. Serve warm or at room temperature with Garlic-Oregano Mayonnaise.

—*Tracey Seaman*

Garlic-Oregano Mayonnaise

This is a splendid condiment for any roast and a tasty spread for cold meat sandwiches. You can roast the garlic alongside the veal.

Makes About 1 Cup

1 medium head of garlic
   (1½ ounces)
2 teaspoons olive oil
2 tablespoons minced fresh
   oregano
1 cup mayonnaise

1. Preheat the oven to 350°. With a sharp knife, cut ½ inch off the top of the head of garlic. Place on a 6-by-6-inch square of aluminum foil and drizzle the olive oil over the top. Seal the garlic in the foil and bake for 60 to 70 minutes, until tender when pierced with a skewer. Remove from the oven, unwrap and let cool.

2. Separate the garlic cloves. Squeeze the stem ends to release the roasted garlic pulp. In a small bowl, combine the oregano, mayonnaise and 2 tablespoons of the roasted garlic (or more if desired). Mix until well blended. Reserve the remaining roasted garlic for another use.

—*Tracey Seaman*

Roast Beef with Pan Gravy

Serve this Roast Beef with Mini-Yorkshire Puddings (p. 128) and Roast Potatoes and Shallots (p. 90). If you choose to make one or both of these side dishes, reserve the rendered beef fat from Step 4 for use in the recipes.

🍷 California Merlot, such as Rutherford Hill

8 Servings

4 to 4½ pounds eye of round,
   including a thin layer of fat,
   rolled and tied
½ teaspoon freshly ground
   pepper
4 ounces beef suet
3 tablespoons all-purpose
   flour
2 tablespoons Madeira or
   port (optional)
2 cups beef stock or canned
   broth

1. Preheat the oven to 350°. Heat a heavy roasting pan over moderate heat until very hot.

2. Sprinkle the meat with the pepper and place it, fat-side down, in the hot pan. Increase the heat to high and cook the roast, turning without piercing the meat, until browned all over, about 8 minutes.

3. Add the piece of suet to the pan, turn the roast fat-side up and place the pan on the middle rack of the oven. Roast for 20 minutes.

4. Remove the roasting pan from the oven. Tilt the pan and draw off the melted, or rendered, fat with a bulb baster. Return to the oven and roast for 40 minutes for rare roast beef, 120° to 125° on an instant-reading thermometer; for medium rare, roast about 20 minutes longer to 135°.

5. Transfer the roast to a carving board, cover very loosely with aluminum foil and let rest for 20 to 30 minutes before carving into thin slices. Meanwhile discard the suet in the roasting pan. Pour off the melted fat in the pan and add it to the fat already collected.

6. Place the roasting pan over moderately low heat. Measure out 3 tablespoons of the reserved rendered beef fat and add it to the pan. Sprinkle in the flour and cook, stirring constantly, over moderately low heat until lightly browned, 2 to 3 minutes.

7. Whisk in the Madeira and beef stock. Bring to a boil, reduce the heat and simmer, stirring occasionally, for 3 minutes. Add any juices that may have collected on the platter on which the roast is resting.

8. Season with salt and pepper to taste. Strain and serve in a sauceboat.

—*Diana Sturgis*

vegetables & salads

Tarragon Beets

The snappy, sharp flavors of tarragon, capers and vinegar balance the natural sweetness of the beets. Tarragon varies in strength, so you may want to add more or less, depending on individual taste. In any case, this sauce should have a pronounced tarragon flavor.

8 Servings

3 pounds beets without tops
⅓ cup tarragon vinegar
1 tablespoon finely chopped fresh tarragon or 1½ teaspoons dried
5 tablespoons unsalted butter, cut into pieces
2 tablespoons drained capers
Salt and freshly ground pepper

1. Place the beets in a large saucepan with water to cover and bring to a boil over moderately high heat. Cook until tender when pierced with a fork, 30 to 40 minutes (depending on the size of the beets). Alternatively, wrap the beets in aluminum foil and bake in a 400° oven for about 1¼ hours, until tender. Peel the beets and cut into 1-inch pieces.

2. In a large nonreactive saucepan, combine ¼ cup of water with the vinegar and tarragon and bring to a boil over high heat. Reduce the heat to moderate and simmer for 3 minutes. Add the butter and stir until melted. Add the beets and cook, stirring, until heated through, about 8 minutes.

3. Remove from the heat, stir in the capers and season to taste with salt and pepper. Toss, transfer to a warmed serving dish and serve hot.
—*Marion Cunningham*

Dilled Beets and Cucumbers

8 Servings

4 bunches of small beets (about 20), with their leafy tops
4 cucumbers—peeled, halved lengthwise and seeded
4 tablespoons unsalted butter
2 tablespoons white wine vinegar
2 tablespoons minced fresh dill or 2 teaspoons dried dillweed
½ teaspoon salt
¼ teaspoon freshly ground pepper

1. Preheat the oven to 350°. Cut off the leafy beet tops (reserving the greens), leaving about 2 inches of the stem intact. Wrap the beets in aluminum foil and bake for about 25 minutes, or until the beets are tender when pierced with a knife. Unwrap and let stand until cool enough to handle. Peel off the skins. Quarter the beets.

2. Pick out about 12 unblemished beet leaves and wash and dry them; discard the remainder or reserve for another use. Working from the outside edge in, arrange the leaves on a large serving platter.

3. Cut the cucumbers crosswise in half. Trim the corners to form long ovals.

4. In a large heavy skillet, melt 2 tablespoons of the butter over moderately high heat until sizzling. Add the beets and cook until they are heated through, 2 to 3 minutes. Add 1 tablespoon of the vinegar, 1 tablespoon of the dill, ¼ teaspoon of the salt and ⅛ teaspoon of the pepper and toss until coated. Mound the beets in the center of the platter.

5. In another large skillet, melt the remaining 2 tablespoons butter over moderately high heat. Add the cucumbers and cook until heated through, 2 to 3 minutes. Add the remaining 1 tablespoon vinegar, 1 tablespoon dill, ¼ teaspoon salt and ⅛ teaspoon pepper and toss until coated. Arrange the cucumbers around the beets. Serve warm.
—*Anne Disrude*

Sweet-and-Sour Beets with Mushrooms

6 Servings

1 pound beets (about 6 medium)
1 stick (4 ounces) unsalted butter
3 tablespoons minced shallots
1 pound mushrooms, thinly sliced
2 tablespoons honey
2 tablespoons red wine vinegar
1 cup chicken, turkey or veal stock
1½ tablespoons green peppercorns packed in brine or water, drained

1. Cook the beets in a medium saucepan of boiling water until just tender, about 15 minutes. Drain, peel and cut the beets into thin slices.

2. In a medium skillet, melt 6 tablespoons of the butter over moderate heat. Add the shallots and sauté until softened, about 2 minutes. Increase the heat to high and add the beets and mushrooms. Sauté, stirring frequently, for 2 minutes.

3. Add the honey, vinegar and stock. Reduce the heat and simmer, uncovered, until the beets are tender, about 2 minutes. With a slotted spoon, remove the vegetables to a serving bowl.

4. Boil the sauce over high heat until it is reduced to ⅓ cup, about 2 minutes. Swirl in the remaining 2 tablespoons butter, add the peppercorns and pour on the sauce.
—*Silvio Pinto*

Green Beans with Walnuts and Lemon

This simple recipe makes green beans, such as Kentucky Wonders or Blue Lakes, come alive. Though they remain a lovely bright green, the beans are cooked enough to remove the raw, grassy taste they sometimes have, leaving them tender and full of flavor. Use the same dressing with other green vegetables, such as broccoli or small leeks.

Serve the beans immediately after they're dressed so that the acid of the lemon juice won't make their bright green color fade.

4 Servings

⅓ cup walnut halves
1 pound green beans, cut on the diagonal into 2-inch pieces
3 tablespoons unsalted butter
1 tablespoon fresh lemon juice
1 teaspoon finely grated lemon zest
Salt and freshly ground pepper

1. Preheat the oven to 450°. Toast the walnuts on a baking sheet until golden, about 3 minutes. Chop coarsely.

2. In a steamer or wok, bring 2 inches of water to a boil. Steam the beans, covered, until tender but still bright green, about 8 minutes. Drain well. Transfer the beans to a medium bowl and add the butter, lemon juice and lemon zest. Toss until the butter melts. Season to taste with salt and generous amounts of pepper and toss again.

3. Transfer the beans to a serving dish, sprinkle the walnuts on top and serve.
—*Susan Herrmann Loomis*

Green Beans with Pimiento Butter

In the South, pimiento refers to fresh red bell peppers, not the bottled and pickled peppers also called pimiento.

6 Servings

1½ pounds young green beans
1 teaspoon light brown sugar
3 red bell peppers, halved
1 stick (4 ounces) unsalted butter, melted
1 teaspoon salt
½ teaspoon freshly ground black pepper
1 tablespoon cider vinegar or 2 tablespoons fresh lemon juice
1 teaspoon granulated sugar
½ teaspoon sweet paprika, preferably imported
½ cup heavy cream, whipped

1. Put the beans in a small amount of boiling water, add the sugar and stir once. Cook briskly, covered, for 4 or 5 minutes, or until beans are just slightly crunchy. Drain the beans and refresh under cold running water; drain well.

2. Preheat the oven to 400°. Cover a baking pan with foil and lay the pepper halves in the pan, cut-sides down. Cover with another layer of foil. Roast for 30 minutes, until the skins will slip off easily and the peppers are soft. Remove from the oven, peel off the skins and cut and reserve 6 strips of pepper, ½ inch wide, for garnish.

3. In a blender or food processor, place the roasted peppers, butter, salt, black pepper, vinegar, granulated sugar and paprika. Puree until smooth and light. Correct all seasonings. Place in a saucepan.

4. When ready to serve, heat the pimiento butter until warm and reheat the beans by dipping them briefly in boiling water. Fold the whipped cream into the sauce and pour over the beans. Garnish with the reserved strips of roasted pepper.
—*Pearl Byrd Foster*

Broccoli Spears with Lemon-Butter Sauce

8 Servings

2 bunches of broccoli
4 tablespoons unsalted butter
1 tablespoon fresh lemon juice
½ teaspoon salt
¼ teaspoon freshly ground pepper

1. Separate the broccoli into spears. Cut off the bottom inch or so and peel the stalks.

2. Steam until crisp-tender, 8 to 10 minutes.

3. Meanwhile, in a small saucepan, warm the butter, lemon juice, salt and pepper over moderate heat, stirring, until the butter melts. Transfer the broccoli to a serving bowl and pour the hot sauce over the broccoli.
—*Diana Sturgis*

Broccoli with Pine Nuts and Raisins

6 Servings

1 head of broccoli
¼ cup olive oil
1 dried hot red pepper
2 garlic cloves, cut into slivers
½ cup (3 ounces) pine nuts
½ cup raisins
2 large tomatoes—peeled,
  seeded and roughly chopped
  (about 1 cup)
½ teaspoon salt
⅛ teaspoon freshly ground
  black pepper

1. Cut the broccoli top into florets. Trim and peel the stalks and cut them on the diagonal into thin slices.

2. Heat the oil with the not pepper and garlic in a medium skillet. Add the pine nuts and raisins and sauté over moderate heat until the nuts just begin to color, about 2 minutes. Add the broccoli and sauté until tender, about 5 minutes.

3. Add the tomatoes and cook just until they are heated through, about 1 minute. Season with the salt and pepper.
—*Silvio Pinto*

Cauliflower and Broccoli with Cream Sauce

Use this tasty cream sauce for other vegetables if you prefer. The recipe makes almost 4 cups.

8 to 10 Servings

2 medium carrots, chopped
2 celery ribs, chopped
1 medium onion, chopped
2 large imported bay leaves,
  broken up
12 white peppercorns
1¼ teaspoons salt

⅛ teaspoon freshly grated
  nutmeg
1 quart milk
4 tablespoons unsalted butter,
  cut into pieces
⅓ cup all-purpose flour
1 large cauliflower (about 2½
  pounds), cut into 1½-inch
  florets
2½ pounds broccoli, cut into
  1½-inch florets

1. In a heavy medium saucepan, combine the carrots, celery, onion, bay leaves, peppercorns, salt, nutmeg and milk. Cover partially and place the pan over moderately low heat, to infuse for 1 hour. Do not boil. Strain the milk and discard the solids.

2. In a heavy medium saucepan, melt the butter over moderate heat. Whisk in the flour and cook, whisking constantly, until foaming, about 3 minutes; do not let the mixture brown. Whisk in 1 cup of the infused milk until completely smooth. Repeat with the remaining milk. Increase the heat to moderately high and bring the sauce to a boil, whisking constantly. Reduce the heat to low and simmer, stirring, until the sauce is satiny and has lost its raw taste, 3 to 5 minutes. *(The recipe can be prepared to this point up to 2 days ahead. Pour the sauce into a medium bowl, place a piece of plastic wrap directly on the surface to prevent a skin from forming, and refrigerate.)*

3. In a large casserole or pot, steam the cauliflower over moderately high heat, covered, for 3 minutes. Add the broccoli, cover and steam until the broccoli is bright green and both vegetables are fork-tender, about 8 minutes.

4. Rewarm the sauce over moderate heat, stirring occasionally. (Thin it with a little water if desired.) Transfer the vegetables to a large heated bowl and pour the sauce on top. Serve at once.
—*Diana Sturgis*

Steamed Brussels Sprouts and Red Grapes

6 to 8 Servings

2 pints brussels sprouts,
  trimmed and halved
  lengthwise
2 cups seedless red grapes
2½ tablespoons unsalted
  butter
1 tablespoon fresh lemon
  juice
½ teaspoon salt
¼ teaspoon freshly ground
  pepper

In a steamer basket, steam the brussels sprouts, covered, until tender, about 15 minutes. Add the grapes and steam 1 minute longer; drain well. Put the brussels sprouts and grapes in a serving bowl, add the butter, lemon juice, salt and pepper, and toss well.
—*Marcia Kiesel*

Shredded Brussels Sprouts

Brussels sprouts have been the most maligned of vegetables—probably because they are usually overcooked. If cooked quickly, they will retain their pleasing yellow-green color and crisp texture.

6 to 8 Servings

2 pints brussels sprouts,
  trimmed
1 stick (4 ounces) unsalted
  butter, at room temperature
1 teaspoon lemon juice

½ teaspoon salt
¼ teaspoon freshly ground
    white pepper
⅛ teaspoon cayenne pepper

1. With a small sharp knife, cut each sprout into 3 or 4 slices. (The sprouts can be sliced, covered and refrigerated 1 day ahead if desired.)

2. Drop the sprouts into a medium saucepan of boiling salted water. After the water returns to a boil, cook the sprouts until crisp-tender, about 2 minutes; drain. Toss with the butter, lemon juice, salt, white pepper and cayenne.
—Camille Glenn

Shredded Brussels Sprouts Sautéed in Cream

6 Servings

4 tablespoons unsalted butter
2 teaspoons finely minced
    garlic
2 packages (10 ounces each)
    frozen brussels sprouts,
    coarsely shredded
1 teaspoon salt
¼ teaspoon freshly grated
    nutmeg
Freshly ground white pepper
⅓ cup heavy cream

In a large skillet, melt the butter over moderate heat. Add the garlic and sauté for 30 seconds. Add the shredded brussels sprouts and salt and toss well. Cook, stirring frequently, for 3 to 5 minutes, until the brussels sprouts are wilted and just tender. Season with the nutmeg and pepper to taste. Add the cream, stir well and cook for 2 minutes more.
—F&W

Cabbage with Pine Nuts

Since it cooks for less than half a minute, the cabbage retains its lovely green color and crisp texture. Toasted pine nuts look pretty on top and add a little crunch and a sweet nutty flavor.

8 Servings

½ cup pine nuts
1 large head of green cabbage,
    coarsely chopped
4 tablespoons unsalted butter,
    melted
2 tablespoons fresh lemon
    juice
Salt

1. Preheat the oven to 350°. Spread the pine nuts on a baking sheet and toast for 10 to 12 minutes, until golden and fragrant.

2. Meanwhile, bring a large pot of salted water to a boil. Plunge the cabbage into the water and return to a boil. Cook for 20 seconds. Drain well in a colander and transfer to a warmed bowl. Stir in the butter and lemon juice. Season with salt to taste and toss well to combine. Sprinkle the toasted pine nuts on top. Toss lightly again before serving.
—Marion Cunningham

Braised Red Cabbage with Maple-Glazed Chestnuts

This recipe combines sweet glazed whole chestnuts, tangy red cabbage and smoky Canadian bacon.

8 Servings

1 pound (about 2½ cups)
    fresh chestnuts or 10 ounces
    dried chestnuts (about 1¼
    cups) *
1 head of red cabbage (2
    pounds), shredded
4 large garlic cloves, minced

4 large shallots, thinly sliced
½ pound Canadian bacon, cut
    into ½-inch dice
1 teaspoon caraway seeds
¼ teaspoon freshly grated
    nutmeg
½ teaspoon salt
¼ teaspoon freshly ground
    pepper
2 cups unsweetened apple
    cider
½ cup red wine vinegar
2 cups milk
1 teaspoon vanilla extract
3 tablespoons unsalted butter
⅓ cup maple syrup
*Available at Italian markets
    and some specialty food
    shops

1. Preheat the oven to 350°. If using fresh chestnuts, cut a small X into the flat side of each one. Arrange the chestnuts in a shallow pan in a single layer. Roast in the oven until the X opens slightly, about 10 minutes. Peel the chestnuts. If using dried chestnuts, place them in a medium saucepan and cover with 4 cups of cold water. Bring to a boil over high heat, remove from the heat and let soak overnight; drain well. (The chestnuts can be prepared to this point up to 3 days ahead and refrigerated in a covered container.)

2. In a large nonreactive flameproof casserole, combine the red cabbage, garlic, shallots, bacon, caraway seeds, nutmeg, salt, pepper, apple cider and vinegar. Bring to a boil over moderately high heat. Reduce the heat to moderately low, cover and cook, stirring occasionally, until the cabbage is tender and the liquid is reduced to ½ cup, about 2 hours.

3. Meanwhile, in a medium saucepan, combine the chestnuts with the milk, vanilla and 2 cups of water. Bring to a boil over moderately high heat. Reduce the heat to moderately low, cover and simmer until the chestnuts are just tender, about 40 minutes. Drain well, rinse under warm water and drain again. *(The recipe can be prepared to this point up to 2 days ahead. Cover and refrigerate the cabbage and chestnuts separately.)*

4. In a large skillet, melt the butter. Add the chestnuts and maple syrup and cook over moderately high heat, tossing frequently, until the chestnuts are glazed and lightly caramelized, about 8 minutes.

5. Meanwhile, reheat the cabbage. Spoon the cabbage onto a serving platter and sprinkle the chestnuts over the top.
—*Mimi Ruth Brodeur*

Winter Vegetable Wreath

The vegetables for this attractive platter can be cooked early in the day, or a day ahead.
8 to 10 Servings

1 medium head of cauliflower
1 medium head of broccoli
½ pound brussels sprouts
½ pound green beans
12 ounces baby carrots, peeled and trimmed
3 medium parsnips, peeled and cut into ½-inch dice
4 small beets, trimmed, leaving 1 inch of the stem and the root
1½ sticks (6 ounces) unsalted butter
½ cup dry white wine
1 teaspoon tarragon

¼ teaspoon salt
⅛ teaspoon freshly ground pepper
Sprigs of watercress, for garnish

1. Trim the cauliflower, leaving the head whole with only enough of the central core to keep the florets intact. Separate the broccoli florets from the stalk, peel the stalk and cut on the diagonal into thin slices.

2. In a large saucepan of boiling salted water, cook the cauliflower until crisp-tender, about 10 minutes. Remove and rinse under cold running water; drain. Add the brussels sprouts to the same saucepan of boiling water and cook until crisp-tender, about 5 minutes. With a slotted spoon, transfer the sprouts to a colander and rinse under cold running water; drain. Add the broccoli stems to the saucepan and cook for 3 minutes; add the florets and cook for 2 to 3 minutes longer until both are crisp-tender. Drain into a colander and rinse under cold running water; drain.

3. Cook the remaining vegetables one at a time until crisp-tender: Cook the green beans for about 5 minutes, the carrots for about 12 minutes and the parsnips for about 7 minutes, rinsing each under cold water after cooking.

4. Meanwhile, in another saucepan, cook the beets for about 25 minutes, then rinse under cold running water until cool enough to handle. Slip off the skins and slice the beets. Place each vegetable in a separate bowl and refrigerate, covered until 1 hour before you plan to serve. Let the vegetables return to room temperature before proceeding.

5. Place the cauliflower in the center of a large, round heatproof platter and arrange the remaining vegetables separately around the out-

side to form a wreath around the cauliflower.

6. Preheat the oven to 300°. In a medium skillet, melt the butter over moderate heat. Add the wine, tarragon, salt and pepper. Simmer for 1 minute. Moisten the vegetables with ¼ cup of the butter sauce. Cover the vegetable platter tightly with foil and place in the oven until the vegetables are heated through, about 30 minutes.

7. Just before serving, reheat the remaining butter sauce and pour over the vegetables. Garnish with watercress if desired. Serve hot.
—*Melanie Barnard*

Parslied Carrots

One of the simplest and tastiest side dishes is this combination of cooked carrots with a gloss of butter and a sprinkling of chopped parsley.
8 Servings

2½ pounds carrots, peeled and cut on the diagonal into ½-inch chunks
4 tablespoons unsalted butter
Salt
¼ cup finely chopped parsley

Bring a large saucepan of salted water to a boil. Add the carrots and cook over moderate heat until just tender, about 10 minutes. Drain off the water. Add the butter to the saucepan and toss to coat the carrots. Season to taste with salt, add the parsley and mix well. Transfer to a bowl and serve hot.
—*Marion Cunningham*

Carrot and Squash Puree

2 Servings

*12 medium carrots, cut into
1-inch chunks
1 medium butternut squash,
cut into 1-inch chunks
(about 3 cups)
½ cup light cream or half-
and-half
1 stick (4 ounces) unsalted
butter
2 teaspoons salt
1 teaspoon freshly grated
nutmeg
½ teaspoon freshly ground
white pepper*

1. Place the carrots and squash in a large, heavy saucepan along with 2 cups of water. Cover the pan and bring the mixture to a boil. Reduce the heat and simmer, partially covered, over low heat until the vegetables are fork-tender, 15 to 20 minutes. Drain off and discard the liquid or reserve it for use in soups or stocks.

2. Puree the cooked vegetables in a food mill or the container of a food processor or blender. Transfer the puree to a large mixing bowl and beat in the cream, butter, salt, nutmeg and pepper. Serve hot.
—*Martha Stewart*

Cassis-Glazed Carrots

For this recipe, the carrots may be boiled several hours ahead. Let them return to room temperature before glazing and broiling. The cassis syrup may also be prepared ahead of time; cover and refrigerate.

8 Servings

*16 medium carrots, peeled
3 tablespoons plus a pinch of
sugar
¾ cup crème de cassis
3 tablespoons red wine
vinegar
4 scallions, cut into 1½-inch-
long julienne strips*

1. In a large heavy saucepan of boiling salted water, cook the whole carrots with the pinch of sugar until tender but still firm, about 20 minutes. Immediately drain and rinse under cold running water until cool. Halve the carrots lengthwise and arrange flat-side up on a broiler pan.

2. Preheat the broiler. In a medium, nonreactive saucepan, combine the remaining 3 tablespoons sugar, the cassis and vinegar. Bring to a boil over high heat, stirring to dissolve the sugar. Boil until thick and syrupy, 3 to 5 minutes.

3. Brush the carrots heavily with the cassis syrup. Broil 4 inches from the heat, until caramelized and brown, 4 to 5 minutes. Transfer the carrots to a platter and sprinkle the scallions on top. Serve hot or at room temperature.
—*Anne Disrude*

Glazed Carrots with Pearl Onions

6 Servings

*4 tablespoons unsalted butter
1 pound (about 18) small
white onions (1 inch in
diameter), peeled
1 pound carrots, cut into
¼-inch slices
1 can (13¾ ounces) chicken
broth
2 teaspoons sugar
Salt and freshly ground
pepper
¼ cup minced parsley*

1. In a large, heavy skillet, melt the butter over moderate heat. Add the onions and cook for about 10 minutes, shaking the pan occasionally to brown them evenly.

2. Add the carrots and cook, stirring, for 5 minutes. Pour in the chicken broth, bring to a boil, reduce the heat and simmer until the carrots are just tender, about 5 minutes.

3. Remove the vegetables with a slotted spoon. Add the sugar to the liquid in the skillet and bring the mixture to a boil over high heat; reduce the liquid to about ¼ cup.

4. Return the vegetables to the pan. Stir to coat with the glaze. Season with salt and pepper to taste and stir in the parsley.
—*F&W*

Braised Celery with Almonds

This recipe is inspired by a surviving menu from Monticello. Those who never think of celery standing on its own as a vegetable will be pleasantly surprised at how appropriate the clean, herbal flavor and crunch of this dish are in a Thanksgiving menu traditionally filled with rich and tender-textured dishes.

8 Servings

*3 cups chicken stock or
  canned broth*
1 cup dry white wine
*1 medium onion, finely
  chopped*
1 large carrot, finely chopped
6 sprigs of flat-leaf parsley
3 whole cloves
10 peppercorns
1 bay leaf
*3 bunches of celery (16 or 18
  large outer ribs)*
*1 large red bell pepper, finely
  diced*
2 tablespoons unsalted butter
*2 ounces (about ½ cup)
  slivered blanched almonds*

1. In a medium nonreactive saucepan, bring the chicken stock, wine, onion, carrot, parsley, cloves, peppercorns and bay leaf to a boil. Reduce the heat to moderately low and boil gently, uncovered, until reduced to 1 cup, 30 to 40 minutes.

2. Strain and reserve the stock. *(The recipe can be prepared to this point 24 hours in advance of serving. Let cool, cover and refrigerate.)*

3. Peel away the celery strings and cut the ribs crosswise on the diagonal into 2-inch pieces. In a large skillet, bring the reserved stock, celery and red pepper to a boil. Reduce the heat to a simmer, cover and cook, stirring often, until the celery is tender but still retains a slight crunch, about 30 minutes.

4. Meanwhile, in a small skillet, melt the butter over moderate heat. Add the slivered almonds and cook, stirring often, until golden brown, about 5 minutes. Set aside.

5. When the celery is tender, transfer it to a heated vegetable dish with a slotted spoon and cover to keep warm. Return the pan with the stock to high heat and boil rapidly until reduced to a few syrupy spoonfuls, about 5 minutes. Stir the almonds and any butter remaining in the small skillet into the reduced juices. Pour over the celery and serve hot.
—*Michael McLaughlin*

Gratin of Leeks

4 to 6 Servings

8 medium leeks
2 cups milk
¾ teaspoon salt
¾ teaspoon thyme
*¼ teaspoon freshly grated
  nutmeg*
2 whole cloves
1 bay leaf
6 peppercorns
*7½ tablespoons unsalted
  butter*
¼ cup all-purpose flour
Freshly ground white pepper
*½ cup grated Gruyère or
  Swiss cheese*
*2 tablespoons freshly grated
  Parmesan cheese*
Dash of cayenne pepper

1. Trim the leeks, cutting off the root end but leaving the base intact. Trim off the tough green tops, leaving about 1½ inches of the tender green above the white part. Split each leek lengthwise down to about ½ inch from the base and rinse well. Tie the leeks into 2 or 3 bundles with kitchen string.

2. Cook the leeks in a large pot of boiling salted water until just tender, 10 to 15 minutes. Drain and refresh under cold running water. Wrap each bundle in paper towels and gently squeeze out excess moisture. Remove the strings and set the vegetables aside on several layers of paper towels while you make the sauce.

3. In a medium saucepan, combine the milk, salt, thyme, nutmeg, cloves, bay leaf and peppercorns. Bring to a simmer over moderate heat. Meanwhile, in another heavy saucepan, melt 6 tablespoons of the butter. Add the flour and cook, stirring, over moderate heat without coloring for about 3 minutes to make a roux. Whisk the hot milk with the spices into the roux, reduce the heat to moderately low and simmer, stirring frequently, for 25 minutes. Strain the sauce. Season with additional salt and nutmeg and white pepper to taste.

4. Preheat the oven to 375°. Generously butter a shallow baking dish large enough to hold the vegetables in a single layer. Spoon a few tablespoons of the sauce over the bottom of the dish. Arrange the leeks in the dish and pour the remaining sauce over them. Sprinkle on the Gruyère and then the Parmesan cheese. Dot with the remaining 1½ tablespoons butter. Sprinkle lightly with cayenne pepper.

5. Bake for 15 to 20 minutes, or until heated through and bubbly. Increase the temperature to broil and

transfer the gratin to the broiler about 4 inches from the heat. Broil for about 3 minutes, checking frequently to prevent burning, until the top is glazed a rich golden brown. Serve hot.

—F&W

Buttered Okra

In this simple preparation, suggested by Anne Friar Thomas, from Cuero, Texas, the gentle cooking brings out the flavor and incomparable texture of the okra.

When buying okra, look for small—three- to four-inch-long—buds that are evenly green. Trim the stem ends, but don't cut into the body of the okra bud itself. The tiny amount of vinegar in this recipe was suggested to keep the okra from developing its characteristic slippery texture, but there's little likelihood of slipperiness as long as you don't cut into the bud. Regardless, use the vinegar because it adds a subtle tang. Serve this with just about any roast meat or fish.

4 to 6 Servings

1 pound okra
½ teaspoon apple cider vinegar
2 tablespoons unsalted butter
½ teaspoon salt
½ teaspoon freshly ground pepper

1. In a medium nonreactive saucepan, combine the okra, vinegar and ½ cup of water. Cover and bring to a boil over moderately high heat. Reduce the heat to moderate. Add the butter, salt and pepper, cover partially and cook, stirring occasionally, until the okra changes from bright to olive green and is tender, about 8 minutes.

2. Season with additional salt and pepper to taste. Transfer to a platter, and pour any cooking juices on top. Serve immediately.

MICROWAVE VARIATION: Place the okra, water and cider vinegar in a microwave-safe bowl. Cover tightly, and cook on High or at full power for 6 minutes, until the okra has softened. Remove from the oven and let stand, covered, until the okra is crisp-tender, about 3 minutes. Season with the butter, salt and pepper and serve immediately.

—*Susan Herrmann Loomis*

Pearl Onions in Creamy Onion Sauce

Frozen small whole onions are a terrific holiday time-saver because they're already peeled.

8 Servings

1 stick (4 ounces) unsalted butter
1 cup dry bread crumbs
3 medium onions, finely chopped
¼ cup all-purpose flour
2 cups milk
2 teaspoons salt
½ teaspoon freshly ground pepper
2 packages (16 ounces each) frozen small whole onions

1. Preheat the oven to 350°. Melt the butter in a medium saucepan. Pour half of the butter into a small bowl and stir in the bread crumbs. Set aside.

2. Add the chopped onions to the remaining butter in the saucepan and cook over low heat, stirring occasionally, until the onions are soft but not brown, about 5 minutes.

3. Sprinkle the flour over the onions and whisk to combine, about 1 minute. Increase the heat to moderate, slowly add the milk and cook,

whisking constantly, until the sauce is smooth and thickened, about 5 minutes. Stir in the salt and pepper.

4. Place the whole onions in a 2-quart baking dish. Pour the onion sauce over them and mix well, spreading the onions in an even layer. Sprinkle the reserved buttered bread crumbs over the top. Bake for 40 to 50 minutes, or until the topping is crisped and the sauce is bubbling around the edges. Serve hot.

—*Marion Cunningham*

Swiss Chard-Stuffed Onions

2 Servings

2 medium onions, about 2½ inches in diameter
3 tablespoons unsalted butter
½ teaspoon freshly ground pepper
½ cup chicken stock or canned broth
1 pound Swiss chard or spinach, stems removed
1 tablespoon olive oil
1 large garlic clove, finely chopped
1 tablespoon minced parsley
¼ teaspoon freshly grated nutmeg
1 teaspoon salt

1. Cook the whole, unpeeled onions in a large saucepan of boiling water for 10 minutes. Drain and rinse under cold running water. Peel off the outer skin and trim off the root ends. Cut off the top third of each onion. Hollow out the centers to make a shell about ⅜ inch thick. Chop the onion removed from the centers and set aside.

2. Preheat the oven to 350°. Arrange the onion shells, cut-side up, in a single layer in a shallow baking dish. Dot with 2 tablespoons of the butter and season with ¼ teaspoon

of the pepper. Pour the stock around the onions. Cover the dish with foil and bake, basting occasionally, until the onion shells are tender but still hold their shape, about 30 minutes.

3. Meanwhile, wash the Swiss chard or spinach well; do not drain. Place in a medium nonreactive saucepan, cover and cook in the water that clings to the leaves over low heat until wilted and tender—5 to 10 for the chard, 3 to 5 minutes for spinach. Drain and rinse under cold running water; drain well. Squeeze with your hands to remove excess moisture.

4. In a large skillet, heat the oil. Add the garlic and sauté over low heat for about 30 seconds, until fragrant Add the reserved chopped onion, the Swiss chard or spinach, parsley, nutmeg, salt and the remaining 1 tablespoon butter and ¼ teaspoon pepper. Cook, stirring constantly, for 5 minutes. Remove from the heat and puree in a food processor or blender.

5. Fill the baked onion shells with the puree. Spoon the onion braising liquid over the tops and serve hot.
—*Martha Stewart*

Puree of Green Peas with Capers

8 Servings

4 packages (10 ounces each) frozen peas, partially thawed
1 cup boiling water
¼ teaspoon light brown sugar
Salt and freshly ground pepper
4 tablespoons unsalted butter
2 tablespoons drained capers
8 strips of pimiento, for garnish

1. Place the partially thawed frozen peas) in a saucepan that has a tight-fitting lid. Add the boiling water, brown sugar and a light sprinkling of salt and pepper. Cover the pot and steam the peas until tender, about 8 to 10 minutes.

2. Drain the peas over a saucepan, reserving the cooking liquid. In a food processor, puree the peas until very smooth. Add the butter and season with salt and pepper to taste. If the puree is too thick, blend in a little of the cooking liquid, a spoonful at a time. Reheat the puree.

3. Rinse the capers in a strainer and gently pat them dry with a paper towel. Stir the capers into the puree and turn the puree into a serving dish. Garnish, if you like, with the pimiento strips.
—*Pearl Byrd Foster*

Stir-Fried Snow Peas with Carrots

6 Servings

2 medium carrots, cut into 2½-by-¼-inch julienne strips
1 pound snow peas
1½ tablespoons unsalted butter
1½ tablespoons minced shallot
Salt and freshly ground pepper

1. Blanch the carrots in boiling water until slightly tender, about 2 minutes. Refresh under cold running water and drain well. String the snow peas.

2. In a medium skillet, melt the butter over moderate heat. Add the shallot and sauté until soft, 1 to 2 minutes. Add the carrots and snow peas and cook, stirring, for 30 seconds. Add 1½ tablespoons water, cover and cook for 2 to 3 minutes, stirring once or twice, until the vegetables are just tender. Season with salt and pepper to taste.
—*Ken Hom*

Roast Potatoes and Shallots

8 Servings

4 large baking potatoes, peeled and halved crosswise
1½ teaspoons salt
16 shallots (about 1¼ pounds), unpeeled
⅓ cup unsalted butter, melted (see Note)
½ teaspoon freshly ground pepper

1. Place the potatoes in a medium saucepan with 1 teaspoon of the salt and water to cover by 1 inch. Bring to a boil, reduce the heat and simmer, covered, for 15 minutes (they will finish cooking in the oven). Drain.

2. Preheat the oven to 350°. When the potatoes are cool enough to handle, cut them in half lengthwise to yield 16 wedges.

3. Place the potatoes in a single layer in a 13-by-9-inch baking dish. Pick off any loose, broken shallot skin and add the unpeeled shallots to the baking dish. (*The recipe may be prepared ahead to this point.*)

4. Drizzle the butter over the potatoes; turn to coat the potatoes. Sprinkle with the remaining ½ teaspoon salt and the pepper.

5. Bake for 35 minutes. Increase the oven temperature to 400°. Remove the baking dish from the oven, and transfer the shallots, which should be tender, to a plate; cover and keep warm until serving time. Turn the potatoes and return them to the oven. Cook for 25 to 30 minutes, until browned and crisp.

NOTE: These potatoes were designed to be served with Roast Beef with Pan Gravy (p. 80). If you choose to make the roast beef, use ⅓ cup of melted beef fat from that recipe in place of the butter here.
—Diana Sturgis

Whipped Potato with Chestnut Puree

8 to 10 Servings

1 pound chestnuts
2 pounds all-purpose potatoes, peeled and quartered
2 sticks (8 ounces) plus 2 tablespoons unsalted butter, melted
3 egg yolks
1 cup crème fraîche or ¾ cup heavy cream
¼ teaspoon freshly grated nutmeg
Salt and freshly ground pepper
3 cups chicken broth
Sprigs of parsley, for garnish

1. With a small sharp knife, cut an X across the flat side of each chestnut. In a large saucepan of boiling water, cook the chestnuts until the cut shells begin to curl, 15 to 20 minutes; drain. With a small sharp knife, trim off the outer shell and the inner brown skin.

2. Meanwhile, place the potatoes in a medium saucepan and add cold water to cover. Bring to a boil and cook over moderate heat until tender, about 15 minutes. Drain, return to the pan and shake over moderately high heat until dry. Rice the potatoes or press them through a sieve or the medium disk of a food mill. Beat ½ cup of the butter into the potatoes; add the egg yolks, one at a time, beating well after each ad-

dition. Stir in half of the crème fraîche, the nutmeg and salt and pepper to taste.

3. Place the chestnuts in a medium saucepan. Add the chicken broth and enough water, if necessary, to cover them by 1 inch. Bring to a boil, reduce the heat and simmer until tender, about 20 minutes; drain. Toss the chestnuts with ½ cup of the remaining butter. When the chestnuts are coated, puree the buttered chestnuts in a food processor or blender until smooth; blend in the remaining crème fraîche and season to taste with salt and pepper.

4. Preheat the oven to 400°. Spoon the potatoes into a buttered 2-quart shallow baking dish or casserole. Fill a pastry bag fitted with a ¼-inch plain tip (#2) with the chestnut puree and pipe the mixture decoratively around the potatoes or over them in a lattice pattern. Drizzle the remaining 2 tablespoons butter evenly over the top.

5. Bake for about 10 minutes, or until the potatoes are heated through and lightly golden on top. Garnish with sprigs of parsley.
—Melanie Barnard

Scalloped Potatoes with Bacon and Cheese

On a farm in Pennsylvania, Barbara Fischer cooks three meals a day for her family of nine. She serves this variation of scalloped potatoes in winter, and sometimes she makes it into a main course, adding beef, ham, corn or peas. In this version, the flavor of the potatoes is heightened by bacon and celery seed.

Get top-quality potatoes. Baking potatoes give a fluffy result, but try Urgenta or Maine potatoes, which fall somewhere between a fluffy and waxy potato. Depending on their age and quality, the potatoes may not al-

ways absorb all the milk and cream. You may want to add only the milk at first. Check the potatoes halfway through cooking. If they have absorbed all the milk, then add the cream and continue baking.

6 to 8 Servings

1 garlic clove, halved lengthwise
8 large baking potatoes (about 4 pounds total), peeled and halved crosswise
6 ounces thick-sliced bacon, cut crosswise into ¼-inch strips
¾ teaspoon salt
¾ teaspoon freshly ground pepper
2 cups milk
½ cup heavy cream
Heaping ¼ teaspoon celery seeds
2 ounces Gruyère cheese, shredded (about ½ cup, packed)
2 ounces sharp Cheddar cheese, shredded (about ½ cup, packed)

1. Preheat the oven to 350°. Rub the garlic clove over the inside of a 12-by-8-inch or 13-by-9-inch nonreactive baking dish.

2. In a large steamer over boiling water, steam the potatoes over high heat until nearly cooked through but still slightly firm in the center, about 15 minutes. Remove from the heat and set aside to cool.

3. In a heavy medium skillet, fry the bacon over moderately high heat until lightly golden but not crisp, about 5 minutes. Using a slotted spoon, transfer the bacon to paper towels; reserve the bacon fat.

4. Grate half the potatoes into the prepared baking dish using the large holes on a hand-held grater. Season with half of the salt and pepper and

sprinkle half of the bacon and 2 teaspoons of the bacon fat on top. Repeat with the remaining potatoes, salt, pepper, bacon and 2 more teaspoons of the bacon fat.

5. Combine the milk and cream and pour evenly over the potatoes. Sprinkle the celery seeds and then the cheeses on top. Cover with aluminum foil and bake in the middle of the oven for 25 minutes. Remove the foil and bake for 20 minutes longer, until the cheese has melted and the potatoes are golden at the edges. Set aside to cool for 5 minutes before serving.

—*Susan Herrmann Loomis*

Potato Puree with Scallions

6 Servings

2 pounds baking potatoes
1 stick (4 ounces) unsalted
*   butter, at room temperature*
About 1 cup half-and-half or
*   light cream*
¼ cup minced scallions
Salt and freshly ground
*   pepper*

1. Peel the potatoes and cut them into 1½-inch cubes. Place the potatoes in a medium saucepan and add enough water to cover them by 2 inches. Heat to boiling and cook until tender, 15 to 20 minutes. Drain and transfer the potatoes to a mixing bowl.

2. Add the butter and ½ cup of the half-and-half to the potatoes. Using an electric mixer, beat until smooth, gradually adding enough additional half-and-half to make a puree with a creamy consistency. Blend in the scallions and season to taste with salt and pepper.

—*Ken Hom*

Gratin of Pumpkin

Pumpkin may seem unusual in a savory gratin, since it is generally served as a dessert in the United States, but it is an excellent vegetable. If pumpkin is not available, butternut or acorn squash can be substituted. Although the same recipe can also be made with frozen or canned pumpkin puree, it is better with fresh.

The mixture of pumpkin puree, cream, milk, nutmeg, salt, pepper, eggs and Swiss cheese can be assembled a few hours ahead or even the day before, but the gratin should not be cooked more than a few hours before it is served.

This recipe can also be prepared in individual gratin dishes. The cooking time will be about 20 minutes.

12 Servings

4 pounds fresh pumpkin, cut
*   into 3-inch pieces and peeled*
1 cup heavy cream
1 cup milk
⅛ teaspoon freshly grated
*   nutmeg*
2½ teaspoons salt
¾ teaspoon freshly ground
*   pepper*
6 eggs, lightly beaten
½ cup grated Swiss cheese
2 tablespoons freshly grated
*   Parmesan cheese*

1. Put the pumpkin in a large saucepan with cold water to cover. Bring to a boil over high heat. Reduce the heat to low, cover and simmer until tender, about 25 minutes; drain well. Puree in a food processor while still hot. *(The recipe can be prepared to this point up to 1 day ahead. Reheat before proceeding.)*

2. Preheat the oven to 375°. In a large mixing bowl, combine the pureed pumpkin, cream, milk, nutmeg, salt and pepper. Beat in the eggs, 1 at a time, and stir in the Swiss cheese.

3. Pour into a buttered 7- to 8-cup shallow baking dish. Sprinkle the Parmesan cheese on top. Set the baking dish in a larger pan and add enough hot water to reach halfway up the sides of the baking dish. Bake for 40 to 45 minutes, until the gratin is set.

—*Jacques Pépin*

Shallots Braised in Red Wine

These mild shallots are a nice alternative to the more traditional holiday dish of onions in cream sauce.

8 to 10 Servings

2½ pounds shallots, peeled
5 tablespoons unsalted butter
¾ cup dry red wine
1 tablespoon sugar

Combine all the ingredients in a large, heavy nonreactive saucepan. Cover and cook over moderate heat, stirring occasionally, until the shallots are tender, about 40 minutes. Uncover and reduce the heat to low. Cook, stirring occasionally, until the liquid reduces to a syrupy glaze, about 15 minutes. *(The recipe can be prepared up to 3 days ahead. Transfer the shallots to a baking dish, cover with foil and refrigerate. Reheat, covered, in a 325° oven for about 20 minutes.)*

—*Diana Sturgis*

Cabbage with Pine Nuts (p. 85).

Parslied Carrots (p. 86).

Mashed Potatoes with Onions and Garlic

6 to 8 Servings

*1 stick (8 ounces) plus 2
  tablespoons unsalted butter*
2 pounds onions, thinly sliced
8 garlic cloves, minced
*5 pounds Idaho potatoes,
  peeled and cut into 2-inch
  chunks*
1 cup milk
½ cup heavy cream
1½ teaspoons salt
*1¼ teaspoons freshly ground
  pepper*

1. In a large skillet, melt the butter. Add the onions, cover and cook over low heat, stirring occasionally, until softened, about 20 minutes. Stir in the garlic, cover and cook until the onions are golden, about 10 minutes longer; set aside.

2. Meanwhile, in a large saucepan, cover the potatoes with hot water and cook over high heat until tender, about 15 minutes. Drain well and return the potatoes to the pan. Cook over high heat, tossing the potatoes until completely dry, about 1 minute.

3. Turn off the heat and mash the potatoes with a potato masher. Stir in the milk and heavy cream until thoroughly combined and fluffy. Stir in the onion-garlic mixture, salt and pepper.
—*Jim Brown*

Glazed Roasted Shallots and Garlic

Be sure to buy large firm shallots and heads of garlic; avoid any that are sprouting. Roast the shallots and garlic with a sprinkling of sugar to release their nutty sweetness. When tender and caramelized, quickly sauté with butter to add the final glaze.

10 to 12 Servings

*3¾ pounds large shallots,
  peeled*
*2 large heads of garlic (about
  32 cloves), separated into
  cloves and peeled*
*¾ cup chicken stock or
  canned low-sodium broth*
*2 tablespoons fresh lemon
  juice*
2 tablespoons sugar
1 teaspoon salt
*½ teaspoon freshly ground
  pepper*
3 tablespoons unsalted butter

1. Preheat the oven to 375°. Place the shallots and garlic in a single layer in a shallow baking pan. In a small nonreactive saucepan, combine the chicken stock and lemon juice and bring to a boil over high heat. Pour the hot stock over the shallots and garlic and sprinkle with the sugar, salt and pepper. Cover with aluminum foil and bake for 45 minutes. Remove the foil, stir gently and bake uncovered for 20 to 30 minutes, or until the shallots are very tender.

2. In a large nonstick skillet, melt 1½ tablespoons of the butter over moderate heat. Add half of the shallots and garlic and some of their cooking liquid. Increase the heat to moderately high and cook, shaking the pan frequently until the shallots and garlic are golden brown and caramelized all over, 5 to 7 minutes. Transfer to a heatproof serving dish. Rinse out the skillet and repeat with the remaining butter, shallots, garlic and cooking liquid. Serve hot. *(The recipe can be prepared up to 1 day ahead. Let cool, cover and refrigerate. Let return to room temperature before reheating in a 375° oven for about 10 minutes. Serve warm.)*
—*Sheila Lukins*

Spinach Ring Filled with Creamed Chestnuts

For most recipes I prefer fresh spinach over frozen, but not when it comes to preparing this recipe, which would require eight pounds of fresh spinach and endless preparation. By using frozen chopped spinach I'm way ahead of the game and free to concentrate on the rest of the dinner.

6 to 8 Servings

Creamed Chestnuts:
*1 pound frozen shelled and
  peeled Italian chestnuts* *or
  1 can (1 pound) whole
  unsweetened chestnuts*
2 cups heavy cream
½ teaspoon salt
*⅛ teaspoon freshly ground
  pepper*

Spinach Ring:
*8 packages (10 ounces each)
  frozen chopped spinach*
1½ teaspoons salt
*⅛ teaspoon freshly ground
  pepper*
*¼ teaspoon freshly grated
  nutmeg*
1 cup heavy cream
Paprika, for garnish
**Available at specialty food
  shops*

1. Make the creamed chestnuts: If using the frozen chestnuts, place

them in a large heavy saucepan with 3 cups of water. Bring to a simmer over moderate heat, cover, reduce the heat to low and simmer until tender, 8 to 10 minutes. Drain well. If using canned, simply drain.

2. Place 10 whole chestnuts in a food processor and process to a fine powder. Empty the chestnut powder into a heavy medium saucepan. Add the cream, salt and pepper and boil, uncovered, until reduced to about 1¾ cups, 20 to 30 minutes.

3. Halve or quarter the remaining chestnuts, depending on their size, and add to the chestnut cream. Set aside off heat while you prepare the spinach ring. *(The creamed chestnuts can be made ahead to this point. Cover and refrigerate, then bring to room temperature while you cook the spinach.)*

4. Meanwhile, prepare the spinach ring: Place the frozen spinach in a large heavy kettle; add the salt but no water. Cover and simmer over moderate heat, stirring occasionally to break up any large frozen clumps, until the spinach is thawed and heated through, about 30 minutes. If it threatens to boil dry at any time, reduce the heat and add a little water.

5. As soon as the spinach is steaming hot, dump into a very large fine sieve and press to extract as much liquid as possible. When the spinach is very dry, return it to the kettle. Add the pepper, nutmeg and cream. Cook over moderate heat, stirring, for 3 to 4 minutes, until heated through. Reheat the creamed chestnuts.

6. Just before serving, pack the hot spinach mixture into a lavishly buttered 6-cup ring mold.

7. To serve, loosen the spinach ring around the edges with a thin-bladed spatula and invert onto a heated round plate (see Note). Fill the center of the spinach ring with the creamed chestnuts, ladling a little of the sauce over the ring at intervals and arranging a few chestnuts about the base. For a holiday touch, add a blush of paprika.

NOTE: If any bits of spinach should cling to the ring mold, no harm done. Simply lift them out and replace on the spinach ring, smoothing the surface with a spatula.
—*Jean Anderson*

Baked Squash with Butter and Maple Syurp

A tasty complement to the dark meat of a turkey, this comes directly from the Northeast, the cradle of the Thanksgiving celebration. The maple syrup lends a distinct sweetness and seems to heighten the buttered squash flavor. For special effect, serve in scooped-out and baked acorn squash halves.

6 to 8 Servings

*6 pounds acorn or butternut
   squash, halved lengthwise
   and seeded
Salt and freshly ground
   pepper
4 tablespoons unsalted butter
¼ cup maple syrup*

1. Preheat the oven to 400°. Place the squash cut-sides down on a baking sheet and bake for 45 minutes to 1 hour, or until the squash is easily pierced with a fork. Scoop the flesh into a bowl and mash the squash with a potato masher or a fork until fairly smooth. Season to taste with salt and pepper. Keep warm.

2. In a small saucepan, combine the butter and maple syrup and cook over low heat, stirring, until the butter is melted and blended with the syrup, about 2 minutes.

3. Stir half of the syrup mixture into the squash. Transfer the squash to a shallow serving dish. Pour the rest of the syrup mixture over the top. Serve hot. *(The recipe can be prepared up to 2 days ahead. Cover and refrigerate. Reheat in a 350° oven until hot, about 20 minutes.)*
—*Marion Cunningham*

Spiced Butternut Squash

Butternut squash is a winter vegetable that lends itself to a wide range of flavors and preparations while still retaining its integrity. This warming puree is spiced for the Christmas season and is a creamy complement to the rest of the meal.

12 Servings

*4 pounds butternut squash (4
   medium)—halved, peeled,
   seeded and cut into 2-inch
   chunks
1 cup chicken stock or canned
   low-sodium broth
6 tablespoons unsalted butter,
   cut into small pieces
½ teaspoon ground ginger
¼ teaspoon mace
¼ teaspoon ground coriander
Pinch of cayenne pepper
½ teaspoon salt
¼ teaspoon freshly ground
   black pepper
1 to 2 tablespoons fresh
   lemon juice
3 tablespoons crème fraîche
   or sour cream*

1. In a large heavy saucepan, combine the squash, chicken stock and 3 cups of water. Bring to a boil over high heat. Reduce the heat to

moderately low, cover partially and simmer until the squash is tender, about 20 minutes. Drain, reserving ¼ cup of the cooking liquid.

2. In a large bowl, combine the squash, butter, ginger, mace, coriander, cayenne, salt, black pepper, 1 tablespoon of the lemon juice and the reserved squash cooking liquid.

3. Preheat the oven to 350°. In a food processor, puree the squash mixture in 2 batches just until smooth; do not overprocess. Transfer the puree to an ovenproof 3-quart serving dish and fold in the crème fraîche. Season with additional lemon juice, and salt and pepper to taste. *(The recipe can be prepared up to 2 days ahead to this point. Let cool, then cover and refrigerate. Let return to room temperature before baking.)*

4. Cover the dish with foil and bake until heated through, about 25 minutes. If desired, uncover and broil about 5 inches from the heat for 1 minute, or until lightly browned. Serve immediately.
—*Sheila Lukins*

Sweet Potato and Butternut Squash Puree

The rich flavor of sweet potatoes is enhanced by the juiciness and light texture of butternut squash.
8 to 10 Servings

4 pounds medium sweet
  potatoes
1 butternut squash (2
  pounds), halved lengthwise,
  seeds scooped out
½ teaspoon salt
¼ teaspoon freshly ground
  pepper

1. Preheat the oven to 400°. Place the sweet potatoes on a large baking sheet. Place the squash, cut-sides down, on the same sheet. Bake until tender, about 1 hour. Let cool slightly.

2. Scoop the pulp from the squash and sweet potatoes into a food processor; discard the skins. Add the salt and pepper and puree until smooth.

3. Spread the puree in an 8-by-10-inch baking dish and swirl decoratively with a spoon if desired. *(The recipe can be prepared up to 2 days ahead. Let the puree cool, then cover with foil and refrigerate. Reheat, covered, in a 375° oven for about 20 minutes.)*
—*Diana Sturgis*

Sweet Potatoes with Cider and Brown Sugar

Here is a deliciously easy treatment for a trusty Thanksgiving standby, inspired by a surviving Jeffersonian menu. As this recipe does not use a lot of sugar, the natural tartness of the cider comes through. (Natural unsweetened cider, by the way, fresh and unfiltered, is preferable to bottled cider or to apple juice.)
8 Servings

4 pounds sweet potatoes,
  peeled and cut into 1-inch
  chunks
2½ cups unsweetened apple
  cider
½ cup (packed) dark brown
  sugar
1 stick (4 ounces) unsalted
  butter
2-inch piece of cinnamon
  stick

1. In a large nonreactive saucepan, combine the potatoes, cider, brown sugar, 6 tablespoons of the butter and the cinnamon stick. Bring to a boil over moderate heat. Reduce the heat to a simmer, partially cover and cook, stirring occasionally, until the potatoes are very tender, about 45 minutes.

2. Let cool slightly, remove the cinnamon stick and force the potatoes through the medium disk of a food mill or puree in batches in a food processor. Transfer to an ovenproof serving dish. *(The potatoes can be prepared to this point several days in advance of serving. Cover tightly and refrigerate. Return to room temperature before proceeding.)*

3. Preheat the oven to 325°. Dot the surface of the potatoes with the remaining 2 tablespoons butter, cover tightly with foil and bake, stirring once or twice, until steaming, about 20 minutes. Remove the foil and bake for 5 minutes longer.
—*Michael McLaughlin*

Sweet Potato Sham

The recipe for this sweet side dish hails from Don Patterson in Texas. The cooking time for the potatoes depends on their age. At the beginning of the season—early fall—they will cook more quickly because they are still quite full of moisture. As the year progresses they lose moisture and take longer to cook.

If you have a source for good sweet potatoes, buy and store them in a cool place to have the year through.
8 to 10 Servings

6 sweet potatoes (about 12
  ounces each)
1 tablespoon plus ¾ teaspoon
  salt
4 tablespoons unsalted butter,
  softened
½ cup granulated sugar
½ cup (packed) brown sugar
1 egg
½ cup milk

½ teaspoon freshly grated
  nutmeg
½ teaspoon cinnamon

1. Preheat the oven to 350°. Place the sweet potatoes in a large saucepan and add enough water to cover. Add 1 tablespoon of the salt. Bring to a boil over high heat and cook until the potatoes are soft, 30 to 50 minutes. Drain well.

2. When the potatoes are cool enough to handle, peel them and place in a large bowl. Using a potato masher or a fork, mash the potatoes until smooth.

3. In a medium bowl, mix the butter and the granulated and brown sugars. Whisk in the egg until blended, then add the milk and mix well. Add to the potatoes and mix thoroughly. Season with the nutmeg, cinnamon and the remaining ¾ teaspoon salt.

4. Transfer the mixture to a large baking dish and smooth the top. Bake for about 1 hour, or until lightly golden. *(The sham can be made up to 1 day ahead and refrigerated, covered. Return to room temperature and reheat in a 350° oven.)*
—Susan Herrmann Loomis

Sherried Sweet Potatoes

I do not enjoy overly candied sweet potatoes, but there must be enough butter and sugar to make a beautiful glaze.

6 to 8 Servings

8 medium sweet potatoes
⅓ cup sugar
¼ teaspoon salt
4 tablespoons unsalted butter,
  cut into small pieces
⅓ cup medium-dry Spanish
  sherry, such as amontillado

1. Preheat the oven to 350°. In a large saucepan, cover the sweet potatoes with hot water. Boil until the potatoes are tender but still firm, about 20 minutes. *(The sweet potatoes can be cooked 1 day ahead; cover and refrigerate.)*

2 Peel the skins off the sweet potatoes and cut them in half. Place in a large baking dish. Sprinkle the sugar and salt over the sweet potatoes. Dot with the butter and drizzle on the sherry.

3. Bake, basting occasionally, until the sweet potatoes are light brown and the glaze is bubbling.
—Camille Glenn

Gratin of Sweet Potatoes Flambéed with Bourbon

This easy dish is only slightly sweet and can make a grand entrance, if you choose to flambé it in front of your guests. For the best presentation, use a very large round or oval ovenproof dish.

6 to 8 Servings

3 pounds large sweet potatoes
4 tablespoons unsalted butter,
  at room temperature
¼ teaspoon salt
⅛ teaspoon freshly ground
  pepper
2 tablespoons sugar
¼ cup bourbon

1. Put the potatoes in a large pot of cold water. Bring to a boil over moderately high heat and cook until the potatoes are just tender around the edges but still firm in the center, 15 to 20 minutes. Drain and rinse under cold water. When the potatoes are cool enough to handle, peel them with a knife (the skins will come off easily).

2. Preheat the oven to 475°. Use 1 tablespoon of the butter to grease a large shallow baking dish, preferably a round or a large oval gratin dish. Cut the sweet potatoes into ¼-inch rounds. Arrange the slices, overlapping slightly in concentric circles. Spread the remaining 3 tablespoons butter all over the potatoes, covering them as well as you can. Season with the salt and pepper. Sprinkle the sugar evenly over the potatoes. *(The recipe can be prepared ahead to this point. Set aside at room temperature for up to 3 hours or cover and refrigerate overnight. Let return to room temperature before proceeding.)*

3. Bake the sweet potatoes for 20 minutes. Reduce the heat to 350° and bake for 20 minutes longer, or until the potatoes are tender and lightly glazed.

4. Pour the bourbon into a large metal ladle or small saucepan. Warm over low heat for about 20 seconds. Carefully ignite the bourbon and drizzle over the sweet potatoes.
—Susan Wyler

Sweet Potato and Turnip Puree

This is a great recipe for those people who don't like their sweet potatoes too sweet.

8 to 10 Servings

3 pounds sweet potatoes
2 pounds turnips, peeled and
  quartered
2 tablespoons (packed) dark
  brown sugar
4 tablespoons unsalted butter
¼ teaspoon salt
Dash of freshly grated nutmeg
3 egg whites

1. Preheat the oven to 350°. Bake the sweet potatoes for 1½ to 2 hours,

until soft throughout. Leave the oven on.

2. Meanwhile, in a large saucepan of lightly salted water, simmer the turnips until tender, about 25 minutes; drain.

3. Peel and cut the sweet potatoes into chunks and put in a food processor. Add the turnips to the sweet potatoes. Add the brown sugar, butter, salt and nutmeg. Puree until smooth. Season with more brown sugar, butter and/or salt to taste. *(The recipe can be prepared to this point up to 4 hours ahead. Set aside, covered, at room temperature.)*

4. Beat the egg whites until stiff but not dry. Fold into the sweet potato-turnip puree. Turn into a greased shallow 2½- to 3-quart baking dish.

5. Bake the sweet potato and turnip casserole for 25 minutes, or until heated through. Serve at once.
—*Lee Bailey*

Flageolets with Garlic Cloves

Flageolets, dried French beans, resemble small navy beans, but they are pale green and have a very subtle flavor. They are the classic accompaniment to a roasted leg of lamb, but are equally good with roasted goose. Substitute white navy beans if flageolets are not available.

6 to 8 Servings

1 pound flageolets* (about 2 cups)
6 tablespoons unsalted butter
6 garlic cloves, quartered
1 tablespoon salt (see Note)
¼ teaspoon freshly ground pepper
Several sprigs of fresh thyme or ½ teaspoon dried
*Available at specialty food stores

1. Put the flageolets in a large saucepan with cold water to cover. Bring to a boil over moderately low heat; drain.

2. Return the beans to the pan and add the butter, garlic, salt, pepper, thyme and 6 cups of water. Bring to a boil, cover and cook over moderate heat until the flageolets are tender, 1 to 2 hours.

3. Drain the flageolets, reserving the broth. *(The beans can be cooked 1 day ahead and refrigerated.)* Before serving, reheat them in the reserved broth.

NOTE: It is important to salt the beans before they cook to bring out their flavor. Don't worry about the amount of salt that is added here; it sounds like a lot, but most of it is drained off, and you won't taste it in the end.
—*Lydie Marshall*

Salad of Winter Greens

Based on a recipe from a farmer in California, this salad is made with lively winter greens, which have their own cheering and distinct character not present at any other time of year. They have a pleasant bitterness and meaty texture that are particularly satisfying when good, fresh vegetables are rare.

The keys to this salad are careful washing of the greens so absolutely no grit remains, drying them completely so the dressing will adhere, tearing them in bite-size pieces to get the most out of their flavor, and tossing them just before serving, so the dressing doesn't wilt the greens.

6 to 8 Servings

2 tablespoons balsamic vinegar
1 garlic clove, minced
½ teaspoon salt
¼ teaspoon freshly ground

pepper
⅓ cup extra-virgin olive oil
1 medium fennel bulb, cored and cut into ¼-inch dice (1 cup)
7 cups (loosely packed) mixed winter greens—such as curly endive, escarole and broccoli rabe (leaves and buds only), torn into bite-size pieces
2 cups radicchio leaves (from 1 medium head), torn into bite-size pieces

1. In a large serving bowl, combine the vinegar, garlic, salt and pepper; whisk well. Whisk in the olive oil in a thin, steady stream so the dressing emulsifies. *(The dressing can be made up to 1 day ahead and refrigerated in a jar. Shake well before using.)* Add the fennel and toss to coat. Set aside to marinate for at least 15 minutes and up to 1 hour.

2. Add the greens and radicchio to the bowl and toss to coat thoroughly. Serve immediately.
—*Susan Herrmann Loomis*

Field Salad with Mushrooms and Walnuts

This is an excellent holiday salad, as the expensive but quite flavorful field salad, also called mâche or lamb's lettuce, is a winter green. If it is unavailable, a mixture of greens—from arugula to romaine or Boston lettuce—can be substituted.

12 Servings

½ pound large mushrooms, stems removed
1 tablespoon fresh lemon juice
1 tablespoon Dijon mustard
½ teaspoon salt
1 teaspoon freshly ground pepper
¼ cup plus 1½ teaspoons

peanut oil
1½ cups walnut pieces (about
6 ounces)
1½ tablespoons unsalted
butter, melted
¼ cup plus 2 tablespoons
extra-virgin olive oil
1½ tablespoons red wine
vinegar
9 cups mâche or a mixture of
Boston lettuce, romaine
lettuce and arugula

1. Preheat the oven to 400°. Slice the mushroom caps horizontally about ¼ inch thick. Stack the slices and cut them into ¼ inch sticks.

2. In a medium bowl, combine the lemon juice, mustard, ¼ teaspoon of the salt and ½ teaspoon of the pepper. With a fork, beat in the peanut oil. Add the mushrooms and toss to combine. *(The mushrooms can be prepared up to 3 hours ahead. Set aside at room temperature.)*

3. On a baking sheet, toss the walnuts with the melted butter. Sprinkle with a pinch of salt and bake until golden brown, about 10 minutes. *(The nuts can be prepared up to 10 hours ahead. Let cool, then store in an airtight container.)*

4. In a medium bowl, stir together the olive oil, vinegar and the remaining ¼ teaspoon salt and ½ teaspoon pepper. *(The dressing can be prepared up to 1 day ahead. Let return to room temperature before using.)*

5. Just before serving, put the salad greens in a large bowl and toss with the dressing. Arrange the salad on 12 serving plates. Spoon equal amounts of the mushrooms in the center and scatter the walnuts over the top.
—*Jacques Pépin*

Christmas Salad with Red and Green Vinaigrette

The leaf lettuce, radicchio and watercress can be washed the day before being served and stored, refrigerated, in a large plastic bag. Be sure the lettuce is dry and layer with paper towels to prevent spoilage.

12 Servings

2 medium anchovies, rinsed
well and minced
1 medium garlic clove,
minced
¼ teaspoon salt
½ teaspoon freshly ground
pepper
¼ cup white wine vinegar
1 tablespoon balsamic vinegar
2 sun-dried tomatoes packed
in oil, minced (about 2
tablespoons)
1 tablespoon minced flat-leaf
parsley
2 teaspoons grainy mustard
⅔ cup extra-virgin olive oil
1 medium head of green leaf
lettuce, torn into bite-size
pieces
1 large head of radicchio, torn
into bite-size pieces
1 large bunch of watercress,
large stems removed
1 medium Belgian endive,
sliced crosswise into 1-inch
pieces

1. In a medium bowl, mash the anchovies, garlic and salt to form a coarse paste; add the pepper. Whisk in the wine vinegar, balsamic vinegar, sun-dried tomatoes, parsley and mustard until thoroughly combined. Whisk in the oil in a slow, steady stream until well blended. *(The dressing can be made days ahead. Refrigerate in a glass jar and allow to come to room temperature before serving. Shake well before using.)*

2. In a large salad bowl, combine the leaf lettuce, radicchio and watercress in a large bowl. Add the endive and toss to mix the greens. Just before serving, add the dressing and toss again.
—*Tracey Seaman*

Mixed Salad with Kumquats and Pecans

Sliced fresh kumquats add a tart, orangey zip to this winter salad. Marinating them in the dressing for half an hour softens their skins nicely. The lettuces can be washed and dried the day before serving. Wrap them loosely in paper towels, pack them in a roomy plastic bag and refrigerate until needed.

8 to 10 Servings

½ cup olive oil
3 tablespoons white wine
vinegar
1 tablespoon Dijon mustard
1 small garlic clove, crushed
¼ teaspoon salt
¼ teaspoon freshly ground
pepper
10 small fresh kumquats,
thinly sliced into rounds,
pits removed
1½ cups pecans (about 5
ounces)
1 head of romaine lettuce,
torn into pieces
1 head of red oak leaf lettuce,
torn into pieces
1 small red onion, sliced into
thin rings
4 Belgian endives—2 thinly
sliced crosswise, 2 separated
into leaves

1. Preheat the oven to 400°. In a jar, combine the olive oil, vinegar, mustard, garlic, salt and pepper. Cover and shake well. *(The dressing can be made 1 day ahead.)* Add the kumquats to the dressing, shake to coat and set aside to macerate for 30 minutes.

2. Meanwhile, spread the pecans on a cookie sheet and bake for 5 minutes, until fragrant and lightly toasted. Let cool, then break the nuts into large pieces.

3. Just before serving, in a large salad bowl, combine the romaine and red oak leaf lettuces with the onion, sliced endives and pecans. Shake the dressing and pour it over the salad. Toss well to combine. Arrange the endive spears around the salad and serve at once.
—*Diana Sturgis*

Salad of Watercress, Arugula and Fennel

I like to serve salad after the main course. I also present a choice of cheeses—possibly a Brie, a chèvre and a Roquefort.
6 to 8 Servings

1 large bunch of arugula, trimmed
2 bunches of watercress, trimmed
1 small fennel bulb, halved and cut into long thin strips
1 garlic clove, crushed through a press
1½ teaspoons Dijon mustard
2 tablespoons red wine vinegar
¾ teaspoon salt

¼ teaspoon freshly ground pepper
⅓ cup light olive oil, such as Bertolli
2 tablespoons minced fresh tarragon or 2 tablespoons minced parsley combined with ½ teaspoon dried tarragon

1. In a salad bowl, combine the arugula, watercress and fennel.

2. In a small bowl, combine the garlic, mustard, vinegar, salt and pepper. Gradually whisk in the olive oil. Whisk in the minced tarragon.

3. Just before serving, pour the dressing over the salad and toss.
—*Lydie Marshall*

Endive and Romaine Salad with Mango Wedges and Cheddar Fingers

Serve this salad with a simple vinaigrette made with fresh lemon juice.
6 Servings

3 tablespoons sugar
6 large Belgian endives
1 large head of romaine lettuce
2 large mangoes, peeled and cut from the pit in ¾-inch slices
½ pound Vermont or other aged Cheddar cheese, cut into 3-by-½-inch fingers
Fresh watercress or parsley, for garnish

1. Fill a bowl with ice water and add the sugar, stirring to dissolve it. Add the untrimmed endives and refrigerate for 2 hours (this removes any bitterness). Drain and rinse well with cold water. Dry the endives well with paper towels. Cut off the bases and separate into spears.

2. Remove the outer leaves from

the romaine (reserve them for a tossed salad). Arrange the tender inner leaves in a circle on a large, chilled salad platter. Lay the spears of endive over the romaine.

3. Pile the mango wedges in the center of the platter and arrange the cheese fingers around the outside. Garnish with watercress or parsley and serve with vinaigrette dressing.
—*Pearl Byrd Foster*

Citrus Green Bean Salad

The light, fresh sweetness of orange is a sunny surprise in this crisp, any-time-of year salad.
12 Servings

2 pounds green beans, cut into 1-inch pieces
½ cup fresh orange juice
1 tablespoon finely grated orange zest (from 1 medium navel orange)
3 tablespoons balsamic vinegar
1 teaspoon granulated sugar
1 teaspoon grainy mustard
¾ teaspoon salt
¾ cup olive oil
½ cup finely chopped red onion
Freshly ground pepper (optional)

1. In a large pot of boiling salted water, cook the beans until just crisp-tender, about 3 minutes. Drain in a colander and rinse under cold water until cool. Pat dry; transfer the beans to a large nonreactive bowl and set aside.

2. In a medium bowl, whisk together the orange juice, orange zest, balsamic vinegar, sugar, mustard and salt. Gradually whisk in the oil in a slow, steady stream until incorporated. Stir in the red onion. Pour the dressing over the beans and toss to coat thoroughly. *(The recipe can be made 1 day ahead; cover and refrigerate overnight. Let the beans sit at room temperature about 1 hour before serving.)*

3. Transfer the beans to a serving bowl and season with pepper if desired. Toss once more and serve.

—*Tracey Seaman*

Beet and Chicory Salad

6 to 8 Servings

3 pounds beets (weighed
   without tops)
1 teaspoon grated lemon zest
¼ cup fresh lemon juice
3 tablespoons olive oil
1 teaspoon salt
½ teaspoon freshly ground
   pepper
1 head of chicory, torn into
   bite-size pieces
¼ cup chopped parsley
Red Wine Vinaigrette (recipe
   follows)
½ cup toasted (see Note)
   coarsely chopped walnuts,
   for garnish

1. Preheat the oven to 450°. Wrap the beets tightly in aluminum foil. Place on a baking sheet and bake about 45 minutes, or until the beets are tender when pierced with a small knife. Let cool slightly.

2. Rub the skins off the beets under cold running water. Cut in half crosswise; cut each half into ¼-inch slices. In a medium bowl, toss the beets with the lemon zest, lemon juice, olive oil, salt and pepper. Let

marinate at room temperature for at least 20 minutes, or up to several hours.

3. In a large bowl, toss the chicory and parsley with enough of the Red Wine Vinaigrette to coat lightly; place in a serving bowl or on a platter. Remove the beets from the marinade and arrange them over the greens. Scatter the walnuts over the top, if desired. Drizzle any remaining beet marinade over the salad. Pass any remaining Red Wine Vinaigrette separately.

NOTE: To toast the walnuts, preheat the oven to 350°. Scatter the nuts in a baking pan and bake, turning the nuts frequently, until lightly toasted, about 10 minutes.

—*F&W*

Red Wine Vinaigrette

Makes About ⅔ Cup

2 tablespoons red wine
   vinegar
1½ tablespoons fresh lemon
   juice
1½ teaspoons Dijon-style
   mustard
½ garlic clove or small
   shallot, minced
¼ teaspoon salt
¼ teaspoon freshly ground
   pepper
¼ cup olive oil
¼ cup vegetable oil

In a small bowl, whisk the vinegar, lemon juice, mustard, garlic, salt and pepper until blended. Gradually whisk in the oils in a slow, thin stream.

—*F&W*

Citrus Salad with Fresh Horseradish Dressing

12 to 15 Servings

4 large grapefruit
6 navel oranges
2 tablespoons fresh lemon
   juice
½ cup peanut or safflower oil
½ cup Lillet or dry vermouth
¼ cup finely shredded fresh
   horseradish
¼ teaspoon salt
⅛ teaspoon freshly ground
   white pepper
2 medium heads of chicory
   (curly endive), torn into
   small pieces
2 medium heads of romaine
   lettuce, shredded

1. With a sharp knife, cut away the peel of the grapefruit and oranges, removing all the white pith. Squeeze the peelings over a small bowl to reserve the juices (about 1 cup total).

2. Cut the fruit crosswise into ¼-inch slices; then cut each round in half. Place the fruit slices in layers in a large baking dish. Strain the reserved juices and pour over the fruit. Cover with plastic wrap and chill. *(The slices can be held overnight in the refrigerator.)*

3. Drain the fruit juice from the sliced fruit, reserving ¼ cup. Make the dressing by whisking together the reserved fruit juice, the lemon juice, oil, Lillet, horseradish, salt and white pepper.

4. To assemble the salad, line a large platter with the greens, tossed together. Arrange concentric circles of overlapping fruit slices on top, then drizzle the dressing over the fruit.

—*Anne Disrude*

Black-Eyed Pea Salad with Orange-Jalapeño Dressing

The Southwestern flavors in this salad add a refreshing twist to the holiday menu.

8 Servings

1 pound dried black-eyed
  peas
1 bay leaf
1 large red onion, finely diced
2 teaspoons grated orange
  zest
¼ cup fresh orange juice
5 garlic cloves, minced
2 tablespoons unsulphured
  molasses
⅓ cup red wine vinegar
¼ teaspoon hot pepper sauce
½ teaspoon thyme
1 teaspoon salt
½ teaspoon freshly ground
  black pepper
¾ cup light olive oil
1 large cucumber—peeled,
  seeded and cut into ½-inch
  dice
1 small jalapeño with its
  seeds, minced

1. In a large saucepan, cover the peas with 4 inches of cold water. Add the bay leaf and bring to a boil over moderate heat. Reduce the heat to low and simmer, stirring occasionally, until the peas are tender, about 50 minutes; add water if the peas look dry. Drain in a colander and rinse well under cold water; discard the bay leaf. Transfer the peas to a large bowl and toss with the red onion.

2. In a medium bowl, combine the orange zest, orange juice, garlic, molasses, vinegar, hot sauce, thyme, salt and black pepper. Whisk in the olive oil. Add the dressing to the peas and toss well. Set aside at room temperature until serving time. (*The recipe can be prepared up to 1 day ahead. Cover and refrigerate.*) Just before serving, fold in the cucumber and jalapeño.
—Marcia Kiesel

Beet, Leek and Zucchini Salad with Radicchio and Romaine

To save time on the day you plan to serve this, cook all of the vegetables the night before; cool and wrap individually, then refrigerate. Cut into matchstick strips when you prepare the salad, not before. Make the dressing several hours ahead of time (or the day before) so that its flavors have a chance to mingle and mellow.

6 to 8 Servings

6 medium beets, with root
  ends and 1 inch of the tops
  left on
4 medium leeks (white and
  tender green)
4 medium zucchini
1 small head of romaine
  lettuce, washed and patted
  very dry
1 medium head of radicchio,
  washed and patted very dry
Lemon-Dill Dressing (recipe
  follows)

1. In a heavy medium saucepan, cook the beets in boiling water to cover over moderate heat until fork-tender, 30 to 45 minutes. Drain, let cool to room temperature, then peel and cut into matchstick strips; set aside.

2. Quarter each leek lengthwise, cutting to within 1½ inches of the base. Fan out, plunge into tepid water and slosh gently up and down to remove all grit and sand. Lay the leeks flat in a heavy medium skillet and add water to cover. Simmer, covered, until tender, 10 to 15 minutes. Drain and let cool to room temperature; cut into matchstick strips.

3. In a covered medium saucepan, cook the whole zucchini in boiling water to cover until crisp-tender, about 10 minutes. Drain and let cool to room temperature; cut into matchstick strips.

4. To assemble the salad, wreathe the romaine and radicchio leaves around the edge of a round plate; place additional leaves in the center. Arrange clusters of the beets, leeks and zucchini strips on top. Shake the dressing well, then drizzle evenly over the salad. Let marinate at room temperature for about 30 minutes before serving.
—Jean Anderson

Lemon-Dill Dressing

Makes About 1 Cup

¼ cup fresh lemon juice
2 teaspoons honey
½ teaspoon salt
⅛ teaspoon freshly ground
  pepper
⅔ cup olive or safflower oil
1 teaspoon distilled white
  vinegar
2 tablespoons minced fresh
  dill or 1 teaspoon dried
  dillweed

Place all of the ingredients in a jar with a tight-fitting lid; shake well to combine. Store tightly covered at room temperature. Shake well again before using.
—Jean Anderson

grains, stuffings and breads

Fragrant Barley

Rarely would we think of putting a bowl of barley on a holiday table, but when decorated and enlivened with pasta bow ties, studded with toasted pine nuts and a confetti of carrots, these pearly grains belong on the most festive tables.

12 Servings

8 ounces bow-tie pasta
3 tablespoons extra-virgin olive oil
1 cup pine nuts (4½ ounces)
4 medium carrots, cut into ¼-inch dice
1 large onion, cut into ¼-inch dice
2 cups pearl barley (about 14 ounces)
4 cups beef stock or canned low-sodium broth
½ cup dried currants (optional)
1 cinnamon stick (optional)
1 teaspoon salt
½ teaspoon freshly ground pepper
2 tablespoons chopped fresh mint

1. In a large pot of boiling salted water, cook the pasta until al dente, about 11 minutes. Drain, rinse under cold running water and set aside. (*The pasta can be cooked up to 1 day ahead. Let cool, toss with a little olive oil to prevent sticking, cover and refrigerate overnight.*)

2. In a large heavy saucepan, heat the oil over moderately low heat. Add the pine nuts and cook, stirring, until just golden, about 5 minutes. Reduce the heat to low. Add the carrots and onion and cook, stirring occasionally, until the onion is translucent, about 5 minutes. Add the barley and stir until the barley is hot, about 2 minutes.

3. Add the stock, currants, cinnamon stick, salt, pepper and 2 cups of water. Increase the heat to high and bring to a boil. Reduce the heat to moderately low, cover and simmer until the liquid has been absorbed and the barley is tender but not mushy, about 55 minutes.

4. Stir in the cooked pasta and 1 tablespoon of the mint. Cover and simmer until the pasta is heated through, about 5 minutes. Spoon the barley into a serving bowl and garnish with the remaining 1 tablespoon mint.
—*Sheila Lukins*

Barley-Almond Pilaf

6 Servings

¾ cup (3½ ounces) slivered almonds
6 tablespoons unsalted butter
1 medium onion, chopped
1 tablespoon caraway seeds
1 cup barley, rinsed and drained
1½ teaspoons salt
Freshly ground pepper

1. Place the almonds in an ungreased, medium skillet and toast them over moderate heat, stirring frequently, until they are lightly browned, about 3 minutes.

2. In a medium saucepan, melt 4 tablespoons of the butter over moderate heat. Add the onion and sauté until the pieces begin to soften, about 2 minutes. Add the caraway seeds and cook for 2 minutes longer. Add the barley and sauté, stirring frequently, for 3 to 4 minutes, until the barley begins to smell toasted. Add 3 cups of water and the salt and bring to a boil. Stir once, reduce the heat to low and cook, covered, for 1 to 1¼ hours, until all the water is absorbed.

3. Stir in the remaining 2 table-spoons butter, ½ cup of the toasted almonds and pepper to taste. Transfer the pilaf to a serving bowl and sprinkle with the remaining ¼ cup almonds.
—*Maria Piccolo & Rosalee Harris*

Baked Wild Rice with Carrots and Mushrooms

You will probably not need to add any salt to this recipe because of the saltiness of the broth and the bacon.

6 to 8 Servings

2½ cups chicken broth
1 cup wild rice, rinsed well in cool water
6 slices lean double-smoked bacon, cut crosswise into julienne strips
1 medium onion, coarsely chopped
2 small carrots, cut into ¼-inch dice
¼ pound mushrooms, finely diced
½ teaspoon thyme
½ teaspoon marjoram
⅛ teaspoon freshly ground pepper
1½ tablespoons unsalted butter

1. In a heavy medium saucepan, bring the broth to a boil. Add the wild rice and when the broth returns to a boil, reduce the heat to low, cover and simmer just until tender (the rice will cook further in the oven), 35 to 40 minutes. Remove from the heat and reserve; do not drain.

2. In a large heavy skillet, fry the bacon over moderate heat until crisp and brown, 5 to 8 minutes. Remove the bacon and drain on paper towels.

3. Pour off all but 3 tablespoons of the bacon drippings from the skil-

let (if your bacon is exceptionally lean and there is not enough fat in the skillet, add enough butter to equal 3 tablespoons). Add the onion and carrots and sauté, stirring, over moderate heat until the carrots are crisp-tender, 3 to 4 minutes. Add the mushrooms, thyme, marjoram and pepper and cook for 2 minutes longer.

4. Dump the rice and any remaining cooking liquid into the skillet; add the reserved bacon and toss lightly to mix. *(The rice can be prepared ahead to this point. Cover and refrigerate; return to room temperature before proceeding.)*

5. Preheat the oven to 350°. Transfer the rice mixture to a generously buttered 2-quart casserole. Cover and bake for 25 to 30 minutes, or until the rice is tender. Dot the surface of the rice with the butter and toss lightly. Serve at table from the casserole.

—*Jean Anderson*

Ten Thousand Lakes Wild Rice, Mushroom and Carrot Dressing

More than 25 years ago when I was researching my first cookbook, *The Art of American Indian Cooking*, a Chippewa from Minnesota gave a wild rice casserole recipe to my Indian co-author, the late Yeffe Kimball. We featured it in the book, and it's still a favorite of mine. I then got to thinking that with an addition here and a subtraction there, it could be turned into a casserole dressing. Quite so. This version is better if made 1 day ahead and then reheated at 350° for 35 to 40 minutes.

10 to 12 Servings

2 cups wild rice (12 ounces)
1½ teaspoons salt
¼ cup corn oil

1 large onion, coarsely
  chopped
6 medium scallions, thinly
  sliced
3 large celery ribs, coarsely
  diced
2 medium carrots, coarsely
  chopped
1 teaspoon marjoram,
  crumbled
½ teaspoon rosemary, very
  finely crumbled
½ teaspoon thyme, crumbled
½ teaspoon freshly ground
  pepper
1 pound small mushrooms,
  thinly sliced
2 tablespoons unsalted butter
3 tablespoons all-purpose
  flour
1⅔ cups chicken or beef stock
  or canned low-sodium broth
2 cups Melba Toast Cubes
  (recipe follows)

1. In a large heavy saucepan, combine the wild rice, salt and 7 cups of water and bring to a rolling boil over moderately high heat. Reduce the heat to moderately low and simmer, partially covered, until the rice has popped and the grains are tender but slightly chewy, about 55 minutes. Drain well and set aside.

2. Meanwhile, in a large heavy skillet, heat the oil over moderately high heat for 1 minute. Add the onion, scallions and celery and cook, stirring frequently, until limp and golden, about 10 minutes. Add the carrots, marjoram, rosemary, thyme and pepper and reduce the heat to low. Cover and cook for 10 minutes. Using a slotted spoon, transfer the vegetables to a large bowl and set aside.

3. Add the mushrooms to the skillet and increase the heat to moderately high. Cook, stirring occasionally, until the mushrooms have

released their juices and the juices have evaporated, about 7 minutes. Add the mushrooms to the bowl of vegetables.

4. Preheat the oven to 350°. Butter a large oval casserole and a large square of heavy-duty aluminum foil.

5. In a small heavy saucepan, melt the 2 tablespoons butter over moderate heat. Whisk in the flour until the mixture is smooth and hot. Whisk in the stock and cook, stirring frequently, until the sauce boils and thickens, about 3 minutes. Reduce the heat so that the sauce bubbles gently; simmer, stirring, until the sauce is as thick as gravy, about 5 minutes longer.

6. Add the sauce to the large bowl along with the Melba Toast Cubes and the reserved wild rice; toss very well. Lightly spoon the dressing into the prepared casserole and cover with the foil; crumple around the casserole to seal tightly. Bake in the middle of the oven for 1 hour and serve at once.

—*Jean Anderson*

Melba Toast Cubes

Small cubes of melba toast impart a nutty flavor and welcome crunch to stuffings. The cubes couldn't be easier to make, and they can be double-bagged in plastic and stored in a 0° freezer for up to three months. These little croutons can also be tossed into green salads or scattered on top of soups.

Makes About 6 Cups

1 loaf (1 pound) firm-textured
  white bread

1. Preheat the oven to 250°. Stack 3 slices of bread and cut into ¼-inch strips with a large serrated knife; then cut the strips crosswise at ¼-inch intervals to form ¼-inch cubes.

Repeat with the remaining slices of bread.

2. Spread the cubes out in a large roasting pan or jelly-roll pan and bake in the middle of the oven, stirring occasionally, for 1 hour or until uniformly crisp and golden. Let cool to room temperature; then store in an airtight container.
—*Jean Anderson*

Cajun Rice Dressing with Ham and Sausage

This dressing resembles jambalaya; in fact, if you doubled the amount of ham and sausage, you'd have jambalaya. Like most good Cajun recipes, this one begins with a roux, which should be browned slowly so that it will develop the proper rich caramel flavor. Rushing the job is likely to produce a bitter taste. This dressing may seem like a lot of work, but it can all be done 1 day ahead. Begin the rice as the roux reduces so that both will be done at the same time.

10 to 12 Servings

Roux Mixture:
2 tablespoons vegetable oil, bacon drippings or lard
3 tablespoons all-purpose flour
1 medium onion, minced
1 medium green bell pepper, finely diced
1 celery rib, finely diced
¼ pound bulk sausage
¼ pound smoked ham, finely ground

Rice Mixture:
2 tablespoons vegetable oil
1 garlic clove, minced
1 small onion, minced
1 large celery rib, diced
¼ to ½ teaspoon cayenne pepper, to taste
¼ teaspoon freshly ground black pepper
2½ cups converted rice (1 pound)
5 cups chicken stock or canned low-sodium broth
⅓ cup very thinly sliced scallion greens
3 tablespoons minced parsley
3 tablespoons unsalted butter

1. Make the roux mixture: In a large heavy saucepan, combine the vegetable oil and flour and cook over moderately low heat, stirring frequently to prevent sticking or scorching, until the roux is a rich rust brown, about 30 minutes.

2. Mix in the onion, green pepper and celery and cook until they stop sizzling, about 5 minutes. Remove from the heat, cover and let stand for 15 minutes.

3. Add 2 cups of water to the roux and cook over moderate heat, stirring, until the mixture boils and thickens, about 3 minutes. Reduce the heat to moderately low so that the mixture bubbles gently; simmer, stirring frequently, until very thick and reduced by at least three-quarters with no more than one inch remaining in the saucepan, about 45 minutes.

4. Meanwhile, in a small heavy skillet, cook the sausage and ham over moderately high heat for 3 minutes, stirring to break up any clumps. Remove from the heat, cover and keep warm. When the roux has thickened properly, stir in the meats and set aside.

5. Make the rice mixture: While the roux is reducing, in a heavy medium casserole, heat the vegetable oil over moderate heat for 1 minute. Add the garlic, onion, celery, cayenne and black pepper and cook, stirring frequently, until the vegetables are slightly softened and fragrant, about 5 minutes. Add the rice and cook, stirring, until well coated and heated through, about 3 minutes. Add the stock and bring it to a rolling boil over moderately high heat, stirring occasionally.

6. Reduce the heat to low so that the liquid bubbles gently; simmer for 15 minutes, stirring once. Stir well, cover and cook until all the liquid has evaporated and the rice is just tender, about 7 minutes longer. Stir in the scallion greens, parsley and butter. As soon as the butter melts, stir in the reserved roux mixture. Transfer the stuffing to a casserole or serving dish and serve immediately. *(The recipe can be prepared up to 1 day ahead. Let cool, then cover and refrigerate. Before serving, cover tightly with foil and bake at 375° for about 30 minutes, or until heated through.)*
—*Jean Anderson*

Double Rice and Mushroom Dressing

Rich and earthy tasting, this dressing requires turkey or chicken livers and is a natural with poultry. The dish can be assembled in advance and heated along with the main course.

Makes About 8 Cups

½ pound turkey and/or chicken livers, trimmed
½ cup milk
1 stick (4 ounces) unsalted butter
½ cup chopped pecans
¾ cup chopped cooked ham (about 4 ounces)
1 pound mushrooms, chopped
8 large scallions, chopped (about 1½ cups)
4 cups chicken stock or 2 cups canned broth diluted with 2 cups water

¾ cup brown rice
¾ cup wild rice, well rinsed
1½ teaspoons thyme
1 teaspoon salt
½ teaspoon freshly ground
    pepper

1. Place the livers in a small bowl and cover with the milk. Refrigerate for 30 minutes, or overnight.

2. In a large heavy saucepan, melt 2 tablespoons of the butter over high heat. Add the pecans and sauté until fragrant, about 2 minutes. Using a slotted spoon, transfer the nuts to a bowl.

3. Add the ham to the saucepan and sauté until lightly browned, about 2 minutes. Transfer to the bowl with the sautéed pecans.

4. Drain the livers and pat dry. In the same pan, melt 2 tablespoons of the butter over high heat. Add the livers and sauté, tossing, until browned on the outside, about 2 minutes. Transfer to a plate.

5. Melt the remaining 4 table-spoons butter in the pan. Add the mushrooms and sauté over moder-ately high heat, stirring occasionally, until most of their juices have evapo-rated, about 15 minutes. Stir in the scallions and cook until wilted, about 2 minutes.

6. Stir in the chicken stock and brown rice and bring to a boil. Re-duce the heat to moderately low, cover and simmer for 20 minutes. Stir in the wild rice, thyme, salt and pepper. Simmer, covered, until the wild rice is tender, 20 to 25 minutes.

7. Preheat the oven to 350°. Cut the livers into ½-inch pieces. Add to the hot rice. Stir in the ham and pecans and turn the mixture into a large well-buttered casserole. *(The recipe can be prepared to this point 1 day ahead. Cover and refrigerate. Let return to room temperature be-fore baking.)*

8. Bake the dressing, covered, for about 30 minutes, or until heated through. Fluff up with a fork before serving and season with additional salt if desired.
—*Diana Sturgis*

Oriental Stuffing

The glutinous rice for this stuffing must be soaked overnight, but the stuffing itself does not take long to prepare.

Makes About 15 Cups

3 cups glutinous rice*
2 tablespoons peanut oil
1 cup minced shallots (about
    ½ pound)
½ cup minced scallions
½ cup Chinese rice wine or
    pale dry sherry
½ pound Chinese pork
    sausage,* cut into ¼-inch
    dice
½ pound Chinese duck liver
    sausage* (see Note), cut into
    ¼-inch dice
3 cups Rich Turkey and
    Chicken Stock (p. 63)
1 teaspoon salt
¼ teaspoon freshly ground
    black pepper
1½ pounds fresh water
    chestnuts,* or ½ pound
    jicama, peeled and coarsely
    chopped (2 cups)
1 small red bell pepper, diced
1½ teaspoons tarragon
1 teaspoon thyme
¼ cup chopped fresh Chinese
    chives,* chives or scallion
    greens
*Available at Asian markets

1. Place the rice in a large bowl. Add 6 cups of water and let soak overnight. Drain well.

2. In a large skillet or wok, heat the peanut oil over moderately high

heat. Stir-fry the shallots and scal-lions for about 30 seconds, until soft-ened. Add the wine and cook until almost no liquid remains in the skil-let, about 4 minutes. Add the pork and liver sausages and cook, stirring once or twice, for 1 minute. Add the rice, the Rich Turkey and Chicken Stock and the salt and black pepper. Cook, uncovered, stirring occasion-ally to prevent sticking, until all the stock is absorbed, about 8 minutes.

3. Add the water chestnuts, red pepper, tarragon, thyme and chives and cook, stirring frequently, for 3 minutes. Remove from the heat and let the stuffing cool to room temper-ature. You should have about 8 cups.

4. Reserve 4 cups of the stuffing to fill the turkey. Spoon the remain-der into a greased baking dish and, before serving, bake at 350° for 45 minutes.

NOTE: Use another ½ pound of Chinese pork sausage if duck liver sausage is unavailable.
—*Ken Hom*

Fruited Couscous Dressing

This side-dish dressing, a light com-bination of quick-cooking couscous, prunes, lemon zest, pine nuts and ap-ples, makes a great match for either sausage or lamb.

Makes About 8 Cups

2 cups chicken stock or 1 cup
    canned broth diluted with 1
    cup water
1 cup chopped pitted prunes
    (8 ounces)
½ cup chopped parsley
1 teaspoon grated lemon zest
½ teaspoon cinnamon
½ teaspoon cumin
½ teaspoon freshly ground
    pepper
1⅔ cups instant couscous
½ cup pine nuts (2½ ounces)

½ pound slab bacon, cut into
    ¼-inch dice
6 tablespoons unsalted butter
2 medium onions, chopped
2 medium tart green apples—
    peeled, cored and chopped
    (about 1½ cups)

1. In a medium saucepan, combine the stock, prunes, parsley and lemon zest. Slowly bring to a boil over low heat. Simmer, covered, for 5 minutes. Add the cinnamon, cumin and pepper and stir in the couscous. Remove from the heat and let stand, covered, until the couscous absorbs all the liquid, about 15 minutes.

2. Meanwhile, in a large heavy skillet, cook the pine nuts over moderate heat, tossing, until lightly toasted, about 3 minutes. Place the nuts in a large bowl.

3. Preheat the oven to 350°. Add the bacon to the skillet and sauté over moderately high heat, stirring, until golden brown, about 3 minutes. With a slotted spoon, add the bacon to the nuts; discard the fat in the pan.

4. Add the butter to the skillet and melt over high heat. Add the onions and apples and cook until softened but not browned, about 5 minutes. Scrape the mixture into the bowl.

5. Fluff up the couscous with a fork and add it to the bowl. Toss well to combine. Turn the mixture into a buttered large shallow baking dish. *(The recipe can be prepared to this point 1 day ahead. Cover and refrigerate. Let the dressing return to room temperature before baking.)*

6. Bake the dressing, covered, for about 20 minutes, or until heated through. Fluff with a fork before serving.
—Diana Sturgis

Bulgur, Toasted Walnut and Dried Fruit Dressing

An acquaintance from California once served me a superb casserole of cracked wheat and dried fruits. It serves as the basis of this dressing, which also contains toasted walnuts, orange and lemon zests, fresh herbs and the woodsy-flavored dried Polish mushrooms available at many supermarkets in little plastic cups.

12 to 14 Servings

¼ cup olive oil, plus some for
    brushing
1½ cups walnuts (6 ounces)
1 ounce dried Polish
    mushrooms
3½ cups boiling water
2 cups bulgur (cracked wheat)
2 cups boiling chicken stock
    or canned low-sodium broth
3 large garlic cloves, minced
1 large onion, coarsely
    chopped
4 large celery ribs, coarsely
    chopped
1 pound carrots, coarsely
    chopped
1 tablespoon minced fresh
    marjoram or 1 teaspoon
    marjoram, crumbled
1 tablespoon minced lemon
    thyme or ¾ teaspoon thyme,
    crumbled
1 teaspoon minced fresh
    rosemary or ½ teaspoon
    rosemary, crumbled
1 teaspoon finely grated
    orange zest
1 teaspoon finely grated
    lemon zest
½ teaspoon freshly ground
    pepper
1 box (11 ounces) mixed
    dried fruits, coarsely
    chopped
1½ teaspoons salt

1. Preheat the oven to 350°. Brush a deep 3½-quart casserole with olive oil and set aside. Spread the walnuts in a pie plate and toast in the middle of the oven for about 12 minutes, or until crisp and lightly browned. Coarsely chop and set aside. Increase the oven temperature to 375°.

2. Place the dried mushrooms in a small heatproof bowl, add 2 cups of the boiling water and let stand for 20 minutes. Place the bulgur in a large heatproof bowl, add the boiling chicken stock and the remaining 1½ cups boiling water and set aside until all the liquid has been absorbed, about 30 minutes.

3. Meanwhile, remove the mushrooms from the soaking liquid with a slotted spoon. Strain the liquid through a fine sieve lined with a moistened paper towel; set aside. Rinse the mushrooms and pat dry. Cut off any tough bits and discard; coarsely chop the mushrooms and set aside.

4. In a large heavy skillet, heat the ¼ cup olive oil over moderate heat for 1 minute. Add the garlic, onion and celery and cook, stirring frequently, until slightly softened, about 5 minutes. Add the carrots, marjoram, thyme, rosemary, orange and lemon zests, pepper and ½ cup of the reserved mushroom soaking liquid. Reduce the heat to low, cover and cook for 15 minutes.

5. When the bulgur is tender, add the dried fruits, chopped mushrooms, remaining mushroom soaking liquid and the salt; toss well to mix. Add the vegetable mixture and the reserved toasted walnuts and toss well again. Lightly spoon the dressing into the prepared casserole and cover tightly with foil. Bake in the middle of the oven for 40 minutes, until steaming hot. Fluff with a large fork and serve immediately.
—Jean Anderson

Ten Thousand Lakes Wild Rice, Mushroom and Carrot Dressing (p. 109).

Chesapeake Oyster Stuffing (p. 125).

Southwest Corn and Pepper Stuffing (p. 125).

Brioche and Oyster Pudding (p. 119).

Apricot-Walnut Stuffing

If you are making this stuffing to go with Roast East Hampton Golden Goose (p. 49), use the liver from the goose you are stuffing. If not, substitute chicken or turkey livers.

Makes Enough for a
12-Pound Goose

½ pound (1½ cups) extra-
large dried apricots and/or
prunes, washed and drained
in a sieve
½ cup dark raisins, washed
and drained
1 cup port wine
1 lemon, thinly sliced
4 tablespoons unsalted butter,
melted
1 goose liver
1 medium onion, chopped
1 large tart apple, coarsely
chopped
1 cup walnuts, coarsely
chopped
½ teaspoon mace
Salt and freshly ground
pepper
2 tablespoons fresh lemon
juice
½ cup minced celery, with
leaves
2 cups ½-inch cubes of soft
white or whole-wheat bread

1. Soak the apricots and raisins in the port wine and refrigerate overnight. In a large nonreactive saucepan, combine the apricots, raisins, port and lemon slices and simmer until almost tender, 5 to 6 minutes. Drain well. (Reserve the port if you are making the gravy for the Roast East Hampton Golden Goose, p. 49)

2. Chop the cooked apricots, lemon and raisins coarsely and place them in a large bowl.

3. In a medium skillet, heat 1 ta-blespoon of the butter and sauté the goose liver until firm but not browned. Chop the liver and add it to the fruit.

4. Add 1 tablespoon of the butter, add the onion and sauté until just translucent. Add the onion, the apple, walnuts and mace to the bowl. Season with salt and pepper to taste and add the remaining 2 tablespoons of butter, the lemon juice, celery and bread cubes. Toss all together.
—Pearl Byrd Foster

Potato, Celery and Melba Toast Stuffing

In the old days on the Eastern Shore of Maryland, a simple bread-and-potato mixture was used to stuff fowl, especially game birds. This version is a bit fancier but still is easy to make. If the flavor is to be right, however, you must make the melba toast yourself. Also, use fresh herbs if they're available; they give the stuffing a bouquet no dried herbs can.

10 to 12 Servings

8 ounces stale, sliced firm-
textured white bread (about
7 slices)
6 tablespoons unsalted butter,
melted
3 large bay leaves, preferably
fresh
2½ teaspoons fresh lemon
thyme or ½ teaspoon thyme,
crumbled
2 teaspoons minced fresh
rosemary or ½ teaspoon
rosemary, crumbled
4 large baking potatoes (2½
pounds), peeled and cut into
½-inch cubes
¼ teaspoon freshly grated
nutmeg
¼ teaspoon freshly ground
pepper
2 medium onions, minced

3 large celery ribs, finely diced
⅓ cup minced parsley
2½ cups hot milk
1¾ teaspoons salt

1. Make the melba toast crumbs: Preheat the oven to 300°. Spread the bread out on a large baking sheet and bake in the middle of the oven for 30 minutes, or until crisp and golden brown. Let cool to room temperature, then break the toast into chunks and place in a food processor. Pulse until the mixture is the texture of coarse crumbs with some large pieces remaining. Set aside.

2. Increase the oven temperature to 425°. Butter a high-sided 3-quart casserole. Place 2 tablespoons of the melted butter and the bay leaves in the bottom. If using fresh herbs, add the thyme and rosemary. Add the potatoes and sprinkle with the nutmeg, pepper and dried herbs, if using. Scatter the onions and celery evenly on top. Cover and bake in the middle of the oven for 20 minutes.

3. Stir the potatoes up from the bottom, cover and bake for 20 minutes longer, or until the potatoes are just tender. Remove the casserole from the oven and preheat the broiler. Remove the bay leaves and discard. Add the parsley and 2 more tablespoons of the butter and toss lightly but thoroughly. Combine the hot milk and salt and gently fold into the potatoes alternately with 2 cups of the melba toast crumbs, the mixture will be very moist. Transfer the stuffing to a 14-inch oval gratin dish.

4. In a small bowl, using a fork, toss the remaining melba toast crumbs with the remaining 2 table-spoons melted butter. Scatter the crumbs evenly over the stuffing and broil 7 inches from the heat for about 30 seconds, or until tipped with brown. Serve at once.
—Jean Anderson

Plantation-Stuffing Patties with Pecans

The idea for this recipe comes from a South Carolina friend who shapes a moist dressing (as stuffing is known down South) into burgers and bakes them. She uses a half-and-half mix of bread stuffing mix and crumbled homemade corn bread plus "gobs of chopped onion, celery and giblet stock." Here melba cubes are substituted for the stuffing mix and chicken stock for the giblet stock (but by all means use giblet stock if you have it on hand). I also added pecans, which, my friend admits, are a nifty addition.

Makes 18 to 20 Patties

Melba Toast Cubes (p. 109)
6 cups dry, coarsely crumbled Old-Fashioned Corn Bread for Stuffing (p. 132)
1½ cups finely chopped pecans (6 ounces)
2 tablespoons poultry seasoning
1 teaspoon salt
¼ teaspoon freshly ground pepper
¼ cup corn oil
1½ large onions, finely chopped
6 large celery ribs, finely chopped
1 stick (4 ounces) unsalted butter, melted
About 3¾ cups chicken stock or canned low-sodium broth

1. Lightly spray two baking sheets with nonstick vegetable cooking spray and set aside.

2. In a very large bowl, combine the Melba Toast Cubes, Corn Bread, pecans, poultry seasoning, salt and pepper; toss well and set aside.

3. In a large heavy skillet, heat the corn oil over high heat for 1 minute. Add the onions and celery and cook, stirring occasionally, until golden but still a bit crisp, about 5 minutes. Add to the bowl along with the melted butter; toss well. Stir in 3¾ cups of the chicken stock; the stuffing should be very moist, about like porridge, but should hold together nicely when you squeeze a bit of it in your hand. Season with additional salt and pepper to taste and let stand for 10 minutes. If the mixture seems dry at this point, add a bit more chicken stock.

4. Preheat the oven to 400°. Using a ½-cup measure, lightly scoop up the stuffing mixture and shape it into patties about 3 inches across and ½ inch thick. Arrange the stuffing patties on the prepared baking sheets, spacing them evenly. *(The patties can be prepared to this point up to 1 day ahead. Cover and refrigerate.)*

5. Bake the stuffing patties on the middle and lower racks of the oven for 15 minutes. Turn the patties over, switch the baking sheets and bake for about 15 minutes longer, or until the patties are lightly browned. Serve hot.
—Jean Anderson

Chestnut Dressing

Makes About 11 Cups

2 pounds large chestnuts in the shell
2 cups chicken stock or low-sodium canned broth
1½ sticks (6 ounces) unsalted butter
6 tender, pale celery ribs, finely chopped
2 medium onions, finely chopped
10 cups coarse bread crumbs (from 1 pound 5 ounces firm-textured white bread)
2 teaspoons marjoram
1 teaspoon thyme
2 teaspoons salt
1 teaspoon freshly ground pepper

1. Slash the brown shells of the chestnuts on both sides. Drop the chestnuts in a large saucepan of boiling water and cook for 5 minutes. Drain and remove the shells and brown skins while the chestnuts are hot so that they will peel off easily. Cut the chestnuts in half.

2. In a medium saucepan, bring the chicken stock to a simmer over moderate heat. Add the peeled chestnuts and cook until just tender but still firm, about 8 minutes. Drain, reserving the stock. *(The chestnuts can be prepared up to 2 days in advance. Refrigerate covered.)*

3. In a large saucepan melt 1 stick of the butter. Add the celery, onions and 1½ cups of the reserved stock. Cook over moderately high heat until the broth has boiled away, about 15 minutes. Do not allow the celery, onions or butter to brown.

4. In a small saucepan, melt the remaining 4 tablespoons butter over moderately low heat or in a heat-proof glass bowl in a microwave oven. In a large bowl, combine the celery and onions with the bread crumbs. Add the cooked chestnuts, the melted butter, marjoram, thyme, salt and pepper. Mix well with a large fork. If the dressing is too crumbly or dry, add the remaining stock. The dressing should be pleasingly moist but not wet.
—Camille Glenn

Chestnut and Sausage Stuffing

This makes enough stuffing for one large chicken or a small turkey.
Makes About 3½ Cups

½ pound fresh chestnuts
1 tablespoon unsalted butter
7 medium shallots, chopped
1 medium celery rib, chopped
½ pound country sausage
   meat
½ pound mushrooms,
   chopped
½ cup chicken stock or
   canned broth
Salt and freshly ground
   pepper

1. Preheat the oven to 350°. Using a sharp paring knife, cut a small X into the flat side of each chestnut, cutting through the woody outer shell; try not to cut into the meat. Place the chestnuts in a shallow pan in a single layer. Roast until the X opens slightly, about 10 minutes. Peel off the shell and the tough inner skin while the chestnuts are still hot. Chop the chestnuts.

2. In a large skillet, melt the butter over moderately high heat. Add the shallots and celery; sauté until softened and lightly browned, about 15 minutes.

3. Add the sausage meat and stir to break up the meat. Cook until lightly browned, about 10 minutes.

4. Add the mushrooms and chestnuts and cook for 10 minutes, stirring occasionally.

5. Add the chicken stock and season to taste with salt and pepper. Continue cooking until most of the liquid has evaporated, about 10 minutes. Let cool completely before using as a stuffing.
—*John Robert Massie*

Wild Mushroom-Sage Stuffing

Makes About 4 Cups

2 pounds fresh wild
   mushrooms, such as
   shiitakes and chanterelles,
   stems removed
2 tablespoons extra-virgin
   olive oil
4 large shallots, coarsely
   chopped
8 large garlic cloves, coarsely
   chopped
1¼ teaspoons thyme
½ cup coarsely chopped fresh
   sage
2 tablespoons unsalted butter
1½ teaspoons freshly ground
   pepper
1 to 1½ tablespoons finely
   grated lemon zest
Salt

1. Wipe the stemmed mushrooms with a damp cloth and cut into ½-inch pieces; set aside.

2. In a large nonstick skillet, heat the olive oil over moderately low heat. Add the shallots, garlic and thyme and cook, stirring, until the shallots soften slightly, about 3 minutes. Increase the heat to moderately high and stir in the mushrooms. Cover and cook until the mushrooms soften, 5 to 6 minutes.

3. Add the sage, butter, pepper and lemon zest. Cook, stirring, until the mushrooms give off some of their liquid, 4 to 5 minutes. Season with salt and additional pepper to taste. Transfer the stuffing to a large bowl and let cool to room temperature before using. *(The stuffing can be made up to 1 day ahead. Cover well and refrigerate.)*
—*Sheila Lukins*

Brioche and Oyster Pudding

This creamy stuffing, made with lightly buttered brioche slices, provides a perfectly delicious repast by itself, coupled with a steamed artichoke or a salad and perhaps a glass of chilled white wine.
8 Servings

6 tablespoons unsalted butter,
   softened
1 medium leek (white and
   tender green), chopped
¼ cup chopped celery
4 ounces smoked ham,
   coarsely chopped
12 parsley stems
1 sprig of fresh thyme or ⅛
   teaspoon dried
1½ cups milk
1 cup heavy cream
6 brioche rolls (about 10
   ounces total), ends trimmed,
   sliced lengthwise ⅜ inch
   thick
2 whole eggs
3 egg yolks
2 tablespoons minced fresh
   chives
1½ tablespoons minced
   parsley
½ teaspoon salt
4 to 5 drops of hot pepper
   sauce
1 dozen oysters, shucked and
   coarsely chopped, liquor
   reserved

1. Preheat the oven to 350°. In a large skillet, melt 1 tablespoon of the butter. Add the leek, celery, ham, parsley stems and thyme and cook over moderate heat until the leek softens, about 5 minutes. Add the milk and cream and cook at a bare simmer for 45 minutes.

2. Meanwhile, lightly butter both sides of the brioche slices using 4 tablespoons of the butter. Place on a

cookie sheet and bake for about 15 minutes, turning once, until lightly browned. Leave the oven on.

3. Use the remaining 1 tablespoon butter to grease a 9-inch springform pan. Arrange the toasted brioche slices in the pan in 3 overlapping rows.

4. Strain the flavored milk and cream, pressing the solids to extract as much liquid as possible. *(The recipe can be prepared to this point 1 day ahead. Cover and refrigerate. Reheat the milk before proceeding.)* In a medium bowl, beat together the whole eggs and egg yolks. Slowly whisk in 1 cup of the hot milk, then whisk in the remainder. Add the chives, parsley, salt, hot sauce and oysters with their liquor.

5. Wrap the outside of the springform pan in a double sheet of aluminum foil. Pour the oyster mixture into the pan, distributing the oysters evenly if necessary. Place the springform in a roasting pan and set in the oven. Pour in enough hot water to reach one-third up the sides of the springform pan. Bake for 35 to 40 minutes, or until a knife inserted 3 inches from the center comes out clean.

6. Transfer to a rack, uncover and let rest for 10 minutes. Run a knife around the edge and remove the outer ring of the pan. Using a large spatula, carefully slide the dressing onto a large round platter. Serve warm or at room temperature.
—*Anne Disrude*

Sweet Pepper Charlotte with Tomatoes and Currants

This colorful charlotte makes a superb and decorative pairing with chicken or pork as well as with turkey. It's quite an elegant dish, with crusty bread triangles encasing a bright, tangy filling.

8 Servings

3 tablespoons sherry wine
  vinegar
3 tablespoons dried currants
  or raisins
6 large red bell peppers
¾ cup extra-virgin olive oil
1 large onion, chopped
3 garlic cloves, chopped
1½ teaspoons oregano
1 can (14 ounces) Italian
  peeled tomatoes, drained
  and crushed
18 slices of firm-textured
  white bread, crusts removed
¾ teaspoon salt
¼ teaspoon coarsely ground
  black pepper
1 egg, beaten

1. In a small nonreactive saucepan, bring the vinegar and currants to a boil. Remove from the heat and let stand until the currants plump up and soften, about 15 minutes.

2. Meanwhile, roast the peppers over a gas flame or under the broiler, turning frequently, until completely charred, 10 to 15 minutes. Place in a paper bag to steam for 10 minutes.

3. Peel the peppers under running water. Core them and remove the membranes and seeds over a bowl to catch the juices. Coarsely chop the peppers. Strain the juices into a large bowl.

4. In a large skillet, heat ¼ cup of the oil. Add the onion, garlic, chopped roasted peppers, oregano and currants with vinegar. Cook over moderately high heat, stirring frequently, until the onion and peppers are slightly browned, about 20 minutes. Add the tomatoes and cook for 5 minutes longer. Set aside.

5. Cut 9 slices of bread into 1½-by-3-inch rectangles; reserve the trimmings. Cut 8 slices into triangles. Cut the remaining slice of bread and all trimmings into ½-inch pieces, add to the bowl of reserved pepper juices and toss. Add the pepper-tomato mixture, salt, black pepper, egg and ¼ cup of the oil. Mix lightly to blend.

6. Preheat the oven to 350°. Lightly oil a 9-inch round cake pan at least 2 inches deep. Brush one side of all the bread pieces liberally with the remaining ¼ cup oil. Placing the oiled side against the pan, line the bottom with the triangles, tips pointing inward. (There will be a little space between the triangles.) Line the sides of the pan with rectangles. Fill with the pepper mixture, packing lightly with a spatula. *(The recipe can be prepared to this point 1 day ahead. Cover and refrigerate. Let return to room temperature before baking.)*

7. Bake the stuffing in the lower third of the oven for 45 minutes, or until the bread is well browned. Invert onto a large round platter and serve hot or at room temperature.
—*Anne Disrude*

Fruit-and-Nut Stuffing

Since the dried fruits in this recipe must soak overnight in bourbon, plan your time accordingly.

Makes About 9 Cups
Enough for a 20-Pound Turkey

18 pitted prunes
½ cup dried currants
1 cup dark raisins
24 dried apricot halves
¼ cup bourbon
3 tart cooking apples—
  unpeeled, cored, and
  chopped
3 large onions, diced
2 celery ribs, diced
4 tablespoons unsalted butter,
  melted
⅔ cup macadamia nuts
⅔ cup cashews
1 cup walnut pieces
2 cups fresh or frozen thawed
  cranberries
1 teaspoon ground cloves
¼ teaspoon cayenne pepper
1 teaspoon ground ginger
1 teaspoon cinnamon
1 teaspoon chervil
1 teaspoon summer savory
1 cup finely minced parsley
  (no stems)
2 teaspoons salt
½ teaspoon freshly ground
  black pepper
2 eggs, lightly beaten

1. Place the prunes, currants, raisins and apricots in a plastic bag and pour the bourbon over the fruit. Seal the bag with a twist tie. Place the bag in a bowl and macerate the mixture overnight.

2. In a large skillet, cook the apples, onions and celery in the butter over moderate heat, stirring occasionally, until the onions are softened and the celery is tender, about 10 minutes.

3. Transfer the sautéed onion mixture to a large bowl. Add the macerated fruit, nuts, cranberries, spices, herbs, salt, pepper and eggs. Gently mix until evenly blended. Set the stuffing aside while you prepare the turkey for roasting.
—*Martha Stewart*

Apple and Prune Stuffing with Almonds

Makes About 6 Cups
Enough for a 12- to 16-Pound Turkey

1 cup cider vinegar
½ cup sugar
2 cups pitted prunes
  (12 ounces)
1 cup slivered almonds
  (4 ounces)
1¾ pounds Granny Smith
  apples—peeled, cored, cut
  into 8 wedges and halved
  crosswise
1 teaspoon crumbled sage
1 teaspoon salt
1 teaspoon freshly ground
  pepper

1. In a small nonreactive saucepan, bring the vinegar and sugar to a boil over moderately high heat, stirring to dissolve the sugar. Remove from the heat, add the prunes and set aside to cool, turning occasionally.

2. Meanwhile, preheat the oven to 350°. Spread the almonds in a baking dish and toast in the oven, shaking the pan once or twice, until golden, 8 to 10 minutes.

3. In a medium bowl, combine the prunes and their liquid, the apples, almonds, sage, salt and pepper; toss well. Drain off the vinegar syrup before using the stuffing.
—*Anne Disrude*

Pecan Stuffing

To make this stuffing as a side dish, pack it into a baking dish and bake at 375° until heated through, 10 to 20 minutes.

Makes Enough for
Two 4½-Pound Roasters

2½ sticks (10 ounces)
  unsalted butter
2 chicken livers, chopped (see
  Note)
1½ cups minced shallots or
  onions
2 cups diced celery, with
  leaves
2 garlic cloves, minced
1 tablespoon salt
1 teaspoon freshly ground
  black pepper
Pinch of cayenne pepper
1 teaspoon crumbled
  rosemary
2 tablespoons chopped
  parsley (no stems)
2 cups (about 7 ounces) large
  pecan halves
1 loaf (about 1 pound) good-
  quality white bread, cut into
  ¼-inch cubes

1. In a small saucepan, melt 1 stick of the butter, then set it aside.

2. In a large skillet or flameproof casserole, melt the remaining 1½ sticks butter. Sauté the chicken livers for about 2 minutes over moderately high heat, then remove the livers with a slotted spoon and set them aside, leaving the butter in the skillet. Add the shallots to the skillet and sauté, stirring, until slightly softened, about 4 or 5 minutes. Add the celery and garlic; toss them to coat with the butter. Sauté for 3 or 4 minutes longer or until the vegetables are slightly translucent (they should retain some crispness).

3. Remove the vegetables from

the heat and season with the salt, black pepper, cayenne, rosemary and parsley. Stir in the pecans, then add the cubed bread and the reserved livers and toss everything together.

4. Add just enough of the reserved melted butter to bind the mixture lightly. Correct all seasonings; the flavoring should be assertive but not overpowering.

NOTE: If you are making this stuffing for Chutney-Glazed Roast Chickens (p. 67), use the livers reserved from the chickens.
—*Pearl Byrd Foster*

Country Ham and Wild Mushroom Stuffing

This stuffing is designed to be baked in the oven and served alongside a turkey, and thus calls for the pan juices for basting in Step 6. If you are making this as a stand-alone side dish, substitute the mushroom soaking liquid from Step 4, instead.

8 Servings

1½ ounces (about 1½ cups) dried porcini mushrooms (see Note)
2 cups chicken stock or canned broth
10 cups crumbled day-old white bread
6 tablespoons unsalted butter
½ pound Smithfield ham (see Note), cut into ½-inch cubes
2 medium onions, chopped
1 teaspoon thyme
1 cup finely chopped flat-leaf parsley
½ teaspoon salt
1 teaspoon freshly ground pepper
1½ cups pan juices from Roast Fresh Turkey (p. 57)

1. Rinse the porcini thoroughly under cold running water and place in a small bowl. In a small saucepan, bring the stock to a boil. Pour over the mushrooms and let stand, stirring occasionally, for 1 hour.

2. Put the crumbled bread in a large mixing bowl. In a medium skillet, melt 2 tablespoons of the butter over moderate heat until foaming. Add the ham and cook, stirring, until browned, about 10 minutes. With a slotted spoon, transfer the ham to the bowl with the bread.

3. Return the skillet to moderate heat, add the remaining 4 tablespoons butter and heat until foaming. Add the onions and thyme, cover and reduce the heat to moderate. Cook, stirring occasionally, until the onions are tender and lightly colored, 10 to 15 minutes. Pour the onions and butter over the bread in the bowl.

4. With a slotted spoon, lift the whole mushrooms from their soaking liquid and transfer to the mixing bowl. Strain the soaking liquid through a funnel lined with a coffee filter or a strainer lined with several thicknesses of dampened cheesecloth. (If making this dish to accompany the Roast Fresh Turkey on p. 57, reserve the mushroom soaking liquid for the gravy. If not, use the liquid to baste the stuffing in Step 6.)

5. Add the parsley to the stuffing, season with the salt and pepper and stir well to mix. Transfer to a medium baking dish, preferably with a tight-fitting lid. (*The stuffing can be prepared to this point several hours in advance of baking. Refrigeration is not necessary.*)

6. Preheat the oven to 325°. Spoon the pan juices (or mushroom soaking liquid) evenly over the stuffing, cover tightly and bake for 35 to 45 minutes, until the stuffing is steaming and the sides and bottom are crunchy and brown.

NOTE: Dried cèpes, morels or shiitake mushrooms can all be used to good effect if porcini are unavailable. Any good-quality, firm, smoky ham can be substituted for Smithfield ham.
—*Michael McLaughlin*

Apricot-Sausage Stuffing

The blend of flavors in this stuffing—tart apricots, sweet apple juice, nutty whole wheat, savory pork—is addictive. The fruit must be marinated overnight, so plan accordingly.

Makes About 8 Cups
Enough for an 18-Pound Turkey

4 ounces dried apricots (about 1 cup)
⅓ cup golden raisins
¾ cup apple juice
1 tablespoon cider vinegar
4 tablespoons unsalted butter
1 medium onion, finely chopped
8 ounces whole wheat bread (about 9 slices), toasted and cut into ½-inch cubes
1 pound bulk pork sausage
½ cup coarsely chopped walnuts
½ cup minced parsley
1 teaspoon thyme
1 teaspoon freshly ground pepper

1. Quarter the apricots or cut into ½-inch pieces. In a small bowl, combine the apricots, raisins, apple juice and vinegar. Cover and allow the fruit to marinate at room temperature overnight.

2. In a medium skillet, melt the butter over moderate heat. Add the onion and cook, stirring occasionally, until softened but not browned, 3 to 5 minutes. Scrape into a large bowl and add the bread cubes and toss briefly.

3. In the same skillet, cook the

sausage over moderate heat, stirring to break the meat up into small pieces, until golden brown, about 5 minutes. Strain to drain off the fat.

4. Add the sausage to the bread and toss lightly. Add the walnuts, parsley, thyme, pepper and marinated fruit with its liquid; toss to mix.

NOTE: When you are ready to use the stuffing, pack it loosely into the turkey; any leftover stuffing may be baked, covered, in a buttered dish alongside the turkey until heated through, about 30 minutes.
—Diana Sturgis

Yankee Ham and Lemon Stuffing Balls

Once when researching early New England recipes, I came across stuffing balls that were served at Old Sturbridge Village in Massachusetts. They contained nearly a pound of ground suet—in addition to half a pound of ham and two egg yolks. What follows is a lower-cholesterol version that's every bit as good as the original. These are traditionally cooked covered; if you would prefer a very crusty exterior, cook them uncovered.

Makes 16 Stuffing Balls

¼ *pound thick-sliced bacon,*
  cut into ¼-inch dice
4½ *cups soft, fresh white*
  bread crumbs (from a
  14-ounce loaf)
½ *pound smoked ham,*
  ground
2 *tablespoons unsalted butter,*
  melted
2 *tablespoons fresh lemon*
  juice
1 *teaspoon marjoram,*
  crumbled

½ *teaspoon thyme, crumbled*
½ *teaspoon finely grated*
  lemon zest
¼ *teaspoon freshly ground*
  pepper
¼ *teaspoon freshly grated*
  nutmeg
1 *egg*
3 *tablespoons vegetable oil*

1. Preheat the oven to 325°. Heat a large heavy skillet over moderately high heat. Add the bacon and fry, stirring frequently, until crisp, about 5 minutes. Drain well on paper towels. Pour off the bacon fat from the skillet and wipe clean.

2. In a medium bowl, combine the bacon with the bread crumbs, ham, melted butter, lemon juice, marjoram, thyme, lemon zest, pepper, nutmeg, egg and 2 tablespoons of water. Mix lightly with your hands until well blended. Shape the stuffing into 16 balls about the size of golf balls.

3. In the skillet, heat the oil over moderate heat until bubbly, about 1 minute. Add half of the stuffing balls and fry, turning frequently, until evenly browned and crisp, about 7 minutes. As the stuffing balls are done, transfer them to an ungreased 9-by-13-inch baking pan. Make sure that they do not touch each other or the sides of the pan. Repeat with the remaining stuffing balls.

4. Cover the pan snugly with aluminum foil and bake in the middle of the oven for 35 minutes, until piping hot. Transfer the stuffing balls to a platter and serve at once.
—Jean Anderson

Great Plains Sage and Sausage Stuffing

Many of the settlers of America's breadbasket were Germans who doted on the sausages of their homeland. Not surprisingly, the Thanksgiving stuffings they developed were rich ones filled with sausage. It's important that you use a firm-textured bread for this particular stuffing and that the bread be good and dry; otherwise it will turn to mush when you mix everything together.

10 to 12 Servings

1 *pound bulk sausage*
1 *stick (4 ounces) unsalted*
  butter, melted
1 *large onion, coarsely*
  chopped
3 *large celery ribs, finely diced*
10 *cups stale ½-inch cubes of*
  firm-textured white bread
  (from a ¾-pound loaf)
½ *cup minced parsley*
2 *teaspoons rubbed sage*
2 *teaspoons poultry seasoning*
½ *teaspoon thyme, crumbled*
½ *teaspoon salt*
½ *teaspoon freshly ground*
  pepper
¾ *cup chicken stock or*
  canned low-sodium broth

1. Preheat the oven to 375°. Butter a deep 3-quart casserole and a large square of heavy-duty aluminum foil; set aside.

2. In a large heavy skillet, fry the sausage meat over moderately high heat, breaking up the clumps, until lightly browned and no trace of pink remains, about 5 minutes. Using a slotted spoon, transfer the sausage to paper towels to drain.

3. Add 2 tablespoons of the butter to the skillet along with the onion and celery. Cook over moderate heat, stirring frequently, until the

onion is soft and golden, about 15 minutes.

4. Scrape the vegetable mixture into a large bowl and add the bread cubes, parsley, sage, poultry seasoning, thyme, salt and pepper and toss well. Add the reserved sausage meat and the remaining 6 tablespoons butter and toss again. Drizzle ½ cup of the chicken stock over the stuffing and toss.

5. Lightly spoon the stuffing into the prepared casserole and drizzle the remaining ¼ cup stock evenly on top. Lay the foil on top of the stuffing, buttered-side down, and crumple around the casserole to seal tightly. *(The recipe can be prepared to this point up to 1 day ahead and refrigerated.)* Bake the stuffing in the middle of the oven for 40 to 45 minutes, until steaming hot. Serve at once.
—*Jean Anderson*

Three-Bread Stuffing

Makes About 11 Cups
Enough for a 14- to 16-Pound Turkey

½ pound rye bread, cut into 1-inch cubes
½ pound pumpernickel bread, cut into 1-inch cubes
½ pound sourdough bread, cut into 1-inch cubes
1 stick (4 ounces) unsalted butter
1 large onion, chopped
2 large celery ribs, chopped
1 teaspoon sweet Hungarian paprika
1 pound spicy sausage, such as Hungarian, hot Italian or chorizo

1 Granny Smith apple—peeled, cored and chopped
3 tablespoons chopped green olives
1 small jalapeño pepper, seeded and minced (optional)
¼ cup chopped parsley
1 tablespoon chopped fresh thyme or 1 teaspoon dried
½ teaspoon freshly ground pepper
½ teaspoon salt
2 eggs, lightly beaten

1. Spread the bread cubes out in a large baking pan and let them dry overnight, uncovered.

2. In a large skillet, melt the butter over moderate heat. Add the onion and celery, reduce the heat to low and cook until soft but not brown, about 12 minutes. Sprinkle on the paprika and cook for 2 minutes longer.

3. In a medium saucepan, cover the sausage with 2 cups of water and poach over moderately high heat until cooked through, about 10 minutes. Drain, reserving 1 cup of the poaching liquid. Coarsely chop the sausage.

4. In a large bowl, combine the dried bread cubes with the cooked onion and celery, sausage, apple, olives, jalapeño, parsley, thyme, pepper, salt, the reserved sausage poaching liquid and the eggs. Mix until well blended. Let cool completely before stuffing the turkey.
—*Tina Ujlaki*

Rich Chicken Liver Stuffing

Because it is so rich and moist, this stuffing tastes almost like a mousse.
Makes About 3¼ Cups

4 tablespoons rendered goose fat or unsalted butter
2 onions, finely chopped
3 cups fresh bread crumbs (from 4 to 5 slices of firm-textured white bread, crusts removed)
½ cup chopped parsley
¾ pound chicken livers, trimmed
1 goose gizzard and goose liver (reserved from Roasted Goose with Chicken Liver Stuffing, p. 49)
2 teaspoons salt
1 teaspoon oregano
2 eggs, lightly beaten

1. In a large skillet, warm the rendered goose fat over moderate heat. Add the onions and cook, stirring, until softened but not browned, about 10 minutes.

2. Add the bread crumbs and parsley. Cook, stirring occasionally, until lightly toasted, about 5 minutes. Remove from the heat and let cool for 15 minutes.

3. Put the chicken livers and reserved goose liver in a food processor. Add the bread and onion mixture, salt, oregano, eggs and reserved gizzard. Turn the machine quickly on and off 10 to 12 times to chop finely. *(The stuffing can be prepared 2 days ahead. Cover and refrigerate.)*
—*Lydie Marshall*

Sausage, Fruit and Nut Stuffing

This can be used to stuff a bird or baked separately in a lightly greased covered casserole at 350° until heated through, about 30 minutes.

Makes About 12 Cups
Enough for an 11-Pound Goose

1 pound bulk pork sausage
1 stick (4 ounces) unsalted
  butter
2 large onions, chopped
2 celery ribs, chopped
6 ounces medium
  mushrooms, sliced
½ cup minced parsley
1 cup (4 ounces) coarsely
  chopped pecans
¾ teaspoon marjoram
¾ teaspoon rosemary
¾ teaspoon thyme
1½ teaspoons salt
Freshly ground pepper
4 cups crumbled, stale corn
  bread
2½ cups crumbled, stale, firm-
  textured white bread or egg
  bread
5 tangerines—peeled,
  sectioned and halved
  crosswise
1¼ cups (8 ounces) fresh or
  frozen cranberries
½ pound fresh or frozen
  lingonberries

1. In a large skillet, cook the sausage over moderately high heat, stirring to break up large lumps, until the meat is browned, about 15 minutes; remove the sausage with a slotted spoon.

2. Melt the butter in the pan drippings, add the onions and celery and sauté over moderate heat until the onions are soft and translucent, about 4 minutes.

3. Add the mushrooms, parsley, pecans, marjoram, rosemary, thyme, salt and pepper to taste. Cook, stirring, for about 3 minutes or until the mushrooms start to darken.

4. In a large bowl, combine the sausage meat, corn bread and white bread. Add the mushroom mixture, tangerines, cranberries and lingonberries. Toss until well mixed. Season with additional salt and pepper to taste.
—Melanie Barnard

Chesapeake Oyster Stuffing

This recipe was double-starred in Mother's recipe file. It came from an old farm woman who lived near our summer cottage on Chesapeake Bay.

10 to 12 Servings

1½ pints (about 3 dozen)
  shucked oysters, with their
  liquor
5 cups dry, coarsely crumbled
  Old-Fashioned Corn Bread
  for Stuffing (p. 132)
4 cups coarsely crumbled
  saltines (about 6 ounces)
4 medium celery ribs, coarsely
  chopped
1 medium onion, coarsely
  chopped
¼ cup minced parsley
1 tablespoon snipped fresh
  dill
2 teaspoons poultry seasoning
1 teaspoon freshly ground
  pepper
½ teaspoon finely grated
  lemon zest
½ teaspoon salt
1½ sticks (6 ounces) unsalted
  butter, melted
1 tablespoon fresh lemon
  juice

1. Preheat the oven to 350°. Butter a deep 3-quart casserole and a large square of heavy-duty aluminum foil and set aside.

2. Pour the oysters into a strainer set over a bowl. Measure out 1 cup of oyster liquor and set aside; if there isn't enough liquor, add enough water to equal 1 cup. Coarsely chop the oysters.

3. In a large bowl, combine the oysters with the Corn Bread, saltines, celery, onion, parsley, dill, poultry seasoning, pepper, lemon zest and salt; toss to mix. Add the melted butter, lemon juice and ½ cup of the reserved oyster liquor and toss again. Season with additional salt and pepper if necessary.

4. Spoon the stuffing lightly into the prepared casserole and drizzle the remaining ½ cup oyster liquor evenly on top. Lay the foil on top of the stuffing, buttered-side down, and crumple around the casserole dish to seal. Bake in the middle of the oven for 40 minutes, until steaming hot.
—Jean Anderson

Southwest Corn and Pepper Stuffing

This stuffing also makes a fine accompaniment to barbecue.

12 to 14 Servings

6 strips of bacon (6 ounces),
  very thinly sliced crosswise
1 large onion, coarsely
  chopped
1 large red bell pepper, finely
  diced
4 tablespoons unsalted butter,
  melted
1 package (16 ounces) frozen
  corn kernels or 4 cups fresh
  kernels
½ cup pine nuts (3 ounces)
Old-Fashioned Corn Bread
  for Stuffing (p. 132), dried
  and crumbled

2 cups coarsely shredded
  longhorn or sharp white
  Cheddar cheese (6 ounces)
⅓ cup chopped cilantro (fresh
  coriander)
1½ tablespoons poultry
  seasoning
1½ teaspoons rubbed sage
1½ teaspoons chili powder
1 teaspoon oregano, crumbled
¾ teaspoon cumin
¾ teaspoon salt
¼ teaspoon freshly ground
  black pepper
1 can (4 ounces) chopped
  green chiles, drained
1½ cups chicken stock or
  canned low-sodium broth

1. Preheat the oven to 350°. Butter a deep 4-quart casserole and a
large square of heavy-duty aluminum foil; set aside.

2. In a heavy medium skillet, fry
the bacon over moderately high heat,
separating the pieces, until crisp and
browned, about 7 minutes. Using a
slotted spoon, transfer the bacon to
paper towels to drain.

3. Add the onion and red bell pepper to the bacon drippings and cook,
stirring frequently, until the onion is
limp and golden, about 10 minutes.
Using a slotted spoon, transfer the
onion-and-pepper mixture to a small
bowl and set aside. Add 2 tablespoons of the melted butter to the
skillet and reduce the heat to low.
Add the corn and cook, stirring often, until tender, about 15 minutes.

4. Meanwhile, spread the pine
nuts in a pie plate and toast them in
the middle of the oven until pale tan,
about 7 minutes. Let the pine nuts
cool slightly, then coarsely chop
them.

5. In a very large mixing bowl,
combine the crumbled Corn Bread,
bacon, pine nuts, cheese, coriander,
poultry seasoning, sage, chili pow-

der, oregano, cumin, salt and black
pepper. Toss well to mix. Add the
chiles, reserved onion-and-pepper
mixture and corn, the remaining 2
tablespoons melted butter and 1 cup
of the stock; toss again.

6. Lightly spoon the mixture into
the prepared casserole and drizzle
the remaining ½ cup chicken stock
evenly over all. Cover with the foil,
buttered-side down, and crumple
around the casserole to seal snugly.
Bake in the middle of the oven for 40
to 45 minutes, until steaming hot.
Serve at once.
—Jean Anderson

Corn Bread-Sausage Dressing

Half of the dressing can be used to
stuff the cavity of the turkey, and the
second half can be spooned into a
baking dish and baked for about 25
minutes in a preheated 350° oven, or
until golden brown. This second
method makes a drier stuffing than
the one inside the turkey.

Makes 14 Cups

White Cornmeal Corn Bread
  (p. 132), coarsely crumbled
1 pound bulk pork sausage
4 medium onions, finely
  chopped
4 tender, pale celery ribs,
  finely chopped
1¼ teaspoons thyme
½ teaspoon sage
½ teaspoon baking powder
1¾ teaspoons salt
1¼ teaspoons freshly ground
  pepper
2 eggs, lightly beaten
½ cup chicken broth or water

1. Put the crumbled Corn Bread
in a large bowl.

2. Form the sausage into 2-inch
flat cakes and cook in a heavy skillet
over moderate heat, turning, until

light brown, about 5 minutes per
side. Drain the sausage on paper
towels and let cool; then break into
small pieces. Add to the corn bread.

3. In a medium saucepan, combine the onions and celery. Add cold
water to cover. Bring to a boil over
high heat and cook until the vegetables are tender but still crisp, about 3
minutes. Drain well. Add to the corn
bread and sausage.

4. Sprinkle the thyme, sage, baking powder, salt and pepper over the
dressing. Add the eggs and stock and
mix the dressing thoroughly with a
large cooking fork to moisten evenly
without packing the dressing.
—Camille Glenn

Spicy Cornbread and
Pumpkin Seed Stuffing

This hearty, wholesome stuffing, full
of rich tastes—chorizo, pumpkin
seeds, coriander seeds—is sure to
liven up any substantial meal. It
teams particularly well with roasted
pork or poultry.

It's best to make the corn bread
for this the day before so it can dry
out.

Makes About 8 Cups

Corn Bread:
1½ cups yellow cornmeal
½ cup all-purpose flour
1 tablespoon baking powder
1 teaspoon salt
3 eggs
1¼ cups milk
1 tablespoon sugar
4 tablespoons unsalted butter,
  melted

Stuffing:
1 pound Mexican-style soft-
  cured chorizo, casings
  removed
1 tablespoon whole coriander
  seeds

½ teaspoon ground coriander
¼ cup hulled, unsalted
  pumpkin seeds*
1 cup chicken stock or canned
  broth
2 eggs
Pumpkin Seed Puree (p. 24)
*Available at health food
  stores and Mexican markets

1. Make the corn bread: Preheat the oven to 400°. Lightly grease a 13-by-9-inch baking dish.

2. In a large bowl, sift together the cornmeal, flour, baking powder and salt. In another bowl, beat the eggs with the milk and sugar. Add the egg mixture to the dry ingredients and mix thoroughly. Stir in the melted butter and pour the batter evenly into the prepared pan.

3. Bake the corn bread for 15 to 18 minutes, or until a toothpick inserted in the center comes out clean. When the corn bread is cool enough to handle, cut it into 1-inch cubes and spread it on a tray to dry out. (The recipe can be prepared to this point several days ahead.)

4. Make the stuffing: In a large skillet, fry the chorizo over moderately high heat, breaking up the meat with a spoon, until lightly browned, about 10 minutes. Stir in the whole and ground coriander seeds and set aside.

5. Preheat the oven to 375°. In a small dry skillet, toast the pumpkin seeds over moderately high heat, tossing frequently, until they begin to brown and pop, 2 to 3 minutes. Transfer to a small bowl.

6. In a large bowl, lightly whisk together the stock and eggs. Add the corn bread, chorizo and 1 cup of the pumpkin seed puree; toss well. Add the toasted pumpkin seeds and toss again. Scrape the stuffing into a large buttered baking dish. (The recipe can be prepared to this point 1 day ahead. Cover and refrigerate. Let return to room temperature before baking.)

7. Bake the stuffing for 40 minutes, or until the top is crisp. To serve, garnish the top of the stuffing with the remaining pumpkin seed puree.

—John Robert Massie

Lemon-Corn Bread Stuffing

Stuffing a Thanksgiving turkey with homemade corn bread is a popular bit of Americana, but this stuffing can become a little heavy. By adding the zest and juice from a few lemons, however, the stuffing and the whole bird take on an unusually light and refreshing flavor.

Be sure to make the corn bread for this recipe 1 day ahead so it can dry overnight.

Makes About 6 Cups

Corn Bread:
1½ cups yellow cornmeal
½ cup all-purpose flour
1 tablespoon baking powder
1 teaspoon salt
3 eggs
1¼ cups milk
1 tablespoon honey or sugar
4 tablespoons butter, melted

Stuffing:
¼ cup olive oil
1 stick (4 ounces) unsalted
  butter
2 cups finely chopped onion
1½ cups chopped celery
1 tablespoon minced garlic
1 cup minced parsley (no
  stems)
1 tablespoon grated lemon
  zest
½ cup fresh lemon juice
1 tablespoon salt
1 teaspoon freshly ground
  pepper
4 eggs
½ cup chicken or turkey
  stock

1. Make the corn bread: Preheat the oven to 400°. Lightly grease a 13-by-9-inch baking pan.

2. In a large bowl, sift together the cornmeal, flour, baking powder and salt. In another bowl, beat the eggs with the milk and honey. Add the egg mixture to the dry ingredients and mix thoroughly. Stir in the melted butter and pour the batter evenly into the prepared pan. Bake for 15 to 18 minutes, or until a toothpick inserted in the center comes out clean.

3. Cut the corn bread into rectangles about 3 by 4 inches, place them on a rack and let dry overnight.

4. Preheat the oven to 350°. Cut the corn bread into ¾-inch croutons; you should have about 7 cups. Place the croutons on a baking sheet and bake for 35 to 40 minutes until dry, golden brown and crisp.

5. Make the stuffing: In a large heavy skillet, heat the olive oil and butter over moderate heat until the butter melts. Add the onion and celery and sauté about 10 minutes, until the onion is softened and translucent. Add the garlic and sauté for 2 minutes. Stir in the corn bread croutons and cook, stirring, for 2 to 3 minutes, until they are heated through. Remove the skillet from the heat and stir in the parsley, lemon zest, lemon juice, salt and pepper.

6. In a medium bowl, whisk the eggs with the stock until blended. Stir the egg mixture into the stuffing and mix well.

—F&W

Mini Yorkshire Puddings

The batter in this recipe can be baked in a 9-inch square pan, but it will take 35 to 40 minutes to cook.

Makes 12 Small Puddings

¾ cup all-purpose flour
½ teaspoon salt
2 eggs
¾ cup plus 2 tablespoons
  milk
¼ cup melted beef fat,
  reserved from Roast Beef (p.
  80), or butter

1. Place the flour and salt in a medium bowl. Add the eggs and pour in half of the milk. Beat well with a wooden spoon until fairly smooth, about 1 minute.

2. Add the remaining milk and beat for 2 minutes. The batter need not be perfectly smooth. Cover and set aside for 30 minutes to 1 hour.

3. Preheat the oven to 400°. Spoon 1 teaspoon of the melted beef fat into each of twelve 3-inch muffin tins . Place the muffin tin in the hot oven and heat until the fat is sizzling and slightly smoking, about 3 minutes.

4. Stir the batter, then ladle about ¼ cup into each muffin cup to fill halfway. Promptly return to the top third of the oven and bake until the puddings are puffed, golden brown and crisp, about 20 to 25 minutes. Serve warm.
—*Diana Sturgis*

Honey Oat Bread

This eggy yeast bread combines elements of Jewish challah and Italian semolina bread. It is a perfect international candidate for French toast.

Makes 1 Large Loaf

1 envelope active dry yeast
⅔ cup lukewarm water (105°
  to 115°)
¼ teaspoon sugar
2½ cups old-fashioned rolled
  oats
About 1½ cups durum wheat
  flour*
1½ teaspoons salt
4 eggs, at room temperature
⅓ cup honey
2 tablespoons unsalted butter,
  melted, or corn oil
1 to 2 tablespoons poppy
  seeds or sesame seeds
  (optional)
*Available in Italian or
  specialty food markets

1. In a small bowl, sprinkle the yeast over the warm water. Add the sugar and let stand until frothy, 5 to 10 minutes.

2. Meanwhile, in a food processor, process the rolled oats until finely ground. On a work surface, toss together the ground oats, 1 cup of the flour and the salt and form into a mound. Make a wide well in the center.

3. In a small bowl, lightly beat 3 of the eggs with a fork. Stir in the honey and butter. Pour the egg mixture into the well and add the yeast mixture.

4. Stirring with the fingers of one hand, begin incorporating the dry ingredients into the liquid in the well. With a pastry scraper in the other hand, combine the ingredients, forming the dough into a ball. Scrape the work surface clean and dust lightly with flour. Knead the dough, adding the remaining flour as necessary, 2 tablespoons at a time, until the dough is smooth and elastic, 7 to 10 minutes (you may have some flour left over).

5. Rinse out a large bowl with warm water, transfer the dough to the bowl and cover with plastic wrap. Let rise in a warm place until doubled in bulk, about 1 hour.

6. Punch down the dough. Turn out onto a work surface and shape into a thick loaf, about 15 inches long. Transfer to a large ungreased baking sheet. Cover with a towel and let rise until doubled in bulk, about 45 minutes.

7. Preheat the oven to 375°. In a small bowl, beat the remaining egg with 1 tablespoon of water. Gently brush the egg glaze on the risen loaf. Sprinkle the poppy seeds on top, if desired, and bake for 35 minutes or until the bread is deep golden brown. Transfer the loaf to a wire rack to cool completely before slicing.
—*Tracey Seaman*

Golden Squash and Sesame Loaf

I have been making variations of this bread every fall for many years (it makes great French toast). To get a well-rounded top, be sure to shape the dough as described here, rolling it out and then up again. This keeps tension in the dough, which, because it contains both cornmeal and squash, isn't as elastic as some.

I've been known to sieve two or three tablespoons of brown sugar over the rolled dough to give the bread a sweet swirl.

Makes 2 Loaves

2 cups cubed, peeled
  butternut squash (from a
  1-pound squash)

1½ cups milk
⅓ cup sugar
1 envelope active dry yeast
¼ cup lukewarm water (105°
   to 115)
1 teaspoon finely grated
   lemon zest
1 cup yellow cornmeal,
   preferably stoneground
2 cups whole wheat flour
1 egg, lightly beaten
4 tablespoons unsalted butter,
   softened
1 tablespoon salt
3½ to 4¼ cups unbleached
   all-purpose flour
¼ cup toasted sesame seeds
1 cup raisins
Egg wash: 1 egg, beaten with
   2 tablespoons milk

1. In a medium saucepan, cover the squash with 4 cups of water. Bring to a boil, cover and reduce the heat to moderately low. Cook the squash until very tender, about 15 minutes; drain.

2. In a blender or food processor, puree the squash until smooth. Scrape the puree into a large mixing bowl and set aside.

3. In a small saucepan, scald the milk over moderate heat. Remove from the heat and mix in the sugar, stirring until dissolved. Whisk the milk into the pureed squash. Let cool to lukewarm (105° to 115°).

4. In a small bowl, sprinkle the yeast over the lukewarm water. Let dissolve for 10 minutes, then stir into the squash mixture along with the lemon zest. Add the cornmeal and whole wheat flour and beat vigorously with a wooden spoon for 1 minute. Cover this sponge with plastic wrap and set aside in a warm place for about 30 minutes.

5. With a wooden spoon, beat the egg, butter and salt into the sponge. Beat in about 3 cups of the un-bleached flour, 1 cup at a time, until the dough becomes too stiff to work. Turn the dough out onto a floured surface and knead with floured hands for 12 minutes, incorporating enough of the remaining flour to keep the dough from sticking. The dough should be smooth and able to hold its shape fairly well, though it won't be extremely elastic. Place the dough in a lightly oiled bowl, cover with plastic wrap and let rise in a warm, draft-free spot until doubled in bulk, about 45 minutes.

6. Butter two 8½-by-4½-inch loaf pans. Sprinkle the sides and bottom of each pan with 1 tablespoon of the toasted sesame seeds.

7. Spread half of the raisins over the top of the dough and punch down. Add the remaining raisins, punching and kneading them into the dough. Divide the dough in half. Keeping one half covered in the bowl, knead the other half briefly on a lightly floured surface, then roll into an oblong about ½ inch thick and 8 inches wide at the widest point. Starting at a long edge, roll the dough up like a carpet, keeping a little tension on it. Pinch the seam together, tucking the ends under. Lift the dough roll into one of the prepared pans, seam-side down, and cover loosely with plastic wrap. Repeat for the other half of the dough, then set aside in a warm, draft-free spot until doubled in bulk, about 30 minutes.

8. When the breads are nearly doubled, preheat the oven to 375°. Very lightly brush each loaf with a little of the egg wash. Using a serrated knife, make 3 or 4 shallow, diagonal slits in the tops of the loaves. Sprinkle the top of each loaf evenly with 1 tablespoon of the sesame seeds.

9. When fully doubled, brush the loaves again with the egg wash and bake in the lower third of the oven for 45 to 50 minutes, or until they are well browned and have a soft, hollow sound when gently tapped with a finger. Check the loaves halfway through to be sure they're browning evenly; turn the pans if necessary. Unmold the loaves and let cool on a rack for at least 30 minutes before slicing. To store, cool thoroughly before placing in plastic bags.
—Ken Haedrich

Shaker Fresh Herb Bread

This is a lovely bread, one that makes great toast and savory sandwiches. The pronounced herb flavor goes especially well with fresh vegetable sandwich fillings, chicken salad and cold cuts, too. The dough itself is easy to handle and has enough body to hold a well-rounded shape in the oven. These loaves can be baked directly on a baking sheet, as described, or slid onto baking tiles. Dried herbs can be substituted, halving the quantities.

Makes 2 Free-Form Loaves

1 envelope active dry yeast
¼ cup lukewarm water (105°
   to 115°)
½ cup old-fashioned rolled
   oats
½ cup buttermilk
1½ cups milk
1 tablespoon sugar
3 tablespoons minced fresh
   dill
2 teaspoons minced fresh
   thyme
2 teaspoons minced fresh sage
1 teaspoon caraway seeds
1 cup whole wheat flour
About 4 cups unbleached
   all-purpose flour
1 egg, lightly beaten
3 tablespoons unsalted butter,
   melted

2 teaspoons salt
Cornmeal or semolina, for the
 baking sheet
Egg wash: 1 egg, beaten with
 1 tablespoon milk

1. In a small bowl, sprinkle the yeast over the water and set aside to proof. Put the oats into another bowl. Warm the buttermilk to about body temperature and pour it over the oats. Stir and set aside until softened, about 10 minutes.

2. In a small saucepan, scald the milk. Transfer the hot milk to a large mixing bowl and stir in the sugar, dill, thyme, sage and caraway seeds. Let cool to lukewarm (105° to 115°) then blend in the softened oats and the yeast.

3. Add the whole wheat flour and 1 cup of the unbleached flour and beat vigorously with a wooden spoon for 1 minute. Cover this sponge with plastic wrap and set aside in a warm draft-free spot for about 30 minutes.

4. With a wooden spoon, beat the egg, melted butter and salt into the sponge. Beat in 3 cups of unbleached flour, 1 cup at a time, until the dough is too stiff to stir, then turn the dough out onto a floured surface. With floured hands, knead the dough, using just enough additional flour to prevent sticking, until it is smooth, soft and moderately elastic, about 10 minutes. Place the dough in a lightly oiled bowl; turn to coat the entire surface. Cover and set aside in a warm spot, until doubled in bulk, about 45 minutes.

5. While the dough rises, very lightly oil a large baking sheet and dust it heavily with cornmeal or semolina.

6. Punch the dough down and turn it out onto a floured surface. Divide the dough in half, knead each half briefly and form them into tight balls. Place the balls on the prepared baking sheet, leaving plenty of room between them for expansion. Cover loosely with plastic and set aside in a warm spot until almost doubled in bulk, about 45 minutes.

7. Preheat the oven to 375°. Brush each loaf sparingly with the egg wash; try not to let it run down the sides and onto the sheet. Using a sharp, serrated knife, make 4 or 5 shallow slashes, 3 to 4 inches long, on the surface. Bake for 45 minutes, until the crust is nicely browned and the bottom sounds hollow when tapped with a finger. (For uniform browning, it is often a good idea to turn the baking sheet 180 degrees about midway through the baking.) Transfer the loaves to a rack. To store, cool thoroughly before placing in plastic bags.
—Ken Haedrich

Toasting Bread

The bread I make for toasting is very simple and quick. It has only one rising and can be baked two to three weeks ahead of time. Slice it and freeze it to simplify last-minute preparations.

Makes 2 Loaves

1 tablespoon active dry yeast
2¼ cups lukewarm water
 (105° to 115°)
1 teaspoon sugar
5 to 5½ cups unbleached
 all-purpose flour
½ cup whole wheat flour
1 tablespoon salt

1. In a large bowl, sprinkle the yeast over ¼ cup of the warm water; stir in the sugar. Let stand until foamy, about 5 minutes.

2. Add the remaining 2 cups warm water, then gradually stir in 2½ cups of the all-purpose flour, about ¼ cup at a time. Mix in the whole wheat flour and the salt. Gradually mix in 2 more cups of the unbleached flour.

3. Turn the dough out onto a floured surface and knead, adding more of the remaining flour to prevent sticking, until the dough is smooth and silky to the touch, about 5 minutes.

4. Cut the dough into 2 equal pieces; shape each piece into a sausage. Put the dough into two well-buttered 6-cup loaf pans, preferably black tin. Cover the pans with plastic wrap, set in a warm place and let stand until the dough has risen three-fourths of the way up the sides of the pans, about 1 hour.

5. Preheat the oven to 400°. Bake the loaves until they are golden and sound hollow when turned out and tapped, about 30 minutes if using black pans or about 40 minutes for shiny metal or glass. Unmold onto a rack and let cool for about 1 hour before slicing. (Or wrap the cooled bread in aluminum foil and freeze until needed. To thaw, put in a 300° oven, still wrapped in the foil, for 15 minutes.)
—Lydie Marshall

Holiday Fig-and Nut Bread

Makes 2 Loaves

Dough:
7 to 8 cups all-purpose flour
2 envelopes active dry yeast
2 cups milk
½ cup honey
1 stick (4 ounces) unsalted
 butter
2 teaspoons salt
2 eggs

Filling:
¼ cup honey
4 tablespoons unsalted butter

1½ teaspoons cinnamon
1 teaspoon ground cloves
1 cup chopped dried figs
1 cup (4 ounces) finely
  chopped walnuts

Glaze and Decoration:
½ cup red currant jelly
Candied pineapple—red,
  green and yellow*
Candied angelica*
Glacéed apricots*
*Available at specialty food
  shops

1. Make the dough: In a large bowl, combine 3 cups of the flour with the yeast. In a small saucepan, heat the milk, honey, butter and salt over low heat until the butter is melted. Cool to lukewarm (about 110°); then add to the flour and yeast. Stir briefly to mix and add the eggs. With an electric mixer, beat the batter on high speed for 3 minutes.

2. Stir in 3 to 4 cups of the remaining flour, 1 cup at a time, to form a stiff dough. Turn the dough out onto a well-floured surface. Gradually work in as much of the remaining flour as necessary to prevent sticking. Knead for 8 to 10 minutes, or until the dough is smooth and elastic. Place the dough in a greased bowl and turn it over to coat. Cover the bowl with a kitchen towel, place in a warm, draft-free place and let the dough rise for about 1 hour, or until doubled in bulk. Punch down the dough, turn it out onto a lightly floured surface and knead briefly. Divide the dough in half and let rest for 10 minutes.

3. Prepare the filling: In a small saucepan, warm the honey and butter over low heat until the butter melts. Remove from the heat and stir in the cinnamon and cloves; set aside. In a small bowl, combine the figs and walnuts; set aside.

4. Preheat the oven to 350°. Grease two 9-by-5-by-3-inch loaf pans. Roll out one piece of the dough on a lightly floured surface into a rectangle about 15 by 8 inches. Spread the rectangle with half the honey-butter mixture, leaving a 1-inch border all around the edge. Cover the honey-butter with 1 cup of the fig and walnut mixture. Starting at one of the short ends, roll up the dough tightly like a jelly roll. Moisten the edges with a little water and pinch the ends of the loaf and along the seam to seal. Place the loaf, seam-side down, in one of the prepared pans. Repeat with the remaining dough and filling. Cover, place in a warm place and let rise until doubled in bulk, about 45 minutes.

5. Bake the loaves for 50 minutes to 1 hour, or until they sound hollow when tapped. Remove from the pans and cool completely on a rack before glazing.

6. Make the glaze and decorate the bread: In a small saucepan, melt the jelly over low heat. Cut the pineapple, angelica and apricots into decorative shapes. Brush the loaves with the jelly and decorate as desired. Lightly brush the decorations with jelly after applying them. Allow the glaze to set before serving.

NOTE: This bread may be made a day or two ahead, but the glaze and decorations should not be applied until about 1 hour before serving.
—*Maria Piccolo & Rosalee Harris*

Steamed Winter Squash and
Date Nut Bread

This bread reminds me of the harvest moon: big and round, colored a radiant shade of orange. I love it with cream cheese and honey for breakfast or with a brothy soup and green salad for lunch or supper. I like to add dates and walnuts to the batter, but there's plenty of room here for substitutions. Raisins and pecans are nice. So are chopped, dried apricots. Wrapped tightly in plastic, this bread has good keeping qualities. You will need a one-pound coffee can for steaming it.

Makes 1 Loaf

2 cups cubed, peeled
  butternut squash (from a
  1-pound squash)
2 tablespoons unsalted butter,
  softened
⅓ cup honey
Grated zest of 1 orange
½ cup yellow cornmeal,
  preferably stoneground
½ cup whole wheat flour
½ cup unbleached all-purpose
  flour
1½ teaspoons baking powder
¾ teaspoon salt
½ teaspoon cinnamon
½ cup chopped, pitted dates
½ cup chopped walnuts

1. In a medium saucepan, cover the squash with 4 cups of water. Bring to a boil, cover and reduce the heat to moderately low. Cook until very tender, about 15 minutes; drain.

2. In a blender or food processor, combine the squash with the butter and puree until smooth. Scrape the puree into a mixing bowl and whisk in the honey and orange zest; set aside.

3. Butter the insides of a 1-pound coffee can, including the plastic lid.

Pour about 3½ inches of water into a saucepan or stockpot (the pot should be tall enough to accommodate the coffee can standing on a trivet or steaming rack). Put a trivet or rack in the center of the pot, cover and bring to a boil.

4. In a medium bowl, combine the cornmeal, whole wheat flour, unbleached flour, baking powder, salt and cinnamon. Toss well to mix. Toss in the dates.

5. Make a well in the dry ingredients and add the squash puree. Stir just until blended, then fold in the walnuts. Spoon the batter into the prepared coffee can, then put on the lid. Press a double layer of foil over the top and secure it with twine.

6. When the water comes to a boil, reduce the heat to an active simmer. Place the can on the trivet; the water should come about halfway up the sides of the can. Cover the pot and steam the bread until the top is springy to the touch and a cake tester emerges clean, about 1 hour and 40 minutes.

7. Remove the foil and lid and let cool on a rack for 5 minutes. Invert the can and let the bread slide out. Let cool on a rack for at least 15 minutes before slicing with a serrated knife. To store, cool thoroughly, then wrap in plastic.
—Ken Haedrich

White Cornmeal Corn Bread

This recipe combines flour and cornmeal to make an exceptionally light corn bread perfect for stuffings.
Makes About 12 Cups Crumbled Corn Bread

4 eggs
1½ cups milk
1½ cups white cornmeal (not stoneground)
1½ cups all-purpose flour
1½ sticks (6 ounces) unsalted butter, melted
1 tablespoon plus 1 teaspoon baking powder
1½ teaspoons salt
1½ teaspoons sugar

1. Preheat the oven to 450°. Lightly grease two 9-inch round cake pans. In a large bowl, combine the eggs and milk. Whisk lightly to blend.

2. In a medium bowl, mix together the cornmeal and flour. Add to the eggs and milk, whisking to blend well. Add the butter, baking powder, salt and sugar. Mix thoroughly. Spoon the batter into the prepared pans.

3. Bake the corn bread in the center of the oven for 20 minutes, or until it is golden brown on top and a cake tester inserted in the center comes out clean.

4. Invert the corn bread onto a rack to cool. Crumble coarsely. Spread out on a baking sheet to dry completely. *(It's a good idea to do this a day in advance. The corn bread can be baked, cooled, wrapped in aluminum foil and frozen up to 2 weeks in advance.)*
—Camille Glenn

Old-Fashioned Corn Bread for Stuffing

This basic corn bread is firm enough to use for all kinds of stuffings. It's good to eat out of hand too. For best results when making stuffing, turn the slightly cooled corn bread out onto a rack and let air-dry uncovered for two days at room temperature or for three in the refrigerator before crumbling and using. Better still, make it up to one month ahead and freeze, covered with freezer wrap.
Makes About 10 Cups Coarsely Crumbled Corn Bread

2 cups sifted all-purpose flour
2 cups cornmeal
2 tablespoons baking powder
1 tablespoon sugar
1½ teaspoons salt
2 eggs, lightly beaten
2 cups milk
½ cup vegetable oil, bacon drippings or melted lard

1. Preheat the oven to 400°. Spray a 13-by-9-by-2-inch baking pan with nonstick vegetable cooking spray and set aside.

2. In a large mixing bowl, combine the flour, cornmeal, baking powder, sugar and salt. Make a well in the center. In a large measuring cup, whisk the eggs, milk and oil until blended. Pour all at once into the well of the dry ingredients and stir briskly until just combined; the batter will be slightly lumpy.

3. Scrape the batter into the prepared pan and bake in the middle of the oven for 30 minutes, or until firm and lightly browned. Cut the corn bread into large squares if serving right away. Or, let cool on a rack for 10 minutes, then turn it out of the pan and air-dry thoroughly before crumbling.
—Jean Anderson

Prosciutto-Wrapped Hearts of Palm (p. 27).

Cranberry-Raspberry Sorbet (p. 199).

Skillet Corn Bread

If I use this corn bread for stuffing, I generally make it the night before and leave it out, uncovered, to dry out so that it will absorb the stock and seasonings and retain a nice coarse texture.

8 Servings

¼ cup safflower or corn oil
1¼ cups yellow cornmeal
¾ cup all-purpose flour
1 teaspoon sugar
½ teaspoon salt
4 teaspoons baking powder
1 cup milk
1 egg, lightly beaten

1. Preheat the oven to 450°. Put 2 tablespoons of the safflower oil in a 9-inch cast-iron skillet and place in the oven while it is preheating, about 10 minutes.

2. Meanwhile, sift together the cornmeal, flour, sugar, salt and baking powder. In a small bowl, blend the milk, egg and remaining 2 tablespoons safflower oil. Add this liquid to the sifted dry ingredients and mix briefly just until blended; do not overmix. Pour the batter into the heated skillet. The oil should be hot enough to make it sizzle; this will give the corn bread a nice crust.

3. Return the skillet to the oven and reduce the oven temperature to 425°. Bake for 20 to 25 minutes, or until the corn bread is golden and crusty around the edges and has pulled away from the sides of the pan.
—Lee Bailey

Spanish Corn Bread

From Art Director Elizabeth Woodson's mother, Irene, this corn bread is loaded with chopped chiles and Cheddar cheese.

9 Servings

1 cup yellow cornmeal
1 cup all-purpose flour
¼ cup sugar
1 tablespoon baking powder
1 teaspoon salt
1 egg, lightly beaten
1 cup milk
1 cup cottage cheese
⅓ cup corn oil
1 can (4 ounces) peeled whole green chiles—drained, patted dry and coarsely chopped
1½ cups (about 6 ounces) grated sharp Cheddar cheese

1. Preheat the oven to 400°. Butter a 9-inch square baking pan.

2. In a large bowl, sift together the cornmeal, flour, sugar, baking powder and salt.

3. In a medium bowl, combine the egg, milk, cottage cheese and oil. Mix until blended. Add to the dry ingredients and stir gently until just mixed. Spread half the batter into the prepared pan. Scatter the chiles evenly over the top and sprinkle with the cheese. Cover with the remaining batter.

4. Bake in the lower third of the oven for 35 minutes, or until the corn bread is golden brown. Cut into squares and serve slightly warm.
—Elizabeth Woodson

Serrano Chile Blue Corn Bread

12 Servings

2 teaspoons vegetable oil
3 serrano chiles or 2 small jalapeños—stemmed, seeded and minced
1 small red bell pepper, cut into ¼-inch dice
1 small green bell pepper, cut into ¼-inch dice
3 garlic cloves, minced
1 cup all-purpose flour
1¼ cups blue cornmeal
2 tablespoons sugar
1 tablespoon baking powder
1 teaspoon salt
2 eggs
6 tablespoons shortening, melted and cooled
6 tablespoons unsalted butter, melted and cooled
1 cup buttermilk, at room temperature
Pinch of baking soda
3 tablespoons chopped cilantro (fresh coriander)

1. Preheat the oven to 375°. In a small skillet, heat the oil. Add the serrano chiles, red and green peppers and garlic and sauté over moderately high heat until softened, about 2 minutes. Let cool.

2. In a large bowl, sift together the flour, cornmeal, sugar, baking powder and salt.

3. In a medium bowl, beat the eggs lightly and stir in the melted shortening and butter. In a small bowl, mix the buttermilk with the baking soda, then stir into the eggs. Pour this liquid into the flour mixture and stir just until blended; do not overmix. Fold in the sautéed vegetables and the coriander.

4. Pour the batter into a lightly buttered 8-by-12-inch baking pan

and bake for 50 minutes, or until the top is golden brown and a toothpick inserted in the center comes out clean. Let cool on a rack. If using the cornbread for stuffing a bird, crumble it onto a cookie sheet and let it stand overnight or dry out in a 350° oven for 10 minutes.

—*Stephan Pyles, Routh Street Cafe, Dallas*

Sally Lunn Corn Bread

The South's beloved Sally Lunn is not usually made with cornmeal. Nor is it baked in muffin tins, although it often was in England during the 19th century. This corn bread Sally Lunn is one I worked out with another Sally, my friend and fellow southerner Sally Rian.

Makes 1 Dozen Rolls

⅓ *cup lukewarm water (105°*
  to 115°)
2 *envelopes active dry yeast*
¼ *teaspoon granulated sugar*
⅔ *cup milk*
1 *stick (4 ounces) unsalted*
  butter, at room temperature
¼ *cup (firmly packed) light*
  brown sugar or ⅓ cup
  granulated maple sugar*
4 *eggs, at room temperature*
1 *teaspoon salt*
3 *cups sifted all-purpose flour*
1¼ *cups sifted stoneground*
  yellow cornmeal
**Available at specialty food*
  shops

1. Place the water in a small bowl, sprinkle on the yeast and granulated sugar and stir well. Let stand until bubbly.

2. Meanwhile, scald the milk; let cool to lukewarm (105° to 115°). Combine the milk with the yeast mixture. Set aside.

3. Cream the butter until light. Add the brown sugar and beat until fluffy. Add the eggs, one at a time, beating well after each addition. Mix in the salt.

4. Combine the flour and cornmeal and add alternately with the yeast mixture to the butter mixture, beginning and ending with the dry ingredients. Beat until smooth and elastic. (If you use a food processor, do not beat longer than 60 seconds or the dough will overheat and kill the yeast.)

5. Scrape the dough into a well-buttered bowl, cover with a dry kitchen towel and set to rise in a warm draft-free spot until doubled in bulk, about 1 hour.

6. Stir the dough down, then beat hard with a wooden spoon, about 100 strokes. (Because the dough is too sticky to knead, you must beat the very daylights out of it to develop the gluten.)

7. Divide the dough equally among 12 well-buttered 2-inch muffin-tin cups. Cover with a cloth and again let rise until doubled in bulk, 25 to 30 minutes.

8. About 10 minutes before the end of the rising period, preheat the oven to 350°. Bake the Sally Lunn for 15 to 20 minutes, or until the rolls are nicely browned and sound hollow when thumped.

9. Cool the rolls in their pans on a wire rack for 5 minutes. Turn out and serve hot with plenty of butter.

NOTE: The rolls can also be made ahead of time and frozen. To reheat, wrap the rolls in foil and set in a 350° oven for 10 to 15 minutes.

—*Jean Anderson*

Southern Corn Sticks

If you do not have corn stick pans, cut the recipe in half and bake the corn bread in a 10-inch iron skillet or a 9-by-13-inch baking pan, preheating the greased pan as directed below in Step 5. The top of the bread will be crisper if browned under a broiler briefly after baking.

Makes 2 Dozen

2 *eggs*
2 *cups milk*
⅔ *cup plain yogurt or*
  buttermilk
3 *cups yellow cornmeal*
4 *teaspoons baking powder*
1 *teaspoon baking soda*
1½ *teaspoons salt*
1 *stick (4 ounces) unsalted*
  butter, melted

1. Generously grease heavy cast-iron corn stick pans with shortening.

2. Beat the eggs until light; beat in the milk and yogurt.

3. Mix together thoroughly the cornmeal, baking powder, soda and salt. Stir these dry ingredients by hand into the egg mixture just until moistened. Fold in the melted butter. Let stand 30 minutes. *(The batter can be made ahead of time and frozen or refrigerated. If the batter seems too thick when it comes time to bake, thin it with a little milk.)*

4. Preheat the oven to 400°.

5. Place the greased pan in the oven; heat until sizzling hot. Remove from the oven, stir the batter well and spoon it carefully into the indentations of the pans. (If a skillet or baking pan is used, smooth the top of the batter.)

6. Bake in the lower third of the oven for 12 to 15 minutes, or until the sides of the corn sticks come away from the pan and the tops are lightly golden. If the tops are not

golden but the sticks are baked through when pierced with a cake tester, run them under the broiler for a moment, until lightly browned. Serve piping hot.
—*Pearl Byrd Foster*

Double-Corn and Cheddar Muffins

Like all muffins, these are best eaten hot from the oven. They are the thing to serve with a bowl of spicy chili or a hearty soup and salad. If your corn kernels are tender, you can fold them into the batter uncooked. But if they happen to be a bit tough, better cook them briefly in a little water, drain and cool before proceeding. You can substitute frozen, thawed corn kernels. Just be sure to pat them dry.

Makes 1 Dozen

1½ cups unbleached
  all-purpose flour
⅔ cup yellow cornmeal,
  preferably stoneground
2 tablespoons sugar
1 tablespoon baking powder
1 teaspoon salt
2 eggs
1 cup milk
5 tablespoons unsalted butter,
  melted
1 cup corn kernels
1 cup grated Cheddar cheese
  (4 ounces)

1. Preheat the oven to 400°. Butter 12 muffin cups, 2½ inches in diameter.
2. In a large mixing bowl, combine the flour, cornmeal, sugar, baking powder and salt.
3. In a separate bowl, beat the eggs lightly. Then whisk in the milk and melted butter. Make a well in the dry ingredients, pour in the liquids and stir gently, just until combined. Fold in the corn and cheese.

Divide the batter among the 12 cups, filling each about three-quarters full.
4. Bake the muffins in the middle of the oven for about 25 minutes, until lightly browned. Transfer the muffin pan to a rack and let cool for several minutes before removing the muffins.
—*Ken Haedrich*

Carolina Potato Rolls

Adding cooked potatoes will make almost any dough moist, flavorful and nutritious.

To freeze the rolls, cool, then wrap in aluminum foil. They will keep for up to two weeks. When ready to use, place the frozen or thawed rolls in a 325° oven. They will crisp up beautifully.

Makes 30 Rolls

1 envelope active dry yeast
¼ cup lukewarm water (105°
  to 115°)
½ cup hot mashed potatoes
1 stick (4 ounces) plus 1
  teaspoon unsalted butter
3 tablespoons sugar
1¼ teaspoons salt
1 egg
½ cup lukewarm milk (105°
  to 115°)
3 cups all-purpose flour
2 to 3 tablespoons poppy
  seeds, for garnish

1. In a small bowl, combine the yeast with the warm water.
2. Put the hot mashed potatoes in a large mixer bowl, add 5 tablespoons plus 1 teaspoon of the butter, the sugar, salt and egg. Beat well.
3. Beat in the yeast. Add the milk alternately with the flour. Beat well.
4. Turn out the dough onto a lightly floured surface. Knead thoroughly by hand for 5 minutes, adding just enough additional flour if

needed to prevent the dough from being overly sticky.
5. Put the dough into a greased bowl and turn to coat the top. Cover with plastic wrap and set aside in a warm place to rise until doubled, about 1½ hours.
6. Punch down the dough. Place on a lightly floured surface and divide into two pieces. Roll out one piece of dough ¼ inch thick. Cut into disks with a round 2½-inch cutter.
7. Melt the remaining 3 tablespoons butter and pour into a shallow bowl. Dip one side of each disk in the melted butter. Fold over, buttered-side in, like a pocketbook. In an 8- or 9-inch square baking pan, place the rolls, seam-side up, touching each other lightly. Sprinkle half of the poppy seeds over the potato rolls. Repeat with the second half of the dough in a second pan.
8. Cover the rolls with plastic wrap and let stand until doubled in bulk, about 1 hour. Preheat the oven to 375°.
9. When the rolls have risen, place them in the middle of the oven and bake for 18 minutes, or until golden brown. Serve warm.
—*Camille Glenn*

Crescent Rolls

There is a secret to the tenderness of my grandmother's rolls. Because the dough is very soft, you will want to add more flour than the recipe calls for, but resist the temptation, or they will toughen. Also, avoid working the dough too much. Just mix it enough so that the flour is thoroughly incorporated; then knead the dough a few times. Let it rise slowly. The final rising of four hours, once the rolls are shaped, is important. Don't stint on it.

If you bake these rolls right before sitting down at the table, they can be enjoyed warm from the oven. In any case, they are best the day they are made.

Makes 32 Rolls

1 cup milk, scalded
1 stick (4 ounces) unsalted
  butter, softened
1 envelope active dry yeast
½ cup sugar
4½ cups all-purpose flour
2 eggs
1 teaspoon salt

1. In a large bowl, combine the scalded milk and the butter. Stir until the butter melts and let stand until lukewarm. Stir in the yeast and sugar. Whisk in 1 cup of the flour. Add the eggs, one at a time, whisking well after each addition. Add the salt and 1 more cup of flour. Mix vigorously with a wooden spoon until the dough is elastic and smooth, about 6 minutes. Alternatively, mix the dough at medium-high speed for 3 minutes.

2. Work in the remaining 2½ cups flour until the dough is a little firmer; it will still be very soft. Turn the dough out onto a lightly floured work surface and knead just until smooth, about 2 minutes. Place the dough in a bowl, cover and let rise in a warm place until doubled in bulk, about 2 hours.

3. Punch down the dough and turn out onto a well-floured work surface and divide it in half. Roll each half into a disk about 16 inches in diameter. Cut each disk into quarters, then cut each quarter into 4 equal wedges. Beginning at the wide ends, roll up the wedges. Seal the pointed end of each wedge underneath so it won't pop up during rising and baking.

4. Arrange the rolls 2 inches apart on 3 lightly floured baking sheets. Cover with a dry kitchen towel and set aside to rise in a warm place until nearly doubled in size, about 4 hours.

5. Preheat the oven to 350°. Bake the rolls in 2 batches in the middle of the oven for 10 to 12 minutes, or until golden. Serve immediately.
—*Susan Herrmann Loomis*

Whole Wheat-Bacon Biscuits

Makes About 3 Dozen

½ pound thick-sliced bacon,
  cut into ½-inch squares
¾ cup chopped onion (1
  medium)
1½ cups chopped mushrooms
  (about 6 ounces)
¾ cup all-purpose flour
¾ cup whole wheat flour
4 teaspoons baking powder
1 teaspoon salt
⅛ teaspoon freshly ground
  pepper
1 teaspoon thyme, crumbled
4 tablespoons unsalted butter,
  cut into thin slices
½ cup sour cream
1 egg, beaten

1. In a large skillet over medium heat, sauté the bacon until crisp, remove with a slotted spoon and set aside on paper towels to drain.

2. Pour off all but 2 tablespoons of the bacon fat from the skillet. Place the skillet over medium heat. Add the onion and mushrooms and cook until the vegetables are soft, 3 to 4 minutes. Let the mixture cool in the pan.

3. Preheat the oven to 425°. Into a large mixing bowl, sift the all-purpose flour, whole wheat flour, baking powder and salt. Stir in the pepper and thyme. Using a pastry blender or two knives, cut in the butter until the mixture resembles coarse meal. Lightly mix in the sour cream, bacon, cooled onions and mushrooms.

4. Turn the dough out onto a lightly floured work surface and quickly roll or pat it to a ½-inch thickness. Using a lightly floured 1½-inch biscuit cutter or small glass, cut out the biscuits. Gather the scraps and quickly pat them to a ½-inch thickness; cut as many additional biscuits as possible. Lightly grease a baking sheet, place the biscuits on it and brush the tops with the beaten egg. Place the pan on the middle rack of the oven and bake for 10 to 12 minutes, or until the biscuits are golden. Serve while still warm.
—*F&W*

Lemon-Parsley Biscuits

Makes About 3 Dozen

1½ cups all-purpose flour
4 teaspoons baking powder
1 teaspoon salt
6 tablespoons unsalted butter,
  cut into thin slices
2 teaspoons grated lemon zest
¾ cup finely chopped parsley
2 tablespoons fresh lemon
  juice
½ cup plain yogurt
1 egg, beaten

1. Preheat the oven to 425°. Sift the flour, baking powder and salt into a large mixing bowl. Using a pastry blender or two knives, cut in the butter until the mixture resembles coarse meal. Blend in the lemon zest.

2. Sprinkle the parsley with the lemon juice and add it to the flour mixture along with the yogurt. Using a fork, quickly mix the dough.

3. Turn the dough out onto a lightly floured work surface and quickly roll or pat it to a ½-inch thickness. Using a lightly floured 1½-inch biscuit cutter or small glass, cut out the biscuits. Gather the scraps and quickly pat them to a ½-inch thickness; cut as many additional biscuits as possible. Lightly grease a baking sheet, place the biscuits on it and brush the tops with the beaten egg. Place the pan on the middle rack of the oven and bake for 10 to 12 minutes, or until the biscuits are golden. Serve while still warm.
—F&W

Chili-Corn Biscuits

Makes About 3 Dozen

1 cup fresh corn kernels (from
  2 ears)
1 garlic clove, minced
6 tablespoons unsalted butter
1½ cups all-purpose flour
¼ cup yellow cornmeal
4 teaspoons baking powder
1 tablespoon sugar
½ teaspoon salt
½ cup sour cream
1 can (4 ounces) chopped
  mild green chiles, well
  drained
1½ cups grated Monterey
  Jack cheese (6 ounces),
  chilled
1 egg, beaten

1. In a small pan over low heat, sauté the corn and garlic in 2 tablespoons of the butter for 5 minutes; set aside to cool.

2. Preheat the oven to 425°. In a large mixing bowl, sift together the flour, cornmeal, baking powder, sugar and salt. Cut the remaining 4 tablespoons butter into pieces. Using a pastry blender or two knives, cut the butter into the flour mixture until it resembles coarse meal. Using a fork, stir in the sour cream, chiles, cheese, reserved corn and garlic; do not overmix.

3. Turn the dough out onto a lightly floured work surface and quickly roll or pat it to a ½-inch thickness. Using a lightly floured 1½-inch biscuit cutter or small glass, cut out the biscuits. Gather the scraps and quickly pat them to a ½-inch thickness; cut as many additional biscuits as possible. Lightly grease a baking sheet, place the biscuits on it and brush the tops with the beaten egg. Place the pan on the middle rack of the oven and bake for 10 to 12 minutes, or until the biscuits are golden. Serve while still warm.
—F&W

Tomato-Basil Biscuits

Makes About 3 Dozen

1½ cups all-purpose flour
4 teaspoons baking powder
½ teaspoon salt
6 tablespoons unsalted butter,
  cut into thin slices
1½ cups shredded mozzarella
  cheese (6 ounces), chilled
3 tablespoons finely chopped
  onion
1½ teaspoons oregano
1½ teaspoons basil
3 tablespoons tomato paste
  dissolved in ⅓ cup milk

2 tablespoons milk
3 tablespoons grated
  Parmesan cheese

1. Preheat the oven to 425°. Into a large mixing bowl, sift together the flour, baking powder and salt. Using a pastry blender or two knives, cut the butter into the flour until the mixture resembles coarse meal.

2. Stir in the cheese, onion, oregano and basil. Pour in the tomato-paste mixture and stir lightly with a fork until the dough can be formed into a ball; do not overmix.

3. Turn the dough out onto a lightly floured work surface and quickly roll or pat it to a ½-inch thickness. Using a lightly floured 1½-inch biscuit cutter or small glass, cut out the biscuits. Gather the scraps and quickly pat them to a ½-inch thickness; cut as many additional biscuits as possible. Lightly grease a baking sheet, place the biscuits on it and brush the tops with the milk. Sprinkle each biscuit with a pinch of Parmesan cheese. Place the pan on the middle rack of the oven and bake for 10 to 12 minutes, or until the cheese is golden brown. Serve while still warm.
—F&W

pickles, relishes & preserves

Bread and Butter Pickles

Makes About 1 Quart

5 pickling (kirby) cucumbers,
  each about 4 inches long,
  thinly sliced
5 small white onions (about
  ½ pound), thinly sliced and
  separated into rings
3 tablespoons coarse (kosher)
  salt
1 cup distilled white vinegar
¾ cup sugar
2 teaspoons mustard seed
¼ teaspoon turmeric
¼ teaspoon celery seed

1. In a large bowl, toss the cucumbers and onion rings with the salt. Cover with water and let rest for about 3 hours. Drain and, without rinsing, place in a quart jar or nonreactive bowl.

2. In a small nonreactive saucepan, bring the vinegar, sugar, mustard seed, turmeric, celery seed and 3 tablespoons of water to a boil. Remove from the heat, pour over the cucumbers, cover and refrigerate for 3 days.
—*F&W*

New Dill Pickles

Makes About 1 Quart

5 pickling (kirby) cucumbers,
  each about 4 inches long
2 garlic cloves, crushed
  through a press
2 to 3 large sprigs of dill
½ cup distilled white vinegar
¼ cup coarse (kosher) salt
½ teaspoon dill seed

1. Wash the cucumbers and place in a quart jar or bowl with the garlic and dill.

2. In a small, nonreactive saucepan, bring the vinegar, salt, dill seed and 3 cups of water to a boil; cover and simmer for 5 minutes. Cool and pour over the cucumbers. Submerge the cucumbers by weighting them with a heavy glass jar, cover with cheesecloth and let rest for 48 hours. Skim off any foam that may accumulate.
—*F&W*

Pickled Vegetables with Pink Peppercorns

Makes About 1 Quart

½ pound carrots, cut into 3-
  by-¼-inch julienne strips
½ pound green beans
¼ pound snow peas
8 sprigs of cilantro (fresh
  coriander), lightly crushed
⅔ cup distilled white vinegar
2 tablespoons sherry vinegar
  or cider vinegar
2 teaspoons salt
2 teaspoons sugar
2 teaspoons pink pepper-
  corns, lightly crushed

1. In rapidly boiling water, blanch the carrots and green beans separately for 2 minutes each and the snow peas for 30 seconds. Remove with a slotted spoon.

2. Place the vegetables, standing upright, in a quart jar. Distribute the cilantro sprigs evenly among the vegetables.

3. In a small bowl, combine the vinegars, salt and sugar with 1 cup water, stirring until the salt and sugar have dissolved. Pour half the mixture over the vegetables, add the peppercorns and the remaining liquid and refrigerate, covered, for 3 days.
—*F&W*

Victory Pickles

Makes About 1 Quart

5 pickling (kirby) cucumbers,
  each about 4 inches long,
  peeled and trimmed
3 tablespoons coarse (kosher)
  salt
¼ teaspoon white pepper
2 whole cloves
1 large bay leaf, broken into
  several pieces
1 garlic clove, lightly crushed
6 large sprigs of dill
About 1 cup cider vinegar
About 1 cup white wine

Quarter the cucumbers lengthwise and place in a colander. Toss with 2 tablespoons of the salt and let drain for 2 hours; rinse and place in a quart jar or in a bowl. Add the remaining 1 tablespoon salt, the pepper, cloves, bay leaf, garlic and dill. Fill the jar with the vinegar and wine; or, if using a bowl, add enough of each to cover and submerge the cucumbers by weighting them down with a plate. Refrigerate, covered, overnight.
—*F&W*

Pickled Brussels Sprouts

Makes About 3 Cups

1 carton (10 ounces) brussels
  sprouts, trimmed and halved
  (about 2½ cups)
3 tablespoons plus 1 teaspoon
  salt
½ cup olive oil
⅓ cup fresh lemon juice
2 garlic cloves, sliced
1 teaspoon dried thyme or 1
  tablespoon chopped fresh
2 large bay leaves
½ teaspoon instant coffee
  dissolved in 1 tablespoon
  water

1. In a large bowl, combine the
brussels sprouts with 3 tablespoons
of the salt and 1 tablespoon of water.
Cover and let rest overnight.

2. Drain and rinse the brussels
sprouts. Blanch them in a pan of
rapidly boiling water for 2 minutes.
Drain and transfer to a bowl or jar.

3. In a small nonreactive saucepan, combine the olive oil, lemon
juice, garlic, thyme, bay leaves, dissolved coffee and remaining 1 teaspoon salt. Bring to a boil over high
heat. Remove from the heat, pour
the hot liquid over the brussels
sprouts and let cool, uncovered, to
room temperature.

4. Strain the liquid into a small
nonreactive saucepan and bring to a
boil over high heat. Pour the liquid
over the brussels sprouts, cool to
room temperature, cover and let rest
overnight.
—F&W

Christmas Refrigerator Pickles

Makes About 1½ Quarts

8 cups small unwaxed
  cucumbers, unpeeled but
  sliced
1 cup sliced celery
1 cup thinly sliced onion rings
3 small carrots, thinly sliced
  or coarsely grated
1 red bell pepper, diced
1½ teaspoons salt
2 cups sugar
1½ cups white wine vinegar
1 teaspoon celery seed

1. Combine the cucumbers, celery, onion rings, carrots, bell pepper
and salt and let stand in a colander to
drain for 30 minutes.

2. While the vegetables drain,
blend sugar, vinegar and celery seed
until the sugar dissolves. Refrigerate
for 30 minutes.

3. Combine the vegetables with
the cold syrup. Pack in one or more
clean, dry Mason jars and cover with
tight-fitting lids. (If more liquid is
needed to cover vegetables, just add
vinegar.) The pickles should be
stored in the refrigerator.
—Michele Evans

Cauliflower in Honey Mustard

Makes About 1 Quart

⅔ cup cider vinegar
⅓ cup olive oil
¼ cup grainy mustard,
  preferably Pommery
2 tablespoons honey
½ teaspoon curry powder
Salt
4 cups cauliflower florets
½ medium green bell pepper,
  cut into ¼-inch strips, 1½
  inches long

1. In a small bowl, whisk together
the vinegar, oil, mustard, honey and
curry; beat in salt to taste.

2. Blanch the cauliflower for 2
minutes in a pan of rapidly boiling
water. Drain and transfer to a bowl
or jar. Combine the marinade with
the cauliflower and green bell pepper, cool to room temperature, cover
and refrigerate for 48 hours, stirring
occasionally.
—F&W

Pickled Cauliflower and Broccoli with Lime

The vegetables marinate overnight,
so plan accordingly.

6 Servings

2 cups dry white wine
½ cup sugar
1 tablespoon coarse (kosher)
  salt
1 tablespoon oregano
2 large bay leaves
1 small head of cauliflower
  (about 1 pound), cut into
  1½-inch florets
1 bunch of broccoli (about 1
  pound), cut into 1½-inch
  florets
¼ cup olive oil

2 tablespoons fresh lime juice
Salt and freshly ground
   pepper
6 thin slices of lime

1. In a large nonreactive pot, combine the wine, sugar, salt, oregano and bay leaves with 2 cups of water. Simmer over moderately low heat for 20 minutes.

2. Add the cauliflower and broccoli florets and bring to a boil. Reduce the heat to moderately low and simmer slowly until the vegetables are tender but still slightly firm, 8 to 10 minutes. Remove from the heat and let cool overnight in the liquid. (The recipe can be made to this point 2 or 3 days ahead. Keep the vegetables refrigerated and tightly covered.)

3. Before serving, remove the vegetables and discard the marinade. Let the vegetables come to room temperature. Just before serving, toss the vegetables in the olive oil and lime juice. Season with salt and pepper to taste and garnish with the lime slices.
—W. Peter Prestcott

Tarragon-Pickled Beets

Makes About 3 Cups

1½ cups distilled white
   vinegar
½ cup sugar
½ teaspoon salt
1 teaspoon allspice berries
2 sprigs of tarragon, each 3
   inches, or 1 teaspoon dried
9 medium beets, peeled and
   each cut into 8 wedges
   (about 2½ cups)
6 scallions (white and tender
   green), cut into ½-inch
   lengths (about ½ cup)

1. In a medium nonreactive saucepan, bring the vinegar, sugar, salt, allspice and 1½ cups water to a simmer over moderate heat. (If using dried tarragon, add it.) Reduce the heat and simmer for 10 minutes. Add the beets, cover and, over moderate heat, cook 10 to 15 minutes, or until just tender.

2. Cool the beets in the liquid for about 30 minutes. Transfer the beets and liquid to a quart jar or bowl and add the scallions and fresh tarragon sprigs. Cover with cheesecloth and let rest overnight.
—F&W

Cracked Radishes

Makes About 3 Cups

1 tablespoon sugar
5 tablespoons soy sauce
1½ tablespoons Oriental
   sesame oil
2½ tablespoons distilled
   white vinegar
¼ teaspoon hot pepper sauce
   or to taste
30 radishes, washed and
   trimmed

In a medium bowl, dissolve the sugar in the soy sauce. Beat in the oil, vinegar and hot pepper sauce. Score both ends of each radish with an X about ⅛ inch deep and toss with the marinade. Cover and refrigerate at least 5 hours, tossing occasionally.
—Jessica Weber

Marinated Mushrooms

Makes About 1 Quart

2 pounds mushrooms,
   quartered
¼ cup lemon juice
2 cups distilled white vinegar
1 cup olive oil
1 tablespoon salt
½ teaspoon pepper
3 garlic cloves, lightly crushed
2 teaspoons dried oregano or
   2 tablespoons chopped fresh
2 teaspoons dried basil or 2
   tablespoons chopped fresh

1. Place the mushrooms in a bowl and cover with water; add the lemon juice.

2. In a medium nonreactive saucepan, bring the vinegar, olive oil, salt, pepper, garlic, oregano and basil to a boil; remove from the heat.

3. Drain the mushrooms, discarding the liquid. Return them to the bowl and pour the hot marinade over. Cool to room temperature, cover and let rest 8 hours or overnight, tossing occasionally.
—F&W

Vermouth-Pickled Pearl Onions

Makes 2 to 2½ Cups

1 pound pearl onions, peeled
   and trimmed (about 4 cups)
4 tablespoons coarse (kosher)
   salt
1 cup dry vermouth
½ cup distilled white vinegar

1. Bring a large pot of water to a boil, add the onions and 1 tablespoon of the salt. When the boiling resumes, cook for 3 minutes. Drain and transfer to a large bowl; add 1 cup cold water and the remaining

salt, stirring until the salt is dissolved. Let rest, covered, overnight.

2. Drain and rinse under cold water. Add the vermouth and vinegar and let rest, covered, overnight.
—F&W

Pearl Onions in Wine

These sweet preserved onions keep for months in the refrigerator.

Makes About 1 Pint

*2 pints (1¼ pounds) tiny
   white boiling (pearl) onions
1 bottle Gewürztraminer or
   other spicy white wine
½ cup sugar
5 imported bay leaves*

1. In a large saucepan, bring 2 quarts of water to a boil. Add the onions. When the water returns to a boil, drain the onions. Slip off the skins and trim the root ends.

2. In a medium nonreactive saucepan, bring the wine, sugar and bay leaves to a boil over high heat. Boil until the liquid is reduced to 2 cups, about 15 minutes.

3. Add the onions and reduce the heat to moderate. Simmer for about 10 minutes, until an onion can be easily pierced with the tip of a knife.

4. With a slotted spoon, remove the onions to a 1-pint jar. Boil the liquid until it is syrupy and reduced to about ¾ cup. Pour the syrup over the onions and add the bay leaves. Let stand uncovered until cool. Cover and refrigerate.
—Anne Disrude

Pickled Pears

Makes About 2 Pints

*3 pounds firm Bosc or Anjou
   pears—peeled, quartered
   and cored
1 tablespoon fresh lemon
   juice
3 cups sugar
2 cups cider vinegar
2 thin slices of lemon
1 tablespoon whole cloves
1 tablespoon allspice berries
1 to 2 pieces of dried stem
   ginger or 3 quarter-size
   slices of fresh ginger
2 cinnamon sticks*

1. Put the pears in a bowl with cold water to cover. Add the lemon juice to prevent discoloration.

2. In a large nonreactive saucepan, combine the sugar, vinegar, lemon slices, cloves, allspice, ginger, cinnamon and 3 cups of water. Bring to a boil over high heat, stirring to dissolve the sugar.

3. Drain the pears and add them to the spiced syrup. Bring to a boil, reduce the heat to moderate and simmer until the pears are tender but still firm, about 3 minutes.

4. Remove from the heat and let the pears macerate in the syrup overnight. The next day, using a slotted spoon, transfer the pears to 2 clean pint canning jars. Boil the syrup over high heat until it registers 200° on a candy thermometer and is almost at the thread stage, about 35 minutes. Pour the syrup over the pears. Let cool, then cover and refrigerate until ready to serve. *(The pears will become a more beautiful color after 2 or 3 days in the syrup. They keep well in the refrigerator for up to 1 month.)*
—Camille Glenn

Sweet-and-Sour Prunes

These tart-sweet preserved prunes are a delicious accompaniment to roast game or pork. They keep well for months in the refrigerator.

Makes About 1 Pint

*2 cups pitted prunes (about
   12 ounces)
1 cup red wine vinegar
⅔ cup sugar
Zest of 1 orange, cut into
   1-inch-long julienne strips
12 allspice berries*

1. Place the prunes in a bowl and pour in 2 cups of boiling water. Set aside for 15 minutes; then drain.

2. Meanwhile, in a small nonreactive saucepan, combine the vinegar and the sugar. Bring to a boil over moderately high heat, stirring to dissolve the sugar. Reduce the heat to moderate and simmer for about 4 minutes.

3. Scald a 1-pint canning jar with boiling water and drain well. Fill the jar with the prunes, interspersing the orange zest and allspice berries. Pour in the hot vinegar mixture; the liquid should overflow the jar. Wipe the rim, seal the jar and let stand until cool. Store in a cool dark place for at least 3 weeks before opening. Refrigerate after opening.
—Patricia Wells

Olive-Oregano Relish

Makes About 1½ Cups

2 tablespoons dried currants
2 tablespoons boiling water
1½ tablespoons chopped fresh
  oregano
1 tablespoon fresh lemon
  juice
¾ teaspoon grated lemon zest
1½ teaspoons anchovy paste
1 teaspoon honey
1 cup Calamata olives (about
  ½ pound), pitted and
  chopped
2 garlic cloves, peeled and
  lightly crushed
¼ cup olive oil

1. In a small bowl, cover the currants with the boiling water. Let soften for about 5 minutes.

2. Meanwhile, in a medium bowl, combine the oregano, lemon juice, lemon zest, anchovy paste and honey. Stir well to dissolve the anchovy paste.

3. Drain and coarsely chop the currants. Add the currants, olives and garlic to the lemon mixture and stir to combine. Add the olive oil and stir well. Cover and refrigerate overnight. Before serving, bring to room temperature. Remove the garlic and stir well.
—*Marcia Kiesel*

Time-Honored Pepper Relish

This is a delicious, typically southern condiment that is compatible with turkey, chicken, braised beef, veal or ham.

Makes About 2 Pints

2 large red bell peppers
1 medium green bell pepper
1 medium Bermuda onion
1 tender celery rib
¼ cup plus 2 tablespoons
  sugar
¾ cup cider vinegar

1. In a food processor, combine the red and green bell peppers, onion and celery. Process until the vegetables are coarsely chopped. Transfer to a colander and let drain for 10 minutes.

2. In a medium nonreactive saucepan, combine the sugar and vinegar. Bring to a boil over moderate heat and cook for 2 minutes. Add the drained vegetables. Return to a boil and cook for 2 minutes.

3. Ladle the relish into impeccably clean or sterilized pint jars; cover. Let cool, then refrigerate.
—*Camille Glenn*

Cranberry-Bourbon Relish

This tangy cranberry relish makes a good accompaniment to any pâté or cold or smoked meat. It is also quite at home beside turkey and stuffing.
10 to 12 Servings

1 cup bourbon
¼ cup minced shallots
Grated zest of 1 orange
1 package (12 ounces)
  cranberries
1 cup sugar
1 teaspoon freshly ground
  pepper

1. In a small nonreactive saucepan, combine the bourbon, shallots and orange zest. Bring to a boil over moderate heat, lower the heat and simmer, stirring occasionally, until the bourbon is reduced to a syrupy glaze on the bottom of the pan, about 10 minutes.

2. Add the cranberries and sugar, stirring well, until the sugar dissolves. Reduce the heat slightly and simmer, uncovered, until most of the cranberries have burst open, about 10 minutes.

3. Remove from the heat and stir in the pepper. Transfer to a bowl, let cool to room temperature, cover and refrigerate. *(This relish can be prepared several days in advance of serving.)*
—*Michael McLaughlin*

Gingered Cranberry Relish

Cranberries, which can be a bit predictable, are not when combined with tart and sweet dried Michigan cherries and crystallized ginger.
Makes About 2½ Cups

1½ cups dried cherries* (9
  ounces)
1 cup fresh cranberries
1 cup sugar
¼ cup coarsely chopped
  crystallized ginger* (about
  1¼ ounces)
½ cup plus 2 tablespoons
  fresh orange juice
1 tablespoon finely grated
  lemon zest
*Available at specialty food
  stores

In a heavy, medium, nonreactive saucepan, combine all the ingredients with 6 tablespoons of water and bring to a boil over moderately high heat. Reduce the heat to moderate and cook, stirring occasionally and

skimming as necessary, until the cranberries pop, about 8 minutes. Transfer to a small serving bowl and let cool. Cover and refrigerate for up to 3 days. Serve the relish at room temperature.
—*Sheila Lukins*

Fresh Cranberry and Orange Relish

Makes About 2¾ Cups

¾ cup sugar
1 large navel orange, with the
    peel on, cut into eighths
2 cups (½ pound) cranberries

1. In a food processor, combine the sugar and orange wedges. Turn the machine on and off quickly for 30 seconds to chop very coarsely. Add the cranberries and continue to pulse for 45 seconds, or until all the ingredients are coarsely chopped and well mixed.
2. Transfer the relish to a serving bowl. Refrigerate until chilled before serving.
—*Camille Glenn*

Tipsy Cranberry Relish

Makes About 2 Cups

2 cups fresh or frozen
    cranberries
1 large orange, chopped
2 tablespoons grated orange
    zest
½ cup gin
⅓ cup sugar

1. Place the berries in a saucepan with the chopped orange sections, 1 tablespoon of the orange zest, the gin and sugar. Cook the relish over moderately high heat only until the berries pop, stirring occasionally. Turn off the heat, stir once again to

thoroughly combine the ingredients and set aside to cool. Refrigerate, preferably overnight to allow the relish time to mellow, until ready to serve.
2. Just before serving, stir the remaining 1 tablespoon orange zest into the relish.
—*F&W*

Pear-Walnut Relish

Makes About 1 Quart

¾ cup chopped walnuts
    (about 3 ounces)
3 pounds Bartlett pears
    (about 6 large), peeled,
    cored and cut into 1-inch
    cubes
2 celery ribs, halved
    lengthwise and cut crosswise
    into thin slices
Zest of ½ medium orange,
    cut into 1-by-⅛-inch
    julienne strips (about
    1½ tablespoons)
⅓ cup sugar
2 tablespoons cider vinegar
½ teaspoon cinnamon
¼ teaspoon mace
¼ teaspoon allspice

1. Toast the walnuts in a small, ungreased skillet over moderate heat, stirring several times, until they are golden brown and crispy, about 5 minutes.
2. In a large saucepan, combine the pears, celery, orange zest, sugar, vinegar, cinnamon, mace and allspice. Add ½ cup of water and bring to a boil over moderately high heat. Boil, stirring gently several times, until the relish has thickened, about 15 minutes.

3. Remove from the heat and stir in the nuts. Let cool to room temperature, cover and refrigerate until chilled.
—*Maria Piccolo & Rosalee Harris*

Cranberry Coffee Pear Relish

Adding chunks of coffee-poached pears to the usual fresh cranberry sauce gives it an unexpected spark of flavor.

8 Servings

1 package (12 ounces)
    cranberries
2½ cups sugar
3 large firm-ripe Bosc pears
    (about 1¼ pounds)
1 lemon, cut in half
3 cups strong brewed coffee

1. In a medium nonreactive saucepan, combine the cranberries, 1 cup of the sugar and 1 cup of water. Bring to a boil over high heat. Reduce the heat to moderately low and simmer, stirring occasionally, until thickened, about 10 minutes. Remove from the heat and let cool.
2. Peel, halve and core the pears. As you cut them, rub with the lemon to prevent discoloration.
3. In a small saucepan, combine the coffee and the remaining 1½ cups sugar. Bring to a simmer over moderate heat, stirring to dissolve the sugar. Add the pears and simmer until tender, about 15 minutes.
4. As soon as the pears are cool enough to handle, cut into large chunks and add to the cooked cranberries. Let cool completely, then cover and refrigerate for up to 2 days before serving.
—*Lee Bailey*

Pear and Apple Chutney

Makes About 1 Cup

2½ cups apple juice
2 tablespoons cider vinegar
2 tablespoons (packed)
  brown sugar
3 large shallots, chopped
1 tablespoon minced
  fresh ginger
½ teaspoon mustard seeds
½ teaspoon cumin
¼ teaspoon crushed hot
  red pepper
½ teaspoon salt
1 large Granny Smith
  apple, peeled and cut into
  ½-inch dice
1 large firm pear, preferably
  Bartlett, peeled and cut into
  ½-inch dice
1 teaspoon finely grated
  lemon zest
¼ cup dried cranberries or
  sour cherries*
*Available at specialty food
  stores

1. In a medium nonreactive sauce-pan, combine the apple juice, vinegar, brown sugar, shallots, ginger, mustard seeds, cumin, hot pepper and salt. Bring to a boil over high heat and cook until the mixture has reduced to 1 cup, about 15 minutes.

2. Stir in the apple and pear. Reduce the heat to moderate and simmer until the fruit is tender, about 10 minutes. Remove from the heat. Stir in the lemon zest and dried cranberries. Let the chutney cool to room temperature, then cover and refrigerate overnight before serving.
—Lee Bailey

Cranberry Chutney

Makes About 2 Cups

2 cups (8 ounces) fresh or
  frozen cranberries
½ cup granulated sugar
¼ cup (packed) light brown
  sugar
1 cinnamon stick
4 whole cloves
2 allspice berries
¼ cup raisins
1 small onion, chopped
¼ cup chopped celery
½ cup chopped unpeeled
  tart apple

1. In a medium saucepan, combine the cranberries, granulated sugar, brown sugar and ½ cup of water. Tie the cinnamon, cloves and allspice in cheesecloth and add to the pan. Bring to a boil over moderate heat, stirring to dissolve the sugar. Lower the heat and simmer, partially covered, until the cranberries begin to burst, about 10 minutes.

2. Stir in the raisins, onion, celery and apple. Simmer the chutney, uncovered, until the mixture thickens, about 20 minutes.

3. Remove from the heat and let cool to room temperature; discard the spice bag. Refrigerate the chutney, covered, for at least 24 hours before serving, or up to 2 weeks.
—Melanie Barnard

Cranberry-Walnut Relish

This fresh-tasting, no-cook relish combines the tang and crunch of cranberries and walnuts with unpeeled orange and pear. A meat grinder or food processor makes preparation a snap. This relish is refreshing at any time of year, and if you want to make it in the summer, freeze the cranberries now in double plastic bags. The relish can then be prepared while the cranberries are still frozen.

Makes About 3 Cups

1 juice orange—scrubbed,
  halved, seeded and coarsely
  chopped
1 small Bosc pear—unpeeled
  and coarsely chopped
2¼ cups (½ pound)
  cranberries
½ cup walnut halves
½ cup sugar

Pass the orange, pear, cranberries and walnuts through a meat grinder or coarsely chop in a food processor, turning the machine on and off for 20 to 30 seconds; do not overprocess. Scrape this mixture into a bowl and stir in the sugar. The relish can be stored in the refrigerator in a covered jar for up to 5 days.
—Diana Sturgis

Cranberry Jelly

Makes About 1¼ Cups

½ pound (2 cups) cranberries
1 cup sugar
⅛ teaspoon salt

1. In a medium saucepan, bring 1½ cups of water to a boil. Add the cranberries and boil over moderately high heat for 20 minutes, stirring occasionally.

2. Puree the cranberries in a food processor and strain. Return the puree to the pan and cook over low heat, stirring frequently, for 3 minutes. Add the sugar and salt and cook until the sugar is dissolved, about 2 minutes. Pour into a bowl, let cool and refrigerate until gelled. *(The recipe can be made up to 1 week ahead; keep refrigerated.)*
—*Marion Cunningham*

Spiced Cranberry Jelly

Makes About 3 Cups

4 cups (1 pound) cranberries
2 cups sugar
2 cinnamon sticks
8 allspice berries
20 whole cloves

1. In a large nonreactive saucepan, bring 2 cups of water to a boil over high heat. Add the cranberries, sugar, cinnamon sticks, allspice and cloves. Return to a boil, reduce the heat to moderately low and boil for 20 minutes.

2. Transfer the mixture to a coarse sieve set over a bowl. Press the cranberries through the sieve with a spatula. Discard the spices.

3. Return the strained cranberries to the saucepan. Bring to a boil over moderately high heat. Cook for 5 minutes, stirring constantly.

4. Pour the cranberry jelly into a 3-cup ring mold and set aside to cool. Cover the jelly and refrigerate overnight.

5. To unmold, invert the ring mold onto a serving plate and press a damp hot kitchen towel on top. Carefully lift off the mold and serve.
—*Camille Glenn*

Candied Quinces

Quinces look like yellowish green apples. They are very tart and need lots of sugar to bring out their wonderful flavor. I prefer candied quinces to candied yams when I serve a roast bird. These are perfect with goose.

6 to 8 Servings

2 lemons, halved
4 pounds quinces
2 cups sugar
2 tablespoons unsalted butter

1. Half fill a large bowl with cold water. Squeeze the juice from 1 of the lemons into the bowl and add the lemon halves. One at a time, peel, quarter and core the quinces and add to the bowl of lemon water to prevent discoloring.

2. In a large nonreactive saucepan, combine 6 cups of water with the sugar and the juice of the remaining lemon. Bring to a boil over high heat, stirring to dissolve the sugar. Add the quinces to the syrup. Reduce the heat to moderate and cook, uncovered, until the quinces are soft and the liquid is very syrupy, about 1 hour.

3. Drain the quinces, reserving the syrup (see Note). *(The recipe can be made to this point up to 1 week in advance. Cover and refrigerate the quinces.)*

4. Shortly before serving, melt the butter in a large skillet over moderate heat. Add the candied quinces and cook, stirring, until warmed through.

NOTE: Reserve the syrup in a 1-pint jar. (When cold, it has the consistency of jelly. You can refrigerate the jelly for several months. I use it to glaze fruit tarts.)
—*Lydie Marshall*

Prunes in Red Wine

These wine-poached prunes make a delightful condiment, but they are also the basis of a simple French bistro dessert (either served by themselves or with fresh berries).

Makes About 3 Cups

2 cups pitted prunes
1 cup full-bodied red wine,
   such as Gigondas
¼ cup sugar
2 thin slices of lemon, seeds
   removed
4 thin slices of orange, seeds
   removed

1. The day before serving, place the prunes in a medium bowl with 2 cups of water, cover and let sit at room temperature to plump for 24 hours.

2. Drain the prunes; discard the soaking liquid. In a medium nonreactive saucepan, combine the prunes with the wine, sugar, lemon slices and orange slices. Bring to a boil over high heat, remove from the heat and let cool. The prunes can be served at room temperature or slightly chilled.
—*Patricia Wells*

Blushing Applesauce

This apple-raspberry sauce is a pleasant accompaniment to ham. The flavor and tartness will be determined by the type of apple you use. Any leftover sauce can be sweetened with a little sugar and served as a dessert.

8 to 10 Servings

3½ pounds apples, such as
  Cortland or McIntosh—
  peeled, cored and cut into
  1-inch chunks
1 bag (12 ounces) frozen
  unsweetened raspberries or
  ¾ pint fresh raspberries

1. Place the apples and 2 tablespoons of water in a large nonreactive casserole. Cover tightly and cook over moderately low heat, stirring once or twice, until the apples are almost tender, about 30 minutes.

2. Stir in the raspberries, cover and cook until all the fruit is soft, about 10 minutes. Transfer the fruit to a food processor and puree until smooth. Strain the puree through a sieve in batches to remove the raspberry seeds. Serve warm or at room temperature. *(The sauce can be made up to 2 days ahead. Cover and refrigerate.)*
—*Diana Sturgis*

Apple and Plum Sauce

6 Servings

2 pounds Golden Delicious
  apples (about 4 large)
1 teaspoon fresh lemon juice
1 tablespoon sugar
½ cup (4 ounces) Chinese
  plum sauce*
*Available at Asian markets

1. Peel and core the apples and cut them into 1-inch chunks. Place them in a medium saucepan and toss with the lemon juice.

2. Add the sugar and enough water to barely cover the apples. Bring the water to a boil over moderate heat. Reduce the heat and simmer the apples, uncovered, until soft, about 10 minutes. Drain the apples and let cool to room temperature.

3. Puree the apples with the plum sauce in a blender or food processor.
—*Ken Hom*

Pear and Apple Compote

Comforting, familiar flavors and a chunky texture make this winter compote a favorite with younger as well as older members of the family. Gently fold the ingredients together so that the fruit will retain some of its texture. It is best served at room temperature.

Makes About 10 Cups

¼ cup fresh lemon juice
6 large firm-ripe Anjou or
  Bartlett pears (about 3
  pounds)
4 Granny Smith or other tart
  cooking apples (about 2
  pounds)

⅔ cup sugar
1 cup Riesling or other dry
  white wine
1 cinnamon stick
1 small vanilla bean, split in
  half lengthwise
1 tablespoon red currant jelly
2 teaspoons finely grated
  lemon zest

1. In a large bowl, combine 2 cups of water with the lemon juice. Peel, halve and core the pears and apples. Cut the fruit into ½-inch chunks, dropping them into the lemon water as they are cut.

2. In a large, heavy, nonreactive saucepan, combine the sugar and wine and bring to a boil over high heat. Stir in the fruit and lemon water and bring to a boil. Reduce the heat to moderate, cover partially and simmer, stirring occasionally, until the fruit is just tender but still in chunks, 10 to 15 minutes. With a large slotted spoon, transfer the fruit to a large bowl; set aside.

3. Add the cinnamon stick, vanilla bean and currant jelly to the liquid in the saucepan. Increase the heat to high and bring to a boil; boil until the liquid reduces to 1½ cups, about 10 minutes. Strain the reduced liquid over the fruit. Stir in the lemon zest. Transfer the compote to a serving bowl and let cool. Cover and refrigerate for up to 3 days. Bring to room temperature before serving.
—*Sheila Lukins*

Bacalao Gloria (p. 28).

At left: Gratin of Pumpkin (p. 92)
and Roast Capon with
Date-Nut Dressing and Chestnut
Sauce (p. 66).
Above: Field Salad with Mushrooms
and Walnuts (p. 101).

Frozen Praline Meringue (p. 199).

Apple-Bourbon Butter

Decidedly American, this simple concoction has a familiar and comforting flavor. Try this fruit butter with sausage links, pork loin and roast duck.

Makes About 1⅓ Cups

> 3 medium Granny Smith
> apples (about 1 pound)—
> peeled, cored and coarsely
> shredded
> 2 tablespoons fresh lemon
> juice
> ⅓ cup sugar
> ⅓ cup plus 1 tablespoon
> bourbon
> ⅛ teaspoon cinnamon
> 1½ tablespoons unsalted
> butter
> 1 teaspoon dark molasses

1. In a heavy medium nonreactive saucepan, toss the apples with the lemon juice. Add the sugar, ⅓ cup of the bourbon and the cinnamon. Bring to a boil over moderately high heat, stirring frequently. Reduce the heat to moderate and boil, stirring frequently, until thickened, about 10 minutes.

2. Stir in the butter, molasses and remaining 1 tablespoon bourbon. Let cool to room temperature. Transfer the butter to a crock, cover and refrigerate for up to 10 days.
—*Jim Fobel*

Pear and Ginger Jam

Fresh ginger gives this jam a sharp bite and brings out the full flavor of the pears. Since fresh ginger can be hot or mild, taste it first and add more or less than called for here, depending on its strength. Try this jam on scones or on miniature biscuits topped with slivers of rosy ham. Baked in small cored apples, it makes a fragrant companion to pheasant, duck or turkey.

Makes About 1⅓ Cups

> 3 cups peeled and chopped
> Bosc pears (1½ pounds)
> ¼ cup sugar
> 2 tablespoons fresh lemon
> juice
> 1 tablespoon grated fresh
> ginger

1. In a heavy medium nonreactive saucepan, combine the pears, sugar, lemon juice and ginger. Bring to a boil over moderately high heat, stirring frequently. Reduce the heat to moderate and boil, stirring occasionally, until thick, about 10 minutes.

2. Let the jam cool to room temperature. Cover and refrigerate for up to 10 days.
—*Jim Fobel*

Red Grape and Zinfandel Jam

This chunky jam tastes even better the next day. As delicious as it is for breakfast, it's also the perfect foil for grilled spareribs and game.

Makes About 1⅓ Cups

> 2 pounds seedless red grapes,
> stemmed and halved
> crosswise
> ½ cup plus 1 tablespoon red
> Zinfandel wine
> ⅓ cup sugar
> 2 large strips of orange zest
> 1 cinnamon stick
> 1 imported bay leaf

1. In a heavy medium nonreactive saucepan, combine the grapes, ½ cup of the Zinfandel, the sugar, orange zest, cinnamon stick and bay leaf. Bring to a boil over moderately high heat, stirring frequently. Reduce the heat to moderate and boil rapidly, stirring occasionally, for 15 minutes. Continue to cook, stirring frequently, until the jam is thick, about 10 minutes longer.

2. Let cool slightly. While still warm, stir in the remaining 1 tablespoon Zinfandel. Let cool to room temperature. Remove and discard the orange zest, cinnamon stick and bay leaf. Transfer the jam to a crock, cover and refrigerate for up to 10 days.
—*Jim Fobel*

desserts

Wintry Fruit Salad

16 Servings

3 kiwis—peeled, quartered
  and sliced ¼ inch thick
2 apples—peeled, quartered,
  cored and sliced ¼ inch
  thick
1 firm-ripe pear—peeled,
  quartered, cored and sliced
  ¼ inch thick
1 cantaloupe—halved, seeded
  and scooped into little balls
  with a melon baller
1 honeydew melon—halved,
  seeded and scooped into
  little balls with a melon
  baller
1 papaya—peeled, halved,
  seeded and cut into 2-by-¼-
  inch strips
1 pint fresh raspberries or
  strawberries
¼ cup sugar
3 tablespoons fresh lemon
  juice

In a large glass bowl, combine all
the fruit. Sprinkle on the sugar and
lemon juice and toss gently. Cover
with plastic wrap and refrigerate for
2 hours, or overnight, before serving.
—Mimi Ruth Brodeur

Orange Gelée

This dessert must be refrigerated for
at least 6 hours, so plan accordingly.
8 to 10 Servings

12 navel oranges
3 cups sugar
2 envelopes unflavored gelatin
2 lemons
½ cup dry white wine
¼ cup Grand Marnier
¼ cup Cointreau
4- to 6-ounce semisweet
  chocolate bar (⅜ to ½ inch
  thick)

1. Remove the zest from 6 of the
oranges with a zester (or use a vegetable peeler and then cut into thin
julienne strips). Place 1 cup of the
sugar and 2 cups of water in a heavy
medium saucepan. Bring to a boil to
dissolve the sugar. Add the julienned
zest and boil without stirring for
about 45 minutes, until only 2 to 3
tablespoons of liquid remain and the
zest is candied. Remove the saucepan
from the heat and let the zest cool to
room temperature.

2. Place the remaining 2 cups of
sugar and 4 cups of water in a large
heavy saucepan. Stir to dissolve the
sugar; sprinkle the gelatin over the
mixture. Set aside for about 5 minutes until the gelatin softens.

3. Meanwhile, remove the zest
from the lemons and the remaining 6
oranges in large pieces with a vegetable peeler. Bring the softened
gelatin mixture to a boil, add the orange and lemon zests and return to a
boil. Cook over moderately high
heat for 10 to 15 minutes, until the
syrup thickens slightly and the liquid
and zests measure about 2½ cups.

4. Strain the syrup into a medium
bowl and discard the zest. Add the
wine, Grand Marnier and Cointreau
to the syrup. Refrigerate (30 to 45
minutes) or chill over ice water until
the mixture starts to set.

5. Meanwhile, with a sharp knife,
cut off all the white pith around the
12 oranges from which the zest was
removed. Cut between the membranes to remove the sections. Let
the fruit drain in a colander for at
least 10 minutes; gently pat dry with
paper towels.

6. Put the orange sections in a
glass bowl, sprinkle with the candied
orange zest and pour in the syrup.
Refrigerate for at least 6 hours or
overnight; the syrup will have the
consistency of a jellied consommé.

7. Place the chocolate on a cookie
sheet lined with wax paper in an un-
lighted gas oven with a pilot light or
a warm (about 90°) place for 30 minutes until slightly softened.

8. Using a vegetable peeler and
pressing gently but firmly, shave off
long thin strips of chocolate, which
will curl as you scrape. If necessary,
use a toothpick to help form the curl.
Transfer to wax paper. (If the curls
break, the chocolate is too cold; return to the oven for another 10 minutes and try again. If curls won't
form, the chocolate is too warm; let
it stand outside of the oven for 5 or
10 minutes and try again.) Refrigerate until serving time. Arrange over
the oranges at the last moment.
—Melanie Barnard

Marmalade Apples in Rum Sauce

4 Servings

4 large baking apples, such as
  Rome Beauties
¼ cup Three-Citrus
  Marmalade (p. 266)
¼ cup dry bread crumbs
2 tablespoons unsalted butter
½ cup dark rum
1 tablespoon brown sugar

1. Preheat the oven to 375°. Core the apples to within ½ inch of their bases.

2. Place the apples in a baking dish just large enough to hold them without touching. Place 1 tablespoon Three-Citrus Marmalade in each apple and top each with 1 tablespoon bread crumbs and ½ tablespoon butter. Add ¾ cup water to the pan and bake about 1 hour, or until tender.

3. Place the apples on a serving dish and pour the pan juices into a saucepan. Add the rum and sugar and boil until the liquid is reduced to ⅓ cup. Pour over the apples and serve.
—F&W

Winter Fruit Compote

For a lovely winter dessert, heat the compote with a little Grand Marnier and serve over vanilla ice cream. This versatile dish is a delicious accompaniment to the Thanksgiving dinner.
8 to 10 Servings

1 cup pitted prunes (8
  ounces), quartered
1 cup dried apricots (8
  ounces), quartered
1 cup dried apple slices (3
  ounces), cut into ½-inch
  pieces
4 large pears, such as Bartlett
  or Comice—peeled, cored
  and cut into ½-inch dice
1½ cups fresh orange juice
2 tablespoons brown sugar
2 teaspoons grated orange
  zest plus slivered orange
  zest, for garnish

In a large nonreactive saucepan, combine all the ingredients except the slivered orange zest with ½ cup of water and bring to a boil over high heat. Reduce the heat to low, cover and simmer until all of the fruits are tender, 7 to 8 minutes. Transfer to a bowl, garnish with the slivered orange zest and serve warm.
—Marion Cunningham

Tarte Tatin

6 to 8 Servings

Pastry:
1 cup sifted all-purpose flour
2 tablespoons sugar
Pinch of salt
4 tablespoons cold unsalted
  butter, cut into small pieces
1 egg yolk
1 to 3 tablespoons ice water

Filling and Assembly:
4 medium Golden Delicious
  apples
6½ tablespoons unsalted
  butter
1 cup sugar
¼ teaspoon cinnamon
Whipped cream or crème
  fraîche (optional)

1. Make the pastry: In a medium bowl, combine the flour, sugar and salt. Cut in the butter until the mixture resembles coarse meal. Add the egg yolk and blend. Add the ice water, 1 teaspoon at a time, until the dough masses together. Press into a ball.

2. On a lightly floured surface, pat or roll the dough out into a 9-inch circle. Wrap in wax paper. Refrigerate for 1 hour.

3. Assemble the tart: Core and peel the apples. Cut them in half lengthwise.

4. Preheat the oven to 350°. In a 9-inch cast-iron skillet, melt 5 tablespoons of the butter over moderately high heat. Add all but 2 tablespoons of the sugar and cook, stirring occasionally, until the sugar begins to caramelize, about 5 minutes. Arrange the apple halves, cored-side up, in the skillet: put 7 halves around the outside and 1 in the center. Place a generous ½ teaspoon of the remaining butter in each apple half and sprinkle with the remaining 2 tablespoons sugar and the cinnamon. Continue cooking until the sugar is well caramelized and the apples begin to color, about 5 minutes.

5. Put the skillet on the lowest rack of the oven. Bake for 15 minutes. Remove from the oven and place the circle of dough over the apples, inside the rim of the pan. Return to the oven and bake for 15 minutes longer, or until the dough is lightly browned. Remove from the oven, let cool for 15 minutes in the pan. Then invert onto a round platter. Serve warm or at room temperature with whipped cream if desired.
—John Robert Massie

Mixed Fruit Cobbler

This is a simple, straightforward cobbler with a light biscuit dough. Choose any seasonal fruit for a filling—I personally like a combination of berries in the summer and a mixture of firm ripe pears and apples in the winter.

6 to 8 Servings

6 firm nectarines or pears—
 peeled, pitted or cored and
 cut into ¼-inch slices
¼ cup fresh lemon juice
3 plums—halved, pitted and
 cut into ¼-inch slices
1 pint blackberries or
 blueberries (2 cups)
2 tablespoons amaretto
 liqueur
½ teaspoon minced fresh
 ginger
3 tablespoons (packed) light
 brown sugar
1 tablespoon cornstarch
½ teaspoon cinnamon
Dash of freshly grated nutmeg
1 tablespoon chopped nuts,
 preferably pecans, walnuts
 or macadamia nuts
1½ cups all-purpose flour
⅓ cup plus ¼ cup granulated
 sugar
½ teaspoon salt
1 teaspoon baking powder
½ teaspoon baking soda
4 tablespoons cold unsalted
 butter, cut into pieces
⅓ cup plain yogurt
¼ cup skim or low-fat milk
½ teaspoon vanilla extract
2 to 3 tablespoons milk or
 cream
Heavy cream, crème fraîche
 or vanilla ice cream, for
 serving

1. In a large bowl, combine the nectarines and lemon juice; toss to coat. Stir in the plums, berries, amaretto and ginger.

2. In a small bowl, combine the brown sugar, cornstarch, cinnamon and nutmeg; blend well. Stir in the nuts. Add the mixture to the fruit and toss to mix; set aside.

3. Preheat the oven to 425°. Sift together the flour, ⅓ cup of the granulated sugar, the salt, baking powder and baking soda. Cut in the butter until coarse crumbs form. In a small bowl, stir together the yogurt, skim milk and vanilla. Make a well in the center of the flour and add the yogurt mixture, stirring until a moist, slightly sticky but manageable dough forms. Add additional skim milk if necessary.

4. Turn the dough out onto a lightly floured sheet of wax paper, fold the paper over the dough and pat it gently into a ¾-inch-thick rectangle. Using a floured, 2½-inch round fluted cookie cutter or a glass, cut the dough into 12 rounds.

5. Spoon the fruit mixture into a large heavy saucepan. Cook over moderately high heat, stirring, until almost simmering. Transfer to a 13-by-10-inch baking dish. In a rectangular pattern, arrange the biscuits over the hot fruit, overlapping them slightly. Brush the top of the biscuits with the milk or cream and sprinkle lightly with the remaining ¼ cup granulated sugar.

6. Bake for about 30 minutes, or until the biscuits are golden brown and the fruit is bubbling. Let cool on a rack for about 10 minutes. Serve warm with heavy cream, crème fraîche or vanilla ice cream.
—*Richard Sax*

Apple Quince Crumble with Eggnog Custard Sauce

The crumble can also be served with a scoop of vanilla ice cream in place of the Eggnog Custard Sauce.

6 Servings

½ cup dried currants
¼ Calvados or brandy
2½ pounds firm, tart apples,
 such as Jonathan, Cortland,
 Granny Smith or Rome,
 peeled and sliced about ¼
 inch thick (about 7 cups)
1½ tablespoons fresh lemon
 juice
1 large quince—peeled, cored
 and thinly sliced
⅓ cup pure maple syrup
⅓ cup plus 1 tablespoon
 all-purpose flour
½ teaspoon allspice
½ teaspoon freshly grated
 nutmeg
¼ teaspoon cinnamon
¼ teaspoon salt
½ cup regular or quick-
 cooking oats
½ cup (packed) brown sugar
1 stick (4 ounces) cold
 unsalted butter, cut into
 pieces
⅓ cup coarsely chopped
 walnuts
Eggnog Custard Sauce (recipe
 follows)

1. Preheat the oven to 375°. In a small nonreactive saucepan, place the currants and Calvados. Bring to a boil over high heat; set aside.

2. In a large bowl, toss together the apples, lemon juice, quince and maple syrup.

3. In a small bowl, combine 1 tablespoon of the flour, the allspice, nutmeg, cinnamon and salt. Stir until well blended. Add the seasoned flour and the currants with the Calvados to the apple mixture; toss to combine. Transfer the fruit to a large well-buttered baking dish.

4. In a large bowl or food processor, combine the oats, brown sugar and remaining ⅓ cup flour. Cut in the butter until coarse crumbs form. Stir in the walnuts. Scatter the topping evenly over the fruit in the baking dish.

5. Bake in the center of the oven for about 1 hour or until the topping is golden brown. Let cool on a rack for about 15 minutes. Serve warm with cold Eggnog Custard Sauce.
—Richard Sax

Eggnog Custard Sauce

Pour this delicious custard over sliced fresh fruit or pound cake for a special, quick dessert.

Makes About 2½ Cups

2½ cups milk
1 vanilla bean, split
  lengthwise
5 egg yolks
⅓ cup sugar
1 teaspoon amaretto liqueur,
  rum or bourbon

1. In a small heavy saucepan, bring the milk and vanilla bean just to a boil over moderate heat. Remove from the heat, cover and let steep until the vanilla flavors the milk, about 1 hour.

2. Return the milk to a boil over moderately high heat. In a small bowl, whisk together the egg yolks and sugar until pale and thick, about 3 minutes. Gradually whisk in the hot milk. Return the mixture to the saucepan and cook over moderate heat, stirring constantly, until the custard is thick enough to coat the back of a spoon, 7 to 10 minutes; do not boil.

3. Strain the custard into a medium bowl. Remove the vanilla bean and scrape the seeds into the strained sauce. Stir in the amaretto. Let cool to room temperature, about 45 minutes. Cover and refrigerate for up to 3 days or freeze for up to 2 months.
—Richard Sax

Apple and Prune Cobbler with Buttermilk Biscuit Crust

Really a pie with no bottom crust, this apple and prune cobbler is a perfect way to combine fruit and pastry quickly and easily. Although prunes enter into few American desserts, they are common in France and in Eastern Europe. The prunes and apples marry well, sharing a slight tartness and a melting texture after baking. The Buttermilk Biscuit Crust is thick and buttery—a perfect complement to the tart juices of the prune and apple filling.

Try the cobbler in the summer, substituting peaches or apricots with raspberries or cherries.

8 to 10 Servings

2 pounds firm cooking apples,
  such as Golden Delicious
1 cup pitted prunes, about 8
  ounces
½ cup walnut pieces, coarsely
  chopped
½ cup plus 1 tablespoon
  sugar

½ teaspoon cinnamon
2 tablespoons all-purpose
  flour
2 tablespoons fresh lemon
  juice
2 tablespoons unsalted butter
Buttermilk Biscuit Dough
  (recipe follows)
1 tablespoon milk or
  buttermilk

1. Peel, halve and core the apples. Slice each half into 5 or 6 wedges, from stem to blossom end. Slice each prune into 3 or 4 strips. In a large bowl combine the apples, prunes and chopped walnuts.

2. Preheat the oven to 375°. In a bowl, combine ½ cup of the sugar, the cinnamon and the flour. Toss with the fruit and nut mixture. Pour the filling into a 1½-quart shallow baking dish, sprinkle on the lemon juice and dot with the butter.

3. On a lightly floured surface, roll the Buttermilk Biscuit Dough a little less than ¼ inch thick, slightly larger than the baking dish. Transfer the dough to the top of the filling and trim any overhang even with the rim of the dish. Flute the edge of the dough at the rim. Slash 4 or 5 vent holes about 1 inch long in the center of the crust. Paint the dough with the milk and sprinkle with the remaining 1 tablespoon sugar.

4. Bake the cobbler for 30 minutes, or until the dough is baked through and deep golden and the filling is beginning to bubble. Let the cobbler cool on a rack. Serve warm or at room temperature.
—Nicholas Malgieri

Buttermilk Biscuit Dough

Don't be alarmed if the biscuit dough is soft; if it is too firm, the crust will be tough. Just flour the work surface and the dough well before rolling the dough out. Support the dough with a tart pan bottom or thin, flexible cookie sheet to transfer it to the top of the filling. Unlike flaky pastry, baking powder biscuit dough is rolled out immediately after it is made.

This recipe also makes excellent biscuits for shortcake. For these, roll out the dough ½ inch thick. Cut with a 3-inch round cutter and bake at 400° for 12 to 15 minutes.

Makes One 9-Inch Crust

¾ cup unbleached all-purpose
  flour
¾ cup cake flour
1½ teaspoons baking powder
½ teaspoon salt
4 tablespoons cold unsalted
  butter
¾ cup buttermilk or milk

1. Combine the all-purpose flour, cake flour, baking powder and salt. Sift into a mixing bowl.

2. Cut the butter into 8 or 10 pieces and add to the dry ingredients. Rub the butter in with your fingertips until the mixture resembles coarse meal.

3. Make a well in the center and add the buttermilk. Toss with a fork to moisten evenly. Let the dough stand in the bowl for 1 minute to absorb the liquid. Turn out onto a floured work surface. Fold the dough over on itself 2 or 3 times until it is smooth and less sticky.
—*Nicholas Malgieri*

Post-Holiday Shortcake

This heart-shaped shortcake is the answer to my hankering for gingerbread, which begins when the leaves turn red and lasts until those little green shoots begin to poke out of the ground. Pear, the most delicately flavored of the winter fruits, is the perfect foil for ginger's aggressive bite. Pears poached in a lemon and fresh ginger syrup are set on a gingerbread base with a large dollop of crème fraîche. Glistening filaments of candied lemon zest garnish the top.

5 Servings

2 cups all-purpose flour
¼ cup (packed) light brown
  sugar
1 tablespoon baking powder
½ teaspoon salt
2 tablespoons ground ginger
1 teaspoon cinnamon
½ teaspoon freshly grated
  nutmeg
¼ teaspoon ground cloves
1 stick (4 ounces) cold
  unsalted butter, cut into
  ¼-inch dice
2 teaspoons instant coffee
  powder
2 teaspoons molasses
⅔ cup plus 2 tablespoons
  milk
2 lemons
2 cups plus 1 tablespoon
  superfine sugar
3 Bosc pears—peeled, halved
  and cored
4-inch piece of fresh ginger,
  peeled and cut into thin
  slices
1 cup heavy cream
1 cup crème fraîche
1 teaspoon vanilla extract
2 tablespoons finely chopped
  candied ginger

1. Preheat the oven to 375°. In a medium bowl, sift together the flour, brown sugar, baking powder, salt, ground ginger, cinnamon, nutmeg and cloves.

2. Using a pastry blender, cut in the butter until the mixture is the texture of coarse meal with a few pea-size pieces of butter remaining.

3. In a 1-cup measure, combine the instant coffee, molasses and 1 tablespoon of the milk. Stir to dissolve the coffee; add the ⅔ cup milk and stir to combine.

4. Make a well in the center of the flour mixture and pour in the milk mixture. Using a rubber spatula, quickly combine the ingredients, scraping down the bowl, until the dough comes together, 5 to 6 strokes.

5. Transfer the dough to a lightly floured surface and knead gently 2 or 3 times. Shape the dough into a 12-inch log, scraping the work surface as necessary. Flatten the log into a rectangle 3 inches wide and 1 inch thick. Dip a large heart-shaped cookie cutter in flour and cut out 4 hearts. Gently reknead the dough scraps just enough to gather them together; shape into a triangle 1 inch thick and cut out the last heart. Brush the tops of the shortcakes with the remaining 1 tablespoon milk and place on a heavy baking sheet lined with aluminum foil. Refrigerate for 10 minutes.

6. Bake the shortcakes for 30 minutes, or until golden brown. Let cool on the baking sheet for 10 minutes. Using a metal spatula, gently transfer the shortcakes to a wire rack to cool further.

7. Meanwhile, using a vegetable-peeler, cut the zest from the lemons, being careful to leave behind the bitter white pith. Using a sharp knife, slice the zest lengthwise into very thin julienne strips.

8. In a medium saucepan, combine 2 cups of the superfine sugar with 3 cups of water. Cook over high heat until the sugar dissolves completely, 4 to 5 minutes. Add the pear halves, zest strips and sliced fresh ginger. Reduce the heat to moderately high and simmer, turning the pears occasionally, until tender and easily pierced with a fork, about 10 minutes. Remove the pears with a slotted spoon and set aside.

9. Continue to simmer the syrup, occasionally washing down the sides of the pan with a pastry brush dipped in water, until the zest is transparent and the syrup somewhat thickened, about 30 minutes. Strain the syrup (you should have about 2 cups) and set aside. Discard the ginger but reserve the lemon zest.

10. In a chilled bowl, combine the heavy cream and crème fraîche and beat until the mixture begins to thicken. Add the remaining 1 tablespoon superfine sugar and the vanilla and continue beating until soft peaks form. Set aside.

11. Using a fork, split each shortcake in half. Spoon about 1 tablespoon of the warm lemon-ginger syrup onto each of 5 dessert plates. Place the bottom half of a shortcake on each plate, cover with a ½-inch layer of cream and top with a pear half, the pointy end matching the heart tip. Spoon another tablespoon of syrup over each pear and cover with another layer of cream. Arrange the shortcake tops over the cream, cocked to one side. Garnish with the reserved candied lemon zest and the candied ginger and drizzle with additional syrup.
—Peggy Cullen

Mediterranean Shortcake

Hazelnuts, figs and mascarpone are the winter flavors of Italy. For this shortcake, plump dried figs are poached in a port syrup, which is then reduced to a glistening sauce the color of Dorothy's ruby slippers. Even if you dislike anise, don't be afraid to use it. It brings out the flavor of the toasted hazelnuts.

6 Servings

1 cup hazelnuts
2 cups all-purpose flour
1 tablespoon baking powder
½ teaspoon salt
1 cup plus 3 tablespoons superfine sugar
1 tablespoon anise seeds, finely chopped or freshly ground
1 stick (4 ounces) cold unsalted butter, cut into ¼-inch dice
⅔ cup plus 1 tablespoon milk
1 vanilla bean
12 moist dried Calimyrna figs (about ¾ pound)
2 cups ruby port
½ cup heavy cream
1 cup mascarpone cheese, at room temperature

1. Preheat the oven to 350°. Place the hazelnuts on a baking sheet and toast until the skins crack and the centers are golden, about 15 minutes. While still warm, rub the nuts in a terrycloth towel to remove the skins; chop coarsely and set aside. Leave the oven on.

2. In a medium bowl, sift together the flour, baking powder, salt and 3 tablespoons of the superfine sugar. Stir in the anise seeds. Cut in the butter until the mixture is the texture of coarse meal with a few pea-size pieces of butter remaining. Toss in the cooled hazelnuts.

3. Pour the ⅔ cup of the milk into a measuring cup and scrape the seeds from the vanilla bean into the milk. Make a well in the center of the flour mixture and add the vanilla milk. Using a rubber spatula, quickly combine the ingredients, scraping down the sides of the bowl, until the dough comes together, 5 to 6 strokes.

4. Transfer the dough to a lightly floured surface and knead gently 2 or 3 times. Shape the dough into a 12-inch log. Pat the log into a rectangle 3 inches wide and 1 inch thick. Dip a 3-inch round biscuit cutter in flour and cut out 4 circles. Gently reknead the dough scraps to gather them together. Pat the dough to a 1-inch thickness and cut out another 2 circles. Brush the tops of the shortcakes with the remaining 1 tablespoon milk and place on a heavy baking sheet lined with aluminum foil. Refrigerate for about 10 minutes.

5. Bake the shortcakes for 30 minutes, or until golden brown. Let cool on the baking sheet for 10 minutes. Using a metal spatula, gently transfer them to a wire rack to cool further.

6. Meanwhile, cut the stem tips off the figs. In a medium nonreactive saucepan, combine the port and the remaining 1 cup sugar. Cook over high heat to dissolve the sugar, about 3 minutes. Add the figs, bring just to a boil and reduce the heat to moderately high. Continue to simmer the figs until the skins are very soft, about 20 minutes. Remove the pan from the heat and leave the figs to steep in the syrup until cool, 20 to 30 minutes.

7. Meanwhile, in a medium bowl, whisk the heavy cream into the mascarpone. Remove the figs from the syrup and cut each fig into quarters. Reserve the syrup.

8. Using a fork, split each shortcake in half. Spoon about 1 table-

spoon of the port syrup onto each of 6 dessert plates. Place the bottom half of a shortcake on each plate and cover with ¼ cup of the mascarpone cream. Arrange 4 fig quarters on the cream with their points facing out. Drizzle about 1 tablespoon of syrup over the figs and top with about 3 tablespoons more cream. Set 4 more fig quarters atop the cream and cover with the other shortcake half. Garnish each shortcake with a dollop of cream and drizzle additional syrup over the top so that it runs down the sides.

—*Peggy Cullen*

Miami Beach Shortcake

When sleigh bells give way to slush puddles and winter begins to get a little tiresome, our thoughts turn south to palm trees and a turquoise sea. This tropical shortcake is covered in coconut to resemble a large macaroon. For the filling, sliced ripe bananas are layered with banana-fortified whipped cream and a touch of tangy sour cream. While it won't give you a tan, this dessert is a proven cure for the ubiquitous late-winter malady known as cabin fever.

6 Servings

⅔ cup plus ½ cup sweetened
    shredded coconut
2 cups all-purpose flour
1 tablespoon baking powder
1 teaspoon freshly grated
    nutmeg
½ teaspoon salt
¼ cup superfine sugar
1 stick (4 ounces) cold,
    unsalted butter, cut into
    ¼-inch dice
⅔ cup plus 1 tablespoon milk
2½ teaspoons vanilla extract
4 large bananas

1 cup heavy cream
2 tablespoons sour cream

1. Preheat the oven to 375°. Toast ⅔ cup of the coconut on a heavy baking sheet for 4 to 5 minutes, stirring once, until lightly browned. Let cool completely. Set aside 3 tablespoons of the toasted coconut for garnish.

2. In a medium bowl, sift together the flour, baking powder, nutmeg, salt and 3 tablespoons of the sugar. Using a pastry blender, cut in the butter until the mixture is the texture of coarse meal with a few pea-size pieces of butter remaining. Toss in the toasted coconut remaining on the baking sheet.

3. Make a well in the center of the mixture and pour in ⅔ cup of the milk and 1 teaspoon of the vanilla. Using a rubber spatula, quickly combine the ingredients, scraping down the bowl, until the dough comes together, 5 to 6 strokes.

4. Using a 2-ounce (¼-cup) ice cream scoop, form a rounded ball of dough. Holding the ball in your hand and using a pastry brush, dab the surface with some of the remaining 1 tablespoon milk. Place the remaining ½ cup untoasted coconut in a medium bowl and roll the ball of dough in it, pressing to help the coconut adhere; let the excess coconut fall back into the bowl. Transfer the shortcake to a heavy baking sheet covered with aluminum foil. Repeat with the remaining 5 shortcakes and the remaining milk and coconut. Refrigerate the shortcake balls for 10 minutes.

5. Bake the shortcakes for 30 minutes, or until the coconut is nicely browned and the surfaces are hard to the touch. Let cool on the baking sheet for 10 minutes. Using a metal spatula, gently transfer the shortcakes to a wire rack to cool.

6. Meanwhile, in a small bowl, mash 1 of the bananas and the remaining 1 tablespoon sugar to a puree. In a medium bowl, combine the heavy cream and sour cream and beat at medium-high speed until soft peaks form, about 2 minutes. Fold in the mashed banana and the remaining 1½ teaspoons vanilla.

7. Using a sharp serrated knife, slice each shortcake in half horizontally. Place the bottom half of a shortcake on each of 6 dessert plates and spread with about ½ cup of the banana cream. Slice the remaining bananas into ¼-inch rounds and arrange the slices on the cream, reserving 6 banana slices for garnish. Top with the other shortcake half. Garnish each shortcake with a dollop of banana cream, a banana slice and ½ tablespoon of the reserved toasted coconut; serve immediately.

—*Peggy Cullen*

Upstate Shortcake

This shortcake was inspired by two of my favorite confections: sticky caramel apples from upstate New York and pecan buttercrunch. The pecan-studded triangular shortcake is split and filled with vanilla ice cream and apples in a buttery caramel sauce. Eat this quickly before the sauce melts the ice cream.

6 Servings

2 cups all-purpose flour
3 tablespoons light brown
    sugar
1 tablespoon baking powder
1 teaspoon cinnamon
½ teaspoon salt
1½ sticks (6 ounces) cold
    unsalted butter, the stick cut
    into ¼-inch dice
1½ cups coarsely chopped
    pecans (5 ounces)
⅔ cup plus 1 tablespoon milk

1 teaspoon vanilla extract
4 medium apples, such as
Winesap, Granny Smith or
Golden Delicious—peeled,
cored and sliced into eighths
¾ cup plus 1 tablespoon
superfine sugar
¼ teaspoon lemon juice
¾ cup heavy cream
6 scoops of good-quality
vanilla ice cream (about 1
pint)

1. Preheat the oven to 375°. In a medium bowl, sift together the flour, brown sugar, baking powder, cinnamon and salt. Using a pastry blender, cut in the 1 stick diced butter until the mixture is the texture of coarse meal with a few pea-size pieces of butter remaining. Toss in the pecans.

2. Make a well in the center of the mixture and add ⅔ cup of the milk and the vanilla. Using a rubber spatula, quickly combine the ingredients, scraping down the sides of the bowl, until the dough comes together, 5 to 6 strokes.

3. Transfer the dough to a lightly floured surface and gently knead 2 or 3 times. Shape the dough into a 12-inch log, scraping the work surface as necessary. Pat the log into a rectangle, 3½ inches wide and 1 inch thick. Using a sharp knife, cut out 6 triangles.

4. Brush the tops of the shortcakes with the remaining 1 tablespoon milk. Transfer the shortcakes to a heavy baking sheet lined with aluminum foil and refrigerate for 10 minutes.

5. Bake the shortcakes for 30 minutes, or until golden brown. Let cool on the baking sheet for 10 minutes. Using a metal spatula, gently transfer the shortcakes to a wire rack to cool further.

6. Meanwhile, in a large skillet, melt the remaining 4 tablespoons butter. Add the apples and cook over high heat, stirring frequently, until lightly browned, about 4 minutes. Sprinkle 1 tablespoon of the superfine sugar over the apples and continue cooking, stirring frequently, until softened and browned, about 4 minutes longer. Remove from the heat and set aside.

7. In a medium saucepan and using your fingers, rub the lemon juice thoroughly into the remaining ¾ cup superfine sugar. Stir in 2 tablespoons of water until blended and bring to a boil over high heat. Using a pastry brush dipped in water, wash down any sugar crystals from the sides of the pan and boil the syrup over high heat until it becomes a light caramel, 4 to 5 minutes. Remove from the heat and slowly whisk in the heavy cream. Return the caramel to the heat and continue whisking until the cream is incorporated. Pour the warm caramel sauce into the skillet and stir gently to coat the apples.

8. Using a fork, split each shortcake in half. Place the bottom half of a shortcake on each of 6 dessert plates and spoon on 2 to 3 slices of apple and about 1 tablespoon of the warm caramel sauce. Set a scoop of ice cream on the apples and coat with another tablespoon of caramel sauce. Top with the other shortcake half. Spoon another 2 or 3 slices of apple and 1 tablespoon of caramel sauce over all and serve immediately.
—*Peggy Cullen*

Creamsicle Currant Shortcake

As a cold wind blows and the afternoon light is beginning to fade, there's no better place to be than on a divan taking tea with scones and clotted cream. Stateside, you'll happily settle for this shortcake, inspired both by the classic hot cross bun with its felicitous pairing of currants and orange and the flavors of an old-fashioned Creamsicle, with its smooth blend of vanilla ice cream and orange sherbet.

6 Servings

2 cups all-purpose flour
1 tablespoon baking powder
½ teaspoon salt
¼ teaspoon freshly grated
nutmeg
¾ cup superfine sugar
1 stick (4 ounces) cold
unsalted butter, cut into
¼-inch dice
¾ cup dried currants
⅔ cup plus 1 tablespoon milk
1½ cups fresh orange juice
¼ cup kirsch
1 cinnamon stick
4 large navel oranges, peeled
and cut into sections
1 cup heavy cream

1. Preheat the oven to 375°. In a medium bowl, sift together the flour, baking powder, salt, nutmeg and 3 tablespoons of the sugar. Using a pastry blender, cut in the butter until the mixture is the texture of coarse meal with a few pea-size pieces of butter remaining. Toss in the dried currants.

2. Make a well in the center of the mixture and add ⅔ cup of the milk. Using a rubber spatula, quickly combine the ingredients, scraping down the bowl, until the dough comes together, 5 to 6 strokes.

3. Transfer the dough to a lightly

floured surface and knead gently 2 or 3 times. Shape the dough into a 12-inch log, then pat it out into a 12-by-3-inch rectangle 1 inch thick.

4. Dip a 3-inch round biscuit cutter in flour and cut out 4 circles from the dough. Gently reknead the scraps just enough to gather them together. Pat the dough to an even 1-inch thickness and cut out 2 more circles. Lightly brush the tops of the shortcakes with the remaining 1 tablespoon milk. Arrange the shortcakes on a heavy baking sheet lined with aluminum foil and refrigerate for 10 minutes.

5. Bake the shortcakes for 30 minutes, or until lightly browned. Let cool on the baking sheet for 10 minutes. Using a metal spatula, gently transfer the shortcakes to a wire rack to cool further.

6. Meanwhile, in a medium nonreactive saucepan, combine the orange juice, kirsch, ½ cup of the sugar and the cinnamon stick. Bring to a boil over high heat. Reduce the heat to moderate and boil until reduced by about half and thickened slightly, about 30 minutes.

7. Remove from the heat and discard the cinnamon stick. Let cool for about 5 minutes, then fold in the orange segments. (The syrup will thin out when the oranges are added.)

8. In a chilled medium bowl, beat the heavy cream until it just begins to thicken. Add the remaining 1 tablespoon sugar and continue beating until soft peaks form.

9. Using a fork, split each shortcake in half horizontally. Spoon 1 tablespoon of the orange syrup onto each of 6 dessert plates. Place the bottom half of a shortcake on each plate and cover with a ½-inch layer of whipped cream. Spoon 2 tablespoons of the glazed oranges over the cream, then spoon over another layer of cream. Top with the other shortcake half. Garnish the shortcakes with a dollop of whipped cream and 2 to 3 orange segments and serve immediately.
—*Peggy Cullen*

Ginger Angel Food Cake

Makes One 10-Inch Tube Cake

4 ounces fresh ginger (about a
   4-inch piece), peeled and
   quartered
1½ cups sugar
1 cup cake flour
2 cups egg whites (about 12)
1½ teaspoons cream of tartar
½ teaspoon salt

1. Preheat the oven to 350°. In a food processor, combine the ginger and ¼ cup of the sugar. Process until blended into a thick paste. Set aside.

2. In a medium bowl, sift the cake flour and ¾ cup of the sugar together 3 times. In a large mixer bowl, beat the egg whites on high speed until foamy, about 1 minute. Beat in the cream of tartar and salt. Add the remaining ½ cup sugar, 1 tablespoon at a time, beating continuously. Continue to beat until the egg whites form soft peaks that hold their shape, 8 to 10 minutes longer.

3. Sift the flour mixture evenly over the whites in 2 batches and mix on the lowest speed until barely incorporated, about 5 seconds. Do not overmix. Add the reserved ginger paste and blend in on the lowest

speed for a few seconds. With a rubber spatula, gently fold a few more times to insure blending.

4. Turn the batter into an ungreased 10-inch tube pan. Cut through the center of the batter with the rubber spatula to eliminate air pockets.

5. Bake for 35 minutes, or until a cake tester inserted into the center comes out clean. Remove from the oven and invert the pan until cool. Free the cake from the sides of the pan with a long narrow knife.
—*Marion Cunningham*

Chocolate Angel Food Cake

Angel cake may be iced, or covered with any icing-like glaze of your choice. Or serve the un-iced cake with berries or other seasonal fruit and/or lightly whipped cream. The cake is best the day it is baked, but it keeps its texture well if stored in a covered "cakesaver," or if simply sheltered from drying air by a large upturned pot.

For the most ethereal results, choose a day of low humidity for baking this cake.

10 Servings

⅔ cup sifted cake flour
⅓ cup unsweetened cocoa
   powder
1⅓ cups sifted superfine sugar
½ teaspoon salt
1½ cups egg whites (from
   about 12 large eggs), at
   room temperature
1 teaspoon cream of tartar
1 tablespoon fresh lemon
   juice
2 teaspoons vanilla extract
¼ teaspoon almond extract
   (optional)

1. First make sure your mixing bowl, whisk or beater and a 10-inch tube pan 4 inches deep (preferably one with separate rim and bottom sections) are completely grease-free. Set aside.

2. Preheat the oven to 350°.

3. Sift the flour and cocoa powder with ⅓ cup of the sugar and the salt; sift 3 or 4 times.

4. In a large bow, whisk the egg whites until foamy. Add the cream of tartar, lemon juice, vanilla, almond extract and 1 teaspoon of water and beat at high speed until the whites form stiff but not dry peaks. Beat in the remaining 1 cup sugar, 2 tablespoons at a time, beating well after each addition.

5. Sift about one-fourth of the flour mixture over the egg whites and fold it in with light strokes of a spatula. Repeat three more times with the remaining flour; do not overfold.

6. Lightly pour the mixture into the prepared pan. Run a thin metal spatula twice through the batter, once near the tube and once near the rim, to eliminate air pockets and smooth the top.

7. Bake for 45 minutes, or until the cake has shrunk very slightly from the sides of the pan and springs back when the top is pressed lightly. If you use a cake tester, it will emerge clean from the cake if inserted at this point.

8. Remove the cake from the oven and invert it, still in the pan (some pans have supporting legs; if yours doesn't, support the central tube of the pan on a narrow-necked bottle). Let the cake "hang" for 1½ hours, or until thoroughly cool.

9. Run a sharp knife around the sides of the pan and unmold the cake. To serve, the traditional method is to pull the cake into wedges with two forks held back to back; or divide it with a comblike cake divider. A finely serrated knife, used in a light sawing motion, will cut the cake neatly, despite the time-honored advice never to use a knife.
—F&W

Ginger Génoise with Whipped Cream and Candied Orange Peel

This cake can be made a day ahead and stored, tightly wrapped, at room temperature. To avoid sogginess, fill it with the whipped cream and garnish as close to serving as possible.

8 Servings

Ginger Génoise:
⅔ cup all-purpose flour
2 teaspoons ground ginger
3 eggs
¼ cup dark molasses, heated and cooled to room temperature
2 tablespoons dark brown sugar
½ teaspoon vanilla extract
1½ tablespoons unsalted butter, melted and cooled to room temperature

Orange-Ginger Whipped Cream:
1 cup heavy cream, chilled
1 tablespoon Grand Marnier or other orange liqueur
3 tablespoons confectioners' sugar
2 teaspoons minced orange zest
1 tablespoon minced preserved stem ginger*

Garnish:
Strips of candied orange peel, preferably homemade (see Note)
*Slices of preserved stem ginger**
**Available at specialty food stores*

1. Prepare the génoise: Preheat the oven to 350°. Generously butter a 9-inch, round cake pan. Dust the pan with flour; tap out any excess.

2. Sift together the flour and ground ginger.

3. Place the eggs in a metal mixing bowl and whisk until frothy, about 1 minute. Add the molasses and brown sugar and set the bowl over a saucepan of barely simmering water. With a whisk or portable electric mixer, beat until the sugar is dissolved, about 1 minute. Continue to beat until the eggs are just warm to the touch, 2 to 3 minutes.

4. Remove the bowl from the pan and beat with an electric mixer until the mixture has cooled and is almost triple in volume, 5 to 7 minutes. Add the vanilla and beat 30 seconds longer.

5. Sift one-third of the gingered flour into the batter and fold quickly but gently until incorporated. Be sure to scrape the bottom of the bowl. Repeat 2 more times with the remaining gingered flour. Just before the last addition is completed, quickly fold in the butter. Immediately pour the batter into the prepared pan. Tap gently to settle.

6. Bake for about 25 minutes in the center of the oven, or until the cake has pulled away slightly from the sides of the pan and springs back when pressed in the center. Remove from the oven and cool in the pan on a rack for 3 minutes. Invert the cake onto a rack to cool completely.

7. Prepare the whipped cream: Using a chilled bowl and beaters, begin whipping the cream and Grand Marnier on medium speed until the mixture starts to thicken, about 1 minute. Increase the speed to high and gradually add the confectioners' sugar, 1 tablespoon at a time. Continue beating until the cream is just stiff, 2 to 3 minutes; do not overbeat. Fold in the orange zest and minced ginger. Chill, covered, until ready to use.

8. Assemble and garnish the cake: Using a long, sharp knife, split the cake horizontally into 2 layers. Shortly before serving, spread the bottom layer with half of the whipped cream. Cover with the second cake layer and spread the remaining whipped cream over the top; do not frost the sides. Decorate the cake with the strips of candied orange peel and slices of preserved ginger.

NOTE: To prepare enough candied orange peel to garnish the cake, remove the zest from 1 large navel orange in thin strips with a zester. Combine ¾ cup sugar and ¼ cup water in a small, heavy saucepan. Heat over moderate heat, stirring, until the sugar dissolves and the syrup comes to a boil, about 5 minutes. Reduce the heat to low, add the orange peel and simmer uncovered for 10 minutes. Remove from the heat and, with a fork, transfer the orange peel, 1 strip at a time, to a rack. Let dry for at least 1 hour.
—*Maria Piccolo*

Basic Gingerbread Cake

This is how most of us remember the plain gingerbread cakes of our childhood: simple and even textured, with a pleasantly spicy taste. Serve it with whipped cream, ice cream or toasted and spread with butter for breakfast.

9 Servings

1½ teaspoons ground ginger
1½ teaspoons cinnamon
*¼ teaspoon freshly grated
   nutmeg*
¼ teaspoon ground cloves
1 teaspoon baking soda
½ teaspoon salt
*½ cup dark unsulphured
   molasses*
*1 stick (4 ounces) unsalted
   butter, at room temperature*
*½ cup (packed) dark brown
   sugar*
3 eggs
2 cups all-purpose flour

1. Preheat the oven to 350°. Butter an 8-inch square baking pan.

2. In a small bowl, combine the ginger, cinnamon, nutmeg, cloves, baking soda and salt.

3. In a small saucepan, heat the molasses over low heat until bubbles begin to form around the sides. Remove from the heat and stir in the butter, 1 tablespoon at a time, until melted and blended.

4. Scrape the molasses into a large mixer bowl. Gradually beat in the spice mixture, brown sugar and ¼ cup of water. Add the eggs, 1 at a time, beating until well blended, 3 to 5 minutes. Add the flour and beat on low speed for 1 minute, then increase the speed to moderate and beat until well combined. Pour the batter into the prepared pan and bake for 45 to 50 minutes, or until a skewer inserted into the center of the cake comes out clean.
—*Linda Merinoff*

Prune Cake

This large, moist cake is made with chopped prunes and a brown sugar and walnut filling. It keeps, well-wrapped, for several days and serves many.

12 to 14 Servings

⅔ cup (packed) brown sugar
1 teaspoon cinnamon
½ cup chopped walnuts
*½ cup plus 2 teaspoons
   granulated sugar*
3 eggs
1 cup milk
*1 stick (4 ounces) unsalted
   butter, melted*
2½ cups all-purpose flour
1 tablespoon baking powder
½ teaspoon salt
*1 box (12 ounces) pitted
   prunes, chopped*

1. Preheat the oven to 350°. Butter and flour a 10-inch tube or bundt pan. In a small bowl, mix together the brown sugar and cinnamon, stirring with a fork until the cinnamon is well distributed. Stir in the walnuts and set the brown sugar filling aside.

2. In a large bowl, combine ½ cup of the granulated sugar, the eggs, milk and melted butter. Whisk to blend well. In a medium bowl, stir together the flour, baking powder and salt. Add the dry ingredients to the liquid ingredients. Beat with a wooden spoon until smooth. Fold in the prunes.

3. With a rubber spatula, spread no more than one-third of the batter over the bottom of the prepared pan. Sprinkle half of the brown sugar filling over the batter. Spread another third of the batter on top. Cover with the remaining filling mixture and spread the remaining batter over all.

4. Bake for 1 hour, or until a cake tester inserted into the center comes out clean. Remove from the oven and let cool for 10 minutes in the pan. Then remove from the pan and let cool completely on a rack. Sprinkle the remaining 2 teaspoons granulated sugar over the top.
—*Marion Cunningham*

Pineapple Crumbcake

Many types of fruit can replace the pineapple in this moist cake. Later in the year try it with fresh apricots or sour cherries, then with peaches or nectarines and finally with prune plums in the fall.

10 to 12 Servings

1 medium pineapple (2 to 2½
    pounds)
2 sticks (8 ounces) unsalted
    butter, softened
1¼ cups sugar
1 whole egg
3 egg yolks
1 teaspoon vanilla extract
2½ cups unbleached all-
    purpose flour
1 teaspoon baking powder
¼ teaspoon cinnamon

1. Preheat the oven to 350°. Butter a 10-by-2-inch round cake pan and line the bottom with parchment or wax paper.

2. Cut the skin and "eyes" from the pineapple. Quarter and core the pineapple. Cut the quarters crosswise into ½-inch-thick slices.

3. In a large mixer bowl, beat 1 stick of the butter and ¾ cup of the sugar until light and fluffy. Add the whole egg and continue beating until well blended. Gradually add the egg yolks, 1 at a time, beating well after each addition. Beat in the vanilla.

4. Sift together 1¼ cups of the flour and the baking powder. Stir into the butter mixture. Turn the batter into the prepared pan and spread evenly.

5. Arrange the pineapple slices on top of the batter in concentric circles, overlapping slightly and leaving a margin of about 1 inch around the edge. (Don't be concerned if the pineapple mounds slightly in the center, the top will even out as the cake bakes.)

6. In a small saucepan over low heat or in a glass bowl in a microwave oven, melt the remaining 1 stick butter. Let cool slightly.

7. In a medium bowl, combine the remaining ½ cup sugar, 1¼ cups flour and the cinnamon. Pour the melted butter over the flour mixture and rub together with your fingertips to form coarse, pea-size crumbs. Scatter the crumbs evenly over the pineapple and batter.

8. Bake the cake for 55 to 60 minutes, until a knife inserted in the center comes out clean. Let cool in the pan for 15 minutes. Unmold onto a plate and remove the paper. Invert back onto a rack to cool. Serve warm or at room temperature.
—*Nicholas Malgieri*

Ali Baba

In France for Christmas and New Year's festivities, the classic desserts are *gâteau St-Honoré*, *bûche de Noël* (see page 180) and *savarin*, which is the least well known in the States but is my favorite dessert. It is a light yeast cake soaked in a syrup made of sugar, water and a liqueur. The Ali Baba is a *savarin* soaked with Grand Marnier, decorated with mixed glacéed fruits and served with lightly whipped cream. It is very important to use good glacéed fruits.

6 to 8 Servings

2 teaspoons active dry yeast
¼ cup lukewarm milk (105°
    to 115°), plus 1 tablespoon
    cold milk
1¾ cups plus 4 teaspoons
    sugar
2 eggs, at room temperature,
    lightly beaten
7 tablespoons unsalted butter,
    at room temperature
1½ cups all-purpose flour
½ teaspoon salt
⅓ cup Grand Marnier
½ cup chopped mixed glacéed
    fruits
Grand Marnier-flavored
    whipped cream, for serving

1. In a large bowl, combine the yeast with the ¼ cup lukewarm milk and 1 teaspoon of the sugar. Let stand until foamy, about 5 minutes. Add the eggs and the butter and mix to blend well.

2. In a separate bowl, combine the flour, 2 tablespoons of the sugar and the salt. With a wooden spoon, gradually incorporate the flour into the egg and butter mixture 2 to 3 tablespoons at a time. When all the flour is added, beat the soft dough against the side of the bowl with a wooden spoon or with your hand

until the dough is very smooth and satiny, about 5 minutes. Cover the bowl with plastic wrap or a kitchen towel and let the dough rise in a warm place until doubled in size, about 1½ hours.

3. Butter a 4-cup ring mold and dust it with 1 tablespoon of the sugar. Punch down the dough, divide it into small pieces and arrange them evenly inside the ring mold. Cover the mold with plastic wrap and let stand in a warm place until the dough rises to the top of the mold, about 45 minutes. Meanwhile, preheat the oven to 400°.

4. Sprinkle 1 tablespoon of the sugar over the top of the dough. Bake for 20 to 25 minutes, or until golden brown. Let the cake rest on a wire rack for 5 minutes.

5. Meanwhile, in a small saucepan, combine 1½ cups of the remaining sugar with 1½ cups of water. Bring to a boil over high heat, stirring to dissolve the sugar. Remove from the heat and add ¼ cup of the Grand Marnier.

6. Unmold the cake; you may need to pry the edges loose with the blade of a blunt knife. Return the hot cake to the mold. Prick the top of the cake all over with a fork and gradually drizzle ½ cup of the syrup over the cake. Invert the cake onto a platter, remove the mold and prick the top with a fork and drizzle with another ½ cup of the syrup. Add the remaining Grand Marnier to the syrup left in the pan and set aside.

7. In a small saucepan, combine the remaining 1 tablespoon milk and 1 tablespoon sugar. Bring to a boil over moderate heat, stirring to dissolve the sugar. Brush this glaze all over the cake. Decorate the top with the glacéed fruits. *(The cake can be made 1 day ahead. Wrap in plastic and set aside at room temperature.)*

8. Shortly before serving, fill the center of the cake with the whipped cream. Serve with the remaining Grand Marnier syrup in a sauceboat on the side.
—Lydie Marshall

Poppy Seed Tante Cake

Made solely with egg whites, the starkness of this cake creates a striking contrast to the blue-black poppy seeds.

Makes One 9-Inch Round Cake

1 vanilla bean
⅔ cup milk
⅔ cup poppy seeds
1⅔ cups cake flour
2 teaspoons baking powder
½ teaspoon salt
1½ sticks (6 ounces) unsalted butter, softened
1¼ cups superfine sugar
4 egg whites, at room temperature
Cream Cheese Icing (p. 177)

1. Slit the vanilla bean lengthwise and cut off the tips. In a small saucepan, scald the milk with the vanilla bean. In a small bowl, combine the scalded milk, vanilla bean and poppy seeds. Let cool to room temperature. Scrape the inside of the vanilla bean into the milk mixture and discard the pod.

2. Preheat the oven to 325°. Butter a 9-by-2-inch round cake pan. Sift together the flour, baking powder and salt into a medium bowl.

3. In a large mixer bowl, beat the butter on high speed until light and fluffy, about 2 minutes. Gradually add 1 cup of the sugar and continue to beat until very light and creamy, about 5 minutes. Sift in one-third of the flour mixture; stir to combine. Beat in half of the milk-poppy seed mixture. Repeat 2 more times with

the remaining dry ingredients and milk.

4. In a medium bowl, beat the egg whites on medium speed until frothy. Add a pinch of salt and continue beating until soft peaks form, about 2 minutes. Beat in the remaining ¼ cup sugar, 1 teaspoon at a time, increasing the speed to high before adding the last 2 teaspoons. Beat until the meringue is stiff and shiny, about 1 minute. Fold one-fourth of the meringue into the cake batter. Fold in the remaining meringue.

5. Scrape the batter into the prepared pan and bake for 50 to 55 minutes, or until a tester inserted into the center comes out clean. Let cool in the pan on a rack for 10 minutes. Remove the cake from the pan and let cool, right-side up, on the rack. *(The cake can be baked up to 1 day in advance, wrapped in plastic and stored at room temperature, or frozen for up to 1 month.)*

6. Using a long serrated knife, trim off the crusty top of the cake. Slice the cake horizontally into 3 even layers; set aside the middle layer to use as the top. Place the bottom layer on the inverted cake pan. Spread ¾ cup of the Cream Cheese Icing over the bottom cake layer. Repeat with the second cake layer. Top the cake with the middle layer. Frost the sides of the cake with a thin layer of icing. Refrigerate for 10 minutes, then refrost the sides with enough Cream Cheese Icing to cover completely. If desired, use a pastry bag fitted with a #2 star tip to pipe a decorative border of icing around the top edge of the cake.
—Peggy Cullen

Traditional Roast Stuffed Turkey with Pan Gravy (p. 60).

Coconut Cake with Divinity Icing (p. 179).

Cream Cheese Icing

Makes About 2½ Cups

11 ounces cream cheese, at
  room temperature
2 sticks (8 ounces) unsalted
  butter, at room temperature
1 vanilla bean, split
  lengthwise
¾ cup confectioners' sugar,
  sifted

1. In a medium mixer bowl, beat the cream cheese until light and fluffy. With the mixer on low speed, gradually beat in the butter until well blended, about 4 minutes.

2. Scrape the seeds from the inside of the vanilla bean into the mixture; discard the pod. Sift in the confectioners' sugar and continue to beat on low speed, scraping the bowl frequently, until well blended, about 2 minutes. Refrigerate until ready to use, but do not let harden.
—*Peggy Cullen*

Pecan-Bourbon Torte with
Bourbon Buttercream
Frosting

12 to 14 Servings

Torte:
4 eggs, separated
1 cup sugar
3 tablespoons bourbon
1⅓ cups (6 ounces) ground
  pecans

Buttercream Frosting:
3 egg yolks
1 tablespoon bourbon
¼ teaspoon vanilla extract
Pinch of salt
⅓ cup sugar

6 tablespoons butter, cut into
  ½-inch pieces, at room
  temperature

Decoration:
1½ ounces bittersweet or
  semisweet chocolate
Candied violets (optional)

1. Make the torte: Preheat the oven to 325°. Lightly butter the bottom of a 9-inch springform pan.

2. In a large bowl, beat the egg yolks, sugar and bourbon until the mixture is light and frothy. In another bowl, beat the egg whites until stiff but not dry. Spoon the beaten whites onto the yolk mixture, sprinkle the nuts on top of the whites and fold gently just until no streaks of white remain.

3. Pour the batter into the springform pan; gently smooth the top with a rubber spatula. Bake in the middle of the oven for about 30 minutes, or until the edges of the cake pull away from the pan and the center springs back when lightly touched. Cool the torte completely before removing it from the pan; the layer will be about 1½ inches high.

4. Prepare the buttercream frosting: In a medium bowl, beat the egg yolks, bourbon, vanilla and salt with an electric mixer on medium speed for 2 to 3 minutes, until the mixture begins to thicken.

5. In a small saucepan, combine the sugar with 2 tablespoons of water. Bring to a boil over moderate heat, using a wet pastry brush to wash down any crystals of sugar that cling to the sides of the pan. Reduce the heat to low and simmer until the syrup reaches 250° on a candy thermometer, or until a drop of syrup forms a firm ball when dropped into a glass of cold water, about 5 to 7 minutes.

6. Gradually beat the hot syrup into the egg yolk mixture in a slow, steady stream; continue to beat on medium speed until cooled to room temperature, 2 to 3 minutes. Add the butter, 2 or 3 pieces at a time, and beat on low speed for 5 minutes, or until the butter is thoroughly incorporated and the mixture is completely smooth. Chill for 30 to 45 minutes, until the frosting is of spreading consistency.

7. Frost and decorate the torte: Spread the buttercream evenly over the sides and top of the torte. Refrigerate until the frosting has set (about 30 minutes) before decorating.

8. Melt the chocolate in a double boiler over simmering water. Remove the pan from the heat. Let the chocolate cool for 5 minutes.

9. Make a paper cone: Tear off a 12-inch length of wax paper; fold diagonally in half to make a triangle. Roll up tightly to form a cone that is almost sealed at the tip. Tape the outside so the cone doesn't unfold.

10. Fill the cone with the melted chocolate and fold down the top to seal. Trim the tip on a diagonal to create a ⅛-inch opening and pipe the chocolate onto the frosted torte in concentric circles. Decorate with candied violets, if you wish. Refrigerate if not served immediately. Then let stand at room temperature for 15 to 20 minutes before serving.
—*Maria Piccolo & Rosalee
Harris*

Chocolate Raspberry Fudge Cake

Everyone should be treated to a bit of chocolate during the holidays. After the cake is glazed, let it sit at room temperature for at least two hours so that it retains its shine. Then refrigerate overnight, loosely covered, so that the texture becomes fudgy and the flavors mellow.

10 Servings

Cake:
4 ounces hazelnuts
1 stick (4 ounces) tablespoon unsalted butter, at room temperature
½ cup plus 2 tablespoons sugar
5 large eggs, separated
6 ounces imported semisweet chocolate, finely chopped
2 tablespoons unbleached all-purpose flour
1 tablespoon sirop de framboise or cassis (optional)
Pinch of salt
¼ teaspoon cream of tartar

Chocolate Glaze:
¾ cup heavy cream
7 ounces imported semisweet chocolate
2 teaspoons sirop de framboise or cassis (optional)

For Serving:
1 cup raspberries
Crème fraîche, for serving

1. Make the cake: Preheat the oven to 350°. Place the hazelnuts on a small baking sheet and bake until the skins crack, about 10 minutes. Transfer the hot nuts to a kitchen towel and rub them together to remove the skins. Finely chop enough nuts to yield 3 tablespoons; set aside in a small bowl. Coarsely chop the remaining nuts, place in another small bowl and set aside.

2. Lightly butter the bottom of a 9½-by-3-inch springform pan and line the bottom with wax paper. Butter the paper and dust lightly with flour, tapping out any excess.

3. In a large bowl, using an electric mixer, cream the stick of butter with ½ cup plus 1 tablespoon of the sugar until pale and light, about 2 minutes. Add the egg yolks one at a time, beating well after each addition; set aside.

4. In a small metal bowl set over simmering water or in a double boiler, melt the chocolate. Remove from the heat and let cool for 3 minutes. Stir the chocolate into the butter and egg mixture until blended.

5. Mix the flour into the finely chopped hazelnuts and fold into the batter. Fold in the framboise.

6. In a large bowl, using an electric mixer, beat the egg whites with the salt just until soft peaks form, about 1 minute. Add the cream of tartar and the remaining 1 tablespoon sugar and continue beating until stiff, glossy peaks form, about 1½ minutes. Gently fold the egg whites into the batter until thoroughly incorporated.

7. Pour the batter into the prepared pan and smooth the surface. Bake in the middle of the oven for 30 minutes, or until the cake puffs up and cracks appear on the surface. Transfer to a rack and let cool for 30 minutes.

8. Remove the sides of the springform pan and invert the cooled cake on a wire rack. Carefully remove the bottom of the pan and peel off the wax paper. Invert the cake onto another rack and let cool completely before glazing. The cake will fall to about 1 inch as it cools.

9. Meanwhile, make the glaze: In a medium saucepan, warm the cream over low heat, about 2 minutes. Add the chocolate and cook, stirring constantly, until smooth and creamy, about 2 minutes longer. Remove from the heat and stir in the framboise. *(Set aside covered at room temperature for up to 1 day.)* Warm before using.

10. Carefully transfer the cake to a large serving plate. Pour the warm glaze on the center of the cake and, using a long narrow spatula, spread it evenly over the top and sides of the cake. *(The cake can be prepared to this point up to 1 day ahead. Once the glaze sets, loosely cover the cake and refrigerate.)*

11. Before serving, sprinkle the reserved coarsely chopped hazelnuts over the cake. Decoratively arrange the raspberries on top. Serve in wedges and pass the crème fraîche separately.
—*Sheila Lukins*

Buttermilk Chocolate Fudge Cake

This is my favorite recipe for chocolate cake. It is simple to prepare and absolutely delicious. Frost it with whipped cream or your favorite icing. Because of its rich, dense texture, the cake is at its best when served at room temperature.

Makes One 10-Inch Cake

4 ounces unsweetened chocolate
2 sticks (8 ounces) unsalted butter, softened
1¾ cups (packed) dark brown sugar
3 eggs
1 teaspoon vanilla extract
1½ cups all-purpose flour
½ teaspoon baking soda
½ teaspoon baking powder

⅛ teaspoon salt
1 cup buttermilk, at room
temperature

1. Preheat the oven to 350°. Butter the bottom and sides of a 10-inch springform pan. Line the bottom with parchment or wax paper. Butter the paper and dust the pan with flour.

2. Put the chocolate in a double boiler over hot water; let stand, stirring occasionally, until melted and smooth. Set aside to cool.

3. In a large mixer bowl, beat the butter until lightly and fluffy. With the mixer on high speed, gradually beat in the brown sugar until well blended and light, about 8 minutes. Add the eggs, 1 at a time, beating well after each addition. Beat in the cooled chocolate and the vanilla.

4. In a large bowl, sift together the flour, baking soda, baking powder and salt. On low speed, beat one-third of the dry ingredients into the chocolate mixture until well blended. Beat in one-third of the buttermilk. Repeat 2 more times with the remaining dry ingredients and buttermilk.

5. Scrape the batter into the prepared pan and smooth the surface. Bake for 1 hour and 10 minutes, or until a cake tester inserted in the center comes out clean. Let cool on a rack for 10 minutes before unmolding. Let cool completely before frosting. *(The cake can be prepared 1 day ahead. Cover with plastic wrap and set aside at room temperature, or freeze for up to 1 month. Let the cake return to room temperature before frosting.)*
—*Mimi Ruth Brodeur*

Coconut Cake with Divinity Icing

The recipe for this cake was given to me by Mrs. Curtis McCaskill of Laurel, Mississippi, who is noted thereabouts for her desserts. It makes a very large cake with a marvelous old-fashioned flavor that is delicious served with fruit.

12 to 18 Servings

3 cups sifted all-purpose flour
¼ teaspoon baking soda
2 sticks (8 ounces) unsalted
    butter, softened
3 cups granulated sugar
6 eggs, at room temperature
1 cup sour cream
½ teaspoon vanilla extract
1 teaspoon coconut extract
Divinity Icing (recipe follows)
4 cups unsweetened shredded
    coconut, preferably fresh

1. Preheat the oven to 350°. Grease and lightly flour a 10-inch tube pan or 12-cup bundt pan. Into a medium bowl, sift together the flour and baking soda.

2. In a large mixer bowl, beat the butter and granulated sugar until light and fluffy, about 5 minutes. Add the eggs, one at a time, beating well after each addition. With a rubber spatula, fold in one-third of the flour, half the sour cream, half the remaining flour and then the remaining sour cream and flour. Stir in the vanilla and coconut extracts and pour the batter in the prepared pan.

3. Bake until a cake tester inserted in the center comes out clean, about 1 hour and 15 minutes. Let the cake cool completely on a rack before unmolding. Frost with Divinity Icing. Sprinkle the coconut over the cake.
—*Lee Bailey*

Divinity Icing

Makes About 3 Cups

2 cups sugar
¼ teaspoon cream of tartar
3 egg whites
1½ teaspoons vanilla extract

1. In a medium saucepan, combine the sugar, cream of tartar and ½ cup plus 1 tablespoon of water. Place over moderately high heat and cook, stirring to dissolve the sugar. Bring to a boil and cook without stirring until the syrup reaches a temperature of 238°, about 8 minutes.

2. Meanwhile, in a large bowl, beat the egg whites with an electric mixer until stiff not dry. Slowly beat about one-third of the hot syrup into the egg whites in a thin stream. Return the remaining syrup to a boil and cook until it reaches 248°, about 5 minutes. Beat half of the syrup into the egg whites. Return the remaining syrup to the heat and boil until it reaches 268°, about 5 minutes. Beat into the egg whites. Beat in the vanilla and beat until the frosting is thick but still spreadable, about 3 minutes.
—*Lee Bailey*

Double Vanilla Pound Cake with Walnut Butter

Store this cake, tightly wrapped, at room temperature. It tastes even better the next day, after the flavors have had a chance to mellow. It also freezes well.

10 Servings

Cake:
2¼ cups all-purpose flour
1½ teaspoons baking powder
½ teaspoon baking soda
½ teaspoon salt

¼ teaspoon freshly grated
 nutmeg
1½ sticks (6 ounces) unsalted
 butter, at room temperature
1 cup (firmly packed) brown
 sugar
1 vanilla bean
2 eggs, separated
1½ teaspoons vanilla extract
1 cup plain yogurt

Walnut Butter:
½ cup walnuts
1 stick (4 ounces) unsalted
 butter, at room temperature
2 tablespoons confectioners'
 sugar
½ teaspoon vanilla extract
Pinch of salt

1. Make the cake: Preheat the oven to 350°. Lightly butter a 9-by-5-by-3-inch loaf pan.

2. Sift together the flour, baking powder and soda, salt and nutmeg.

3. In a large bowl, cream the butter and brown sugar with a wooden spoon until light and fluffy. Cut the vanilla bean in half crosswise. Reserve one half of the bean for the walnut butter. Split the other half lengthwise and scrape the seeds out of the pod into the butter-brown sugar mixture. Add the egg yolks and vanilla extract and beat to blend thoroughly.

4. Alternately stir one-fourth of the dry ingredients and one-third of the yogurt into the butter-brown sugar mixture, beating until blended after each addition. Beat the egg whites until stiff but not dry. Fold them into the batter. Turn the batter into the prepared pan.

5. Bake in the middle of the oven for 1 hour and 10 minutes to 1 hour and 15 minutes, or until a toothpick inserted in the center comes out clean. Cool in the pan on a rack at least 30 minutes. Remove the cake from the pan and let cool completely.

6. Prepare the walnut butter: In a food processor, coarsely chop the walnuts, about 5 to 10 seconds. Add the butter and the confectioners' sugar and blend for 10 seconds. Add the vanilla extract and salt and scrape the seeds from the reserved vanilla bean half into the butter. Blend for 5 to 10 seconds longer, until all the ingredients are thoroughly combined. Scrape into a crock or small bowl and refrigerate until needed. Let soften to spreading consistency before serving.

7. Serve the pound cake in slices, accompanied by the walnut butter.
—Maria Piccolo

Bûche de Noël

8 to 10 Servings

1⅓ cups granulated sugar
3 egg whites
Pinch of salt
⅛ teaspoon cream of tartar
12 ounces semisweet
 chocolate, coarsely chopped
⅓ cup strong freshly brewed
 coffee
1 tablespoon vanilla extract
2 to 3 tablespoons dark rum,
 to taste
1 stick (4 ounces) unsalted
 butter, softened
Orange Sponge Cake (recipe
 follows)

3 tablespoons unsweetened
 cocoa powder
1 tablespoon confectioners'
 sugar
Spun Caramel Veil (p. 181)

1. Preheat the oven to 200°. Lightly butter and flour a baking sheet.

2. In a medium saucepan, bring the granulated sugar and ½ cup of water to a boil over moderately high heat. Remove from the heat and swirl until the sugar is dissolved and the liquid is completely clear, about 1 minute. Return the saucepan to the heat, cover tightly and cook until the syrup reaches 238° on a candy thermometer or until a spoonful of syrup dropped into a glass of cold water forms a soft ball, about 5 minutes.

3. Meanwhile, in a medium mixer bowl, beat the egg whites with the salt and cream of tartar until soft peaks form.

4. Gradually beat in the hot sugar syrup in a thin stream. Increase the speed to high and beat until the meringue is cool and very firm, about 5 minutes.

5. Scoop one-fourth of the meringue into a pastry bag fitted with a ⅜-inch plain tip and pipe eight to ten ½-inch domes onto the prepared baking sheet to make "mushroom caps." Hold a ⅛-inch plain pastry tip over the end of the other tip and pipe out eight to ten ¾-inch high conical shapes for the "mushroom stems." (Pipe any meringue remaining in the pastry bag back into the bowl.) Bake for 1 hour, or until the meringues are dry and can be easily removed from the baking pan.

6. In a double boiler over hot water, combine the chocolate and coffee. Let stand, stirring occasionally, until melted and smooth. Remove from the heat and let cool completely.

7. Beat the melted chocolate, vanilla, rum and 4 tablespoons of the softened butter into the meringue. Transfer two-thirds of the mixture to a medium bowl and refrigerate; this is the frosting. Beat the remaining 4 tablespoons butter into the remaining mixture, which will be used as the filling.

8. Unroll the Orange Sponge Cake and spread evenly with the unchilled chocolate filling, leaving a ½-inch border free on all sides. Using the wax paper to help lift, roll up the cake from a short edge to form a 12-inch log.

9. Slice a narrow slanting piece from each end of the log. Carve out a slight indent in the upper side of the log and insert an end-piece to simulate a bump or knot. With 2 long spatulas, transfer the cake to a large platter and slip sheets of wax paper under the sides and ends to catch any frosting spills.

10. Beat 2 tablespoons plus 2 teaspoons of the cocoa into the chilled chocolate frosting. Using a long metal spatula, spread all but 1 tablespoon of the frosting evenly over the cake, leaving the two ends uncovered. Run the tines of a fork, or the spatula, lengthwise across the frosting to simulate bark.

11. Using a small sharp paring knife, pierce a small hole in the bottom of each mushroom cap. Insert a dab of reserved frosting and gently press the pointed end of a meringue stem into place. Repeat with the remaining frosting, mushroom caps and stems.

12. Arrange the mushrooms in clusters on the log, sift on the confectioners' sugar to resemble snow, and dust the tops of the mushrooms with the remaining 1 teaspoon cocoa powder. To complete the picture, drape bunches of the Spun Caramel Veil over the log.
—*Julia Child*

Orange Sponge Cake

Makes One 12-by-18-Inch Cake

¾ *cup blanched almonds (4½ ounces)*
¾ *cup plus 2 tablespoons granulated sugar*
3 eggs, separated
2 teaspoons grated orange zest
2½ tablespoons fresh orange juice
¼ teaspoon almond extract
½ cup cake flour
3 tablespoons confectioners' sugar

1. Preheat the oven to 375°. Lightly butter a 12-by-18-inch jelly-roll pan. Line the bottom and sides with wax paper, leaving a 2-inch overhang at each end. Butter and flour the paper.

2. In a food processor or blender, finely grind the almonds and 3 tablespoons of the granulated sugar.

3. In a medium mixer bowl, beat the egg yolks with ½ cup of the granulated sugar on high speed until pale and thick, about 4 minutes. Beat in the orange zest, orange juice, ground almonds and the almond extract. Slowly sift and stir in the flour until blended.

4. In a medium bowl, beat the egg whites until soft peaks form. Beat in the remaining 3 tablespoons granulated sugar, 1 tablespoon at a time, until stiff.

5. Stir one-fourth of the beaten egg whites into the almond batter to lighten it, then gently fold in the remaining whites. Scrape the batter into the prepared pan and spread into the corners. Bake for 8 to 10 minutes, until the cake is very pale gold in color and the top is springy to the touch. (Do not overbake or the cake will crack when rolled.)

6. Evenly sift 1½ tablespoons of the confectioners' sugar over the top of the cake. Cover with a sheet of wax paper and a lightly dampened towel. Invert the pan onto a tray or baking sheet to unmold the cake; peel off the wax paper. Sift the remaining 1½ tablespoons confectioners' sugar evenly over the cake.

7. Starting from a short edge, roll up the cake with the towel and paper inside to form a 12-inch log. Wrap the cake in plastic wrap and refrigerate until chilled. *(The cake can be prepared 2 to 3 days in advance or frozen for up to 1 month.)*
—*Julia Child*

Spun Caramel Veil

Makes Enough for One Bûche de Noël

1 cup sugar
3 tablespoons light corn syrup

1. Set a clean broomstick handle across a table, with about 2 feet extending over the table edge. Spread a few layers of newspaper beneath the protruding handle to protect the floor.

2. In a small saucepan, combine the sugar, corn syrup and ⅓ cup of water. Stir over moderately low heat until the sugar is dissolved, about 3 minutes. Cover tightly and cook over moderately high heat for 5 minutes. Remove the lid and boil until the mixture turns a pale amber, about 5

more minutes. Let cool for 1 minute, or until it forms strands when lifted with a fork.

3. Place the caramel near the broomstick and, working quickly, dip the fork into the caramel and wave it over the broomstick to form long hanging threads of caramel. Repeat until you have a bunch of threads. If the caramel hardens too quickly, melt it again over moderate heat for 1 or 2 minutes.
—*Julia Child*

Bûche de Saint Bruno

A pastry yule log is as strong a tradition in France as Christmas pudding in England. This version is refreshingly perfumed by all the alpine herbs gathered by the monks of the La Grande Chartreuse Monastery to flavor their old and famous liqueur.

12 Servings

Decoration:
½ cup sliced almonds
1 tablespoon unsalted butter
½ cup shelled, unsalted pistachios
1 cup mixed candied fruit, finely diced
2 tablespoons green Chartreuse liqueur

Cake:
7 eggs
1 cup granulated sugar
2 tablespoons unsalted butter, softened
3 tablespoons brandy or dark rum
1½ cups all-purpose flour
3 teaspoons baking powder
⅛ teaspoon salt

Meringue "Mushrooms":
2 egg whites
1½ cups granulated sugar
⅛ teaspoon salt

½ cup confectioners' sugar
1 tablespoon rum or brandy

Filling:
1½ cups mixed candied fruit, finely diced
¼ cup green Chartreuse liqueur
2 cups heavy cream
⅔ cup confectioners' sugar
3 tablespoons unsalted butter, softened

Frosting:
1 cup heavy cream
⅓ cup confectioners' sugar
2 tablespoons unsalted butter, softened
2 tablespoons green Chartreuse liqueur

1. Make the decoration: In a skillet, cook the almonds in the butter over medium heat, stirring, until almonds are slightly golden. Let cool.

2. In a food processor, mix the almonds and pistachio nuts and pulse on and off until the mixture is in coarse bits resembling bark and moss. Mix with the candied fruit and Chartreuse and set aside.

3. Make the cake: Separate 3 of the eggs. In a mixer bowl, combine the 4 whole eggs with the 3 egg yolks and the granulated sugar. Beat until light and lemon-colored. Then add the softened butter and beat for 1 minute. The mixture will be bubbly. Add the rum and beat for 30 seconds at high speed.

4. Sift the flour with the baking powder; sift the dry ingredients over the egg mixture and beat until well incorporated.

5. In another bowl, beat the 3 egg whites with the salt until firm peaks form. Fold the egg whites into the batter and beat for 1 minute at low speed.

6. Preheat the oven to 350°.

Grease a jelly-roll pan measuring 15½ by 10½ inches. Line the pan with aluminum foil and butter the foil. Pour the batter into the pan, smooth the top and bake for 12 minutes, or until very lightly golden.

7. Meanwhile, dampen 3 thicknesses of paper towels, using enough towels to cover the baking pan completely.

8. Remove the cake from the oven and immediately lay the damp paper towels over it. Then lay dry paper towels over the damp ones and invert a baking sheet over the dry towels. Turn everything over and unmold the cake from the foil.

9. Starting with a short end, roll the cake up, together with the paper towels. Let the cake cool at room temperature.

10. Meanwhile, make the "mushrooms": Preheat the oven to 350°. In a medium bowl, beat the egg whites with the granulated sugar and salt just until mixed. Set the bowl over a pan of warm water and let sit, stirring from time to time, until tepid, about 10 minutes. Whip the egg whites until soft peaks form, about 3 minutes. Leave the egg whites over the pan of warm water.

11. Lightly butter and flour a large cookie sheet. Put the meringue into a pastry bag with a small plain tip and make about 10 little elongated meringues (these will be the mushroom stems) on the cookie sheet, 1 inch apart. (Vary their size.) With a teaspoon, shape 10 smoothly rounded heaps for the caps.

12. Lower the oven temperature to 200° and bake the meringues for 6 minutes. Turn off the heat. (The meringues will look cooked, but they are not.) Let them dry for 20 minutes in the oven. The remove and cool completely.

13. To assemble the mushrooms: Mix the confectioners' sugar and

rum into a thick paste. Attach the meringue stems to the caps with the paste. Let dry. *(The mushrooms can be made several days ahead.)*

14. Meanwhile, make the filling: In a medium bowl, toss the fruit and liqueur together and set aside to macerate for 1 hour.

15. In a mixer bowl, blend the cream, confectioners' sugar and butter and beat until thick. Drain the macerated fruit well and stir into the filling. Set the bowl in the freezer for about 15 minutes; do not let it freeze hard.

16. Assemble the cake: Unroll the cake and remove the paper towels. Spread the filling over the cake and roll up again, being sure not to use any pressure. Wrap in heavy-duty foil and place in the freezer for at least 2 hours, or for up to 10 days.

17. Make the frosting: Within a day of serving the cake, beat the cream, confectioners' sugar, butter and Chartreuse together until the mixture is firm. Frost the cake and return to the freezer for 1 hour to harden the frosting. Then, with the point of a knife, make slightly wavy lengthwise "bark" lines in the coating. Sprinkle with the reserved fruit-nut mixture, wrap loosely and return to the freezer. *(The cake may be stored overnight, or for as long as 10 days.)*

18. Remove from freezer about 15 minutes before serving. When the surface has softened a little, stick the "mushrooms" onto the log in clumps.

—Monique Guillaume

Peach and Ginger Trifle

This trifle has an angel food cake flavored with fresh ginger as its base. The fresh, snappy ginger taste goes well with almost any fruit you might choose to use.

12 to 14 Servings

*Ginger Angel Food Cake
    (p. 168)
Lemon Custard (p. 197)
8 peaches, peeled and sliced
    or 2 packages (16 ounces
    each) frozen unsweetened
    peach slices, thawed
1 cup heavy cream*

1. Using a large serrated knife, slice the Ginger Angel Food Cake horizontally into 3 rings. Cut each ring into 8 wedges. Line the bottom of a 3½- to 4-quart glass serving bowl with 8 of the cake wedges. Spoon about half of the Lemon Custard over the cake.

2. Reserve 1½ cups of the prettiest peach slices for garnish. Arrange the remaining peach slices over the custard. Line the sides of the bowl with 8 more wedges of cake, overlapping if necessary. Place the remaining cake wedges over the peaches and press gently. Spoon the rest of the Lemon Custard over the top and smooth the surface with the back of the spoon. Arrange the reserved peach slices decoratively on top.

3. Refrigerate for at least 6 hours before serving so that the cake softens and the flavors mellow. *(The recipe can be made to this point up to 1 day ahead.)*

4. Whip the cream until stiff. Spoon or pipe over the top.

—Marion Cunningham

Cranberry Jelly Roll

This is the best cake roll recipe I know. It is also the simplest, eliminating the usual time-consuming separate handling of egg yolks and whites. Tart and sweet, this dessert is good after a rich meal.

10 Servings

*½ cup cake flour
½ teaspoon baking powder
¼ teaspoon salt
5 eggs
½ cup granulated sugar
1 teaspoon vanilla extract
2 to 3 tablespoons
    confectioners' sugar, for
    dusting
Cranberry Jelly (p. 151), at
    room temperature
Sweetened whipped cream,
    for garnish*

1. Preheat the oven to 350°. Grease a 15½-by-10½-by-1-inch jelly-roll pan and line with wax paper. Grease and lightly flour the wax paper. Mix the flour, baking powder and salt in a bowl, stirring with a fork to blend well.

2. In a medium mixer bowl, beat the eggs and granulated sugar at high speed until pale, fluffy and light, about 4 minutes. Gradually add the flour mixture and the vanilla and beat on low speed for just a few seconds. Finish folding the flour into the egg mixture with a rubber spatula until no white streaks show.

3. Spread the batter evenly in the jelly-roll pan. Bake for 12 minutes, or until the top of the cake is golden. Spread a kitchen towel (larger than the cake) on the counter, with the long side nearest you, and sift some of the confectioners' sugar on top.

4. Invert the warm cake onto the prepared towel. Remove the wax paper and discard. Roll the cake in the

towel from the long side. Transfer to a rack to cool. Leave the cake rolled up until you are ready to fill it.

5. To assemble, gently unroll the cake and spread the Cranberry Jelly right to the edges. Reroll the cake and place on a serving dish, seam-side down. Dust the top with the remaining confectioners' sugar. Slice the jelly roll and serve with sweetened whipped cream.

—Marion Cunningham

Pumpkin Cheesecake

14 to 16 Servings

2 tablespoons butter, softened
⅓ cup gingersnap crumbs
4 packages (8 ounces each) cream cheese, at room temperature
1½ cups (firmly packed) dark brown sugar
5 eggs
¼ cup all-purpose flour
1 teaspoon cinnamon
1 teaspoon allspice
¼ teaspoon ground ginger
¼ teaspoon salt
1 can (16-ounces) unsweetened solid-pack pumpkin
Maple syrup and walnut halves, for garnish
Unsweetened whipped cream (optional)

1. Generously butter a 9-inch springform pan with the softened butter. Sprinkle the gingersnap crumbs into the pan and shake to coat the bottom and sides evenly.

2. Preheat the oven to 325°. In a large bowl, beat the cream cheese with a wooden spoon until fluffy. Gradually beat in the brown sugar. Add the eggs, 1 at a time, mixing thoroughly after each addition. Sift in the flour, cinnamon, allspice, gin-

ger and salt. Blend well. Beat in the pumpkin puree. Pour the batter into the prepared pan.

3. Bake in the center of the oven for 1½ to 1¾ hours, until the cake pulls away from the sides of the pan and a toothpick inserted in the center comes out clean. Remove from the oven and cool in the pan on a rack for 1 hour. Carefully remove the ring from the springform and let the cake finish cooling to room temperature. Refrigerate, covered, until chilled.

4. Brush the top of the cake with maple syrup and garnish with walnuts. Serve with whipped cream, if desired.

—Maria Piccolo

Gingerbread Cheesecake Swirl

8 to 12 Servings

1 pound cream cheese, at room temperature
½ teaspoon vanilla extract
4 eggs
½ cup plus 2 tablespoons granulated sugar
¼ cup light unsulphured molasses
4 tablespoons unsalted butter, at room temperature
1 teaspoon ground ginger
1 teaspoon cinnamon
⅓ teaspoon freshly grated nutmeg
⅛ teaspoon ground cloves
¼ teaspoon salt
½ cup (packed) light brown sugar
1½ teaspoons baking soda
1 cup all-purpose flour

1. Preheat the oven to 350°. Butter a 9-inch springform pan. In a mixer bowl, beat the cream cheese on high speed until light and smooth, about 3 minutes. With the mixer on,

beat in the vanilla. Add 2 of the eggs, 1 at a time, beating until thoroughly blended. Gradually add the granulated sugar and beat until the mixture is light and fluffy, about 3 minutes; set aside.

2. In a medium saucepan, heat the molasses over low heat until bubbles begin to form around the sides. Remove from the heat and stir in the butter, 1 tablespoon at a time, until completely blended. Scrape the molasses into a medium bowl and stir in the ginger, cinnamon, nutmeg, cloves and salt. Add the brown sugar and beat with a wooden spoon until smooth. Let the mixture cool to room temperature.

3. Beat the remaining 2 eggs into the batter, one at a time, until well blended. Stir in the baking soda, then beat in the flour in three batches until completely incorporated.

4. Using a tablespoon, drop half the gingerbread batter in dollops into the prepared pan. Use one-fourth of the reserved cream cheese mixture to fill in the empty spaces. Dollop the remaining gingerbread batter on top of the cream cheese mounds. Fill in with another one-fourth of the cream cheese mixture. Swirl with the flat edge of a knife to marbleize the batters. (Be careful not to overmix.) Smooth the remaining cream cheese mixture over the top.

5. Bake in the middle of the oven for 50 minutes, or until the top of the cake begins to crack in the center. (The cake may be lumpy since the gingerbread rises and the cheesecake sinks.) Let cool to room temperature. Remove the sides of the springform pan, cover and refrigerate. Serve chilled.

—Linda Merinoff

Christmas Pudding

Christmas puddings may be made up to one year ahead. Aging improves the flavor. Store, tightly wrapped, in a cool, dry place. To serve, reheat by steaming for 1 to 2 hours.

As an alternative to steaming on top of the stove, this pudding can be placed in a deep roasting pan filled with boiling water to reach halfway up the sides of the pudding basin. Cover and steam in a 300° oven for 4 to 7 hours, depending on the size of the puddings, replenishing the boiling water at regular intervals.

16 Servings

2 cups dark raisins
2 cups golden raisins
2 cups dried currants
½ cup finely chopped
  blanched almonds (about 2
  ounces)
1½ cups (loosely packed)
  grated suet (about 4 ounces)
2 cups fresh bread crumbs
2 teaspoons grated orange
  zest
1 teaspoon grated lemon zest
½ cup (packed) brown sugar
½ cup grated carrot
1 cup all-purpose flour
1 teaspoon cinnamon
1 teaspoon freshly grated
  nutmeg
½ teaspoon ground ginger
¼ teaspoon ground cloves
4 eggs, lightly beaten
½ cup dark ale or milk
⅓ cup brandy
Brandy Sauce (recipe
  follows), Hard Sauce
  (p. 185) or whipped cream

1. In a large bowl, mix the dark and golden raisins, currants, almonds, suet, bread crumbs, orange and lemon zests, brown sugar and carrot. Sift in the flour, cinnamon, nutmeg, ginger and cloves; mix well. Stir in the eggs and ale until well blended.

2. Butter a 6- to 8-cup pudding basin. Line the bottom with a small circle of buttered wax paper. Spoon the pudding mixture into the basin. Cover with a sheet of buttered wax paper and a sheet of aluminum foil, pleated together in the center to allow for expansion. Twist and crimp the foil tightly around the rim or tie securely with string to seal. Tie the basin in a kitchen towel sling (see Note) and lower it onto a rack or folded towel in a steamer or large, deep pot filled with enough boiling water to reach halfway up the sides of the basin.

3. Cover and steam over moderate heat for 7 hours, replenishing the boiling water as needed, about every 30 minutes. This pudding will get darker the longer it steams.

4. Store the pudding in its basin, covered, until ready to use. Before serving, steam for up to 2 hours to reheat. Just before serving, unmold the pudding onto a platter. Heat the brandy, light it with a match and pour it over the top of the pudding. When the flames die out, cut the pudding into wedges and serve with Brandy Sauce, Hard Sauce or whipped cream.

NOTE: To make a "sling" with a kitchen towel, place the covered pudding basin in the center of a linen or cotton kitchen towel. Bring up two diagonal corners of the towel and knot the ends securely. Tie the other two corners of the towel in the same fashion.
—Diana Sturgis

Brandy Sauce

Makes About 1⅓ Cups

1 tablespoon cornstarch
1¼ cups milk
2 tablespoons sugar
1 tablespoon unsalted butter
3 tablespoons brandy

1. Place the cornstarch in a small, heavy saucepan. Blend in ¼ cup of the milk with a wooden spoon until smooth. Stir in the remaining milk; add the sugar and butter.

2. Bring the mixture to a boil over moderate heat, stirring constantly. Reduce the heat to low and simmer, stirring, for 4 minutes. Remove from the heat and stir in the brandy.

3. Pour into a sauceboat and serve at once; or pour into a small bowl, cover with waxed paper and hold in a saucepan of hot water for up to 1 hour.
—Diana Sturgis

Hard Sauce

To prepare the hard sauce well in advance, chill it until almost firm, form into a log 1 inch in diameter, wrap tightly and freeze.

Makes About 1 Cup

1 stick (4 ounces) unsalted
  butter, at room temperature
½ cup (packed) brown sugar
3 tablespoons brandy

Beat the butter with the sugar until they are soft and well combined. Gradually beat in the brandy. Place the sauce in a small crock and refrigerate it for at least 1 hour or for several days.
—Diana Sturgis

Golden Syrup and Ginger Pudding

This traditional English pudding is made with an imported product called Golden Syrup. You may use this or substitute a homemade facsimile for which we include a recipe.

6 Servings

Golden Syrup (recipe follows)
1 stick (4 ounces) unsalted
 butter, at room temperature
½ cup sugar
2 eggs, lightly beaten
1 cup plus 2 tablespoons all-
 purpose flour
1 teaspoon baking powder
1 teaspoon ground ginger
2 tablespoons milk
2 tablespoons diced (¼-inch)
 preserved ginger (optional)
Custard Sauce (p. 188)

1. Pour the Golden Syrup into the bottom of a buttered 4-cup pudding basin.

2. In a medium bowl, beat together the butter and sugar until they are pale and creamy. Beat in half of the eggs. Sift together the flour, baking powder and ground ginger and stir half of these dry ingredients into the egg mixture. Stir in the remaining eggs and then the rest of the dry ingredients. Stir in the milk and the preserved ginger.

3. Spoon the batter into the basin. Cover the basin with a sheet of buttered wax paper and a sheet of aluminum foil, pleated together in the center, to allow for expansion. Twist and crimp the ends tightly around the rim of the basin or tie securely with string. Place the basin in a kitchen towel sling (see Note) and lower it onto a rack or folded towel in a steamer or large, deep pot filled with enough boiling water to reach halfway up the sides of the basin.

4. Cover and steam the pudding over moderate heat for 1½ hours. Replenish with boiling water at regular intervals. To test for doneness at the end of the cooking time, remove from the heat, uncover and carefully raise an edge of the papers. Insert a skewer or sharp knife into the center; it should come out almost clean. If there is wet batter clinging to it, re-cover and steam the pudding a bit longer.

5. To serve, unmold the pudding with its syrup onto a serving platter. Cut into wedges and serve hot with Custard Sauce.

NOTE: To make a "sling" with a kitchen towel, place the covered pudding basin in the center of a linen or cotton kitchen towel. Bring up two diagonal corners of the towel and knot the ends securely. Tie the other two corners of the towel in the same fashion.
—*Diana Sturgis*

Golden Syrup

Makes About ⅓ Cup

¼ cup sugar
½ teaspoon distilled white
 vinegar or white wine
 vinegar
⅓ cup light corn syrup

1. Place the sugar in a small, heavy saucepan. Shake gently to form an even layer. Add the vinegar and 1 tablespoon of water. Cook, without stirring, over low heat for 5 minutes.

2. Increase the heat to moderate and cook for 5 minutes longer, or until the syrup has caramelized to a golden liquid. Immediately remove from the heat and pour in the corn syrup. The mixture will bubble up but do not stir. When all the bubbles have subsided, after 2 or 3 minutes, stir with a wooden spoon for a minute or so, until the caramel and corn syrup are thoroughly mixed.

3. Let cool to room temperature before using. If made ahead, store in a covered jar at room temperature.
—*Diana Sturgis*

Marbled Pudding

6 Servings

1 stick (4 ounces) unsalted
 butter, at room temperature
½ cup sugar
3 eggs, lightly beaten
1 cup plus 2 tablespoons
 all-purpose flour
1 teaspoon baking powder
½ teaspoon almond extract
⅓ cup semisweet chocolate
 chips
3 tablespoons milk
¼ cup unsweetened cocoa
 powder
½ teaspoon vanilla extract
Chocolate-Amaretto Sauce
 (recipe follows)

1. In a medium bowl, beat the butter and sugar with a wooden spoon until pale and creamy. Beat in half of the eggs. Sift together the flour and baking powder and stir half into the butter mixture. Stir in the remaining eggs and then the rest of the flour and baking powder. Transfer half of the batter to another bowl.

2. Add the almond extract and half of the chocolate chips to one bowl of batter; stir to mix well.

3. In a small bowl, stir the milk, cocoa and vanilla extract until blended. Add this cocoa mixture and the remaining chocolate chips to the second bowl of batter; stir to mix well.

4. Butter a 4-cup pudding basin. Drop alternating heaping tablespoons of batter from each bowl into the basin; it will be about three-fourths full.

5. Cover the basin with a sheet of buttered wax paper and a sheet of aluminum foil, pleated together in the center to allow for expansion. Twist and crimp the foil tightly around the rim or tie securely with string to seal. Tie the basin in a kitchen towel sling (see Note) and lower it onto a rack or folded towel in a steamer or large, deep pot filled with enough boiling water to reach halfway up the sides of the basin.

6. Cover and steam over moderate heat for 1½ hours, replenishing the boiling water at regular intervals. To check for doneness, remove from the heat, uncover and carefully raise an edge of the paper. Insert a skewer or sharp knife into the center of the pudding; it should come out almost clean. If there is wet batter clinging to it, replace the cover and steam the pudding a bit longer.

7. Unmold the pudding onto a platter. Serve hot with warm Chocolate-Amaretto Sauce.

NOTE: To make a "sling" with a kitchen towel, place the covered pudding basin in the center of a linen or cotton kitchen towel. Bring up two diagonal corners of the towel and knot the ends securely. Tie the other two corners of the towel in the same fashion.
—Diana Sturgis

Chocolate-Amaretto Sauce

This sauce is also marvelous at room temperature over ice cream.
Makes About ¾ Cup

2 ounces semisweet chocolate
1 tablespoon sugar
½ cup heavy cream
1 tablespoon unsalted butter
3 tablespoons amaretto
    liqueur

Place the chocolate, sugar and cream in a small, heavy saucepan. Warm gently over very low heat just until the chocolate melts. Whisk until the mixture is smooth. Do not allow the sauce to boil. Remove from the heat. Add the butter and stir until melted. Stir in the amaretto.
—Diana Sturgis

Apple Layer Pudding

A nice change from apple pie, this pudding also may be made with sweet pitted plums or sweetened rhubarb when they are in season.
6 Servings

Apple Filling:
1 pound tart cooking apples,
    such as Greening or Granny
    Smith—peeled, quartered,
    cored and cut into ¼-inch
    slices (about 3 cups)
3 tablespoons fresh lemon
    juice
1 teaspoon minced lemon zest
⅓ cup raisins
½ cup (packed) brown sugar
½ teaspoon cinnamon

Suet Pastry:
1 cup plus 2 tablespoons
    all-purpose flour
1 teaspoon baking powder
¼ teaspoon salt
⅔ cup (loosely packed) grated
    suet (about 2 ounces),
    chilled

*Custard Sauce (recipe
    follows), for serving*

1. Make the filling: Place the apples in a medium bowl and toss them with the lemon juice. Add the lemon zest, raisins, brown sugar and cinnamon and stir to mix.

2. Prepare the pastry: In a medium bowl, sift together the flour, baking powder and salt. Stir in the suet. Sprinkle 6 tablespoons of cold water over the surface and stir quickly and lightly with a fork to form a soft, but not sticky, dough; do not overmix.

3. Assemble the pudding: Turn the dough out onto a lightly floured surface and divide it into 3 slightly graduated pieces of dough. Roll out each circle ¼ inch thick. Place the smallest piece in the bottom of a well-buttered 4-cup pudding basin and top with half the apple mixture. Place the smaller of the remaining pastry circles over the apples, trim to fit the basin if necessary. Add the remaining apple mixture and any liquid from the apples. Top with the largest circle of pastry; trim to fit the inside of the basin if necessary.

4. Cover the basin with a sheet of buttered wax paper and a sheet of aluminum foil pleated together in the center to allow for expansion. Twist and crimp the foil tightly around the rim or tie securely with string to seal. Tie the basin in a kitchen towel sling (see Note) and lower the pudding into a steamer or large, deep pot filled with enough boiling water to reach halfway up the sides of the basin.

5. Cover and steam over moderate heat for 2 hours; replenish the boiling water at regular intervals.

6. Loosen the sides of the pudding with a knife. Unmold the pudding onto a serving platter and serve hot with Custard Sauce.

NOTE: To make a "sling" with a kitchen towel, place the covered pudding basin in the center of a linen or cotton kitchen towel. Bring up two diagonal corners of the towel and knot the ends securely. Tie the other two corners of the towel in the same fashion.

—Diana Sturgis

Custard Sauce

Makes About 1 Cup

1 whole egg
2 egg yolks
2 tablespoons sugar
1 cup milk
½ teaspoon vanilla extract

1. In a small bowl, beat the whole egg, egg yolks and 1 tablespoon of the sugar together until well blended.

2. In a double boiler, bring the milk to a boil with the remaining 1 tablespoon sugar. Remove from the heat and stir about 2 tablespoons of the hot milk into the egg mixture. Gradually stir the egg mixture into the remaining milk and cook over boiling water, stirring constantly with a wooden spoon, until the custard thickens enough to lightly coat the back of the spoon. Immediately transfer the saucepan to a bowl of ice water to stop the cooking. Stir in the vanilla. Serve warm.

—Diana Sturgis

Jam Roly-Poly

6 Servings

1½ cups all-purpose flour
1½ teaspoons baking powder
½ teaspoon salt
1 cup (loosely packed) grated suet (2½ ounces), chilled
¾ cup plum jam, at room temperature
Custard Sauce (at left)

1. Sift the flour, baking powder and salt into a medium bowl. Add the suet, toss with a fork and stir in enough cold water (about ⅔ cup) to make a soft, but not sticky, dough; do not overmix.

2. Turn the dough out onto a lightly floured surface and roll out into an 8-by-10-inch rectangle. Spread the dough to within 1 inch of the edges with the jam.

3. Dampen the edges of the dough with water and roll up from one of the long sides like a jelly roll. Press along the seam and at both ends to seal in the jam. Tear off a sheet of aluminum foil 16 inches long. Lay a sheet of wax paper the same size on top of the foil and butter the wax paper. Place the jam roll lengthwise in the center of the paper. Fold and crimp the edges of both sheets to seal, leaving room around the roll to allow for expansion.

4. Place a rack in a large steamer or turkey roaster. Add enough boiling water to come just below the rack. Lower the jam roll onto the rack, cover and steam over moderate heat for 1½ hours, replenishing the water at regular intervals.

5. Remove the foil and wax paper and place the pudding on a platter. Cut into slices and serve hot with Custard Sauce.

—Diana Sturgis

Steamed Pumpkin-Pecan Pudding with Ginger Sabayon

I've always been fond of steamed pudding, although not the traditional English plum pudding. So I decided to develop a thoroughly American pumpkin-pecan pudding and to sauce it with a sabayon instead of the more usual hard sauce.

6 to 8 Servings

2 cups sifted all-purpose flour
1½ teaspoons baking soda
1 teaspoon salt
1½ teaspoons cinnamon
¾ teaspoon ground ginger
½ teaspoon freshly grated nutmeg
¼ teaspoon ground cloves
1 cup finely ground pecans (4 ounces)
3 eggs
1 cup (firmly packed) light brown sugar
¼ cup molasses
1½ cups canned unsweetened solid-pack pumpkin
3 tablespoons unsalted butter, melted
Ginger Sabayon (recipe follows)

1. Sift the flour, baking soda, salt, cinnamon, ginger, nutmeg and cloves together into a large bowl; stir in the pecans.

2. In a mixer bowl, beat the eggs and brown sugar until thick and light, about 3 minutes at high speed. Slowly beat in the molasses and pumpkin.

3. Make a well in the center of the dry ingredients; dump in the pumpkin mixture and stir lightly just until combined (there will be some lumps but this is how it should be). Drizzle in the melted butter and stir lightly just to mix.

4. Pour the batter into a lavishly

buttered 2-quart steamed pudding mold (preferably a fluted one) and snap the lid on tight (the inside of the lid should be well buttered, too). Lower the mold onto a rack or a folded towel in a kettle containing enough boiling water to reach about one-fourth of the way up the pudding mold.

5. Cover the kettle and steam the pudding for 2 hours, adding more boiling water, if necessary, to keep the level of the water from reducing too drastically. Keep the water at a good boil as the pudding steams.

6. When the pudding has steamed for 2 hours, transfer it to a wire rack and let stand upright, covered, for 15 minutes.

7. To serve, remove the lid from the pudding mold and invert the pudding onto a dessert platter. Decorate with sugar-frosted grapes or sprigs of holly, if desired. Whisk the Ginger Sabayon for 5 to 10 seconds. Pour into a large heated sauceboat and pass separately.
—Jean Anderson

Ginger Sabayon

Makes About 2 Cups

4 egg yolks
1 whole egg
½ cup sugar
½ cup fresh orange juice
2 tablespoons orange liqueur, such as Grand Marnier
1 tablespoon finely minced preserved stem ginger* (see Note)
1 tablespoon preserved stem ginger liquid
*Available at specialty food shops

In the top of a large double boiler, place all of the ingredients and whisk slowly to combine. Set over simmering water and whisk slowly until the mixture begins to thicken and mount in volume. Continue to cook, whisking briskly, until the mixture is about the consistency of boiled icing and nearly fills the double boiler top, about 10 minutes. Remove from the heat and let the sabayon rest over the hot water 1 minute before serving.

NOTE: If the stem ginger is unavailable, use 1½ tablespoons finely minced crystallized ginger and omit the ginger liquid.
—Jean Anderson

Christmas Bread Pudding with Amaretto Sauce

Easily made a day ahead of time, bread pudding is the ideal finale to Christmas dinner. If panettone is not available, substitute another similar, fruit-studded sweet bread. Just before serving, spread the amaretto sauce over the pudding and broil until golden brown and bubbly.

12 Servings

Bread Pudding:
1 panettone or other fruit-studded sweet bread (about 1 pound), cut into 1-inch slices
1 quart light cream
3 eggs
1 cup granulated sugar
1 tablespoon plus 2 teaspoons vanilla extract
1 teaspoon almond extract

Amaretto Sauce:
1 stick (4 ounces) unsalted butter, cut into pieces
1 cup confectioners' sugar
3 tablespoons amaretto liqueur
2 egg yolks

1. Make the bread pudding: Preheat the broiler. Arrange the bread slices on 2 baking sheets and toast 2 inches from the heat for about 1 minute a side, or until lightly browned. Set aside for at least 1 hour.

2. Tear the toasted panettone into 1½-inch pieces and place in a large bowl. Pour the light cream over the bread, making sure all the pieces are moistened. Set aside for 1 hour until all the liquid has been absorbed.

3. Preheat the oven to 325°. Generously butter the bottom and sides of a 9-by-13-by-2-inch baking dish and set aside. In a medium bowl, whisk the eggs with the granulated sugar, vanilla and almond extracts until blended. Stir into the soaked bread. Transfer the mixture to the prepared baking dish and bake in the middle of the oven for about 1 hour, or until the pudding is set and the top is golden brown. Let cool to room temperature. *(The pudding can be prepared 1 day ahead. Cover and set aside at room temperature.)*

4. Make the amaretto sauce: In a medium bowl set over a small saucepan of simmering water or in the top of a double boiler, melt the butter. Slowly whisk in the sugar until the mixture is creamy, about 30 seconds. Add the amaretto and then the egg yolks, one at a time, whisking constantly. Cook, whisking constantly until the sauce is the consistency of honey and reaches 160°, about 4 minutes. Let cool to room temperature. *(The sauce can be made up to 1 day ahead. Cover and refrigerate. Let return to room temperature before using.)*

5. Preheat the broiler. Just before serving, spoon the amaretto sauce over the pudding and broil 3 to 4 inches from the heat until bubbly and lightly browned, about 2 minutes. Cut the pudding into 12 rectangular pieces and serve immediately.
—Sheila Lukins

Orange and Honey Bread Pudding

If you like, peel and slice the oranges after using their zest to flavor the pudding. Sprinkle them with a little sugar and orange liqueur and serve them along with the pudding.

8 Servings

1 stick (4 ounces) unsalted
* butter*
24 to 30 slices of French
* bread, 1½ inches in*
* diameter, cut ⅛ to ¼ inch*
* thick*
2 cups milk
1 cup heavy cream
⅔ cup honey, preferably
* orange blossom*
3 navel oranges
5 eggs

1. Preheat the oven to 325°. Melt the butter and let cool slightly. Dip one side of each bread slice into the butter and arrange the bread, buttered-side up, overlapping slightly in a shallow 1½-quart baking dish.

2. In a medium saucepan, combine the milk, cream and honey. Strip the zest from the oranges with a swivel-bladed vegetable peeler and add to the pan. Bring to a boil over moderate heat, remove from the heat and let stand for 5 minutes.

3. In a large mixing bowl, whisk the eggs until liquefied. Gradually whisk in the hot milk and cream mixture. Do not overbeat, or the custard will have a great deal of foam on the surface. Strain the custard back into the pan and skim off the foam with a large spoon. Pour the custard evenly over the bread in the dish; the bread will rise to the top.

4. Place the baking dish in a larger pan and pour warm water into the pan to reach halfway up the sides of the baking dish. Bake the bread pudding for 45 minutes, or until the custard is set and the bread is an even golden brown.
—*Nicholas Malgieri*

Indian Pudding with Brandy Butter Sauce

This sweet, dense pudding is a traditional New England dessert. It can be made a day ahead and served slightly warm, with brandy butter sauce (as here), whipped cream or vanilla ice cream.

6 to 8 Servings

Pudding:
6 cups milk
1 cup yellow cornmeal
2 eggs
½ cup dark unsulphured
* molasses*
4 tablespoons unsalted butter
* at room temperature*
¼ cup granulated sugar
1½ teaspoons cinnamon
1½ teaspoons freshly grated
* nutmeg*
½ teaspoon salt
¼ teaspoon baking powder

Brandy Butter Sauce:
1 stick (4 ounces) unsalted
* butter, at room temperature*
¼ teaspoon salt
2 cups confectioners' sugar
2 tablespoons heavy cream
2 tablespoons Cognac

1. Make the pudding: Preheat the oven to 300°. Butter a 1½- to 2-quart casserole or Crockpot. In a large heavy saucepan, scald the milk over moderately high heat.

2. In a medium bowl, combine the cornmeal, eggs, molasses, butter, granulated sugar, cinnamon, nutmeg, salt and baking powder. Stir to blend well. Gradually whisk in all of the scalded milk. Pour the pudding mixture into the saucepan and cook over moderate heat, stirring until it just begins to boil, about 2 minutes. Pour into the buttered casserole.

3. Set a roasting pan on the bottom shelf of the oven and fill with warm water. Place the pudding on the middle shelf and bake until set, 3½ to 4 hours. Replenish the water in the roasting pan if necessary during cooking. *(The pudding can be prepared up to 1 day ahead. Let the pudding cool, then cover and refrigerate. Reheat in a 350° oven until warmed through, about 20 minutes.)*

4. Make the brandy butter sauce: In a small bowl, cream the butter with the salt until light and fluffy. Add the confectioners' sugar, 1 tablespoon at a time, alternating with the cream and Cognac; beat until smooth. The sauce will be creamy. *(If not using right away, cover and refrigerate for up to 3 days.)* Let return to room temperature before serving.

5. Serve the pudding warm with the brandy butter sauce.
—*Warren Picower*

Chocolate Pecan Pudding with Bourbon Sauce

Midway between a chocolate cake and a soufflé, this pudding can be served right from the oven or allowed to cool slightly. Although it sinks a bit when fully cooled, it is still delicious and moist.

6 to 8 Servings

4 ounces semisweet chocolate,
* chopped*
1½ cups pecan pieces (about
* 5½ ounces)*
⅓ cup sugar
¼ cup dry bread crumbs
¼ teaspoon cinnamon
1 stick (4 ounces) unsalted
* butter, softened*

1 tablespoon bourbon
5 eggs, separated
Pinch of salt
Bourbon Sauce (recipe
  follows)

1. Preheat the oven to 350°. Place the chocolate in a small heatproof bowl. Add 3 tablespoons of hot water and set the bowl over a pan of hot but not simmering water. Stir with a whisk until the chocolate is melted and smooth. Remove the bowl from the water and let the chocolate cool to room temperature.

2. Coarsely chop the pecan pieces in a food processor. Remove ½ cup of the pecans and set aside. Add 1 tablespoon of the sugar to the remaining nuts and grind to a fine powder. Combine the finely ground pecans, bread crumbs and cinnamon in a bowl; mix well and set the ground pecan mixture aside.

3. In a large mixer bowl, beat the butter with half the remaining sugar until soft and light. Beat in the cooled chocolate and then the bourbon. Add the egg yolks, 1 at a time, beating until smooth. Stir in the ground pecan mixture.

4. In a large bowl, beat the egg whites with the salt until they form very soft peaks. Gradually beat in the remaining sugar in a slow stream and continue beating until the egg whites hold soft peaks. Stir one-fourth of the beaten egg whites into the chocolate batter, then gently fold in the remaining egg whites.

5. Pour the batter into a buttered 1½-quart baking dish or 8-inch square baking pan. Smooth the top. Scatter the reserved chopped pecans evenly over the surface of the batter. Place the baking dish in a larger pan and pour hot tap water into the larger pan to reach halfway up the sides of the baking dish. Bake the pudding in the middle of the oven for 30 to 35 minutes, or until the pudding puffs and feels slightly firm when pressed with the palm of the hand; do not overbake.

6. To serve, spoon the warm pudding onto dessert plates. Ladle 2 or 3 tablespoons of the Bourbon Sauce over or around the pudding. Pass the remaining sauce separately.
—Nicholas Malgieri

Bourbon Sauce

Custard sauces are so versatile that you can flavor them to your taste. Other variations can be created by substituting a favorite liquor or liqueur. Or omit the alcohol and double the vanilla.

Makes About 2 Cups

1½ cups milk
⅓ cup sugar
4 egg yolks
2 tablespoons bourbon
1 teaspoon vanilla extract

1. In a medium nonreactive saucepan, combine the milk and sugar. Bring to a boil over moderate heat.

2. Beat the egg yolks in a small bowl until liquefied. When the milk boils, gradually whisk one-third of it into the yolks. Return the remaining milk to a boil over low heat and whisk in the yolk mixture. Cook, whisking constantly, until the sauce thickens, 1 to 1½ minutes; do not let boil. Immediately remove from the heat.

3. Whisk the sauce constantly for 1 minute to cool. Strain through a fine sieve into a bowl and whisk for 30 seconds. Stir in the bourbon and vanilla. Serve the sauce warm (see Note).

NOTE: If it is necessary to reheat the sauce, pour it into a heatproof bowl and whisk over a pan of simmering water until just warm, about 2 minutes.
—Nicholas Malgieri

Wild Rice Pudding with
Raisins

To make a lovely garnish for this rice pudding, marinate about 12 orange sections in a small amount of orange liqueur for at least 30 minutes.

6 Servings

Pinch of salt
1 cup wild rice
½ cup raisins, washed and
  drained
2 tablespoons unsalted butter,
  softened
3 tablespoons honey,
  preferably clover
½ teaspoon freshly grated
  nutmeg
2 cups milk
2 eggs, lightly beaten
2 to 3 tablespoons orange
  liqueur, such as Grand
  Marnier
1 cup heavy cream, whipped

1. Bring 1½ cups of water to a simmer and add the salt. Add the wild rice, cover and cook just until tender, about 45 minutes. When tender, uncover and toss with a fork to release the steam. Reserve ½ cup of fluffy grains for garnish.

2. Meanwhile, in a small saucepan, cook the raisins in 1 cup of water until tender, about 15 minutes. Set the raisins aside in their cooking liquid.

3. Combine the cooked rice, the raisins and their liquid, butter, honey and nutmeg.

4. In a double boiler, heat the milk over simmering water. Add the rice mixture and stir in the beaten eggs. Cook, stirring, until the mixture thickens; do not let it boil. Re-

move from the heat and stir in the liqueur. Add more honey and more nutmeg, if desired.

5. Serve warm or cold. Top with the reserved grains of wild rice and the whipped cream.
—*Pearl Byrd Foster*

Lime Sponge Pudding

Here's a variation on the old lemon sponge pudding. As this bakes, the top half magically becomes a light cake and the bottom half a creamy custard.

8 Servings

3 eggs, separated
1½ cups milk, scalded
1 cup sugar
½ cup all-purpose flour
2 tablespoons unsalted butter, melted
⅓ cup lime juice (from about 5 limes)
1 tablespoon grated lime zest

1. Preheat the oven to 325°. In a medium bowl, beat the egg yolks with a whisk. Slowly whisk in the scalded milk. Whisk in the sugar, flour, butter, lime juice and lime zest.

2. In another medium bowl, beat the egg whites until stiff but not dry. Fold the egg whites into the lime mixture. Spoon into eight 6-ounce custard cups.

3. Arrange the cups in a baking pan. Add 1 inch of hot water to the pan and bake for about 15 minutes, or until the tops are dry and lightly golden. Serve at room temperature or chilled.
—*Marion Cunningham*

Tulip Cups

These crisp cookie containers make a lovely dessert filled with mousse (such as the Cranberry Fool that follows), ice cream or sorbet. For a special treat, drizzle a little melted semisweet chocolate into the cups before filling them.

Tulip batter is simple to make, but expect a few misshapen cups before you have 12 perfect tulips. Any remaining cookies may be left flat or rolled into cigar shapes and served another time.

Makes About 12

⅔ cup sugar
½ cup all-purpose flour
1 whole egg
2 egg whites
½ teaspoon vanilla extract
4 tablespoons unsalted butter, melted

1. In a medium bowl, place the sugar, flour, whole egg, egg whites and vanilla. Beat with a wooden spoon until well mixed. Stir in the butter and 1 tablespoon of water; the batter will be thin. *(The recipe can be made to this point 1 day ahead. Refrigerate, tightly covered.)* Stir before using and add up to 1 tablespoon additional water, if necessary, to restore the consistency.

2. Preheat the oven to 425°. Butter a large heavy cookie sheet. Using a tablespoon measure, drop 4 separate tablespoons of the batter onto the sheet, allowing plenty of room for each one to spread. Using the back of a spoon, spread the batter into 4-inch circles, leaving about 1 inch in between.

3. Bake in the lower third of the oven for 6 to 8 minutes, or until the cookies have a golden-brown border about 1 inch wide. Meanwhile, cut four 4-inch-square pieces of alu-

minum foil and set 4 narrow glass jars (such as 2-inch-diameter spice jars) bottom-side up on the work surface.

4. Remove the cookies from the oven. Working quickly, scrape a cookie from the sheet with a wide metal spatula and invert it over the spice jar. Cover with a square of foil to protect your hands and mold the cookie into a tulip shape. Repeat with the remaining cookies. If they should harden on the sheet, return to the oven for 30 seconds to restore pliability. Remove the shaped tulip cups from their molds.

5. Scrape the cookie sheet clean and repeat Steps 2 through 4.
—*Diana Sturgis*

Cranberry Fool

This cranberry mousse from The Shoalwater restaurant in The Shelburne Inn in Seaview, Washington, can be made up to one day ahead.

6 Servings

½ cup sugar
½ cup fresh orange juice
2 cups cranberries (½ pound)
1 cup heavy cream

1. In a medium nonreactive saucepan, stir together the sugar, orange juice and 1¾ cups of the cranberries. Bring to a boil over moderately high heat and cook until the berries split, 4 to 5 minutes. Remove from the heat; let cool to room temperature, about 30 minutes.

2. In a chilled bowl, whip the cream until soft peaks form. Fold the cool cranberry mixture into the whipped cream and spoon the mousse into 6 stemmed dessert glasses. Garnish with the remaining ¼ cup cranberries. Serve chilled.
—*The Shoalwater, Seaview, Washingon*

Creamsicle Currant Shortcake (p. 167).

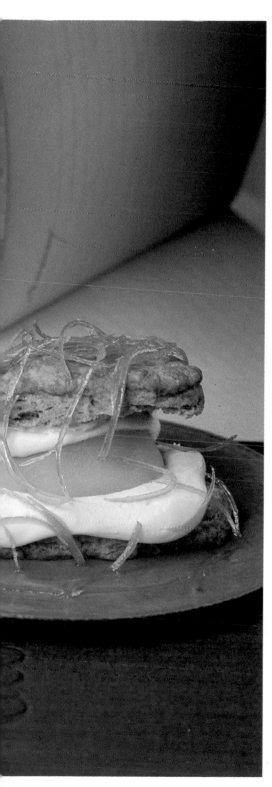

At left, left to right:
Mediterranean Shortcake
(p. 165) and Post-Holiday
Shortcake (p. 164).
Above: Miami Beach Shortcake
(p. 166).

Upstate Shortcake (p. 166).

Chocolate Orange Mousse

The orange zest contributes a surprising amount of flavor to this mousse. Of course you can omit it if you prefer a simple chocolate taste. Cooking the egg yolks and egg whites makes this a light but stable mousse that can be made up to two days ahead.

8 to 10 Servings

12 ounces imported extra-
  bittersweet chocolate, such
  as Tobler, broken into
  pieces
1½ cups milk
4 egg yolks
Finely grated zest of 1 orange
½ cup sugar
6 egg whites
1 cup heavy cream, chilled
Chocolate shavings, for
  garnish

1. Place the chocolate pieces in a food processor and pulse until finely ground, about 20 seconds. Leave the chocolate in the bowl.

2. In a heavy medium saucepan, combine the milk, egg yolks and orange zest. Cook over moderate heat, whisking constantly, until slightly thickened, about 5 minutes; do not let the custard boil. Strain immediately into a pitcher. With the food processor running, pour the hot custard into the chocolate in the bowl; a smooth mixture will form almost at once. Stop the machine and scrape the chocolate mixture into a large bowl.

3. In a small heavy saucepan, combine the sugar and ¼ cup of water. Bring to a boil over moderate heat, stirring occasionally to dissolve the sugar. With a pastry brush dipped in water, wash down any sugar crystals from the sides of the pan. Cook without stirring until the syrup registers 235° on a candy thermometer, about 10 minutes.

4. Meanwhile, place the egg whites in a large heatproof bowl and beat with an electric mixer until soft peaks form. Carefully add the boiling sugar syrup in a thin, steady stream, beating constantly as you pour. Continue to beat the whites at high speed until stiff, glossy peaks form when the beaters are lifted, about 2 minutes.

5. With a large whisk or a spatula, gently fold one-fourth of the egg whites into the chocolate mixture until no white streaks remain. Repeat with the remaining egg whites. Refrigerate the mixture until cool, about 15 minutes.

6. In a medium bowl, beat the cream until stiff. Fold the whipped cream into the cooled chocolate mixture and pour the mousse into a large serving bowl. Cover with plastic wrap and refrigerate until chilled, about 4 hours, or for up to 2 days. Garnish with chocolate shavings before serving.
—Diana Sturgis

Lemon Custard

Makes About 2½ Cups

Juice and grated zest from 2
  large lemons
1 stick (4 ounces) unsalted
  butter, cut into tablespoons
1 cup sugar
4 eggs
1 cup heavy cream

1. In a double boiler, combine the lemon juice, lemon zest, butter and sugar. Stir occasionally over simmering water until the butter melts and the sugar dissolves, about 5 minutes.

2. In a medium bowl, beat the eggs lightly until blended. Gradually whisk about one-third of the hot lemon mixture into the eggs. Stir the warmed eggs back into the remaining lemon mixture in the double boiler. Continue to cook over the simmering water, stirring constantly, until the curd is thick and steaming, about 3 minutes. Remove from the heat, strain and let cool. Cover with plastic wrap touching the surface. Refrigerate until chilled. *(The recipe can be made to this point up to 1 day ahead.)*

3. Whip the cream until stiff. Fold the whipped cream into the cold lemon curd until completely blended. Refrigerate the custard until ready to use.
—Marion Cunningham

Chilled Bourbon Custard

This custard is a clone of the English syllabub, a rich, frothy beverage for which the English designed beautiful syllabub cups that were the size of demitasse cups but with two handles. You can serve this wonderful custard southern-style in small cups, or use it as a sauce, like a crème anglaise. It is delicious with the Brandied Pumpkin Pie (p. 219).

Makes 3½ Cups

6 egg yolks
¼ cup sugar
1 teaspoon all-purpose flour
Pinch of salt
2 cups milk, scalded
1 to 2 tablespoons good
  bourbon
Lightly sweetened whipped
  cream, for serving

1. In a medium nonreactive pan, beat the egg yolks with the sugar, flour and salt until the yolks turn pale, about 5 minutes. Gradually beat the warm milk into the egg yolk mixture.

2. Set the saucepan over moder-

ately low heat and cook, stirring constantly, until the custard thickens enough to coat the back of the spoon, about 5 minutes.

3. Pour the custard into a well-chilled serving bowl. Cover the surface directly with a piece of plastic wrap and refrigerate until cold.

4. Just before serving, stir in the bourbon. Serve in small cups with whipped cream on top if desired.
—*Camille Glenn*

Spiced Pumpkin Ice Cream

This subtle ice cream is best eaten when slightly softened. Move from the freezer to the refrigerator about 10 minutes before serving.

8 Servings

2 egg yolks
¾ cup sugar
1½ cups milk
1 cup canned unsweetened solid-pack pumpkin, pressed through a fine sieve
1½ teaspoons cinnamon
1½ teaspoons freshly grated nutmeg
1 cup heavy cream

1. In a medium bowl, whisk the egg yolks with ½ cup of the sugar until well blended, about 1 minute.

2. In a small heavy saucepan, stir together 1 cup of the milk with the remaining ¼ cup sugar over moderate heat until the liquid boils and the sugar dissolves. Slowly whisk the hot milk into the egg-sugar mixture.

3. Transfer to a medium saucepan. Cook, stirring, over moderately low heat until the custard thickens slightly, about 5 minutes; do not allow to boil. Immediately pour into a large bowl set over ice.

4. Stir in the pumpkin puree, cinnamon, nutmeg, cream and remaining ½ cup milk until blended. Continue to stir over ice until cool.

5. Pour into the canister of an ice cream maker and freeze according to the manufacturer's directions.
—*Diana Sturgis*

Maple Ice Cream

Thomas Jefferson was always intrigued by culinary contraptions, bringing back from his travels to Europe waffle irons, pasta makers and a French ice cream machine. While he was not the first American (nor, indeed, the first president) to indulge in "iced creams," they appeared regularly on his menus and he did much toward turning us into a country of ice cream lovers.

Although maple as an all-purpose seasoning is not used with the frequency it was in centuries past, a hardy cottage industry still exists. Seek out a good-quality syrup for this recipe, since the cooking process used will intensify the flavor.

Makes About 1½ Quarts

2 cups pure maple syrup
2 cups milk
2 cups heavy cream
4 egg yolks

1. In a medium saucepan, bring the maple syrup to a boil over moderate heat. Reduce the heat to very low and simmer until reduced by half, about 45 minutes. (Counteract the tendency of the syrup to boil over by stirring often with a metal spoon.) At the end of the reduction process you will have what appears to be a combination of maple syrup and maple sugar.

2. Let the reduced syrup cool slightly; then slowly whisk in the milk and cream. Return to moderate

heat and bring to a boil, stirring to dissolve the solids.

3. In a medium bowl, whisk the egg yolks thoroughly. Slowly whisk the hot maple syrup mixture into the egg yolks in a thin stream. Return this mixture to the pan and stir constantly over low heat until the mixture is steaming and has thickened enough to coat the back of a spoon heavily, 3 to 5 minutes. Do not let the mixture come close to a boil or it will curdle.

4. Remove from the heat, let cool to room temperature and refrigerate, covered, until very cold, at least 4 hours or preferably overnight.

5. Churn the chilled maple mixture in an ice cream maker, according to the manufacturer's instructions. Transfer to a storage container, cover and freeze. *(This ice cream can be prepared several days in advance. Allow it to soften in the refrigerator for 10 minutes or so, if necessary, before serving.)*
—*Michael McLaughlin*

Pumpkin Maple Ice Cream

This ice cream has a deep, mellow pumpkin flavor that is highlighted by a sprinkling of rum and walnuts.

8 Servings

3 egg yolks
1 cup maple syrup
1 cup milk, scalded
1 cup canned unsweetened solid-pack pumpkin
1½ teaspoons freshly grated nutmeg
1 cup heavy cream
Dark rum and chopped walnuts, for garnish

1. In a large bowl, blend the egg yolks and maple syrup well.

2. Gradually beat the hot milk into the eggs and syrup. Pour the mixture into a heavy medium saucepan and cook, stirring, over moderately low heat until it registers 180° on an instant-reading thermometer, about 15 minutes; do not let boil.

3. Return the hot mixture to the bowl and blend in the pumpkin, nutmeg and cream. Pour the mixture into an ice cream maker and freeze according to the manufacturer's instructions. Transfer to a covered container and let the ice cream ripen in the freezer for at least 2 hours or overnight.

4. To serve, scoop into stemmed glasses. Top with a dash of rum and a sprinkling of chopped walnuts.
—*Diana Sturgis*

Cranberry-Raspberry Sorbet

Beautifully colored and packing a lively flavor wallop, the raspberry taste predominates in this refreshing sorbet.

8 Servings

1 bag (12 ounces) fresh or frozen cranberries
1½ cups sugar
1 bag (12 ounces) frozen unsweetened raspberries

1. Put the cranberries in a nonreactive saucepan, add 1 cup of water and bring to a boil. Reduce the heat and simmer until the berries burst, about 5 minutes. Stir in the sugar and then the raspberries and cook, stirring until the sugar dissolves, about 1 minute. Pour into a bowl, stir in ½ cup of cold water and refrigerate until chilled. *(The recipe can be prepared ahead to this point up to 1 day ahead.)*

2. Strain the fruit mixture in batches, pressing hard on the solids with a wooden spoon. Pour into an ice cream maker and freeze according to the manufacturer's instructions. Transfer the sorbet to a chilled container and freeze, covered, for 2 hours, or for up to 3 days before serving.
—*Diana Sturgis*

Frozen Praline Meringue

The advantage of this dessert is that it can be prepared several weeks ahead. Be sure, however, that after it is decorated with the rosettes of whipped cream, it is frozen hard before wrapping it. Use plastic wrap and two layers of aluminum foil so that the dessert won't pick up any tastes from the freezer.

The longer the meringue is frozen and the colder the freezer, the more time it should spend in the refrigerator to soften before serving. Generally, after it has been in the freezer for more than a couple of days, it should stay in the refrigerator for half an hour before serving.

12 Servings

5 egg whites
1½ cups granulated sugar
1½ cups sliced blanched almonds
1 pint vanilla ice cream
3 cups heavy cream
¼ cup confectioners' sugar, sifted
1½ tablespoons dark rum
Crystallized violets or candied rose petals, for decoration

1. Preheat the oven to 200°. Butter the bottoms of two 11-by-17-inch baking sheets. Line with parchment paper. Using a pencil, draw a 10-inch circle in the center of each sheet of parchment paper.

2. In a large mixer bowl, beat the egg whites until stiff but not dry. Gradually beat in 1 cup of the granulated sugar over a 10-second period and continue beating on high speed for no longer than 10 seconds. (Some of the sugar should remain slightly granular to make a very tender meringue.)

3. Scoop the meringue into a large pastry bag fitted with a 1-inch plain tip. Cover the parchment circles with meringue, starting in the center and piping in a spiral to form a 10-inch disk.

4. Bake the meringues for about 4 hours, until hard. They will be slightly beige in color. Turn the oven off but leave the meringues in to dry until cool.

5. Lightly oil a baking sheet. In a heavy medium saucepan, cook the remaining ½ cup granulated sugar over moderately high heat, stirring occasionally with a wooden spoon as the sugar closest to the sides of the pan begins to melt. Stir the melting sugar into the dry sugar in the center. After 6 to 7 minutes, the mixture will turn a rich caramel color. Add the almonds; this will solidify the caramel a little. Continue cooking to remelt the sugar and brown the almonds, about 2 minutes longer. Pour the praline onto the oiled sheet and let cool.

6. Let the ice cream soften slightly. Meanwhile, break the praline into pieces and process in a food processor until finely ground. Scoop the ice cream into a large bowl and, with a rubber spatula, fold in the praline powder. Freeze the ice cream to firm it slightly.

7. In a large bowl, combine the heavy cream, confectioners' sugar and rum. Beat with an electric mixer until stiff. Cover and refrigerate until needed.

8. Trim the meringues to make them the same size and uniformly round; reserve the trimmings. Put one of the meringue disks flat-side down on a large round cake plate. Scoop the ice cream onto the meringue and spread it evenly to the edge. Spread 1½ cups of the whipped cream over the ice cream, smoothing it evenly. Sprinkle any crumbled meringue trimmings over the cream and top with the second meringue disk, flat-side up. Coat the top and sides with 2⅔ cups of the whipped cream.

9. Spoon the remaining whipped cream into a pastry bag fitted with a star tip. Decorate the top and the base of the cake with whipped cream rosettes. Gently press crystallized violets or rose petals into the rosettes and place the dessert uncovered into the freezer. Freeze for at least 3 hours, until hard. Cover with plastic wrap and aluminum foil and return to the freezer.

10. About 30 minutes before serving time, unwrap the cake. Transfer it to the refrigerator to soften slightly before cutting and serving.
—*Jacques Pépin*

pies

Cranberry Gems

This is a perfect make-ahead sweet for the holidays. The tartlet shells may be baked weeks in advance and frozen. The cranberry filling should be made at least one day in advance; it will keep for several months in the refrigerator. Any leftover filling makes a lovely spread for toast or a relish for turkey, ham or cold meats. You may want to make a second batch of filling just for that purpose. Since there's no need to defrost the shells, these tartlets take just minutes to assemble. The finished product has a sparkling, polished look.

Makes 16 to 20 Tartlets

1 package (12 ounces)
  cranberries, fresh or frozen
⅓ cup orange or pineapple
  juice
1 tablespoon grated orange
  zest
1 tart apple, peeled and
  chopped
1 medium pear, peeled and
  chopped
½ cup raisins
½ cup (3 ounces) dried pears
  or dried pineapple,* finely
  diced
1 cup sugar
1½ teaspoons cinnamon
Pinch of freshly grated
  nutmeg
⅓ cup coarsely chopped
  walnuts, pecans or
  macadamia nuts
3 tablespoons Grand Marnier
  or dark rum
Pâte Brisée (recipe follows)
Whipped cream, for garnish
*Available at health food
  stores

1. In a medium nonreactive sauce-pan, combine the cranberries, orange juice and zest, apple, pear, raisins, dried pears, sugar, cinnamon and nutmeg. Bring to a boil, reduce the heat to moderately low and simmer, stirring occasionally, until thickened, about 20 minutes. Remove from the heat and stir in the nuts and Grand Marnier. Spoon into a 1-quart heat-proof jar; cover and refrigerate.

2. Lightly butter 24 individual tartlet tins 3 inches in diameter and ⅜ inch high. (Any shaped shallow tin of 1½-tablespoon capacity can be used.) On a lightly floured surface, roll out the Pâte Brisée about ⅛ inch thick. Invert a tin on the pastry and cut out a piece ½ inch larger than the tin. Fit the piece of pastry into the tin and cut off the excess around the rim. Repeat with the remaining pastry. Prick the bottom of each shell with a fork and freeze for at least 20 minutes before baking.

3. Preheat the oven to 400°. Place the tins on a cookie sheet and bake on the lowest rack of the oven for 12 to 15 minutes, until golden. Check the tartlets after 7 minutes and prick them with a fork if the centers start to rise. Cool in the tins on a rack for 10 minutes, then unmold. Freeze in an airtight container until ready to fill.

4. To assemble, place 1 table-spoon of the cranberry filling in each pastry shell. If desired, garnish with whipped cream.
—Dorie Greenspan

Pâte Brisée

Makes Enough for About 20 Tarlets

1½ cups all-purpose flour
1 tablespoon sugar
¼ teaspoon salt
1 stick (4 ounces) cold
  unsalted butter, cut into
  pieces
3 tablespoons ice water

1. In a medium bowl, combine the flour, sugar and salt. Cut in the butter until the mixture resembles coarse meal.

2. Sprinkle the dough with 2 ta-blespoons of the ice water, tossing with a fork to evenly distribute the moisture. Sprinkle on the remaining 1 tablespoon ice water and, using your fingertips, blend lightly into the dough. Gather the dough into a ball and flatten to a 6-inch disk. Cover with plastic wrap and refrigerate for at least 1 hour.
—Dorie Greenspan

Cranberry Tartlets

Makes 8 to 10 Tarts

Nut Crust:
1 cup finely chopped walnuts
1 stick (4 ounces) unsalted
  butter, softened to room
  temperature
3 tablespoons sugar
1½ cups all-purpose flour
1 egg yolk, beaten
½ teaspoon vanilla extract

Cranberry Filling:
1 envelope unflavored gelatin
3 cups fresh or frozen
  cranberries
1 cup sugar
½ cup red currant jelly

Topping:
½ cup heavy cream, whipped

1. Prepare the nut crust: Combine the walnuts, butter, sugar and flour in a mixing bowl, using a pastry blender or your fingers. Stir in the egg yolk and vanilla to form a firm pastry dough. If necessary, blend in a drop or two of water.

2. Using your fingers, press the dough firmly against the bottoms and sides of 3-inch tart pans so that it is about ⅛ inch thick. Chill the shells for 1 hour.

3. Preheat the oven to 350°. Place the shells on a baking sheet and bake them until slightly golden and firm, about 12 to 15 minutes. Remove the baking sheet from the oven and set the tart pans on a rack to cool. Then carefully remove the shells from the pans.

4. Prepare the cranberry filling: In a small bowl, sprinkle the gelatin over ¼ cup cold water and set aside to dissolve.

5. In a saucepan, combine the cranberries with the sugar and currant jelly. Gently boil the mixture, uncovered, over moderate heat, stirring occasionally, for 15 minutes. Remove the pan from the heat, cool the mixture slightly and stir in the dissolved gelatin.

6. When the mixture is cool, divide it evenly among the tart shells. Chill the tarts and serve topped with the whipped cream.
—*Martha Stewart*

Apple Tartlets

These lovely tartlets may be kept in the refrigerator for a day or two, but they are best eaten the day they are made.

Makes 8 Tartlets

¼ cup raisins
1 tablespoon dark rum
Pâte Brisée (p. 202)
5 small Granny Smith apples
½ cup apple jelly
1 tablespoon sugar
1 teaspoon cinnamon
1 egg, beaten
Chopped toasted nuts or
  raisins, for garnish

1. In a small bowl, toss the raisins with the rum; set aside to macerate.

2. Lightly butter eight 3-inch tartlet tins. On a lightly floured surface, roll out the pastry about ⅛ inch thick. Using a round cookie cutter, 3½ to 3¾ inches in diameter, cut out eight circles of dough and fit into the tins. With a sharp knife, trim off the excess around the rim of each tin and freeze until ready to fill.

3. Core and peel the apples. Halve them lengthwise, place the halves cut-side down and cut crosswise into 12 slices, keeping the slices together. Cut two of the sliced apple halves in half again lengthwise to make a total of 48 small pieces.

4. In a small heavy saucepan, bring the apple jelly to a boil over moderately high heat, stirring until smooth. Remove from the heat and set aside. In a small bowl, combine the sugar and cinnamon.

5. Preheat the oven to 400°. Brush the inside of each pastry shell with some of the hot apple jelly. Set the remaining jelly aside. Arrange 6 of the small apple pieces pinwheel fashion in the bottom of each tin. Dividing evenly, sprinkle the tartlets with 1 teaspoon of the cinnamon-sugar.

6. Fill the hollowed core of each of the 8 remaining sliced apple halves with one-eighth of the raisins and, holding the slices together, invert quickly onto the center of each tart.

7. Brush the top of each tartlet with the beaten egg and sprinkle all with the remaining 1 tablespoon cinnamon-sugar. Place on a cookie sheet and bake on the lowest rack of the oven for 20 to 25 minutes, or until the crust is golden and the apple, when pierced with a knife, is tender but still slightly firm. Cool the tartlets in the tins on a rack for 10 minutes; then unmold.

8. Reheat the apple jelly (adding a drop of water or rum if it has thickened too much) over low heat until melted. Brush lightly over the tartlets. If desired, garnish with chopped toasted nuts or additional raisins.
—*Dorie Greenspan*

Chocolate-Almond Tartlets

Whether trimmed with whipped cream rosettes, dusted with toasted almonds or served plain straight from the fridge, these are sweets that will please anyone who adores chocolate. My preference is to serve them at room temperature when they're at their creamiest.

Makes 12 Tartlets

½ recipe Cream Cheese
  Dough (p. 30)
1⅓ cups heavy cream
8 ounces bittersweet
  chocolate, preferably Lindt
  or Tobler, finely chopped

¼ cup amaretto liqueur
½ cup whole blanched
  almonds, toasted and finely
  chopped

1. Remove the Cream Cheese dough from the refrigerator and let stand for about 10 minutes, until malleable. Meanwhile, lightly butter twelve 3-inch fluted tartlet molds.

2. On a lightly floured work surface, roll out half the dough about ⅛ inch thick. Using a 3½-inch round cookie or biscuit cutter, cut out 6 circles of dough. Fit the dough into the tartlet molds without stretching. Place in the freezer for at least 30 minutes, or until firm. Meanwhile, repeat with the remaining dough.

3. Preheat the oven to 400°. Line each frozen tartlet with aluminum foil and fill with pie weights or dried beans. Bake for 15 minutes. Remove the foil and weights and bake for 2 to 3 minutes longer, until golden brown. Remove from the oven and let cool in the tins on a rack; then unmold. *(The recipe can be prepared ahead to this point. Refrigerate the pastry shells in an airtight container for up to 3 days or freeze for up to 1 month. Defrost before proceeding.)*

4. In a small saucepan, bring ⅔ cup of the heavy cream to a boil. Remove from the heat, add the chocolate and stir until completely melted, smooth and glossy. Mix in 2 tablespoons of the amaretto and set aside to cool, stirring occasionally. Do not refrigerate.

5. To finish the tartlets, fill with the chocolate-almond cream. Sprinkle with the chopped almonds and refrigerate the tarts until set, at least 30 minutes.

6. Whip the remaining ⅔ cup cream with the remaining 2 tablespoons amaretto and pipe onto the tartlets. Serve chilled or at room temperature.

—*Dorie Greenspan*

Chocolate-Pecan Tartlets

Makes 8 Tarts

Pie Pastry (p. 221)
3 ounces bittersweet
  chocolate
3 tablespoons unsalted butter
¾ cup sugar
1 cup light corn syrup
3 eggs
1 teaspoon vanilla extract
1 cup pecans, coarsely
  chopped, plus 40 pecan
  halves for garnish

1. Preheat the oven to 250°. Divide the Pie Pastry into eighths and roll each portion into a round approximately ⅛ inch thick. Fit each carefully into a 4-inch tart pan. Roll a rolling pin over the top to trim the pastry edge flush to the pan. Place the shells in the refrigerator while you prepare the filling.

2. Place the chocolate and the butter in a shallow ovenproof bowl and place it in the oven for 3 minutes, or until the ingredients have melted. Remove the plate from the oven and stir to blend the ingredients; set aside.

3. In a saucepan, stir the sugar and corn syrup together until the sugar is partially dissolved. Bring the mixture to a boil, and then gently boil it for 2 minutes, stirring constantly with a wooden spoon.

4. In a bowl, beat the eggs and then stir in the melted chocolate and butter. Mix well. Add the hot sugar syrup and stir to combine. Mix in the vanilla and chopped pecans and allow the mixture to cool slightly.

5. Increase the oven temperature to 350°. Remove the tart shells from the refrigerator and place them on a baking sheet. Fill the shells with the chocolate filling, making sure that the nuts are distributed evenly. Decorate the tops with the pecan halves. Place the sheet of tarts in the oven and bake them for 45 minutes, or until the filling has set. Serve chilled.
—*Martha Stewart*

Sauce-Apple Pie

I have never been in agreement with charts claiming to give the best uses for each apple variety. Pie-wise, the results always seem al dente to me, at odds with the quest for a truly tender crust. Instead, I look for an apple that will cook into the meltingly tender, almost custardlike filling my old-fashioned palate prefers.

My first choice for pie is the Cortland, recommended on many apple charts as ideal for sauce, but other varieties—as long as they are listed as not successful for pies or baking whole—will produce a similar effect. I like to serve the pie à la mode, with a scoop of Maple Ice Cream (p. 198).

8 Servings

Filling:
3 pounds Cortland or other
  "sauce" apples—peeled,
  cored and cut into ⅛-inch
  slices
¼ cup unbleached all-purpose
  flour
½ cup sugar
1½ teaspoons cinnamon
½ teaspoon freshly grated
  nutmeg
2 teaspoons vanilla extract
¾ cup raisins

Pastry:
3 cups unbleached all-purpose
flour, measured by sifting
into a dry-measure cup and
sweeping level
½ teaspoon salt
6 tablespoons unsalted butter,
chilled
½ cup lard, chilled
4 to 6 tablespoons cold water
About ⅓ cup whole wheat
flour (see Note)

Glaze:
1 egg, beaten
1 tablespoon sugar

1. Prepare the filling: In a bowl, combine all the ingredients for the filling and let stand at room temperature, stirring occasionally, while you prepare the crust.

2. Make the pastry: In a food processor, combine the all-purpose flour and the salt. Cut the butter and lard into small pieces and add to the processor. With short pulses, cut the butter and lard into the flour until the mixture resembles oatmeal, about 5 seconds. Add the water, 1 tablespoon at a time, pulsing between each addition until a rough dough is formed. (You may not need all the water.)

3. Sprinkle the work surface with 2 tablespoons of the whole wheat flour. Turn the dough out, form it into a ball (it will be crumbly) and divide into two flat 6-inch disks. Wrap each one in plastic wrap and refrigerate for at least 30 minutes.

4. Preheat the oven to 400°. On a work surface lightly sprinkled with whole wheat flour, roll out one pastry disk to form an even circle about 14 inches in diameter. Ease the dough into a 10-inch pie plate. If it tears, patch it by pressing the edges together; it is not necessary to moisten the dough for an effective patch.

5. Spoon the filling and any accumulated juices into the pie shell. Roll out the remaining disk of dough, lightly flouring the work surface with just enough whole wheat flour to prevent sticking. Lay the top crust over the apples. Trim the overhanging dough edges to ½ inch and fold the lower crust over the upper, pinching it gently but firmly to seal. Crimp decoratively if desired and cut 3 or 4 slits into the upper crust.

6. Bake the pie on the lowest rack of the oven for 40 minutes. Brush the crust with the beaten egg, sprinkle evenly with the sugar and bake for another 10 to 15 minutes, or until the juices are bubbling up through the slits in the crust and the pie is a rich golden brown. Let the pie cool to room temperature before serving.

NOTE: The whole wheat flour used to roll out the pastry adds extra texture and color to the crust. Unbleached all-purpose flour can be substituted.
—*Michael McLaughlin*

Best Apple Pie

8 Servings

Flaky Pastry (recipe follows)
made with vegetable
shortening
2½ pounds (5 to 7) tart
cooking apples, such as
Granny Smith or Greening
1 cup plus 2 tablespoons
sugar

¼ cup all-purpose flour
1½ teaspoons cinnamon
½ teaspoon freshly grated
nutmeg
1 tablespoon unsalted butter
½ egg white (1 tablespoon),
lightly beaten

1. On a lightly floured surface, roll out one of the Flaky Pastry rounds to an 11- to 12-inch circle. Fold the circle into quarters or roll it loosely over a lightly floured rolling pin and transfer it to a 9-inch pie plate. Unfold and ease the pastry into the plate without stretching it. Keep the remaining, unrolled portion chilled while you prepare the apples.

2. Peel, core and quarter the apples lengthwise. Cut the quarters lengthwise into ½-inch-thick wedges (you should have about 7 cups). In a medium bowl, mix 1 cup of the sugar, the flour, cinnamon and nutmeg. Add the apples and toss to coat them well. Spoon them into the bottom crust, mounding them in the center. Dot the top of the apples with the butter.

3. Preheat the oven to 425°. On a lightly floured surface, roll out the pastry for the top crust to a 12-inch circle. Moisten the edge of the bottom crust lightly with cold water and place the top crust over the apples. Trim the overhang of both crusts evenly to ½ inch. Turn the excess pastry under the rim and firmly seal the edges by crimping them decorative. Cut three steam vents in the top crust with a knife. Lightly brush the pastry with the egg white and sprinkle the remaining 2 tablespoons sugar over the top.

4. Bake the pie for 40 minutes, or until the top is golden brown and the apples are tender when pierced with a knife. Transfer the pie to a rack and cool before serving.
—*F&W*

Flaky Pastry

All pastry doughs are made from the same basic ingredients: flour, fat and ice water. Most pastry doughs require all-purpose flour; do not substitute another type of flour unless it is specified in a particular recipe. The ratio of fat to flour determines the texture of the dough, and the type of fat—it can be unsalted butter, margarine, shortening or lard—will affect the dough's tenderness and flavor. For example, butter creates the richest, most elegant pastry crust. Lard, on the other hand, creates a flakier, more tender crust. Solid vegetable shortenings do not contribute flavor; however, the texture of the dough will be smooth and the resultant crust flaky.

Makes Two 9-Inch Single Crusts or One Double Crust

2 cups all-purpose flour
¼ teaspoon salt
⅔ cup vegetable shortening, butter or lard, chilled
About ¼ cup ice water

In a large bowl, combine the flour and salt. Cut in the shortening, lard or butter until the mixture resembles coarse meal. Sprinkle the ice water over the mixture 1 tablespoon at a time, tossing with a fork, until the pastry can be gathered into a ball. (Use additional drops of water if necessary.) Divide the ball of dough in half; flatten each half into a 6-inch round, wrap each in wax paper and chill for at least 45 minutes. *(Tightly wrapped in plastic wrap, this pastry will keep for up to 3 days in the refrigerator or for up to 3 months in the freezer.)*
—F&W

Apple-Quince Pie

8 to 10 Servings

4 tart green apples—peeled, cored and cut into ½-inch slices
2 ripe quinces—peeled, cored and cut into ⅛-inch slices
Grated zest and juice of 1 medium lemon
¾ cup sugar
1 tablespoon all-purpose flour
Flaky Pie Dough (recipe follows)
3 tablespoons unsalted butter, cut into ½-inch dice

1. Preheat the oven to 400°. In a large bowl, toss together the apples, quinces, lemon zest, lemon juice, sugar and flour.
2. On a lightly floured surface, roll out one disk of Flaky Pie Dough about ⅛ inch to a 12-inch circle. Fit the pastry into a 9-inch glass pie plate. Roll out the top crust in the same manner.
3. Mound the fruit mixture in the lined pie plate and dot with the butter. Moisten the rim of the pie shell with water and lay the top crust over the fruit.
4. Using scissors, trim the edges of the dough so that they extend no more than ¾ inch beyond the rim of the plate. Roll the dough under and crimp to make an attractive border. Cut at least 5 steam vents in the top crust.
5. Bake the pie in the lower third of the oven for 25 minutes. Reduce the oven temperature to 350° and bake for 35 to 40 minutes longer, or until the crust is golden brown and the fruit is tender. Let cool for at least 2 hours before serving.
—Michael James

Flaky Pie Dough

Makes Two 9-Inch Single Crusts or One Double Crust

2¼ cups all-purpose flour
¾ teaspoon salt
¾ cup chilled shortening
5 to 6 tablespoons ice water

1. In a large bowl, combine the flour and salt. Cut in the shortening until the mixture resembles very coarse meal with some pieces of shortening the size of corn kernels still visible.
2. Sprinkle 5 tablespoons of the ice water over the mixture, tossing to moisten evenly. Gather the dough into a ball, adding up to 1 tablespoon more ice water if the dough is too dry.
3. Divide the dough in half and pat each piece into a 6-inch disk. Wrap separately in plastic wrap and refrigerate for at least 30 minutes.
—Michael James

Meatless Mince Pie with Bourbon

8 to 10 Servings

Flaky Pie Dough (above)
⅔ cup golden raisins
⅓ cup dried currants
¼ cup bourbon
¼ cup apple juice or cider
1 pound tart green apples, peeled and cored
3 tablespoons fresh lemon juice
1 navel orange, unpeeled, coarsely chopped
⅔ cup sugar
½ teaspoon salt

½ teaspoon cinnamon
½ teaspoon ground mace
¼ teaspoon ground cloves
¼ teaspoon ground ginger
2 tablespoons unsulphured
  molasses
1 tablespoon all-purpose flour
4 tablespoons unsalted butter

1. On a lightly floured surface, roll out one disk of the Flaky Pie Dough about ⅛ inch thick to a 12-inch circle. Fit the dough without stretching into a 9-inch glass pie plate. Fold the edge of the dough under and crimp it to form a fluted rim. Refrigerate the pastry shell for at least 30 minutes.

2. Meanwhile, preheat the oven to 400°. In a large bowl, combine the raisins, currants, bourbon and apple juice.

3. In a food processor, very finely chop the apples. Add the apples and lemon juice to the raisin mixture, toss to mix.

4. Without rinsing the bowl, process the coarsely chopped unpeeled orange until it is a fine pulp. Add the orange to the raisin mixture along with the sugar, salt, cinnamon, mace, cloves, ginger, molasses and flour. Mix to blend well.

5. In a small skillet, melt the butter over low heat. Cook until it becomes light brown, about 5 minutes. Stir the browned butter into the mincemeat and pour the filling into the chilled pie shell.

6. Roll out the remaining disk of dough about ⅛ inch thick to a 12-inch circle. Using a crimped dough cutter, cut the pastry into ½- to ¾-inch-wide strips. Moisten the edge of the pie shell with water and with the strips of pastry, weave a lattice top. Press the strips to the moistened rim of the dough to seal the ends.

7. Place the pie on a baking sheet and bake in the lower third of the oven for 25 minutes. Reduce the oven temperature to 350° and bake for 45 minutes longer, or until the crust is golden brown and the filling is bubbling. Let cool completely before serving.
—Michael James

Cranberry-Apple Pie
with an Oatmeal-Almond
Crust

8 Servings

1 package (12 ounces)
  cranberries
1 large Granny Smith apple—
  peeled, cored and chopped
1¾ cups (packed) brown
  sugar
2 teaspoons grated orange
  zest
¼ teaspoon ground cloves
1½ tablespoons quick-
  cooking tapioca
½ cup finely ground almonds
⅓ cup old-fashioned rolled
  oats
2 tablespoons all-purpose
  flour
½ teaspoon salt
3 tablespoons cold unsalted
  butter, cut into ¼-inch dice
Oatmeal-Almond Pie Dough
  (recipe follows)

1. In a large bowl, combine the cranberries, apple, 1¼ cups of the brown sugar, the orange zest, cloves and tapioca; stir well. Set aside at room temperature.

2. In a medium bowl, combine the remaining ½ cup brown sugar with the ground almonds, oats, flour and salt. Work in the butter until large crumbs form; cover and refrigerate.

3. Preheat the oven to 425°. Roll out the Oatmeal-Almond Pie Dough

to form an 11-inch circle, ⅛ inch thick. Fit the dough into a 9-inch pie plate without tearing or stretching. Shape the rim into an even ridge and flute; refrigerate for 10 minutes.

4. Spread the reserved cranberry filling evenly in the shell. Bake the pie in the bottom third of the oven for 15 minutes. Cover loosely with foil and bake for 10 minutes longer. Uncover and spread the pie evenly with the reserved almond-oat topping. Reduce the heat to 350° and bake for 20 to 25 minutes longer, until bubbly. (If the topping begins to get too dark, cover loosely with foil.) Let cool on a rack.
—Ken Haedrich

Oatmeal-Almond Pie Dough

Makes One 9-Inch Crust

¾ cup all-purpose flour
½ cup oat flour* or ⅔ cup
  old-fashioned rolled oats,
  ground in a blender
¼ cup finely ground almonds
½ teaspoon salt
⅓ cup chilled shortening
3 tablespoons ice water
*Available at health food
  stores

1. In a large bowl, combine the all-purpose flour, oat flour, ground almonds and salt; stir well. Cut in the shortening until the mixture resembles coarse meal.

2. Sprinkle on the ice water, 1 tablespoon at a time, tossing with a fork after each addition. Gather the dough into a ball and flatten into a ½-inch-thick disk. Cover with plastic wrap and refrigerate for 30 to 45 minutes.
—Ken Haedrich

Cranberry Pie

This marvelous recipe is from Elizabeth Ryan, a farmer and baker in New York's Hudson Valley. It's one of her most popular Thanksgiving pies, vying with apple and pumpkin. "It's my version of mince pie," she says, "And I like it a lot better."

If you like this pie, too, remember that your freezer need never be without a bag or two of cranberries, so you can make it year-round. (If you use frozen cranberries, don't thaw them.) In this recipe, the cranberries are sweetened just enough to calm their tartness and let the flavors in the filling come through.

8 Servings

*Farmhouse Pie Pastry (recipe
  follows)*
1 cup sugar
¼ cup all-purpose flour
*1 bag (12 ounces) fresh or
  frozen cranberries*
½ cup golden raisins
*⅓ cup coarsely chopped
  walnuts*
¼ cup fresh orange juice
*3 tablespoons unsalted butter,
  melted*
*½ teaspoon finely grated
  orange zest*
*1 egg mixed with 2 teaspoons
  water, for brushing*

1. Preheat the oven to 400°. On a lightly floured surface, roll out half of the Farmhouse Pie Pastry into a 12-inch circle. Place the dough in a 9-inch pie plate, fitting it evenly into the plate without stretching; leave the edges overhanging and refrigerate. On a sheet of wax paper, roll out the remaining pie pastry into another 12-inch circle; transfer the pastry on the wax paper to a baking sheet and refrigerate.

2. In a small bowl, mix the sugar with the flour and set aside.

3. In a food processor, chop the cranberries until some are finely ground and the largest pieces are the size of peas, about 2 minutes for frozen and several pulses for fresh.

4. Transfer the cranberries to a medium bowl and add the raisins, walnuts, orange juice, melted butter and orange zest. Mix until thoroughly combined.

5. Sprinkle ¼ cup of the reserved sugar and flour mixture on the bottom of the pastry-lined pie plate. Pile in the cranberry filling and sprinkle the remaining sugar and flour mixture on top. Cover with the rolled out pie pastry and crimp the edges together to seal. Brush the top of the pie with the egg wash and cut several slits for steam to escape.

6. Place the pie plate on a baking sheet and bake in the middle of the oven for about 50 minutes, until the pastry is golden and the filling bubbles up through the steam vents. Transfer to a rack and let cool to room temperature before serving.
—*Susan Herrmann Loomis*

Farmhouse Pie Pastry

This pastry, so light, buttery and flaky, will make any pie a spectacular success. The most important rules to follow when making it are: do not overmix it once the water is added, and be sure to chill it for at least an hour before rolling. It is quite delicate and can be difficult to work with if the dough is the least bit warm.
Makes One 9-Inch Double Crust

*1¾ cups unbleached all-
  purpose flour*
1 tablespoon sugar
1 teaspoon salt
*1 stick (4 ounces) plus 3
  tablespoons cold unsalted
  butter, cut into small pieces*
*2 tablespoons chilled lard, cut
  into small pieces*
About 3 tablespoons ice water

1. In a food processor fitted with a plastic dough blade, combine the flour, sugar and salt. Pulse just to mix. Add the butter and lard and pulse on and off about 10 times, until the mixture is the texture of coarse meal with a few pea-size pieces of fat remaining.

2. Pour in some of the ice water, 1 tablespoon at a time, and pulse to incorporate it into the flour mixture. Add just enough water for the pastry to hold together in a very loose ball.

3. Turn the dough out onto a large sheet of wax paper and press it into a 5-inch disk. Wrap tightly and refrigerate for at least 1 hour. *(The pastry dough can be made up to 1 week ahead and frozen. Wrap it first in wax paper and then in aluminum foil so it doesn't dry out.)*
—*Susan Herrmann Loomis*

Icy Fresh Cranberry Pie

8 Servings

Graham Cracker Crust:
*1½ cups graham cracker
  crumbs*
*¼ cup confectioners' sugar,
  sifted*
*6 tablespoons unsalted butter,
  melted*
½ teaspoon cinnamon

Filling:
2 seedless, thin-skinned
  oranges (see Note)
2 cups (about ½ pound)
  cranberries
½ cup granulated sugar
1 tablespoon fresh lemon
  juice
1 pint vanilla ice cream,
  softened

Garnish:
1 cup heavy cream, whipped
  and lightly sweetened

1. Prepare the crust: Preheat the oven to 350°. In a bowl or in a food processor, combine the graham cracker crumbs with the confectioners' sugar, melted butter and cinnamon. Press the mixture evenly into a 9-inch pie plate. Bake 10 minutes, then allow to cool completely.

2. Prepare the filling: Cut the oranges up roughly, including the peel. In a food processor, coarsely chop the cranberries and oranges together. Stir in the granulated sugar and lemon juice.

3. Fold the cranberry-orange mixture into the softened ice cream until blended. Fill the baked and cooled pie shell with this mixture and freeze until firm.

4. About 30 minutes before the pie is to be served, transfer it to the refrigerator to soften slightly. Spread the whipped cream over the pie.

NOTE: If the oranges you are using have very thick skins, peel the oranges and remove all the bitter white pith before chopping.
—*Pearl Byrd Foster*

Pear and Ginger Pie

Very often fruit pies are obscured with too many spices. This one is flavored only with fresh ginger, which adds a subtle sparkle.

8 to 10 Servings

Flaky Pie Pastry (recipe
  follows)
2½ pounds firm, ripe pears
1-inch piece of fresh ginger,
  peeled and finely grated
⅓ cup sugar
3 tablespoons unbleached all-
  purpose flour
2 tablespoons unsalted butter
1 egg
Pinch of salt

1. Preheat the oven to 450°. Divide the Flaky Pie Pastry in half. On a lightly floured work surface, roll out half the dough into an 11-inch disk, ⅛ to ¼ inch thick. Fit without stretching into a 9-inch glass pie plate. Trim the dough even with the edge of the pan.

2. Peel, quarter and core the pears and cut each quarter crosswise into 5 or 6 slices. Place the pears in a large bowl and toss with the grated ginger.

3. Combine the sugar and flour and sprinkle 2 tablespoons of the mixture over the pastry in the pan. Pour the remaining sugar and flour over the pears and toss gently to mix. Turn the filling into the prepared pastry shell and smooth the top as much as possible. Dot the filling with the butter.

4. On a lightly floured surface, roll out the remaining dough to an 11-inch disk and fold the dough in half. Place the folded dough on the surface of the filling and line up the fold with the center of the pie. Unfold the dough. Trim the edge of the dough so that there is an even ½-inch edge of overhang. Tuck the excess dough under the edge of the bottom crust. Flute the edge of the crust. Cut 3 or 4 vent holes in the center of the top crust with the point of a paring knife. Beat the egg and salt together and paint the top of the pie with the glaze.

5. Bake the pie on the bottom rack of the oven for 15 minutes. Reduce the oven temperature to 350° and bake for 35 minutes longer, or until the crust is deep golden and the juices are just beginning to bubble up. Let the pie cool on a rack. Serve warm or at room temperature.
—*Nicholas Malgieri*

Flaky Pie Pastry

The greatest problem in making all-butter crusts is to get them flaky and tender at the same time. The addition of the cake flour in this recipe cuts down the gluten development in the all-purpose flour and results in a more tender dough. The bit of baking powder helps the dough to expand very slightly, contributing both to tenderness and to a firm contact between the bottom crust and the pan; it also ensures that the crust bakes evenly throughout.

Makes One 9-Inch Double Crust

2 cups unbleached all-purpose
  flour
¼ cup cake flour
¼ teaspoon baking powder
¼ teaspoon salt
2 sticks (8 ounces) unsalted
  butter
5 to 6 tablespoons ice water

1. Combine the all-purpose flour, cake flour, baking powder and salt in a mixing bowl. Stir well to blend.

2. Cut each stick of butter into 6 or 8 pieces and, using your fingertips, rub the butter into the dry ingredients until the mixture is mealy with no large pieces of butter visible.

3. Sprinkle the water over the flour and butter mixture and toss with a fork to moisten. Add only enough water to make the dough hold together. Knead the dough into a ball and flatten into a 6- to 8-inch disk. Wrap in plastic and refrigerate for about 1 hour, or until firm.
—Nicholas Malgieri

Gingered Pear Pie in a Spiced Whole Wheat Crust

8 Servings

6 large firm-ripe pears (about
  3 pounds)—peeled, cored
  and quartered
2 tablespoons fresh lemon
  juice
½ cup sugar
1½ tablespoons quick-
  cooking tapioca
1 teaspoon ground ginger
Pinch of salt
Spiced Whole Wheat Pie
  Dough (recipe follows)
2 tablespoons unsalted butter

1. Cut the pears into ⅛- to ¼-inch-thick slices and place in a bowl. Sprinkle with the lemon juice, sugar, tapioca, ginger and salt; toss gently to combine.

2. Preheat the oven to 425°. On a lightly floured surface, roll the larger disk of Spiced Whole Wheat Pie Dough into an 11-inch circle, ⅛ inch thick. Fit the dough into a 9-inch pie plate without stretching.

3. Roll the remaining dough into a 10-inch circle, ⅛ inch thick. Spoon the pears into the shell and smooth the surface. Dot with the butter. Moisten the dough rim and place the lid on top; press gently all around the rim to seal. Trim the dough with scissors, leaving a ¼-inch overhang.

4. Fold the rim under to form an even ridge. Prick several steam vents in the lid with a fork and bake the pie in the middle of the oven for 25 minutes. Reduce the heat to 375° and bake for 20 to 25 minutes longer, until thick syrup bubbles through the vents. Let cool on a rack.
—Ken Haedrich

Spiced Whole Wheat Pie Dough

Makes One 9-Inch Double-Crust

1¼ cups whole wheat flour
1¼ cups all-purpose flour
1 teaspoon cinnamon
1 teaspoon freshly grated
  nutmeg
½ teaspoon salt
¾ cup chilled shortening
2 tablespoons cold unsalted
  butter, cut into ¼-inch slices
4 to 5 tablespoons ice water

1. In a large bowl, combine the whole wheat and all-purpose flours with the cinnamon, nutmeg and salt; stir well. Cut in the shortening and butter until the mixture resembles coarse meal.

2. Sprinkle on the ice water, 1 tablespoon at a time, tossing with a fork after each addition. When the dough begins to mass together, form into 2 balls, one slightly larger than the other. Flatten each into a ½-inch-thick disk. Cover with plastic wrap and refrigerate for at least 30 minutes before rolling out.
—Ken Haedrich

Cranberry-Orange Cream Tart

8 to 10 Servings

Crust:
2 cups all-purpose flour
2 tablespoons sugar
½ teaspoon salt
1 stick (4 ounces) cold
  unsalted butter, thinly sliced
3 tablespoons chilled
  vegetable shortening or lard
About 5 tablespoons ice water

Filling:
½ cup sugar
4 egg yolks
4 tablespoons cornstarch
1½ cups milk
½ vanilla bean, split
  lengthwise
1½ tablespoons orange
  liqueur
½ cup heavy cream, chilled

Topping and Assembly:
2 large oranges
1 cup sugar
12 ounces fresh cranberries
1 tablespoon plus 2 teaspoons
  cornstarch blended with 2
  tablespoons water
½ cup chopped walnuts

1. Prepare the crust: In a medium bowl, combine the flour, sugar and salt. Cut in the butter and shortening until the mixture resembles coarse crumbs. Sprinkle on 3 tablespoons of the ice water, tossing lightly until the dough begins to mass together. Gradually add up to 2 more tablespoons of ice water if necessary. Gather the dough into a ball and flatten into a 6-inch disk. Wrap and refrigerate for at least 1 hour.

2. Preheat the oven to 425°. Roll out the dough on a lightly floured surface into a circle about ⅛ inch thick and 13 inches in diameter. Fold into quarters and center in a 10½-inch tart pan with a removable bottom. Unfold and fit against the bottom and sides of the pan. Run a rolling pin over the top of the pan to trim off excess dough. Prick the bottom of the crust with a fork and refrigerate until chilled, about 20 minutes.

3. Line the pastry crust with aluminum foil and fill with dried beans or pie weights. Place on a cookie sheet and bake for 12 minutes. Remove the foil and beans, prick any bubbles with a fork and reduce the oven temperature to 375°. Continue to bake for about 15 minutes, or until the crust is golden brown. Transfer to a rack and let cool for 5 minutes. Remove the sides of the pan and let the crust cool completely before filling. *(The crust can be baked 1 day ahead, wrapped tightly and stored in a cool, dry place.)*

4. Make the filling: In a medium bowl, beat the sugar and egg yolks until thick and light colored. Whisk in the cornstarch until smooth. In a small saucepan, bring the milk with the vanilla bean just to a boil. Strain to remove the vanilla bean and gradually whisk the hot milk into the egg mixture.

5. Scrape into a heavy medium saucepan and bring to a boil over low heat, stirring frequently. Reduce the heat and simmer, stirring, for 1 minute, until the custard is thickened and smooth. Pour into a medium bowl and whisk for about 10 minutes, until light and fluffy and cooled to room temperature. Stir in the orange liqueur.

6. Beat the cream until stiff. Fold the whipped cream into the cooled custard. Cover the pastry cream and refrigerate the pastry cream until the tart is assembled.

7. Make the topping: Remove the zest from the oranges; cut into thin julienne strips. Squeeze the juice from the oranges. There will be about 1 cup; if there is less, add water to make 1 cup.

8. In a small heavy saucepan, simmer the zest in 1 cup of water until softened, about 3 minutes. Strain and return the strips of zest to the pan. Add 1 cup of cold water and the sugar and bring to a boil. Reduce the heat and simmer, uncovered, until the syrup is reduced to ½ cup, about 20 minutes. With a slotted spoon, remove the zest and spread the strips flat on a sheet of wax paper.

9. Add the orange juice to the syrup in the pan and bring to a boil. Add the cranberries, reduce the heat and simmer, uncovered, for 10 minutes. Stir in the cornstarch mixture and simmer, stirring, until the liquid thickens and clears, about 1 minute. Pour into a shallow bowl, cover loosely with wax paper and let cool to room temperature.

10. Assemble the tart: Slide the baked tart shell onto a serving platter. Fill with the pastry cream, spreading evenly. Sprinkle the walnuts over the surface and spread the cranberry mixture on top. Sprinkle the candied orange zest in a border around the edge. Refrigerate, covered, until serving time.
—*Diana Sturgis*

Ricotta-Orange Pie

The inside of this prebaked pie shell is coated with melted chocolate before it is filled. This prevents it from becoming soggy during baking and adds a delicious flavor to the pie.
10 Servings

3 ounces semisweet chocolate
Cookie Crumb Crust (p. 227)
*   made with vanilla wafers*
*   and almonds*
1½ cups ricotta cheese
⅔ cup sugar
½ cup sour cream
3 eggs, separated
1½ tablespoons finely minced
*   orange zest*
½ teaspoon almond extract
¼ teaspoon salt

1. Melt the chocolate in a double boiler. Quickly spread it in an even layer over the bottom of the prepared Cookie Crumb Crust. Chill for 15 to 20 minutes.

2. Meanwhile, preheat the oven to 350°. In a large bowl, blend the ricotta with ½ cup of the sugar, the sour cream, egg yolks, orange zest, almond extract and salt. Beat until smooth and set aside.

3. In another large bowl, beat or whisk the egg whites until soft peaks form. Gradually beat in the remaining sugar and continue beating until stiff peaks form. Do not overbeat. Gently but thoroughly fold the egg whites into the ricotta mixture. Pour the mixture into the pie shell and bake in the center of the oven for 30 minutes, or until the filling is puffy and golden. Cool to room temperature (the pie will settle during cooling) and then chill thoroughly before serving.
—*F&W*

Cherry Custard Pie

8 to 10 Servings

Custard:
5 egg yolks, at room
  temperature
1 cup sugar
⅔ cup all-purpose flour
2 cups milk, scalded
2 teaspoons unsalted butter,
  softened to room
  temperature
2 teaspoons almond extract

Prebaked Sweet Pastry Shell
  (recipe follows)

Cherry Topping:
1 can (16 ounces) tart, pitted
  cherries
4 teaspoons cornstarch
4 tablespoons sugar
2 to 3 drops red food coloring
  (optional)

1. Prepare the custard: Using an electric mixer or a whisk, beat the egg yolks and sugar together in a large bowl until the mixture is pale yellow and forms a ribbon when the beaters are lifted. Gradually beat in the flour until well blended. A few drops at a time, beat in ¼ cup of the scalded milk, then beat in the remainder in a slow, steady stream.

2. Transfer the mixture to a saucepan and, stirring constantly with a whisk, bring the mixture to a boil over moderate heat; cook for 2 minutes. (If the mixture becomes lumpy as you are cooking it, remove the pan from the heat, whisk vigorously until the custard is smooth and then return it to the heat.)

3. Remove the pan from the heat and stir in the butter and almond extract. Let the custard cool, covered, for 10 minutes, and then pour it into the Prebaked Sweet Pastry Shell. Lay a sheet of wax paper on the custard and chill for 1 hour.

4. Prepare the topping: Thoroughly drain the cherries, reserving the juice. Measure the juice and, if necessary, add enough water to make 1 cup. Pour the liquid into a small saucepan and stir in the cornstarch until smooth. Add the sugar and bring the mixture to a boil over moderate heat and cook for 1 minute, stirring once or twice. Remove the pan from the heat. Stir in the food coloring if desired. Cover the glaze to prevent a skin from forming.

5. Assemble the pie: Arrange the cherries on top of the custard in a single layer. Spoon the cherry glaze evenly over the cherries and custard. Chill the pie for at least 1 hour before serving.
—*F&W*

Prebaked Sweet Pastry Shell

Sweet pastry is basic flaky pastry that has been sweetened by the addition of granulated or superfine sugar. In addition, most of the liquid is provided by egg in lieu of water. (It is sometimes necessary to add a few drops of water to make the dough cohere.) This type of dough is quite crumbly and comparatively difficult to work with; however, the flavor and crisp tenderness of the crust will make your efforts worthwhile. If you want to make an extra crust, this recipe can be doubled easily.

Makes One 9-Inch Crust

1 cup all-purpose flour
1½ tablespoons sugar
¼ teaspoon salt
⅓ cup (5 tablespoons plus 1
  teaspoon) unsalted butter
½ large egg, lightly beaten
  (see Note)

1. In a medium bowl, combine the flour, sugar and salt. Cut in the butter until the mixture resembles coarse meal. Gradually add the egg to the mixture, stirring with a fork, until the dough begins to mass together. If necessary add a few drops of cold water. Gently pat into a ball and flatten it into a round about 6 inches in diameter. Wrap in wax paper and chill for at least 1 hour. *(Tightly wrapped in plastic wrap, the pastry will keep for up to 3 days in the refrigerator or for up to 3 months in the freezer.)*

2. Preheat the oven to 400°. Oil or butter a 9-inch pie plate. Roll out the pastry between two sheets of generously floured wax paper to an 11- to 12-inch round. Carefully peel off the top sheet of wax paper. Invert the pastry into the pie plate and peel off the remaining wax paper. Without stretching it, gently fit the pastry into the pie plate and trim off the overhang evenly to ½ inch. Fold the edges under and crimp decoratively. With a fork, lightly prick the dough all over. Refrigerate for 15 minutes.

3. Line the pastry shell with aluminum foil and fill with dried beans, rice or pie weights. Bake for 12 minutes and remove the foil and weights. Reduce the heat to 350° and bake for another 8 minutes. Cool the shell completely on a rack before filling.

NOTE: For ½ an egg, beat 1 egg lightly with a fork and measure out 1½ tablespoons.
—*F&W*

Fudge Pie (p. 228).

Peach and Ginger Trifle (p. 183).

Prune Cake (p. 170).

Banana Cream Pie

10 Servings

6 tablespoons all-purpose flour
1 cup granulated sugar
¼ teaspoon salt
2 cups milk, scalded
3 egg yolks, well beaten
4 tablespoons unsalted butter, cut into ¼-inch slices and softened to room temperature
1 teaspoon vanilla extract
4 small bananas
Cookie Crumb Crust (p. 227) made with vanilla wafers
2 cups heavy cream
¾ cup confectioners' sugar

1. In a medium saucepan, combine the flour, sugar and salt. Gradually stir in the scalded milk until the mixture is smooth. Bring it to a boil over moderate heat, stirring constantly. Boil, stirring, for 1 minute and remove from the heat.

2. Gradually stir about ¼ cup of the hot milk mixture into the egg yolks, then stir the yolk mixture back into the pan. Cook, stirring constantly, over moderate heat for about 3 minutes, or until the custard is very thick. Remove the pan from the heat and stir in the butter and vanilla until smooth. Place a sheet of plastic wrap on the surface of the custard to prevent a skin from forming, and allow to cool for 15 minutes.

3. Cut the bananas into ¼-inch slices and arrange half of them, overlapping slightly, over the bottom of the prepared Cookie Crumb Crust. Cover them evenly with half the custard. Arrange the remaining bananas over the custard layer and cover evenly with the remaining custard. Cover the custard with wax paper and refrigerate for 2 hours.

4. Using a chilled bowl and beaters, beat the heavy cream until soft peaks form. Gradually add the confectioners' sugar ¼ cup at a time, beating on low speed after each addition until it is thoroughly incorporated. Then beat on high speed until the cream is stiff.

5. Spoon all the whipped cream over the pie, or spread about two-thirds of it over the surface, place the remainder in a pastry bag fitted with a decorative tip and pipe decorations around the edge and in the center of the pie.
—F&W

Maple Pecan Pie

8 Servings

1½ cups heavy cream
¾ cup sugar
¾ cup pure maple syrup
2 eggs, lightly beaten
2 teaspoons vanilla extract
2 cups pecan halves
Cornmeal Crust (p. 223), partially baked
Lightly sweetened whipped cream, for serving

1. Preheat the oven to 400°. In a large heavy saucepan, bring the heavy cream and sugar to a simmer over moderate heat. Simmer for 25 minutes, whisking occasionally, until the mixture slightly caramelizes to a light brown. Remove from the heat and whisk in the maple syrup, eggs

and vanilla. Stir in the pecans. Pour the mixture into the partially baked Cornmeal Crust.

2. Bake the pie in the lower third of the oven for 25 to 30 minutes, or until the custard is nearly set and the top is richly browned. Let cool completely. Serve with lightly sweetened whipped cream.
—Michael James

Banana Walnut Tart

I first made this dessert two years ago while planning a tart class that was to take place during the winter when the usual stone fruits and berries would not be available. Since then it has become one of my favorites. When the bananas bake between the walnut filling and the crust, they acquire the consistency of preserves, and their moist texture is in perfect contrast to the crumbly crust and the dense walnut filling.

8 Servings

Sweet Pastry Dough (recipe follows)
3 ripe bananas
1½ cups walnut pieces (about 6 ounces)
½ cup (packed) light brown sugar
4 tablespoons unsalted butter, softened
2 eggs
3 tablespoons unbleached all-purpose flour
¼ teaspoon cinnamon
1 tablespoon dark rum

1. Preheat the oven to 350°. On a lightly floured work surface, roll the Sweet Pastry Dough into a 12- to 13-inch round, ⅛ to ¼ inch thick. Fit the dough into a 10-inch tart pan with a removable bottom and trim the excess dough even with the edge.

2. Cut the bananas into ½-inch-thick slices. Cover the bottom of the dough with the banana slices, fitting them tightly together.

3. In a food processor, coarsely chop the walnuts. Remove ½ cup of the chopped walnuts and set aside. Add the brown sugar to the work bowl and process until the walnuts are very finely ground. Add the butter and process until mixed. Add the eggs, 1 at a time, processing only until the mixture is smooth and scraping down the sides of the bowl occasionally. Add the flour and cinnamon and process until blended.

4. Spread the walnut filling evenly over the bananas, covering as much of the surface as possible. Scatter the reserved chopped walnuts over the top.

5. Bake the tart on the bottom rack of the oven for 40 minutes, or until the pastry is baked through and the walnut filling is set and a deep golden color. Remove the tart from the oven to a rack and immediately sprinkle the rum over the top.
—Nicholas Malgieri

Sweet Pastry Dough

Use this dough for any pie or tart with a raw or liquid filling. The presence of the baking powder makes the dough expand slightly during baking so that it maintains a constant contact with the hot bottom of the pan and bakes through evenly, eliminating raw and soggy bottoms.

Makes One 10-Inch Tart Shell

1 cup unbleached all-purpose flour
¼ cup sugar
½ teaspoon baking powder
Pinch of salt
4 tablespoons unsalted butter
1 egg, lightly beaten

In a bowl, combine the flour, sugar, baking powder and salt. Rub in the butter with your fingertips until the mixture resembles coarse meal. Stir the egg into the dough with a fork to moisten evenly. Press the dough together in the bowl and turn out onto a lightly floured surface. Knead lightly 2 or 3 times, press into a 6-inch disk and wrap in plastic wrap. Refrigerate until firm, about 1 hour.
—Nicholas Malgieri

Walnut Pie

8 to 10 Servings

½ recipe Flaky Pastry made with butter (see Note)
2 cups coarsely chopped walnuts (about 8 ounces)
¼ cup honey
1½ teaspoons cinnamon
¼ teaspoon ground cloves
¾ cup (packed) light brown sugar
¾ cup light corn syrup
1 stick (4 ounces) unsalted butter, melted and cooled to room temperature
3 eggs, well beaten
¼ teaspoon salt

1. On a lightly floured surface, roll out the Flaky Pastry to an 11- to 12-inch circle. Fold the circle into quarters or roll it loosely over a lightly floured rolling pin and transfer it to a 9-inch pie plate. Unfold and ease the pastry into the pie plate without stretching it. Trim the edges evenly to leave a ½-inch overhang. Fold the excess pastry under and crimp the edge decoratively. Refrigerate the pie shell while preparing the filling.

2. Preheat the oven to 350°. In a small bowl, mix the walnuts with the honey, cinnamon and cloves. In a medium bowl, stir the brown sugar with the corn syrup until blended. Stir in the butter, eggs and salt. Stir in the nut mixture until blended.

3. Pour into the prepared pie shell and smooth out the surface. Bake the pie in the center of the oven for about 1 hour, or until the filling is set. Transfer to a rack and cool completely before serving.

NOTE: For ½ recipe of Flaky Pastry, make a full recipe (page 206) and reserve one pastry round for another use; or make the pastry using 1 cup flour, ⅛ teaspoon salt, ⅓ cup butter and about 2 tablespoons ice water, and do not divide the dough in half.
—F&W

Pumpkin Custard Pie

This recipe comes from Linda Stoltzfus, a young Amish woman from northern Pennsylvania. It produces a pie that is light and airy, with a subtle pumpkin taste and delicate edge of cinnamon.

The pie is best made with freshly cooked pumpkin, but pumpkin from a can works well too. You might want to double the recipe and make two pies, thereby using a full recipe of the pastry dough and—if using canned pumpkin—a whole can of pumpkin puree.

8 to 10 Servings

½ recipe Farmhouse Pie Pastry (p. 208)
1 cup fresh or unsweetened canned pumpkin puree (see Note)
2 eggs, separated
1⅓ cups milk
¼ cup plus 2 tablespoons granulated sugar

¼ cup plus 2 tablespoons
(lightly packed) light brown
sugar
1 tablespoon unsalted butter,
melted
¾ teaspoon vanilla extract
Pinch of salt
3 tablespoons all-purpose
flour
¼ teaspoon cinnamon

1. Preheat the oven to 425°. On a lightly floured surface, roll out the Farmhouse Pie Pastry into a 12-inch circle. Place the dough in a 9-inch pie plate, fitting it evenly into the plate without stretching; crimp the edge. Line the pastry with aluminum foil or parchment paper and fill with pie weights, dried beans or rice.

2. Bake the pastry for 15 to 20 minutes, or until the edges begin to turn golden. Remove the foil and weights and bake for about 10 minutes longer, or until lightly browned all over. Transfer to a rack to cool. (The pie shell can be prebaked up to 1 day ahead; store at room temperature.)

3. In a medium bowl, combine the pumpkin puree and egg yolks and whisk until blended. Whisk in the milk, granulated sugar, light brown sugar, butter, vanilla and salt. Sift the flour over the mixture and whisk in until smooth.

4. In another medium bowl, whisk the egg whites just until they are bright white and form very soft peaks. Lightly whisk them into the pumpkin mixture, then pour the filling into the prebaked pie shell. Sprinkle the cinnamon on top.

5. Bake the pie in the middle of the oven for 10 minutes, then reduce the heat to 350° and bake for 25 to 30 minutes longer, or until the filling is nearly set but still moves slightly in the center. Transfer to a rack to cool to room temperature before serving.

NOTE: To make 1 cup of fresh pumpkin puree, steam 7 ounces of peeled fresh pumpkin chunks over boiling water until very soft throughout, about 15 minutes. Puree in a food processor until smooth. Transfer the puree to a medium saucepan and cook over moderately high heat until thick enough to hold its shape on a spoon, 8 to 10 minutes.
—Susan Herrmann Loomis

Brandied Pumpkin Pie

Otto Seelbach, a member of the Louisville Seelbach Hotel family, who knew good food, told me years ago that a pumpkin pie should "cry"—that is, small teardrops of moisture should rise to the top after the pie rests for a while. In other words, a delicious pumpkin pie must be moist and luscious. This is the pumpkin pie that cries.

8 to 10 Servings

Old-Fashioned Pie Crust,
unbaked (recipe follows)
1 cup canned unsweetened
solid-pack pumpkin
1 cup heavy cream or
evaporated milk
3 eggs
1 cup (packed) light brown
sugar
1 teaspoon cinnamon
½ teaspoon ground ginger
¼ teaspoon freshly grated
nutmeg
¼ cup brandy
Chilled Bourbon Custard
(p. 197) or whipped cream,
for serving

1. Preheat the oven to 400°. Cover the Old-Fashioned Pie Crust with aluminum foil and weigh down

with dried beans or pie weights. Place the pie plate on the bottom rack of the oven and bake for 15 minutes, or until the crust is almost dry and lightly colored. Remove the beans and the foil and set the partially baked crust aside to cool for 15 minutes. Leave the oven on.

2. Meanwhile, measure the pumpkin into a large bowl. Gradually whisk in the cream. Add the eggs one by one, whisking until well blended.

3. Combine the sugar with the spices and beat them into the pumpkin mixture. Add the brandy and mix well. Spoon the filling into the partially baked crust.

4. Place the pie on the lowest shelf of the oven and bake for 8 minutes. Reduce the oven temperature to 350° and continue to bake 40 to 45 minutes longer, or until a knife inserted in the middle comes out clean. Serve warm or cold, with Chilled Bourbon Custard or whipped cream.
—Camille Glenn

Old-Fashioned Pie Crust

Makes One 9-Inch Crust

1 cup plus 2 tablespoons all-
purpose flour
¼ teaspoon baking powder
¼ teaspoon salt
6 tablespoons cold unsalted
butter, cut into small pieces
1 tablespoon sugar
1 egg yolk
1 tablespoon ice water

1. In a large bowl, combine the flour, baking powder and salt; mix well. Cut in the butter until the mixture resembles coarse meal. Mix in the sugar. Add the egg yolk and ice water and stir to form a dough. Pat the dough into a 6-inch disk; wrap and refrigerate until chilled, about

20 minutes.

2. On a lightly floured sheet of wax paper, roll out the dough into an 11-inch circle. Invert the pastry into a buttered 9-inch metal pie plate and peel off the paper. Fit the pastry evenly into the dish without stretching. Trim the dough to ½ inch beyond the rim of the pan. Fold the edge under and crimp decoratively. Refrigerate the pie shell while you make the filling. *(The unbaked crust can be formed 1 day ahead.)*
—Camille Glenn

Old-Fashioned Pumpkin Pie

Molasses is the secret ingredient that helps flavor this traditional pumpkin pie. Light textured when freshly made, the pie will be denser, with a deeper flavor, if made the day before and refrigerated overnight.

8 to 10 Servings

Pie Crust:
1 cup plus 2 tablespoons all-purpose flour
¼ teaspoon baking powder
¼ teaspoon salt
6 tablespoons cold unsalted butter, cut into pieces
1 tablespoon sugar
1 egg yolk
1 tablespoon ice water

Filling:
1⅓ cups canned unsweetened solid-pack pumpkin
3 whole eggs
1 cup sour cream
½ cup heavy cream
½ cup unsulphured molasses
1 teaspoon ground ginger
1 teaspoon allspice
1 teaspoon cinnamon

Sweetened whipped cream dusted with cinnamon, for serving

1. Make the crust: In a large bowl, mix together the flour, baking powder and salt. Cut in the butter until the mixture resembles coarse meal. Mix in the sugar. Add the egg yolk and ice water and stir to form a dough. Pat the dough into a 6-inch disk; wrap and refrigerate until chilled, about 20 minutes.

2. On a lightly floured sheet of wax paper, roll out the dough into an 11-inch circle. Invert the pastry into a buttered 9-inch metal pie plate and peel off the paper. Fit the pastry evenly in the dish, trim away any excess and decoratively crimp the edge. Refrigerate the pie shell while you make the filling. *(The crust can be made a day ahead.)*

3. Make the filling: Preheat the oven to 400°. In a large bowl, lightly beat the pumpkin, eggs, sour cream, heavy cream, molasses, ginger, allspice and cinnamon until well blended.

4. Place the pie plate on a baking sheet and pour the filling into the prepared pie shell. Bake in the middle of the oven for 20 minutes. Reduce the oven temperature to 325° and continue to bake for 25 to 30 minutes, until the pie is set but slightly wobbly in the center. Let cool on a rack. Serve at room temperature or chilled with the cinnamon-dusted whipped cream.
—Diana Sturgis

Sour Cream Pumpkin Pie with Butter Pecan Topping

Serve this pie with unsweetened whipped cream on the side.
6 to 8 Servings

Pastry:
1¼ cups all-purpose flour
¼ teaspoon baking powder
¼ teaspoon salt
6 tablespoons cold butter, cut into small pieces
2 tablespoons vegetable shortening
1 egg, lightly beaten

Filling and Topping:
2 cups chopped pecans
¼ cup plus 2 tablespoons (packed) light brown sugar
3 tablespoons unsalted butter, melted
1⅓ cups canned solid-pack pumpkin
1½ teaspoons ground ginger
1½ teaspoons cinnamon
1 teaspoon ground allspice
3 eggs, lightly beaten
⅓ cup unsulphured molasses
2 tablespoons granulated sugar
1 cup sour cream
½ cup heavy cream

1. Make the pastry: In a large bowl, stir together the flour, baking powder and salt. Cut in the butter and then, using your fingertips, work in the shortening until the mixture resembles coarse meal. Stir in the egg and gather the dough into a ball. Flatten the dough into a 6-inch disk, wrap in plastic wrap and refrigerate for at least 30 minutes before rolling out.

2. Make the filling and topping: Preheat the oven to 350°. In a medium bowl, toss together the pecans, brown sugar and melted butter; set aside.

3. In a large bowl, combine the pumpkin, ginger, cinnamon, allspice and eggs. Whisk to blend well. Mix in the molasses, granulated sugar, sour cream and heavy cream until thoroughly blended.

4. Roll out the pastry to a 12-inch circle about ⅛ inch thick. Fit the dough loosely into a 10-inch pie dish, preferably glass. Trim the edge, leaving an extra ½ inch all around. Fold the edge under itself and flute if desired.

5. Pour in the pumpkin filling and bake for 15 minutes. Sprinkle the reserved pecan mixture evenly over the pie and bake for about 30 minutes longer, until the top is brown and crusty and the filling is set. Let the pie cool for at least 2 hours before serving, with a bowl of whipped cream on the side. *(The pie can be made up to 6 hours in advance and refrigerated.)*
—*Marcia Kiesel*

Spiced Butternut Squash Pie

8 to 10 Servings

1 butternut squash, about 2 pounds
½ teaspoon cinnamon
1 teaspoon ground ginger
1 teaspoon salt
¼ cup honey
½ cup molasses
5 eggs
¾ cup heavy cream
Pie Pastry (recipe follows)

1. Cut the squash in half and remove the seeds. Steam the squash in a vegetable steamer until it is fork-tender, 20 to 25 minutes.

2. Remove the squash from the pan, and when it is cool enough to handle, scoop out the flesh with a spoon; discard the shells. Using a food processor, blender or food mill, puree the squash. You should have about 2½ cups.

3. Place the puree in a large bowl and beat in the cinnamon, ginger, salt, honey and molasses. In a separate bowl, whisk together the eggs and cream and blend the mixture into the squash mixture.

4. Preheat the oven to 450°. On wax paper, roll the Pie Pastry into a 12-inch round. Invert it into a 9- or 10-inch pie plate. Press it carefully against the sides and trim the top edge. If your kitchen is warm, chill the pastry shell for 10 minutes; otherwise, proceed with the next step.

5. Place the pie plate on a baking sheet and pour three-fourths of the filling into it. Place the pie on the center shelf of the oven and pour the remaining filling into it. (This method avoids the possibility of spilling the pie while you are transferring it to the oven.)

6. Bake the pie for 10 minutes. Then reduce the temperature to 325° and bake it for an additional 45 minutes, or until the center of the filling is firm when the baking sheet is moved gently back and forth. Serve warm, at room temperature, or chilled.
—*Martha Stewart*

Pie Pastry

Makes One 9-Inch Crust

1½ sticks (6 ounces) cold unsalted butter
2 cups all-purpose flour
½ teaspoon salt
3 to 4 tablespoons ice water

1. In a food processor, cut the butter into small pieces and process it with the flour and salt for 15 seconds. Add 3 tablespoons of the ice water and pulse on and off until the dough just holds together when pressed. If necessary, add up to 1 more tablespoon of the ice water and process very briefly.

2. Form the dough into a flat round about 6 inches in diameter, wrap it in wax paper, and chill it for at least 2 hours.
—*Martha Stewart*

Pumpkin Cheesecake Pie in a Gingersnap Crust

A small slice of this rich and creamy pie feels like an extravagant treat.
12 Servings

½ cup pecans
2 tablespoons granulated sugar
1 cup gingersnap crumbs (from about 20 cookies)
5 tablespoons unsalted butter, melted
1 pound cream cheese, at room temperature
⅔ cup (packed) brown sugar
½ cup sour cream, at room temperature
1 cup canned unsweetened solid-pack pumpkin
3 eggs, at room temperature
1 teaspoon cinnamon
Pinch of ground cloves
Pinch of ground ginger
Pecan halves, for garnish

1. Preheat the oven to 325°. Place the ½ cup pecans and the granulated sugar in a food processor and process until finely chopped, about 20 seconds. Pour into a large bowl, add the gingersnap crumbs and mix. Pour in the butter and stir well to combine. Turn the mixture into a 10-inch pie plate and press evenly against the bottom and sides of the dish to form a crust. Bake for 10 minutes. Set aside to cool. Leave the oven on.

2. In a large bowl, beat the cream cheese and brown sugar until soft and well blended. Stir in the sour cream and pumpkin. Gradually beat in the eggs, 1 at a time, and the cinnamon, cloves and ginger.

3. Place the pie plate on a baking sheet and pour in the filling. Bake in the middle of the oven for 45 minutes, or until the filling is set. Let cool on a rack. Arrange the pecan halves around the edge of the pie. *(The pie can be made 1 day ahead if desired. Refrigerate, covered.)*
—Diana Sturgis

Maple Squash Pie in a Poppy Seed-Corn Crust

8 Servings

Poppy Seed-Corn Pie Dough (recipe follows)
1½ cups cooked and well-drained winter squash or unsweetened canned pumpkin puree
¾ cup pure maple syrup
3 eggs, lightly beaten
¾ cup heavy cream
1 teaspoon cinnamon
½ teaspoon allspice
½ teaspoon ground ginger
½ teaspoon ground cloves
¼ teaspoon salt

1. Roll the Poppy Seed-Corn Pie Dough into an 11-inch circle, ⅛ inch thick. Fit the dough into a 9-inch pie plate, without stretching. Form the edge into an even ridge and flute. Freeze the shell for 15 minutes.

2. Meanwhile, preheat the oven to 450°. In a food processor, puree the squash and maple syrup. Add the eggs, cream, cinnamon, allspice, ginger, cloves and salt; puree until blended.

3. Pour the filling into the partially frozen shell and bake in the lower third of the oven for 10 minutes. Reduce the heat to 325° and bake for 45 to 50 minutes, or until all but the very center of the pie is set. (The center will firm up as the pie cools.) Let cool on a rack.
—Ken Haedrich

Poppy Seed-Corn Pie Dough

Makes One 9-Inch Crust

¾ cup all-purpose flour
½ cup stone-ground cornmeal
2 tablespoons poppy seeds
½ teaspoon salt
¼ cup chilled shortening
2 tablespoons cold unsalted butter
2½ to 3½ tablespoons ice water

1. In a large bowl, combine the flour, cornmeal, poppy seeds and salt; stir well. Cut in the shortening and butter until the mixture resembles coarse meal.

2. Sprinkle on the ice water, 1 tablespoon at a time, tossing with a fork after each addition. Gather the dough into a ball and flatten into a ½-inch-thick disk. Cover with plastic wrap and refrigerate for 30 minutes.
—Ken Haedrich

Southern Yam Pie Topped with Candied Ginger

This delectable pie is an unusual variation on the theme of the pumpkin or sweet-potato pie, with the added warmth and nip of candied ginger.

8 Servings

Pastry:
1½ cups plus 2 tablespoons all-purpose flour
½ teaspoon salt
1 stick (4 ounces) unsalted butter, cut into pieces
1 egg yolk
2 to 3 tablespoons ice water

Filling:
About ¾ pound yams (2 or 3 yams)
¾ cup light cream or milk
⅓ cup superfine sugar
½ cup (packed) light brown sugar
Pinch of salt
1 teaspoon ground ginger
½ teaspoon cinnamon
½ teaspoon freshly grated nutmeg
Pinch of ground cloves
2 large eggs, lightly beaten

Topping:
¾ cup (about 6 ounces) crystallized ginger
4 tablespoons unsalted butter
⅓ cup (packed) light brown sugar
2 teaspoons fresh lemon juice
Whipped cream, for serving

1. Preheat the oven to 350°.

2. Prepare the pastry: In a food processor, combine the flour and salt and cut in the butter until you have formed coarse crumbs. Stir in the egg yolk and just enough ice water to make it possible to press the pastry

together lightly into a cohesive ball. Wrap the ball of pastry in plastic wrap or wax paper and chill for at least 30 minutes.

3. Prepare the filling: Place the yams on a baking pan and bake for 45 minutes to 1 hour, or until very tender.

4. Meanwhile, roll out the chilled pastry on a floured work surface to make a 13-inch round, then fit it into a 9-inch pie plate, crimping or fluting the edge, as you prefer. Chill the pastry until you have completed Step 6.

5. Remove the yams from the oven and increase the oven temperature to 375°. Pinch the yam skins all over without breaking through the skin. (This helps release the skin from the flesh.) Halve the yams and scoop out the cooked flesh. While still hot, puree the flesh in a food processor. Measure out 1½ cups of yam puree and reserve any leftover puree for another use.

6. In a small saucepan, bring the cream or milk to a simmer. Return the yam puree to the food processor, if you have used one) and add the superfine sugar, brown sugar, salt, ginger, cinnamon, nutmeg and cloves. Add half of the beaten eggs at a time, whisking to blend. Stir in the hot cream. Let filling cool slightly.

7. Pour the cooled filling into the pie shell and place on the center shelf of the oven. Bake for 20 to 25 minutes, or until the center is almost set (it will jiggle when you shake the shelf). Remove the pie from the oven and lower the oven heat to 325°. Cool the pie for a few moments while you prepare the topping.

8. Prepare the topping: Gently rinse excess sugar from the crystallized ginger, pat the pieces dry with paper towels and chop the ginger coarsely. In a small bowl, cream the butter with the brown sugar. Add the chopped ginger and lemon juice.

9. With a spatula, spread the topping gently and evenly over the pie. Return the pie to the oven and bake for about 25 minutes, or until the center has set. Check at intervals to keep the topping from burning.

10. Serve the pie at room temperature, garnished with a dollop of whipped cream.
—Pearl Byrd Foster

Sweet Potato Pie

8 to 10 Servings

¾ pound sweet potatoes
1 cup milk
2 eggs, separated
⅓ cup plus 2 tablespoons granulated sugar
2 tablespoons pure maple syrup
½ teaspoon vanilla extract
¼ teaspoon cinnamon
¼ teaspoon freshly grated nutmeg
Salt
1 stick (4 ounces) unsalted butter
Cornmeal Crust (recipe follows), partially baked
1 teaspoon confectioners' sugar
Sweetened whipped cream, for serving

1. Preheat the oven to 350°. Bake the sweet potatoes until tender when pierced with a fork, about 1 hour. Let cool; then peel and cut the sweet potatoes into large dice. *(The recipe can be prepared to this point up to 1 day ahead.)*

2. Preheat the oven to 400°. In a food processor or blender, puree the sweet potatoes, gradually adding the milk to make a smooth mixture.

3. Add the egg yolks, ⅓ cup of the sugar, the maple syrup, vanilla, cinnamon, nutmeg and ¼ teaspoon salt. Mix until well blended, about 1 minute.

4. In a small saucepan, cook the butter over low heat until nut brown, about 5 minutes. Pour the butter into the sweet potato puree, discarding any dark residue at the bottom of the pan; mix well.

5. Beat the egg whites with a pinch of salt until they form soft peaks. Gradually beat in the remaining 2 tablespoons sugar, 1 teaspoon at a time, until firm peaks form. Fold the sweet potato puree into the beaten egg whites.

6. Pour the filling into the partially baked Cornmeal Crust. Bake the pie for 20 minutes. Reduce the oven temperature to 350° and bake for 20 minutes longer, or until the pie filling is set and the crust is nicely browned.

7. Let the pie cool. Lightly dust the crust with the confectioners' sugar. Serve with a bowl of whipped cream.
—Michael James

Cornmeal Crust

Makes One 9-Inch Crust

1 cup plus 2 tablespoons all-purpose flour
¼ cup finely ground yellow cornmeal
½ teaspoon salt
6 tablespoons chilled shortening
About ¼ cup ice water

1. In a medium bowl, combine the flour, cornmeal and salt. Cut the shortening into the flour until the mixture resembles oatmeal with some pieces of shortening the size of corn kernels still visible; do not over-

mix. Sprinkle the ice water over the flour mixture and toss to combine. Squeeze the dough into a ball, adding a few more drops of water if necessary. Handling the dough as little as possible, shape it into a 6-inch disk. Wrap the dough in plastic wrap and refrigerate for at least 30 minutes.

2. On a lightly floured surface, roll out the dough about ⅛ inch thick to a 12-inch circle. Fit the pastry, without stretching, into a 9-inch glass pie plate. Fold under the edge of the pastry until it is flush with the rim and crimp the edge. With a fork, prick the dough all over. Freeze the pastry shell for 30 minutes. Meanwhile, preheat the oven to 450°.

3. For a partially baked pie shell, line the crust with a sheet of aluminum foil and fill with pie weights or dried beans. Bake in the lower third of the oven for 10 minutes, or until the pie shell is very lightly browned. Remove the foil and weights.

4. For a fully baked pie shell, follow the instructions in Step 4. Then reduce the oven temperature to 400° and bake the empty pie shell for 15 minutes longer, or until the shell is golden brown.
—Michael James

Lemon-Lime Meringue Pie

8 to 10 Servings

Filling:
1 cup sugar
6 tablespoons cornstarch
¼ teaspoon salt
5 tablespoons unsalted butter
4 egg yolks, at room
* temperature*
¼ cup fresh lemon juice
¼ cup fresh lime juice
1 teaspoon grated lemon zest
1 teaspoon grated lime zest

Prebaked Sweet Pastry Shell
(p. 212)

Meringue:
4 egg whites, at room
* temperature*
¼ teaspoon salt
¼ teaspoon cream of tartar
½ cup sugar

1. Prepare the filling: In a medium saucepan, place the sugar, cornstarch, salt, butter and 2 cups of water. Bring the mixture to a boil over moderate heat, and then cook for 1 minute, stirring constantly with a wooden spoon until thickened and smooth; remove from the heat.

2. Lightly whisk the egg yolks in a small bowl. Whisk in the lemon and lime juices. Gradually whisk the yolk mixture into the sugar mixture in the saucepan. Over low heat, bring the mixture to a boil, stirring constantly. Remove from the heat and stir in the lemon and lime zests. Let the mixture cool for 10 minutes covered, and then pour it into the Prebaked Sweet Pastry Shell. Lay a sheet of wax paper on the filling and chill for at least 5 hours or overnight.

3. Prepare the meringue: Preheat the oven to 350°. Place the egg whites in a bowl, add the salt and cream of tartar and beat until soft peaks form. Gradually add the sugar and continue beating until the whites stand in stiff peaks and are very glossy; do not overbeat or the meringue will be dry.

4. Assemble and bake the pie: Pile the meringue on the filling, mounding it in the center and spreading it out to the very edge of the crust all around. If desired, make small peaks all over the meringue with the back of a spoon. Bake the pie in the center of the oven for 15 minutes, or until the meringue turns golden. Chill for at least 3 hours before serving. To

slice evenly, dip a knife into hot water before making each cut.
—F&W

Frosty Lime Pie

8 Servings

Graham Cracker Crust:
1¼ cups graham cracker
* crumbs*
¼ cup superfine sugar
4 tablespoons unsalted butter,
* at room temperature*

Filling:
5 eggs, separated
¾ cup superfine sugar
⅔ cup fresh lime juice
2 teaspoons grated lime zest
⅛ teaspoon salt

Topping:
1½ cups heavy cream
Lime slices or strawberries,
* dipped in sugar, for garnish*

1. Preheat oven to 350°.

2. Prepare the crust: Put the graham cracker crumbs and sugar in a bowl. Add the butter and work with a wooden spoon (or your fingers) to blend well.

3. Press the mixture evenly into a 9-inch pie plate with your fingertips (or set an 8-inch pie plate over the mixture and press it down to form an even layer).

4. Bake the crust 10 minutes. Cool to room temperature. Leave the oven on.

5. Prepare the filling: Whisk the egg yolks in a double boiler over hot—not boiling—water until very thick. Gradually beat in ½ cup of the sugar until the mixture is very pale and thick and forms a ribbon when

the beater is lifted.

6. Stir in the lime juice and zest and continue to cook over simmering water, stirring, until the mixture will coat a metal spoon. Do not allow to boil. Turn the filling into a large bowl; cool to room temperature.

7. When the filling is cool, beat the egg whites with the salt until soft peaks form. Gradually beat in the remaining ¼ cup sugar until the meringue is stiff and shiny.

8. Stir one-third of the meringue into the filling, then gently fold in the remaining meringue.

9. Turn the filling into the cooled pie shell and bake for 15 minutes, or until the top is lightly tinged with brown. Cool. Chill, then freeze, uncovered. Once frozen, enclose in plastic wrap and keep frozen until just before serving. *(The pie will keep, frozen, for two to three weeks.)*

10. Remove from the freezer 10 minutes before serving. Whip the cream, pile it onto the pie and garnish with lime slices or strawberries, dipped in sugar.
—*Pearl Byrd Foster*

Coconut Meringue Pie

8 to 10 Servings

2 cups milk
1¼ cups sugar
5 eggs, separated
½ cup all-purpose flour
¼ cup heavy cream
1 teaspoon vanilla extract
2 tablespoons unsalted butter
¾ cup plus 2 tablespoons
  unsweetened shredded
  coconut (about 2½ ounces)*
Prebaked Pie Shell (recipe
  follows)
½ teaspoon cream of tartar

¼ teaspoon salt
*Available at health food stores

1. In a large heavy saucepan, bring the milk to a simmer over moderately low heat.

2. Meanwhile, in a medium bowl, gradually beat ½ cup of the sugar into the egg yolks. Beat until the mixture thickens slightly and lightens in color, about 5 minutes. Beat in the flour.

3. Gradually whisk the hot milk into the egg mixture in a thin stream. Beat in the heavy cream and vanilla.

4. Pour the custard back into the saucepan and cook over moderately high heat, whisking constantly, until it boils and thickens. Continue to beat over heat until the custard is smooth and has no raw flour taste, 1 to 2 minutes. Remove from the heat and beat in the butter. Stir in ¾ cup of the coconut.

5. Pour the coconut custard into the Prebaked Pie Shell, press a piece of plastic wrap directly onto the surface to prevent a skin from forming and refrigerate until chilled and set, about 2 hours.

6. Preheat the oven to 400°. In a large bowl, combine the egg whites, cream of tartar and salt. Set the bowl over a pan of simmering water. Whisk slowly until the egg whites are slightly warmed.

7. Remove the bowl from the heat and beat the egg whites with an electric mixer at medium speed until soft peaks form. At high speed, gradually beat in the remaining ¾ cup sugar, 1 tablespoon at a time, until stiff shiny peaks form.

8. Using a metal spatula, spread the meringue over the coconut custard, swirling it decoratively into standing peaks. Set the pie in the oven and bake for 5 minutes, or until the meringue peaks begin to

brown. Garnish the pie with the remaining 2 tablespoons coconut. Let cool, then cover and refrigerate. Serve the pie well chilled.
—*Michael James*

Prebaked Pie Shell

Makes One 9-Inch Crust

1½ cups all-purpose flour
¼ teaspoon salt
½ cup chilled shortening
3 to 4 tablespoons ice water

1. In a large bowl, combine the flour and salt. Cut in the shortening until the mixture resembles very coarse meal with some pieces of shortening the size of corn kernels still visible; do not overmix. Sprinkle on 3 tablespoons of the ice water, tossing to moisten evenly. Gather the dough into a ball, adding up to 1 tablespoon more ice water if necessary. Flatten into a 6-inch disk, wrap and refrigerate for at least 30 minutes.

2. On a lightly floured surface, roll out the dough about ⅛ inch thick to a 12-inch circle. Fit the pastry into a 9-inch glass pie plate. Trim the dough to ¾ inch beyond the rim of the dish. Fold the excess dough under the pastry and crimp the edge. With a fork, prick the dough all over. Freeze the pastry shell for 30 minutes. Meanwhile, preheat the oven to 450°.

3. Line the pie shell with a sheet of aluminum foil and fill with pie weights or dried beans. Bake for 10 minutes, or until dry. Remove the foil and weights. Reduce the oven temperature to 400° and bake the pie shell for 15 minutes longer, or until lightly browned.
—*Michael James*

Coffee Cream Pie in a Buckwheat Cocoa Crust

8 Servings

¾ cup (lightly packed) light
  brown sugar
¼ cup plus 1 teaspoon
  cornstarch
¼ teaspoon salt
3 cups milk
2 tablespoons plus 2
  teaspoons instant coffee
  granules
4 egg yolks, lightly beaten
2 tablespoons unsalted butter,
  softened
½ teaspoon vanilla extract
Buckwheat Cocoa Crust,
  baked (recipe follows)

1. In a large saucepan, whisk the brown sugar, cornstarch and salt. Place over moderate heat and gradually whisk in the milk. Heat until lukewarm; whisk in the instant coffee and egg yolks.

2. Whisking constantly, cook the mixture until it comes to a boil, about 10 minutes. Boil for 30 seconds, then reduce the heat to moderately low and simmer for 2 minutes, whisking constantly. Remove from the heat and whisk in the butter and vanilla. Place a piece of plastic wrap directly over the filling and set aside for 10 minutes.

3. Remove the plastic wrap and pour the filling into the Buckwheat Cocoa Crust. Let cool to room temperature on a rack, then cover loosely with plastic wrap and refrigerate for at least 2 hours before serving.
—Ken Haedrich

Buckwheat Cocoa Crust

If you want a very intense buckwheat flavor, roast the buckwheat flour in a dry, heavy skillet over moderate heat, stirring constantly, until it darkens a shade or two. Remove from the pan and let cool to room temperature before proceeding.
Makes One 9-Inch Crust

¾ cup buckwheat flour
½ cup all-purpose flour
1 tablespoon sugar
2 teaspoons sifted
  unsweetened cocoa powder
¼ teaspoon salt
3 tablespoons chilled
  shortening
3 tablespoons cold unsalted
  butter, cut into ¼-inch
  pieces
3½ tablespoons ice water

1. In a large bowl, combine the buckwheat and all-purpose flours with the sugar, cocoa and salt; stir well. Cut in the shortening and butter until the mixture resembles coarse meal.

2. Add the ice water, 1 tablespoon at a time, tossing with a fork. Gather the dough into a ball and flatten to form a ½-inch-thick disk. Cover with plastic wrap and refrigerate for 45 to 60 minutes.

3. Roll out the dough to form an 11-inch circle, ⅛ inch thick. Fit the dough into a 9-inch pie plate without stretching. Shape the edge into an even ridge and freeze the shell for at least 30 minutes.

4. Meanwhile, preheat the oven to 425°. Bake the shell in the bottom third of the oven for 20 minutes. Transfer to a rack and let cool completely.
—Ken Haedrich

Irish Coffee Pie

10 Servings

Café au Lait Layer:
1½ cups milk
3 tablespoons finely ground
  coffee or 1½ tablespoons
  instant coffee
4 egg yolks
½ cup granulated sugar
6½ tablespoons all-purpose
  flour
4 tablespoons unsalted butter,
  cut into tablespoons
1 teaspoon vanilla extract

*Cookie Crumb Crust (p. 227)
  made with chocolate wafers*

Irish Coffee Layer:
½ cup (packed) dark brown
  sugar
¼ cup cornstarch
2 tablespoons all-purpose
  flour
1¾ cups strong freshly
  brewed coffee
⅓ cup plus 1 tablespoon Irish
  whiskey
1 ounce unsweetened
  chocolate, broken into
  pieces
1 egg yolk
4 tablespoons unsalted butter

Topping:
2 cups heavy cream
¾ cup sifted confectioners'
  sugar

1. Prepare the café au lait mixture: Scald the milk over low heat in a small saucepan. If using ground coffee, place it in a paper filter and pour the hot milk through it into a bowl—do not stir. Measure the mixture and, if necessary, add more milk to make 1½ cups. If using the instant coffee, simply stir it into the milk.

2. Whisk the egg yolks and granulated sugar in a medium bowl until thick and lemon-colored. Gradually whisk in the flour to form a smooth paste. Whisk in the hot coffee-milk in a slow, steady stream. Transfer the mixture to a medium saucepan and bring it to a boil over low heat, whisking constantly. Boil for 1 minute, whisking constantly. Remove from the heat and whisk vigorously to cool slightly. Add the butter and vanilla and stir until smooth. Pour the filling into the prepared Cookie Crumb Crust, cover with buttered wax paper and chill until the filling is thoroughly set.

3. Prepare the Irish coffee layer: In a medium saucepan, combine the brown sugar, cornstarch and flour. Slowly whisk in the brewed coffee until smooth. Add ⅓ cup of the whiskey and the chocolate. Cook over low heat, stirring constantly, until the mixture thickens and begins to boil. Simmer for 1 minute, stirring constantly. Remove from the heat.

4. Beat the egg yolk with a fork in a small bowl. Beat in 2 tablespoons of the chocolate mixture, then stir the yolk mixture into the chocolate mixture remaining in the pan. Blend in the remaining 1 tablespoon whiskey and the butter.

5. Remove and discard the wax paper from the pie. Pour the Irish-coffee filling evenly over the café au lait layer. Smooth the top with a thin spatula. Cover with buttered wax paper, cool to room temperature and chill thoroughly.

6. Prepare the topping: Using a chilled bowl and beaters, whip the heavy cream at high speed until soft peaks form. Add the confectioners' sugar ¼ cup at a time, beating on low speed after each addition until thoroughly incorporated. Then beat on high speed until the cream is stiff.

7. Complete the pie: Spoon all of the whipped cream over the pie or evenly spread about two-thirds of it over the surface, place the remainder in a pastry bag fitted with a decorative tip, and pipe decorations around the edge and in the center of the pie. Chill before serving.
—F&W

Cookie Crumb Crust

Our cookie crumb crust recipe, which makes one 9-inch shell, requires 1⅓ cups of cookie or wafer crumbs. If you wish, you may replace ⅓ cup of the cookie crumbs with ⅓ cup ground nuts.

Makes One 9-Inch Crust

1⅓ cups crushed cookie
  crumbs, or 1 cup cookie
  crumbs and ⅓ cup finely
  chopped nuts
2 tablespoons sugar
5 tablespoons unsalted butter,
  melted

Preheat the oven to 350°. In a medium bowl, combine the cookie crumbs, or cookie crumbs and chopped nuts, with the sugar. Pour the butter over and blend with a fork until the crumbs are moistened. Butter the bottom of a 9-inch pie plate (not the sides or the shell may fall during baking) and distribute the crumbs evenly over it. Gently press the crumbs evenly over the bottom and then up the sides of the pan. Bake in the center of the oven for 8 minutes. Cool to room temperature before filling.
—F&W

Coffee-Almond Crunch Tart

8 to 10 Servings

2 cups (8 ounces) whole
  blanched almonds
¾ cup all-purpose flour
¼ cup sugar
½ teaspoon freshly grated
  nutmeg
4 tablespoons cold unsalted
  butter, cut into pieces
1 egg
¼ teaspoon almond extract
4 ounces semisweet chocolate
2 pints coffee ice cream
1 tablespoon almond liqueur,
  such as amaretto

1. Preheat the oven to 350°. Lightly butter a 10- or 11-inch tart pan with a removable bottom.

2. Spread the almonds on a jelly-roll pan and toast in the oven, shaking the pan once or twice, for about 12 minutes, or until the nuts are pale brown. Let cool.

3. Place 1 cup of the nuts in a food processor. Add the flour, sugar and nutmeg. Process until the ingredients are mixed and the nuts are finely chopped, 10 to 20 seconds. Add the butter and turn the machine quickly on and off 4 or 5 times, until the butter is well distributed. Add the egg and almond extract and blend until the mixture begins to clump together, about 10 seconds. Remove the dough and wipe out the bowl.

4. Press the dough evenly over the bottom and sides of the prepared tart pan; freeze until firm, at least 30 minutes. Place the bowl and beaters from an electric mixer in the freezer to chill for at least 30 minutes.

5. Increase the oven temperature to 400°. Cover the tart shell with aluminum foil and fill with pie weights or dried beans. Bake for 20 minutes, remove the weights and foil and bake for 5 to 10 minutes longer, or until the crust is golden.

6. Meanwhile, finely chop 2 ounces of the chocolate. Sprinkle the chocolate evenly over the bottom of the hot crust and, as it melts, spread it evenly with a pastry brush. Remove the sides of the tart pan and let the crust cool to room temperature. When the crust is cool, replace the sides of the pan.

7. Put the remaining almonds in a food processor and grind to a paste, 1 to 2 minutes. Place the ice cream in the chilled bowl and beat until slightly softened, about 30 seconds. Add the almond paste and amaretto and continue to beat until the mixture is blended, about 1 minute. Spoon the ice cream mixture evenly into the crust and freeze for at least 30 minutes.

8. Melt the remaining 2 ounces chocolate in a double boiler over hot water. Piping with a small plain decorating tip or drizzling with the tines of a fork, create a design over the top of the tart with the melted chocolate.

9. Cover the tart with plastic wrap and freeze for at least 4 hours before serving.
—Dorie Greenspan

Fudge Pie

Creamy, thick and chocolatey says it all. For a luxurious touch, serve with unsweetened whipped cream.
10 Servings

1 stick (4 ounces) unsalted butter
2 ounces unsweetened chocolate
2 eggs, lightly beaten
1 cup sugar
¼ cup all-purpose flour
¼ teaspoon salt
2 teaspoons vanilla extract
Prebaked Pie Crust (recipe follows)

1. Preheat the oven to 350°. In a small heavy saucepan, combine the butter and chocolate. Cook over low heat, stirring occasionally, until the chocolate is melted. Remove from the heat and let cool.

2. In a medium bowl, whisk together the eggs, sugar, flour, salt and vanilla. Beat until smooth. Stir in the melted chocolate and blend well.

3. Pour into the Prebaked Pie Crust and bake for 30 to 35 minutes, or until the center is just set (it should give a little when you touch it, but it shouldn't be liquid). Let cool on a rack.
—Marion Cunningham

Prebaked Pie Crust

Makes One 9-Inch Pie Crust

1½ cups all-purpose flour
¼ teaspoon salt
½ cup shortening
3 to 4 tablespoons ice water

1. Preheat the oven to 425°. In a medium bowl, mix the flour and salt together. Cut in the shortening until the mixture resembles coarse meal. Add 3 tablespoons of the ice water, 1 tablespoon at a time, stirring lightly with a fork after each addition. Add 1 more tablespoon of water if needed so that the dough holds together. Gather and flatten into a disk.

2. On a lightly floured surface, roll out the dough until it is about ⅛ inch thick. Transfer the dough to a 9-inch pie plate and fit it against the bottom and sides without stretching. Trim to an even ½-inch overhang, fold the overhang under and crimp decoratively.

3. With a fork, prick the bottom and sides of the shell all over at ½-inch intervals. Press a 12-inch square piece of heavy-duty aluminum foil snugly against the bottom and sides of the shell to prevent the dough from shrinking.

4. Place the pie shell in the upper third of the oven and bake for 6 minutes. Remove the foil and continue baking for 8 to 10 minutes longer, or until light brown, dry and crisp. Remove from the oven and let cool completely on a rack.

LARD CRUST: Substitute 1¼ cups all-purpose flour, ⅛ teaspoon salt and ½ cup lard for the quantities listed above. The amount of water is the same.
—Marion Cunningham

cookies

Meringue Kisses

Makes About 5 Dozen

¾ cup whole hazelnuts
½ cup egg whites (about 4
  eggs), at room temperature
Pinch of salt
1 cup sugar
1 teaspoon rum, brandy or
  Cognac
¼ teaspoon cinnamon

1. Preheat the oven to 375°. Spread the hazelnuts out in a single layer on a baking sheet. Roast them for about 20 minutes, turning them occasionally by shaking the pan back and forth. Cool the nuts to room temperature and then rub them between the palms of your hands to remove the skins. Chop the nuts coarsely. Reduce the oven temperature to 200°.

2. Place the egg whites in a large, deep mixing bowl along with the pinch of salt. With an electric mixer, beat at low speed until they are frothy. Increase the speed to medium and beat until soft peaks are formed. Reduce the speed to low and begin to add the sugar, a tablespoonful at a time, making sure that each is incorporated before adding another. When all the sugar has been added, increase the speed to medium and continue to beat until stiff peaks are formed. Do not overbeat or the meringue will become dry.

3. Pour the rum over the cinnamon to dissolve it and then pour it over the meringue. Sprinkle the nuts over the meringue and gently fold all together with a rubber spatula until the nuts are evenly distributed.

4. Line several baking sheets with parchment or wax paper. Using a spoon or a pastry bag fitted with a plain, ¼-inch tip and half-filled with meringue, shape the meringue into kisses, using about 1 tablespoon for each and leaving a 1-inch space between. If you are shaping the kisses with a spoon, dab the back of the spoon against the meringue and then pull it away to give the rochers their traditionally irregular shape. Bake them for 45 minutes to 1 hour, or until they are dry all the way through but not brown on the outside.
—*Nicholas Malgieri*

Spicy Nut Meringues

Makes About 5 Dozen

2 egg whites
1 teaspoon cinnamon
⅛ teaspoon ground cloves
½ cup sugar
2 cups finely chopped walnuts

1. Preheat the oven to 250°.

2. Beat the egg whites until they form soft peaks. Mix the cinnamon, cloves and sugar together and gradually add to the egg whites, beating continuously. Beat until very stiff. Fold in the walnuts.

3. Drop by teaspoonfuls onto nonstick or buttered cookie sheets. Bake for 1¼ hours, then turn off the oven. Open the door and allow the meringues to cool slowly. When cool, store in a tightly covered jar. These keep very well if protected from even the slightest dampness.
—*F&W*

Almond-Lemon Macaroons

These nutty cookies have a pleasant lemony flavor and are ideal with Champagne or espresso.
Makes About 6 Dozen

1 cup sliced, blanched
  almonds
½ cup plus 2 tablespoons
  sugar
3 egg whites
1 teaspoon grated lemon zest

1. Preheat the oven to 275°. Butter 2 large heavy cookie sheets. Sprinkle with flour and tap off any excess.

2. Set aside 2 tablespoons of the almond slices. Place the remaining almonds in a food processor. Add 2 tablespoons of the sugar and process until the nuts are finely ground, about 20 seconds. (Do not overprocess or the nuts will be oily.)

3. Beat the egg whites until soft peaks form. Gradually beat in the remaining ½ cup sugar, 2 tablespoons at a time, until stiff peaks form. Fold in the ground almonds and lemon zest.

4. Spoon rounded teaspoonfuls of the nut mixture onto the prepared cookie sheets, leaving 1 inch between them. Press a reserved almond slice on top of each cookie. Place in the oven and immediately reduce the heat to 200°. Bake until dry and lightly colored, about 1½ hours. Let cool on a rack. Store in an airtight tin.
—*Diana Sturgis*

Macarons de Nancy

Crisp almond cookies called *macarons* (macaroons) are a specialty of the French city of Nancy.

Makes About 4 Dozen

2 egg whites, at room
    temperature
Pinch of salt
1 cup confectioners' sugar,
    sifted
1 teaspoon almond extract
2 cups (9 ounces) finely
    ground blanched almonds
20 to 25 candied cherries,
    halved (3 ounces)
1 egg yolk
3 tablespoons milk

1. Preheat the oven to 275°. In a medium bowl, beat the egg whites with the salt until foamy. Gradually beat in the confectioners' sugar ¼ cup at a time, continuing to beat until stiff peaks form. Beat in the almond extract. Fold in the ground almonds.

2. Using a teaspoon or a pastry bag fitted with a ¼-inch plain tip, form quarter-size mounds on an oiled cookie sheet, spaced 1 inch apart. Place a cherry half on top of each and bake for 20 minutes.

3. In a small bowl, beat the egg yolk with the milk until blended to make a glaze. Remove from the oven and brush each cookie lightly with the glaze. Return to the oven and bake for 5 to 10 minutes longer, or until the cookies are shiny on top and very lightly browned on bottom.

4. Remove to a rack to cool. Store in a tightly covered tin.
— *Monique Guillaume*

French Macaroons with Chocolate Cream Filling

In France macaroons are not made with coconut, but with an almond meringue. The pastry chef at Taillevent, Gilles Bajolles, taught me how to make macaroons that are crisp outside and moist inside. The secret is not to beat the egg whites too stiffly before the sugar is added. These freeze well.

Makes About 3 Dozen

4 egg whites
3 tablespoons granulated
    sugar
2 cups sifted confectioners'
    sugar
1 scant cup of almond
    powder* (see Note)
¼ cup heavy cream
2 ounces bittersweet
    chocolate, broken into small
    pieces
1 tablespoon praline paste* or
    hazelnut butter*
*Available at specialty food
    shops and health food stores

1. Preheat the oven to 425°. In a large bowl, beat the egg whites until soft peaks form. Add the granulated sugar and beat until stiff and shiny. Fold in the confectioners' sugar and the almond powder until blended.

2. Line 2 large cookie sheets with parchment paper. Fit a pastry bag with a plain ¼-inch tip and pipe out 1-inch meringues, or form with 2 teaspoons.

3. Put an empty cookie sheet or jelly-roll pan on the top rack of the oven to absorb some of the heat and prevent the tops of the meringues from burning. Set the meringues in the middle of the oven and bake for 10 minutes, or until they are light golden in color. Set the cookie sheets on a rack and let cool. Then carefully scrape the meringues from the parchment with a wide metal spatula.

4. In a small saucepan, bring the cream to a boil over low heat. Add the chocolate and stir until melted. Remove from the heat and stir in the praline paste. Refrigerate until stiff enough to spread, about 15 minutes.

5. Spread a small dab of the chocolate filling onto the flat side of one meringue and sandwich with another. Repeat to fill all the meringues. Wrap well and freeze until ready to serve.

NOTE: To make your own almond powder, finely grind 5 ounces blanched almonds with 1 tablespoon granulated sugar in a food processor.
—*Lydie Marshall*

Chocolate-Dipped Snowballs

These flourless macaroons are somewhere between a cookie and a confection. They are crunchy on the outside, moist and chewy on the inside. The slight bitterness of semisweet chocolate is the perfect foil for the sweet toasted coconut. These cookies can be stored in an airtight container for about a week and are wonderful for mailing to cool climates.

Makes About 2 Dozen

2½ cups unsweetened
    medium shredded coconut*
1 tablespoon plus 2 teaspoons
    cornstarch
¾ cup sugar
2 tablespoons unsalted butter,
    cut into pieces
¼ cup light corn syrup
1 teaspoon vanilla extract
¼ teaspoon salt
2 egg whites, lightly beaten

5 ounces imported semisweet chocolate, chopped into ½-inch pieces (about 1 cup)
*Available at health food stores.

1. Preheat the oven to 375°. Butter and flour a heavy baking sheet. In a medium bowl, combine the coconut and cornstarch; set aside.

2. In a medium nonreactive saucepan, combine the sugar, butter, corn syrup, vanilla and salt. Bring to a boil over high heat, stirring constantly. Boil for 10 seconds, then remove from the heat and stir in the coconut mixture. Add half of the beaten egg whites, stirring until thoroughly incorporated. Stir in the remaining whites. The mixture will form a ball. Return to high heat and cook, stirring, for 30 seconds. Let cool slightly.

3. With moistened hands, break off tablespoon-size pieces of the mixture and roll into 1-inch balls. Place on the prepared baking sheet about 1 inch apart.

4. Bake for 10 minutes, or until the tops just begin to turn golden brown. Turn the tray halfway through baking to insure even cooking. Let the cookies cool completely on the sheet.

5. Place the chocolate in a small bowl set over a small saucepan filled with ¾ inch of simmering water or in a double boiler. When the chocolate is nearly melted, remove from the heat and, using a rubber spatula, stir until the mixture is completely smooth. Set aside to cool, stirring occasionally. The chocolate is ready for dipping when a small drop placed just below your lower lip feels cool on the skin.

6. Line a baking sheet with parchment paper. Using your fingers, hold a snowball near the top and dip the bottom half into the cooled chocolate. Gently shake off the excess and lightly scrape the bottom over the rim of the bowl. Set the dipped snowball, chocolate-side up, on the parchment paper. By the time you are dipping the 10th one, the first one should have hardened. If not, the chocolate was not quite cool enough. Refrigerate the cookies for just 5 minutes to set the chocolate; store at room temperature.
—*Peggy Cullen*

Champagne Fingers with Raspberry Glaze

Delicate champagne fingers become even tastier when raspberry glaze is sandwiched between them.
Makes About 5 Dozen

5 eggs, at room temperature
1¼ cups sugar plus additional for coating
Pinch of salt
1 teaspoon grated orange or lemon zest
1 teaspoon vanilla extract
2 cups all-purpose flour
1 cup seedless red raspberry jam

1. Beat the eggs slightly and combine them with the sugar and salt in a double boiler over simmering water; the water should not touch the top portion of the double boiler. Stirring constantly with a wire whisk, heat until the mixture is lukewarm (100°) and the sugar has melted completely.

2. Pour the mixture into a large mixing bowl and beat the mixture until it has cooled and quadrupled in volume—it will be almost white in color and form a very thick ribbon when the beater or whisk is lifted from the bowl. Stir in the orange zest and the vanilla.

3. Begin to sift the flour over the egg mixture, gently folding the two together as you sift. When all the flour has been folded in, the batter will be fairly dry; be sure to scrape the bottom as you fold. The final batter should be smooth.

4. Cover several baking sheets with parchment. If you find you don't have enough baking sheets, shape the cookies on parchment and then transfer the paper to the baking sheets as they become available.

5. Fit a pastry bag with a plain, ¼-inch tip and half-fill the bag with batter. Onto the paper-lined baking sheets, squeeze out 2-inch-long finger shapes, leaving about 1 inch of space between them. Continue making fingers until all the batter is used. If desired, you can also pipe stars, letters and other designs.

6. Generously pour sifted sugar over the champagne fingers, making sure that they are well covered (the excess will be poured off later). Let the fingers dry for 2 to 3 hours so that the sugar will become crusty.

7. Preheat the oven to 325°. Carefully pour off the excess sugar, making sure that you hold the parchment to the baking sheet firmly with your thumbs so the cookies won't fall off; save the sugar for another purpose. It is important that no excess sugar remain on the baking sheets.

8. Bake the fingers for 10 to 15 minutes, or until pale blond and firm. Let them cool on the parchment paper.

9. Meanwhile, in a small, heavy saucepan, bring the jam to a boil over moderately high heat, stirring occasionally. When the jam has come to a full rolling boil, allow it to boil, stirring occasionally, for about 4 minutes. Remove from the heat.

10. Sandwich the champagne fingers with the hot glaze.
—*Nicholas Malgieri*

Gilded Chocolate Shortbread (p. 254).

Clockwise from near right:
Linzer Wreaths (p. 255),
Fruitcake Cookies (p. 250),
Granny's Molasses Spice Cookies
(p. 239), Cranberry-Pistachio
Biscotti (p. 251), Chocolate-Dipped
Snowballs (p. 231).

Heavenly Puff Angels (p. 254).

Pfeffernüsse

Although butterless cookies made with eggs, sugar and flour are relatively unknown in the United States, they are traditional favorites in German-speaking countries and in Italy. The method of making this dough is similar to that for making sponge cakes—whole eggs and sugar are beaten together in a warm bowl until the sugar dissolves and the mixture is properly thick. The dry ingredients are then folded in. Enough flour is used to make the dough firm enough to be piped, rolled out or otherwise shaped. The unbaked cookies are allowed to dry overnight so they will hold their shape during baking.

Makes About 3½ Dozen

2 eggs
1⅓ cups superfine sugar
About 1 tablespoon rum
1½ cups plus 2 tablespoons flour
1 teaspoon baking powder
1 tablespoon cinnamon
¼ teaspoon ground cloves
¼ teaspoon freshly grated nutmeg
¼ teaspoon ground ginger
½ cup (about 3 ounces) ground unblanched almonds
1 tablespoon finely minced candied fruit

Lemon Icing:
About 1½ cups confectioners' sugar
About 2 tablespoons fresh lemon juice

1. In a mixing bowl set over a saucepan of boiling water, beat the eggs and sugar until they are thick and mousse-like, about 5 minutes.

2. Remove the bowl from the pan of water and continue to beat the eggs and sugar for another 3 minutes. Add the rum.

3. Sift the flour, baking powder, cinnamon, cloves, nutmeg and ginger together. Then sift the dry ingredients over the eggs and fold them in, using a wooden spoon. Fold in the almonds and candied fruit.

4. Turn the dough onto a lightly floured board and knead it until smooth and cohesive, about 3 minutes; the dough will be quite soft. If the dough is too dry, add a bit more rum. If it is too wet, add a bit more flour.

5. Form the dough into balls 1 inch in diameter. Arrange about 1 inch apart on buttered baking sheets. Let stand, uncovered, to dry out for 15 to 24 hours.

6. Preheat the oven to 375°.

7. Bake a panful at a time in the center of the oven for 12 to 14 minutes, or until firm and light brown. During baking, the balls will "burst" slightly as moisture escapes from the center, forming random cracked patterns on the surface. Transfer to cooling racks.

8. Make the lemon icing: Gradually beat 1½ cups of the confectioners' sugar into 2 tablespoons of the lemon juice and beat for at least 10 minutes, until no graininess remains. If too thin or too thick, adjust the consistency with more confectioners' sugar or lemon juice.

9. Brush the cookies smoothly with icing while still warm. Allow the icing to set firmly before storing the cookies.
—F&W

Chocolate Wreaths

Similar to *Pfeffernüsse* and other German-style butterless cookies, the dough for these wreaths must dry out for at least 24 hours before the cookies can be baked.

Makes About 3½ Dozen

2 eggs
1⅓ cups superfine sugar
About 1 tablespoon rum
1 cup all-purpose flour
1 teaspoon baking powder
¼ cup unsweetened cocoa powder
1 tablespoon cinnamon

1. In a mixing bowl set over a saucepan of boiling water, beat the eggs and sugar until they are thick and mousse-like, about 5 minutes.

2. Remove the bowl from the pan of water and continue to beat the eggs and sugar for another 3 minutes. Add the rum.

3. Sift the flour, baking powder, cocoa and cinnamon together. Then sift the dry ingredients over the eggs and fold them in, using a wooden spoon.

4. Turn the dough onto a lightly floured board and knead it until smooth and cohesive, about 3 minutes; the dough should be soft enough to be piped through a pastry tube. If the dough is too dry, add a bit more rum. If it is too wet, add a bit more flour.

5. Fit a pastry bag with a large star tip and fill the bag with the dough. Pipe wreaths about 2 inches in diameter onto a buttered baking sheet, placing them an inch apart.

6. Allow the wreaths to dry out, uncovered, for 12 to 24 hours. Then turn the wreaths over and allow the undersides to dry out for at least another 12 hours.

7. Preheat the oven to 300°, keep-

ing the oven door slightly ajar with the handle of a wooden spoon. Bake cookies, one panful at a time, in the lower third of the oven, until the wreaths are firm and the color of bleached cocoa. Cool on rack.
—*F&W*

Basic Lebkuchen Dough

The lebkuchen family of cookies is characterized by the use of honey or a dark syrup as a sweetener and a high spice content. In the Middle Ages, lebkuchen were already being made in Germany, generally in cloisters. Honey, which was originally more available than sugar, lends "keeping" quality to baked goods, a special advantage for holiday cookies made weeks ahead of time.

Use this basic dough to make one of the following cookies: Marzipan-Filled Spice Cookies, German Spice Cookies, Filled Spice Hearts or Honey Cake Squares.

Makes Enough for 6 Dozen
Cookies

3¾ cups all-purpose flour
1½ teaspoons baking powder
1 tablespoon cinnamon
½ teaspoon ground cloves
½ teaspoon ground aniseed
½ teaspoon freshly grated
 nutmeg
½ teaspoon ground ginger
1 teaspoon ground cardamom
1¼ cups honey or molasses
1 stick (4 ounces) unsalted
 butter
½ cup candied fruit, finely
 chopped (about 4 ounces)
1 cup ground almonds (about
 6 ounces)

1. Sift together the flour, baking powder, cinnamon, cloves, aniseed, nutmeg, ginger and cardamom. Set aside.

2. In a saucepan, heat the honey or molasses and butter until the butter has melted and the mixture just reaches the boiling point—don't let it boil or it might lose its aroma and the cookies could become too hard. Immediately remove from the heat and cool for about 1 minute. With a wooden spoon, stir in the candied fruit and ground almonds, beating vigorously to break up any clumps of fruit and to blend the mixture well.

3. Now add the sifted flour-spice mixture, stir for a moment and turn the dough out onto a lightly floured board. Knead with your hands until smooth. The dough should be very soft, but not sticky. Wrap tightly in plastic wrap, place in a plastic bag and leave overnight at room temperature before using.
—*F&W*

Marzipan-Filled Spice Cookies

Makes About 3 Dozen

1 package (7 ounces)
 marzipan or almond paste*
½ recipe Basic Lebkuchen
 Dough (at left)
1 egg, lightly beaten
*Available at specialty food
 stores

1. Preheat the oven to 425°. On a lightly floured work surface, roll the marzipan into a log ¾ inch in diameter, lightly reflouring the surface as necessary.

2. Roll out the Basic Lebkuchen Dough ⅓ inch thick, making a strip 3½ to 4 inches wide and the same length as the marzipan log. Roll the marzipan log in the dough, stopping

just short of completing the wrapping. Allowing for an overlap of ¼ inch; trim excess dough. Moisten the overlap with water and press the seam together well.

3. Slice the roll into cookies ⅓ inch thick. Using a spatula or table knife, plump the slices back into a neat circular shape.

4. Brush the top of each round with lightly beaten egg. Transfer the cookies to a buttered cookie sheet and bake for 10 minutes, or until golden brown. Cool on a rack before storing.
—*F&W*

German Spice Cookies

These cookies are at their best two to three weeks after baking; this time allows the flavor of the spices to mingle and ripen. These cookies may be left plain or they may be decorated with sliced almonds or with piped ornaments of white icing.

Makes About 6 Dozen

Basic Lebkuchen Dough (at
 left), made with molasses
Sliced blanched almonds, for
 decoration

1. Preheat the oven to 375°. Butter and flour a baking sheet.

2. Roll out the Basic Lebkuchen Dough as thin as possible on lightly floured board. Cut out with decorative cutters. Decorate the unbaked cookies with sliced almonds.

3. Bake the cookies on the prepared baking sheet for 7 minutes, or until crisp and brown. Cool on racks.
—*F&W*

Filled Spice Hearts

For making these cookies, you will need two heart-shaped cutters, one about ⅓ inch larger than the other; or you can use heart patterns cut from cardboard, one ⅓ inch larger than the other.

*Yield Varies According
to Size of Hearts*

*Basic Lebkuchen Dough
(p. 238)*
*2 cups confectioners' sugar,
sifted, plus additional sugar
for rolling out the filling*
1 egg white, lightly beaten
*1 package (7 ounces)
marzipan or almond paste**
Royal Icing (p. 243)
**Available at specialty food
stores*

1. Preheat the oven to 375°. On a lightly floured surface, roll out the Basic Lebkuchen Dough ¼ inch thick. Cut out large hearts with a cutter or trace around the larger cardboard heart with a sharp knife. Place half of the hearts on a buttered baking sheet.
2. In a food processor, blend 2 cups of the confectioners' sugar and the egg white.
3. Dust a pastry board and rolling pin with confectioners' sugar and roll the marzipan out into a sheet about ⅛ inch thick. Using the smaller cutter or pattern, cut out hearts ⅓ inch smaller than the cookies and place one on each heart on the pan. Brush exposed rims of cookies with water, then top the filling with the remaining cookie hearts, pressing the edges well together. If desired, use the back of a knife to make "stitch" indentations in a decorative pattern around the edges.

4. Bake for 15 minutes, or until light brown. Transfer to a rack and cool.
5. Spoon the Royal Icing into a pastry bag fitted with a fine "writing" point. Pipe names, frills or flower motifs, as desired, onto the cookies.
—F&W

Honey Cake Squares

Makes About 5 Dozen

*Basic Lebkuchen Dough
(p. 238), freshly made*
*1½ cups almonds, coarsely
chopped*
1 cup raisins
1¾ cups apricot jam
*About 3 tablespoons fresh
lemon juice*
Royal Icing (p. 243)

1. Make the Basic Lebkuchen Dough, working quickly so that the dough remains warm. Divide the dough in half and, while still warm, roll out one half directly onto a large, buttered rimless baking sheet, making a rectangle about ⅜ inch thick. (It needn't cover the entire pan.) If your baking pan has a rim, turn it upside down and roll dough out onto the bottom.
2. Roll the second half of dough onto a piece of cooking parchment or wax paper, making the rectangle the same size as the first sheet of dough. Set aside. Preheat the oven to 350°.
3. In a bowl, mix the almonds, raisins, apricot jam and lemon juice together, adding a little more lemon juice if the mixture is too thick to spread.
4. Spread the almond-raisins filling evenly over the dough on the baking sheet. Lay the second sheet of dough over the filling, paper side up.

Peel off the paper. Press the edges of the sheets of dough together well and trim evenly.
5. Bake for 25 minutes, or until the top is golden. Set the pan on a rack and allow the cookies to remain overnight at room temperature. The following day, cut the sheet into 1¼-inch squares.
6. Brush the Royal Icing evenly over the top of each square. Allow the icing to dry before storing the cookies.
—F&W

Granny's Molasses Spice Cookies

It seems as though everyone's granny west of the Mississippi had a recipe for some version of this cookie. As these cookies bake, they puff up, heave a sigh and then collapse as flat as can be. They have a cracked surface and a sugary sheen. Be careful not to overbake them, for burnt molasses is very bitter. The cookies can be stored in an airtight container for a week to 10 days and they travel well.

Makes About 4 Dozen

*1½ sticks (6 ounces) unsalted
butter, cut into ½-inch
pieces*
*¼ cup dark unsulphured
molasses*
1 teaspoon vanilla extract
2 cups all-purpose flour
1⅓ cups sugar
2 teaspoons baking soda
2 teaspoons ground ginger
2 teaspoons cinnamon
*¼ teaspoon freshly grated
nutmeg*
¼ teaspoon ground cloves
¼ teaspoon salt
1 egg, lightly beaten

1. Preheat the oven to 375°. In a small saucepan, melt the butter over low heat. Remove from the heat and stir in the molasses and vanilla. Set aside to cool.

2. In a medium bowl, sift the flour with 1 cup of the sugar and the baking soda, ginger, cinnamon, nutmeg, cloves and salt.

3. Add the beaten egg to the cooled butter mixture and mix well with a fork. Using a rubber spatula, fold the butter mixture into the flour. Cover tightly and refrigerate until firm, about 15 minutes.

4. Put the remaining ⅓ cup of sugar in a small bowl. Scoop out walnut-size pieces of the dough and roll into 1-inch balls. Toss the balls in the sugar to coat completely and place on ungreased baking sheets, about 2 inches apart.

5. Bake for 10 minutes, or until the bottoms begin to brown. The cookies will be a little soft and will remain chewy. Let cool on the baking sheet for about 5 minutes, then transfer to a rack to cool completely.
—Peggy Cullen

Spiced Angel Cookies

These delicious spice cookies are edible ornaments that can be hung on the tree, given as gifts or washed down with plenty of milk. They will keep for up to two weeks sealed in a cookie tin.

Makes About 3 Dozen

2 cups all-purpose flour
⅛ teaspoon salt
½ teaspoon baking soda
1 teaspoon baking powder
1 teaspoon cinnamon
1 teaspoon allspice
1 teaspoon ground ginger

1 stick (4 ounces) unsalted
  butter, at room temperature
½ cup granulated sugar
½ cup unsulphured molasses
1 egg yolk

1. In a medium bowl, whisk together the flour, salt, baking soda, baking powder, cinnamon, allspice and ginger.

2. In another medium bowl, cream the butter and sugar at high speed until fluffy, about 1 minute. Add the molasses and beat on high speed for 1 minute more. Beat in the yolk until incorporated.

3. With the mixer at low speed, beat in the flour and spice mixture in two batches. The dough will be very stiff. Divide the dough in half and place on two large sheets of wax paper. Flatten the dough into disks, wrap and refrigerate for at least 2 hours or overnight.

4. Preheat the oven to 350°. Remove one package of dough from the refrigerator and split in half. On a generously floured work surface, working quickly, roll one portion of the dough to between ⅛ and ¼ inch thick. (The dough tends to become sticky as it comes to room temperature.) Cut out cookies with a 3-inch angel-shaped cookie cutter. With a metal spatula, transfer the angels to a large ungreased cookie sheet. Bake for about 8 minutes, or until firm (but not hard) and golden brown. Be careful not to overbake. With a skewer or toothpick, make a hole in the head of each angel large enough for a string or ribbon to be pulled through. Let the cookies cool on the baking sheet for 2 minutes, then transfer the cookies to a rack to cool completely.

5. Gather up any scraps of dough, wrap in wax paper and chill. Repeat with the remaining cookie dough. Combine all the dough scraps; reroll and cut out more cookies.
—Tracey Seaman

Basic Gingerbread Cookies

These cookies can be cut into any shape and decorated with icing, raisins, nuts or small candies.

Makes About 2 Dozen

3 cups unbleached all-purpose
  flour
2½ teaspoons ground ginger
1¼ teaspoons cinnamon
½ teaspoon ground
  cardamom
½ teaspoon freshly grated
  nutmeg
¼ teaspoon ground cloves
½ teaspoon baking soda
¼ teaspoon salt
¾ cup dark or light
  unsulphured molasses
1 stick (4 ounces) unsalted
  butter, at room temperature
½ cup sugar
1 egg

1. In a large bowl, stir together the flour, ginger, cinnamon, cardamom, nutmeg, cloves, baking soda and salt.

2. In a small saucepan, heat the molasses over low heat until bubbles begin to form around the sides. Remove from the heat and stir in the butter, 1 tablespoon at a time, until completely incorporated. Scrape the molasses into a large bowl. Beat in the sugar and 2 tablespoons of water until well blended. Beat in the egg.

3. Make a well in the center of the dry ingredients and pour in the molasses mixture. Gradually stir in the flour mixture until blended. Turn the dough out onto a floured surface and

knead lightly until smooth. Pat the dough into a 6-inch disk, cover with plastic wrap and refrigerate overnight or for up to 3 days.

4. Preheat the oven to 350°. Roll out half the dough ⅛ inch thick. (Keep the remaining dough well wrapped until ready to use.) Cut out shapes using a cookie cutter. Place the cookies about ½ inch apart on greased cookie sheets and bake for 10 to 12 minutes, until firm and slightly puffed. Transfer the cookies to a rack to cool. Repeat with the remaining dough. Decorate the cookies or leave plain. *(The cookies can be stored in an airtight container for up to 2 weeks.)*
—Linda Merinoff

Gingersnap-Chocolate Sandwich Cookies

You can eat these cookies plain, make them into sandwiches, or spread each cookie with chocolate. I like these best the day they're made; they become harder and less chewy over time, and it's the chewiness that I love.

Makes 30 Sandwich Cookies

¼ cup dark unsulphured
 molasses
6 tablespoons unsalted butter,
 at room temperature
½ cup granulated sugar
¼ cup (packed) dark brown
 sugar
¼ teaspoon ground ginger
¼ teaspoon cinnamon
⅛ teaspoon ground
 cardamom
Pinch of ground cloves

Pinch of freshly grated
 nutmeg
1 whole egg
1 egg yolk
½ cup plus 2 tablespoons all-
 purpose flour
4 ounces bittersweet
 chocolate, cut into pieces

1. Preheat the oven to 350°. In a small saucepan, heat the molasses over low heat until bubbles begin to form around the sides. Remove from the heat and stir in the butter, 1 tablespoon at a time, until completely blended.

2. Scrape the molasses into a large bowl. Add the granulated sugar, brown sugar, ginger, cinnamon, cardamom, cloves and nutmeg. Beat until well blended. Beat in the whole egg and the egg yolk. Add the flour and mix well.

3. Drop level teaspoons of the dough onto buttered and floured cookie sheets, leaving about 2 inches between the cookies. Bake for 8 to 10 minutes, or until the edges are golden brown. Let the cookies cool on the sheets for 5 minutes, then transfer to a rack to cool completely.

4. Place a small saucepan over simmering water and add the chocolate. Remove the pan from the heat and let stand, stirring occasionally, until the chocolate is melted and smooth, about 5 minutes.

5. Spread the flat side of half the cookies with the chocolate. Top with the remaining cookies and press lightly to make them adhere. Refrigerate for 10 minutes to set the chocolate. The cookies can be stored in an airtight container for up to 3 days.
—Linda Merinoff

Vanilla Crescents

Makes About 5 Dozen

2⅓ cups all-purpose flour
1⅓ cups confectioners' sugar
⅛ teaspoon salt
Grated zest of 1 lemon
2 sticks plus 2 tablespoons
 (10 ounces) very cold
 unsalted butter, cut into
 small pieces
2 egg yolks
1 teaspoon vanilla extract
¾ cup ground blanched
 almonds
Confectioners' sugar, for
 dusting

1. Sift the flour, confectioners' sugar and salt into a large mixing bowl. Stir the lemon zest into the dry ingredients.

2. Cut the butter into the dry ingredients just until the mixture forms coarse crumbs.

3. Make a well in the center of the mixture. In a small bowl, beat the egg yolks, vanilla and ground almonds together. Pour the yolk mixture into the well and blend into the butter-flour mixture until you can pull the dough together into a mass. Remove the dough to a lightly floured board and knead it quickly until there are no visible streaks of egg, about 1 minute. Wrap the dough tightly in plastic wrap and refrigerate for at least 30 minutes before using.

4. Roll the chilled dough into a smooth log about 1½ inches in diameter. Wrap the log in plastic and chill for at least 30 minutes.

5. Cut the cylinder of dough into slices ⅜ inch thick. Form each slice into a log shape, then roll it back and forth on the pastry board, slightly tapering the ends, until it is 3 inches long. After shaping 20 pieces in this way, bend each gently into a crescent shape. Form the crescents carefully so they are all uniform in length and size. As the crescents are shaped, place them at least ½ inch apart on buttered and floured baking sheets. When each pan is full, refrigerate the cookies. Preheat the oven to 375°.

6. Bake the cookies, a panful at a time, in the center of the oven for 12 to 14 minutes, or until pale yellow; do not allow them to brown. Remove the crescents immediately to a cooling rack.

7. While still warm, dust the crescents with confectioners' sugar.
—F&W

Basic Butter Cookie Dough

Makes Enough for
About 4 Dozen Cookies

2⅓ cups all-purpose flour
1⅓ cups confectioners' sugar
⅛ teaspoon salt
Grated zest of 1 lemon
2 sticks plus 2 tablespoons
  (10 ounces) very cold
  unsalted butter, cut into
  small pieces
2 egg yolks
1 teaspoon vanilla extract

1. Sift the flour, confectioners' sugar and salt into a large mixing bowl. Stir the lemon zest into the dry ingredients.

2. Cut the butter into the dry ingredients just until the mixture forms coarse crumbs.

3. Make a well in the center of the mixture. In a small bowl, beat the egg yolks and vanilla together, then pour the yolks into the well. Blend the yolk mixture into the butter-flour mixture until you can pull the dough together into a mass. Remove the dough to a lightly floured board and knead it quickly until there are no visible streaks of egg, about 1 minute. Wrap the dough tightly in plastic wrap and refrigerate for at least 30 minutes before using.
—F&W

Cottage Butter Cookies

Makes About 4 Dozen

2 sticks (8 ounces) unsalted
  butter, softened
⅔ cup sugar
1 teaspoon vanilla extract
½ teaspoon lemon extract
1 egg
2½ cups all-purpose flour
1 teaspoon baking powder
Colored crystal sugar, Sugar
  Glaze (recipe follows) or
  Royal Icing (p. 243), for
  decoration

1. In a large mixer bowl, beat the butter and sugar until smooth and fluffy, 3 to 4 minutes. Add the vanilla extract, lemon extract and egg and beat until smooth and light, 2 to 3 minutes.

2. Add 1¼ cups of the flour and ½ teaspoon of the baking powder. Beat until just smooth; add the remaining 1¼ cups flour and ½ teaspoon baking powder and mix to combine. Cover the dough with plastic wrap and refrigerate until firm, at least 1 hour.

3. Preheat the oven to 325°. On a lightly floured surface, roll out one-fourth of the dough ⅛ inch thick. Cut the dough out with decorative cookie cutters and place 1 inch apart on ungreased cookie sheets.

4. Bake the cookies for 20 minutes, or until lightly golden around the edges. Repeat with the remaining dough.

5. To decorate: sprinkle the cookies with crystal sugar while still warm and then transfer to a rack to cool. Or, let the cookies cool and then decorate with Sugar Glaze or Royal Icing. Store in layers, separated by sheets of wax paper, in an airtight tin.
—Quinith Janssen

Sugar Glaze

This frosting may be used for spreading onto simple butter cookies. The cookies may be baked several days ahead, before frosting. Let the glaze harden before storing the cookies.

Makes Enough for 4 to 5 Dozen
  Cookies

3 tablespoons milk
½ teaspoon vanilla extract
3½ cups (1-pound box)
  confectioners' sugar
Food coloring

1. In a medium bowl, combine the milk and vanilla. Slowly stir in the sugar, beating constantly until the frosting becomes thick and creamy. The more this frosting is beaten, the shinier it becomes.

2. Divide the frosting among several small bowls. Stir a few drops of the desired food coloring into each bowl. If the frosting becomes too thin, stir in a few teaspoons of confectioners' sugar. Spread on cooled cookies with a broad flat knife.

NOTE: To prevent the frosting from forming a crust while decorating, keep covered with a dampened cloth.
—*Quinith Janssen*

Royal Icing

Pipe royal icing designs with a paper cone or a pastry bag fitted with a very small plain tip. In a pinch, fill a plastic sandwich bag with the icing, snip a small hole in one of the corners and use it as a makeshift pastry bag.

Makes About 1 Cup

1 egg white
About 1½ cups confectioners'
  sugar, sifted
About 2 tablespoons fresh
  lemon juice

In a bowl, beat the egg white until frothy, then gradually beat in 1½ cups of the confectioners' sugar and 2 tablespoons of the lemon juice. Beat at least 10 minutes to dissolve the sugar; the icing should be very smooth. The icing should be thick enough to hold its shape when piped; add more sugar or lemon juice to adjust the consistency.
—*F&W*

Orange Cookies

Cutting out fanciful holiday shapes and dusting the baked cookies with colored sugars, painting the tops with sugar glaze or piping out royal icing borders and designs can be great family fun.

Makes About 3 Dozen

¾ cup confectioners' sugar
⅔ cup unsalted butter,
  softened
2 tablespoons grated orange
  zest

¼ cup fresh orange juice
1¾ cups all-purpose flour
Pinch of salt
Colored crystal sugar
Sugar Glaze (p. 242) or Royal
  Icing (p. 243), for
  decoration

1. In a large mixer bowl, beat the confectioners' sugar and butter until smooth and fluffy, 3 to 4 minutes. Add the orange zest and juice and beat until smooth.

2. Gradually add the flour and salt, beating until just smooth. Cover with plastic wrap and refrigerate until the dough is firm, at least 1 hour.

3. Preheat the oven to 325°. On a lightly floured surface, roll out one-quarter of the dough ⅛ inch thick. Cut the dough out with cookie cutters and place 1 inch apart on ungreased cookie sheets.

4. Bake the cookies for 25 minutes, or until lightly golden around the edges. To decorate: sprinkle the cookies with crystal sugar while still warm and then transfer to a rack to cool. Or, let the cookies cool and then decorate with Sugar Glaze or Royal Icing. Store in layers, separated by sheets of wax paper, in an airtight tin.
—*Quinith Janssen*

Honey Cookies

Makes About 2 Dozen

1 stick (4 ounces) unsalted
  butter, softened
¼ cup honey
¼ cup granulated sugar
1 teaspoon baking soda
1 egg yolk
1 cup all-purpose flour
½ cup colored crystal sugar

1. In a large mixer bowl, combine the butter, honey, granulated sugar,

baking soda and egg yolk. Beat until smooth. Gradually beat in the flour, mixing well. Form the dough into a ball. Wrap in plastic and refrigerate until firm, about 1 hour.

2. Preheat the oven to 300°. Pinch off large teaspoons of the dough and roll into balls about 1½ inches in diameter. Roll the balls in the crystal sugar and place about 2 inches apart (the cookies will flatten and spread in the oven) on ungreased cookie sheets.

3. Bake for 25 minutes, or until crisp and golden. Let cool for 5 to 7 minutes before transferring to a rack to cool.
—*Quinith Janssen*

Sweetheart Cookies

Makes About 2 Dozen

1½ sticks (6 ounces) unsalted
  butter, softened
½ cup sugar
1 egg yolk
½ teaspoon grated lemon zest
1½ cups all-purpose flour
¼ teaspoon salt
About 2 tablespoons
  raspberry jam

1. In a medium bowl, cream the butter and sugar until fluffy and light. Beat in the egg yolk and lemon zest.

2. Combine the flour and salt and sift into the butter mixture. Stir until well blended. Cover and refrigerate the dough until firm, 2 to 3 hours.

3. Preheat the oven to 350°. Shape the dough into balls 1¼ inches in diameter and place them on ungreased cookie sheets. With your fingertip or the end of a wooden spoon, make a small depression in the center of each cookie. Fill each hollow with ⅛ to ¼ teaspoon raspberry jam.

4. Bake in the middle of the oven for 15 minutes, or until the cookies are lightly browned around the edges. Transfer to wire racks and let cool.

—*Joanna Pruess*

Butter Walnut Crescents

Makes About 2½ Dozen

1 stick (4 ounces) unsalted
  butter, softened
½ cup confectioners' sugar
1 teaspoon vanilla extract
½ cup finely ground walnuts
1 cup all-purpose flour
½ teaspoon salt
Confectioners' sugar, for
  dusting

1. Preheat the oven to 350°. In a medium bowl, cream the butter until light and fluffy. Stir in the confectioners' sugar. Add the vanilla extract and ground walnuts and mix well.

2. Combine the flour and salt and sift over the butter mixture. Stir until smooth.

3. Shape a rounded teaspoon of dough into a ball 1 inch in diameter. Roll each ball between your hands to shape it into an elongated cylinder; pinch the ends to taper. Form into crescents and place on a lightly floured cookie sheet.

4. Bake the cookies in the middle of the oven for about 13 minutes, or until the edges are browned. Transfer to wire racks and let cool to room temperature. Dust with additional confectioners' sugar.

—*Joanna Pruess*

Pogachel

These Hungarian cookies, plain as biscuits and not overly sweet, are especially good for dunking.

Makes About 2½ Dozen

1 stick (4 ounces) unsalted
  butter, softened
¾ cup sugar
1 egg
2 tablespoons sour cream
2 cups all-purpose flour
2 teaspoons baking powder
½ teaspoon salt

1. Preheat the oven to 350°. In a medium bowl, cream the butter and sugar together until fluffy and light in color. Beat in the egg and the sour cream.

2. Combine the flour, baking powder and salt. Sift these dry ingredients over the butter mixture. Using your hands, knead the mixture to make a smooth, soft dough.

3. Working on a lightly floured surface, carefully roll out the dough to an even thickness of slightly more than ¼ inch. Using a round cookie cutter about 2¼ inches in diameter, dipped in flour, cut out the cookies. Carefully transfer to a lightly floured cookie sheet using a spatula dipped in flour. Gather the scraps, reroll them and continue. Prick the center of each cookie in two places with a fork. Bake in the middle of the preheated oven for 18 to 20 minutes, or until lightly browned around the edges. Transfer to wire racks to cool.

—*Joanna Pruess*

Butter-Cookie Pretzels with Lemon Icing

For an extra hit of lemon flavor, grate the zest of a lemon into the Royal Icing before brushing it onto the cookies.

Makes About 6 Dozen

*Basic Butter Cookie Dough
  (p. 242)
Royal Icing (p. 243)*

1. Roll the chilled Basic Butter Cookie Dough into a log 1½ inches in diameter. Chill, well wrapped in plastic, for at least 30 minutes.

2. Cut the log into ¼-inch slices. Form each slice into a log shape, then roll it back and forth on a pastry board until it is 6 inches long. (Use the first strand as a measure for the rest, so that the pretzels will be uniform in size.) Shape the pretzels: Make a circle with the strand of dough, then cross the ends of the strand and lay them, about an inch apart, on the upper rim of the circle. Arrange the pretzels about an inch apart on a buttered and floured baking sheet and refrigerate them while you shape the remaining dough. Refrigerate all the cookies while you preheat the oven to 375°.

3. Bake the cookies, a panful at a time, in the center of the oven for 12 to 14 minutes, or until pale yellow; do not allow them to brown. Remove the cookies to a cooling rack.

4. Meanwhile, prepare the Royal Icing as directed in the recipe. The pretzels should be warm when iced; if they have cooled to room temperature, reheat them on a baking sheet in a 250° oven until warm, about 5

minutes. Brush the cookies carefully with the icing. Allow the icing to set before storing the cookies.
—F&W

Dominoes

Makes About 5 Dozen

Basic Butter Cookie Dough (p. 242)
About 1½ cups sifted confectioners' sugar
About 2 tablespoons fresh lemon juice
⅓ cup chocolate chips

1. Roll the Basic Butter Cookie Dough out ⅜ inch thick, then cut it into rectangles measuring 2½ by 1 inch. Remove the rectangles to buttered baking sheets and place in the freezer or refrigerator for 10 to 20 minutes.

2. Preheat the oven to 350°. Before baking the cookies, trim any ragged edges with a sharp knife. Bake the cookies in the center of the oven, a panful at a time for 10 to 12 minutes, or until pale yellow. Remove to cooling racks.

3. Meanwhile, gradually beat 1½ cups of the confectioners' sugar into 2 tablespoons of the lemon juice until you have a smooth icing; beat for at least 10 minutes. Adjust the consistency with additional confectioners' sugar or lemon juice as needed.

4. Brush the cookies, which should still be slightly warm, carefully with the icing and allow the coating to set. (If the cookies have cooled, rewarm them on a baking sheet in a 250° oven for about 5 minutes before icing them.) Reserve remaining icing.

5. In a small bowl, melt the chocolate chips on a heatproof plate set over a pan of simmering water. Beat the chocolate gradually into the reserved icing—it should become dark brown.

6. Scoop the chocolate icing into a pastry bag fitted with a fine "writing" tip and pipe lines and dots onto the "dominoes." If you prefer not to use a pastry bag, drop frosting from the tip of a small knife or a skewer to make the dots and lines.
—F&W

Biscuits Marquise

These delicate jam-and-butter-cookie sandwiches are the invention of the Marquise de Pompadour's chef at Saint-Cloud.
Makes About 2½ Dozen

2 cups all-purpose flour
1 teaspoon baking powder
Pinch of salt
2 sticks (8 ounces) unsalted butter, at room temperature
6 egg yolks, at room temperature
2 tablespoons light rum or kirsch
1 cup sugar
About ⅓ cup apricot jam

1. Preheat the oven to 350°. Sift together the flour, baking powder and salt.

2. In a large mixer bowl, beat the butter, egg yolks, rum and sugar until smooth.

3. Gradually add the flour mixture to the butter mixture, blending on low speed until smooth.

4. Spoon the dough into a pastry bag fitted with a ¼-inch plain tip. Onto 2 large lightly oiled cookie sheets, pipe out mounds about 1½ inches in diameter, spaced about 2 inches apart. Flatten slightly, using

the back of a fork dipped in water. Bake for 10 minutes, or until slightly golden and browned around the edge. Transfer the cookies to a rack; they will crisp as they cool.

5. In a small saucepan, warm the jam over low heat until melted. When the cookies are cool, sandwich together using about ½ teaspoon of melted jam for each pair of cookies.
—Monique Guillaume

Jam-Filled Butter Cookies

Makes About 4 Dozen

Basic Butter Cookie Dough (p. 242)
Sifted confectioners' sugar, for dusting
About 6 tablespoons raspberry jam
About 6 tablespoons apricot jam
Lemon juice (optional)

1. Preheat the oven to 350°.

2. Roll out the Basic Butter Cookie Dough ⅛ inch thick on a lightly floured board and cut out cookies with a round 2-inch fluted cutter. Using a small round aspic cutter or a thimble, cut 1 or 3 small holes in half the cookies to make the cookie "lids." The solid cookies will be the bases. Place the cookies about an inch apart on buttered baking sheets and put them in the freezer or refrigerator for 10 to 20 minutes.

3. Bake the cookies in the center of the oven, a panful at a time, for 12 to 14 minutes, or until pale yellow; do not allow them to brown. Transfer to racks. While still warm, dust the "lids" with sifted confectioners' sugar. Turn the cookie bases upside down.

4. In separate small saucepans, bring the jams just to a boil to melt them and make them spreadable.

Strain the apricot jam through a sieve; reheat the jam, adding a bit of lemon juice, if necessary, to thin to a spreading consistency.

5. Spread the raspberry jam on half of the cookie bases while they are still warm. Spread the remaining cookie bases with apricot jam. Carefully place a lid on top of each base.
—F&W

Almond Ovals

Makes About 12 Dozen

4 sticks (1 pound) unsalted
  butter, at room temperature
¾ cup granulated sugar
2 cups (about 8 ounces) finely
  ground unblanched almonds
½ teaspoon vanilla extract
¼ teaspoon almond extract
4 cups all-purpose flour
About 1¾ cups confectioners'
  sugar

1. In a large bowl, cream the butter and sugar. Add the ground almonds, vanilla and almond extracts.
2. Add 3 cups of the flour, 1 cup at a time and blend thoroughly. Knead in the last cup of flour by hand.
3. Preheat the oven to 350°.
4. To shape each cookie, roll about a teaspoonful of dough between your palms into the shape of a marble and then into a long oval shape. Place on a nonstick or buttered cookie sheet 1½ inches apart.
5. Bake only one sheet of cookies at a time for about 10 minutes, or until very lightly browned.
6. Roll the cookies in the confectioners' sugar while they are hot from the oven. Set out on large plates to cool and then store in tightly closed jar. These will keep for weeks.
—F&W

Nut Puffs

Makes About 4 Dozen

2 sticks (8 ounces) unsalted
  butter, softened
1½ cups confectioners' sugar
2 cups all-purpose flour
½ cup finely chopped walnuts
  or pecans
Pinch of salt

1. Preheat the oven to 300°. In a large mixer bowl, beat the butter and ½ cup of the confectioners' sugar until smooth and fluffy, 3 to 4 minutes. Add the flour, chopped nuts and salt. Mix until thoroughly blended, 1 to 2 minutes.
2. Roll the dough into balls about 1 inch in diameter. Place 1 inch apart on ungreased cookie sheets.
3. Bake for 25 minutes, until golden. Remove from the cookie sheets while still warm and roll in the remaining 1 cup confectioners' sugar. Let cool, then store in an airtight tin.
—Quinith Janssen

Pecan Icebox Cookies

Makes About 4 Dozen

1 stick (4 ounces) unsalted
  butter, softened
1 cup (packed) dark brown
  sugar
1 egg
1 teaspoon vanilla extract
2½ cups all-purpose flour
½ teaspoon baking soda
½ teaspoon salt
½ cup chopped pecans

1. In a medium bowl, cream the butter and sugar together until light and fluffy. Beat in the egg and vanilla.
2. Combine the flour, baking soda

and salt and sift into the butter mixture. Blend together thoroughly. Stir in the pecans.
3. Shape the dough into a roll 2 inches in diameter. Wrap tightly in plastic wrap and refrigerate overnight or for up to 1 week.
4. Preheat the oven to 350°. Using a sharp thin knife, cut the dough into ¼-inch slices and place on ungreased cookie sheets. Bake in the middle of the oven for about 15 minutes, or until lightly browned and set. Transfer to wire racks and let cool.
—Joanna Pruess

Chocolate Nut Wafers

These delicate cookies are best eaten the day they are made, but they may be frozen or refrigerated for a day or two.

Makes About 4 Dozen

1 cup toasted almonds,
  walnuts or pecans, finely
  chopped
1¾ cups all-purpose flour
¼ teaspoon ground cloves
Pinch of salt
2 sticks (8 ounces) unsalted
  butter, at room temperature
½ cup sugar
½ teaspoon almond or vanilla
  extract
12 ounces (2 cups) semisweet
  chocolate chips

1. In a medium bowl, combine the chopped nuts, flour, cloves and salt.
2. In another bowl, beat the butter until light and fluffy. Gradually beat in the sugar and almond extract until smooth. Gradually add the nut-flour mixture ½ cup at a time, beating after each addition until incorporated. *(The recipe may be prepared ahead to this point and refrigerated.)*
3. Preheat the oven to 350°. Pinch

off heaping teaspoons of the dough and roll into balls about 1 inch in diameter. Place 1½ inches apart on ungreased cookie sheets. Cover with wax paper and, with the bottom of a glass, gently flatten each ball until ⅜ inch thick. Remove the wax paper.

4. Bake for 13 to 15 minutes, or until slightly colored. Transfer to a rack to cool.

5. Melt the chocolate in a double boiler over hot water until smooth. Partially dip each wafer into the chocolate to coat half the cookie. Let any excess chocolate drip back into the bowl. Gently run the edge of each wafer against the rim of the bowl to remove more excess chocolate. Place the dipped wafers on cookie sheets lined with wax paper and refrigerate until the chocolate is set.
—*Dorie Greenspan*

Linzer Sandwiches

Rich with hazelnuts, chocolate and orange liqueur, these will satisfy a sophisticated sweet tooth.
Makes About 2½ Dozen

2 cups hazelnuts
1½ cups all-purpose flour
1 tablespoon unsweetened
   cocoa powder
1¼ teaspoons cinnamon
¼ teaspoon ground cloves
⅛ teaspoon salt
1 stick (4 ounces) unsalted
   butter, at room temperature
½ cup sugar
½ teaspoon grated orange zest
1 egg
2½ teaspoons orange liqueur,
   such as Grand Marnier
3 ounces bittersweet or
   semisweet chocolate
½ cup seedless raspberry jam
Confectioners' sugar, for
   dusting

1. Preheat the oven to 350°. Spread the hazelnuts on a jelly roll pan and toast in the oven, shaking the pan once or twice, until the nuts are pale brown beneath the skin, about 12 minutes. Rub the hot nuts in a dry kitchen towel to remove as much of the brown skin as possible. Chop the nuts fine, but do not grind them.

2. In a medium bowl, combine the hazelnuts, flour, cocoa, cinnamon, cloves and salt.

3. In a large mixer bowl, beat the butter, sugar and orange zest until light and creamy. Add the egg and 1½ teaspoons of the orange liqueur; beat until smooth.

4. Gradually beat in the flour mixture, occasionally scraping the sides of the bowl with a rubber spatula, until incorporated.

5. Divide the dough in half. Place half on a large sheet of wax paper and cover with another sheet of wax paper. Using your hands, flatten the dough into a disk, then roll out ¼ inch thick. Repeat with the other half of the dough. Transfer, still between the wax paper, to two cookie sheets and freeze until very firm, about 45 minutes.

6. Preheat the oven to 375°. Remove the top sheet of wax paper from one of the dough rounds. With a 2-inch round cutter, cut into circles and place on a lightly greased or nonstick cookie sheet. (If the dough becomes too soft or sticky, freeze briefly to firm up.) Place in the refrigerator or freezer while cutting the second half of the dough. Gather up the scraps, roll again between wax paper, chill and cut.

7. Bake the cookies for 11 to 13 minutes, or until pale gold. Transfer to a rack and let cool.

8. Meanwhile, melt the chocolate in a double boiler over hot water. With a small spatula, spread a thin layer of chocolate on each cookie.

9. While the chocolate is setting, place the raspberry jam in a small saucepan and cook over moderate heat, stirring until slightly thickened. Stir in the remaining 1 teaspoon orange liqueur; remove from the heat and let cool.

10. Place about ½ teaspoon of the jam on the chocolate side of half the cookies. Gently press the remaining cookies, chocolate-side down, on top of the filling, rotating to spread the jam evenly.

11. Before serving, sift confectioners' sugar over the cookies.
—*Dorie Greenspan*

Lazy Linzer Squares

In the classic tradition of the linzer torte, these crisp squares of almond pastry and raspberry jam are a sweet addition to any buffet all year long.
Makes About 4 Dozen

1 cup whole blanched
   almonds (4½ ounces)
¼ cup granulated sugar
1⅔ cups all-purpose flour
¼ cup confectioners' sugar
¼ teaspoon salt
⅓ cup cold unsalted butter,
   cut into small pieces
⅓ cup chilled shortening
1 tablespoon vanilla extract
About 2 tablespoons ice water
1 jar (12 ounces) seedless
   raspberry jam
1 cup sliced blanched
   almonds (4½ ounces)

1. Preheat the oven to 350°. Place the whole almonds on a 10-by-15-inch jelly-roll pan and toast in the

oven as it preheats for 10 minutes. Remove from the oven and let the almonds cool completely.

2. In a food processor, combine the toasted almonds and granulated sugar and process until the nuts are finely ground. Add the flour, confectioners' sugar and salt; process briefly to combine. Add the butter and shortening and process to a coarse meal, about 20 seconds. Add the vanilla and 1 tablespoon plus 1 teaspoon of the ice water and continue to process until the mixture begins to form a ball, about 20 seconds longer. If the dough is not coming together at this point, add another teaspoon of ice water.

3. Transfer the dough to a work surface and form into a ball. Roll the dough between 2 sheets of wax paper to form an 11-by-16-inch rectangle, about ¼ inch thick. Remove the top sheet of wax paper and, pulling the bottom sheet, slide the dough onto the jelly-roll pan. Trim off any dough along the sides of the pan with a small sharp knife or a pastry wheel. Bake for 15 minutes. Meanwhile, in a small saucepan melt the jam over moderately low heat.

4. Remove the pan from the oven and drizzle the hot jam over the hot pastry. Working quickly, spread the jam evenly over the surface with a pastry brush. Sprinkle the sliced almonds evenly over the jam and bake for 15 to 20 minutes longer, or until the almonds are golden brown and the jam is bubbly.

5. Transfer the pan to a rack and let cool completely. Cut into fifty 2-by-1½-inch cookies. Store in a cookie tin for up to 1 week or wrap well in foil and freeze for up to 2 weeks.
—*Tracey Seaman*

Apricot-Hazelnut Squares

Makes About 2½ Dozen

1½ cups all-purpose flour
1 teaspoon baking powder
½ teaspoon salt
1 cup old-fashioned rolled oats
½ cup chopped hazelnuts
1 cup (packed) dark brown sugar
1 tablespoon finely minced lemon zest
1½ sticks (6 ounces) unsalted butter, chilled and cut into 12 pieces
1 cup apricot preserves

1. Preheat the oven to 350°. Lightly oil a 13-by-9-by-2-inch baking pan.

2. In a large bowl, sift together the flour, baking powder and salt. Stir in the oats, hazelnuts, brown sugar and lemon zest. Cut in the butter until the mixture resembles coarse meal.

3. Press two-thirds of the mixture firmly into the prepared pan. Evenly spread the apricot preserves over the top and sprinkle with the remaining oat mixture. Press gently to compact the layers.

4. Bake for 45 to 50 minutes, until the top is lightly browned. Remove from the oven and let cool in the pan on a rack for 1 hour. Cut into 2-inch squares.
—*Maria Piccolo & Rosalee Harris*

Sally's Sesame Crisps

Makes About 5 Dozen

1 cup sesame seeds
1½ sticks (6 ounces) unsalted butter, melted and cooled to room temperature
¾ cup (packed) light brown sugar
1 egg
2 tablespoons dark rum
1¼ cups sifted all-purpose flour
¼ teaspoon baking powder
½ teaspoon freshly grated nutmeg
¼ teaspoon salt
⅛ teaspoon freshly ground white pepper

1. Place the sesame seeds in a large skillet and cook over moderate heat, tossing frequently until light brown and toasted, about 5 minutes. Spread out on a plate and let cool.

2. Preheat the oven to 375°. In a medium bowl, combine the butter, sugar, egg, rum and sesame seeds.

3. Combine the flour, baking powder, nutmeg, salt and white pepper and sift over the butter mixture. Blend well.

4. Drop by rounded ½-teaspoon measures about 2 inches apart onto buttered cookie sheets. Bake in the middle of the oven for about 10 minutes, or until the cookies are golden brown with darker edges. Transfer to wire racks and let cool.
—*Joanna Pruess*

Chocolate-Lace Almond Cookies

A simple way to pipe the chocolate decoration onto these charming cookies is with a paper cone. To make one, simply roll a sheet of white paper diagonally into a tight cone and fill with the melted chocolate. Snip off the small end of the cone to create any size tip you like.

Makes About 5 Dozen

⅔ *cup sugar*
½ *cup all-purpose flour*
½ *finely chopped blanched almonds*
1 *whole egg, lightly beaten*
2 *egg whites*
½ *teaspoon vanilla extract*
4 *tablespoons unsalted butter, melted*
4 *ounces semisweet chocolate*

1. In a medium bowl, mix the sugar, flour and almonds. Add the whole egg, egg whites and vanilla and beat with a wooden spoon until well incorporated. Stir in the butter and 1 tablespoon of water, the batter will be thin and slightly granular. (*The batter may be made 1 day ahead and refrigerated, tightly covered. Stir before using and add up to 1 tablespoon additional water, if necessary, to restore the consistency.*)

2. Preheat the oven to 425°. Butter a large heavy cookie sheet. Place in the oven for 1 minute, until the cookie sheet is warm and the butter is melted. Remove from the oven.

3. Using a teaspoon measure, spoon 4 to 6 separate teaspoons of the batter at least 4 inches apart onto the warm cookie sheet. With the back of a spoon, spread the batter into thin circles 2 to 2½ inches in diameter, leaving at least 1 inch between circles to allow for spreading during baking.

4. Bake in the lower third of the oven for 5 minutes, or until the cookies have a golden-brown border ½ inch wide.

5. Remove the cookies from the oven. Slide the back of a wide metal spatula under each cookie, pushing to separate the cookie from the sheet without tearing. Transfer to a wire rack and let cool.

6. Scrape the cookie sheet clean, wipe with a paper towel and lightly butter it. It is not necessary to re-warm the sheet. Repeat Steps 2 through 4 to form and bake the remaining batter.

7. Melt the chocolate in a double boiler over hot—but not boiling—water. Scrape into a small pastry bag fitted with a plain ⅛-inch tip or into a small paper cone. Pipe decorative swirls onto the cooled cookies and let set. (*Although better fresh, the recipe may be made a few days ahead. Store the cookies in an airtight tin or stack them with a sheet of wax paper between each layer, wrap in plastic bags and store in the freezer. Unstack them while still frozen and let come to room temperature before serving.*)
—*Diana Sturgis*

Lacy Ginger Snowflakes

These lacy cookies have a caramel crunch that is offset by the chewy bite of candied ginger and pineapple. The ginger should be soft enough to tear, and the candied pineapple should be moist and pliable. These elegant but fragile wafers will keep for two to three days, stored in an airtight container.

Makes About 2 Dozen

½ *cup instant rolled oats*
½ *cup all-purpose flour*
2 *ounces candied ginger, cut into ⅓-inch dice (⅓ cup packed)*
2 *ounces candied pineapple, cut into ⅓-inch dice (⅓ cup, packed)*
4 *tablespoons unsalted butter, cut into ½-inch pieces*
¼ *cup (lightly packed) light brown sugar*
¼ *cup light corn syrup*
1 *teaspoon ground ginger*
1 *teaspoon dark rum*

1. Preheat the oven to 350°. In a medium bowl, combine the oats and flour. Add the candied ginger and pineapple and toss to coat thoroughly with the flour.

2. In a medium saucepan, combine the butter, brown sugar, corn syrup, ground ginger and rum. Bring to a boil over high heat, stirring, until the butter is completely melted, about 2 minutes. Stir the hot syrup into the dry ingredients and let cool, stirring occasionally, until the batter is somewhat stiff, about 5 minutes.

3. Meanwhile, lightly butter a heavy baking sheet. Scoop out scant tablespoons of the dough and, with moistened hands, roll into 1-inch balls. Place the balls on the baking sheet about 3 inches apart. Bake for 8 minutes, or until the edges are golden. The centers will appear somewhat white and underbaked, but they will continue to cook on the hot baking sheet.

4. Let the cookies cool slightly until they begin to harden, about 3 minutes. Using a metal spatula, transfer the cookies to a rack and let cool completely.
—*Peggy Cullen*

Biscotins d'Albi

From Albin, in the Languedoc region of southwestern France, come *biscotins*, small cookies flavored with orange liqueur and candied fruit.

Makes About 3½ Dozen

1 stick (4 ounces) unsalted
  butter, at room temperature
½ cup granulated sugar
2 eggs, at room temperature
1 cup mixed candied fruit,
  finely chopped (about 3
  ounces)
2 teaspoons vanilla extract or
  orange liqueur
1¾ cups all-purpose flour
1 teaspoon baking powder
Pinch of salt
2 tablespoons orange liqueur
  or light rum
⅔ cup confectioners' sugar

1. Preheat the oven to 350°. In a medium mixer bowl, beat the butter and granulated sugar until light and fluffy, about 4 minutes.

2. Add the eggs, one at a time, beating well after each addition. Stir in the candied fruit and the vanilla.

3. In a separate bowl, sift together the flour, baking powder and salt. Stir the dry ingredients into the butter mixture one-third at a time.

4. Oil 1½- to 2-inch tartlet molds (or same size miniature muffin tins) and fill about two-thirds full with the mixture. Place on a cookie sheet and bake for 12 to 15 minutes, or until lightly browned.

5. Meanwhile, in a small bowl, stir the orange liqueur into the confectioners' sugar to make a fairly thin, smooth icing.

6. While the cookies are still warm, remove from the molds and dip the tops into the frosting to glaze lightly. Let cool on a rack, then store in tightly covered tins.
—*Monique Guillaume*

Galettes du Soir

These after-dinner cookies made with dark rum and currants, come from Morlaix in Brittany.

Makes About 6 Dozen

1 cup dried currants
1½ tablespoons dark rum
1½ sticks (6 ounces) unsalted
  butter, at room temperature
1 cup sugar
2 eggs, at room temperature
2½ cups all-purpose flour
1 teaspoon baking powder
⅛ teaspoon salt

1. In a small bowl, toss the currants with the rum; set aside.

2. In a medium mixer bowl, beat the butter and ⅔ cup of the sugar until light and fluffy, about 4 minutes. Beat in the eggs one at a time until well incorporated. Stir in the currants with the rum.

3. In a separate bowl, sift together the flour, baking powder and salt.

4. Stir the dry ingredients into the butter mixture one-third at a time. The dough will be rather dry, the consistency of pie crust. Form into a ball and refrigerate for at least 30 minutes.

5. Preheat the oven to 350°. On a floured surface, roll out the dough ¼ inch thick and cut into 1½-inch squares.

6. Place on a lightly oiled cookie sheet and bake for 15 minutes, or until very lightly browned.

7. Sprinkle lightly with the remaining ⅓ cup sugar. Remove to a rack to cool and store in a tightly covered tin.
—*Monique Guillaume*

Fruitcake Cookies

As with any good fruitcake, there is only enough batter in this recipe to hold the fruit together. Sticky Medjool dates and moist, plump figs are first choices, but you can substitute other dried fruits. The cookie supporting the fruit remains soft and cakey. These cookies are best eaten a couple of days after they are baked, when the flavors have had a chance to develop. They travel well and will keep for up to two weeks in an airtight container.

Makes About 2 Dozen

1 stick (4 ounces) plus 2
  tablespoons unsalted butter,
  softened
⅓ cup (packed) dark brown
  sugar
½ teaspoon cinnamon
½ teaspoon ground ginger
¼ teaspoon freshly grated
  nutmeg
Pinch of salt
1 cup plus 2 tablespoons all-
  purpose flour
½ cup whole unblanched
  almonds
3 moist dried figs, cut into
  ½-inch pieces (½ cup)
4 large dates, preferably
  Medjool, cut into ½-inch
  pieces (½ cup)
½ cup pecans, coarsely
  chopped
2 tablespoons honey
1 teaspoon plus 1½
  tablespoons dark rum

*1 egg, at room temperature,
lightly beaten*
½ cup confectioners' sugar

1. In a medium bowl, using an electric mixer on high speed, cream 6 tablespoons of the butter with the brown sugar, cinnamon, ginger, nutmeg and salt until light and fluffy. Beat in ¾ cup of the flour on low speed just until incorporated. Wrap the dough tightly and refrigerate until chilled, about 15 minutes.

2. Preheat the oven to 400°. Place the almonds on a heavy baking sheet and toast for about 5 minutes, until golden brown. Let cool, then coarsely chop. In a large bowl, combine the almonds with the figs, dates and pecans; set aside.

3. In a medium bowl, using an electric mixer on high speed, cream the remaining 4 tablespoons butter with the honey and 1 teaspoon of the rum until light and fluffy. Gradually beat in the egg, scraping down the bowl as necessary. Beat in the remaining 6 tablespoons flour on low speed until just combined. Fold the batter into the dried fruit and nuts until completely coated. Set aside.

4. Lightly butter a heavy baking sheet. On a lightly floured surface, roll out the chilled dough ¼ inch thick. Using a 2-inch fluted cookie cutter, stamp out rounds as close together as possible. Reroll the scraps and repeat.

5. Place the cookies on the prepared baking sheet about 1 inch apart. Using your fingers, mound 1 tablespoon of the fruitcake batter on each cookie. Bake the cookies for 10 minutes, until they begin to brown on top.

6. Sift the confectioners' sugar into a bowl and add the remaining 1½ tablespoons rum; stir until smooth.

7. When the cookies are baked, immediately drizzle about ½ teaspoon of the rum glaze over each one. Return to the oven and bake for about 1 minute, or until the glaze bubbles and cracks. Let the cookies cool on the baking sheet for about 5 minutes. Using a spatula, transfer to a rack to cool completely.
—*Peggy Cullen*

Cranberry-Pistachio Biscotti

Makes About 3 Dozen

1¾ cups all-purpose flour
1 cup plus 1 teaspoon sugar
½   teaspoon baking powder
¼ teaspoon salt
½ cup dried cranberries (2½ ounces, see Note)
4 tablespoons cold unsalted butter, cut into ½-inch pieces
1 teaspoon vanilla extract
1½ cups shelled unroasted pistachios* (8 ounces)
2 eggs, lightly beaten
*Available at Indian and Middle Eastern markets

1. Preheat the oven to 350°. Lightly butter a large heavy baking sheet.

2. In a food processor, combine the flour with 1 cup of the sugar, the baking powder and salt. Process for a few seconds to blend. Add the dried cranberries and process until coarsely chopped. Add the butter and vanilla. Pulse until the mixture resembles coarse meal.

3. Add the pistachios and eggs and pulse 10 times to blend. Scrape down the sides of the bowl and pulse 5 times, just until the dough is evenly moistened.

4. On a lightly floured work surface, divide the dough into 4 equal pieces. Roll each piece into an 8-inch log. Transfer the logs to the prepared baking sheet, leaving 2 inches between each. With your hands, flatten the logs to a width of 2 inches and sprinkle with the remaining 1 teaspoon of sugar. Bake for 25 minutes, or until golden brown. Using a metal spatula, transfer the logs to a rack to firm up slightly, 15 to 20 minutes.

5. Transfer the logs to a work surface. Using a sharp knife and a quick single motion, slice each log on the diagonal into ½-inch slices. Return the biscotti to the baking sheet, cutsides down, and bake just until the first hint of golden brown appears, about 7 minutes. Transfer to a rack and let cool completely.

NOTE: Dried cranberries are available at specialty food stores.
—*Peggy Cullen*

Raspberry Snails

Chocolate, which is a traditional companion to raspberry, seems pleasantly surprising in these small packages with intense flavor.
Makes 3 Dozen

½ recipe Cream Cheese Dough (p. 30)
⅔ cup seedless raspberry jam
¼ cup sugar
½ teaspoon cinnamon
¼ cup dried currants
⅔ cup mini-chocolate chips or chopped semisweet chocolate
1 egg

1. Remove half the dough from the refrigerator and let rest at room temperature until malleable, about 10 minutes. Meanwhile, in a small saucepan, melt the raspberry jam over low heat, stirring frequently.

Remove from the heat and let cool while you shape the dough.

2. On a lightly floured surface, roll out the dough into a 10-inch square. Using a pastry brush, spread a thin coating of jam over the dough.

3. Combine 2 tablespoons of the sugar with the cinnamon and sprinkle half of the mixture evenly over the dough. Scatter half the currants and chocolate over the dough. Cover the dough with a sheet of wax paper and, using your hands, gently press the ingredients into the dough.

4. Mark the top and bottom edges of the dough at 2-inch intervals. Using these marks as guides, cut diag- 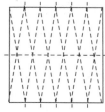 onally across to make a harlequin pattern. Then cut the dough in half crosswise to make 18 triangles. There will be 2 odd pieces of dough at either end. These can be pieced together to make nibbles for the baker.

5. Starting at the wide base of each triangle, roll up the dough. Place the cookies on a buttered cookie sheet, preferably nonstick, with the points tucked underneath. Refrigerate the cookies for at least 30 minutes before baking, or freeze. (The shaped cookies can be frozen and baked without thawing.) Repeat with the remaining dough, jam, cinnamon-sugar, currants and chocolate chips.

6. Preheat the oven to 350°. Beat the egg with 1 teaspoon of cold water to make a glaze. Brush the glaze over each cookie. Sprinkle with the remaining 2 tablespoons sugar.

7. Bake for 25 minutes, or until golden. (Frozen cookies will take 5 to 7 minutes longer.) Transfer to a rack and let cool before serving. The baked cookies can be stored in an airtight container for 2 to 3 days or frozen for up to 1 month.
—*Dorie Greenspan*

Cinnamon Knots

These are the cookies for which the "bet-you-can't-eat-just-one" wager was meant. Equally at home with coffee, tea or mugs of steaming cider, the knots may be made with ginger-sugar for a spicy change.

Makes About 4 Dozen

½ recipe of Cream Cheese
  Dough (p. 30)
1 cup sugar
¼ cup cinnamon

1. Remove half the dough from the refrigerator and let stand at room temperature for about 10 minutes until malleable.

2. In a small bowl, combine the sugar and the cinnamon. Sprinkle about ¼ cup of the mixture on a work surface. Put the dough on the sugared surface and sprinkle with about 2 tablespoons of cinnamon sugar. Roll out the dough into a 13-inch square, sprinkling with more cinnamon sugar and turning the dough several times as you roll.

3. Trim the dough into a 12-inch square. Cut in half crosswise and, working with one half of the dough at a time, fold each piece lengthwise in half into a 12-by-3-inch rectangle. Cut crosswise at 1-inch intervals into 12 strips.

4. Using a small paring knife, cut a slit down the center of each strip leaving a ½-inch margin at the free ends.

5. Holding the cookie by the folded end, fold back both layers of dough and pull through the slit and back down to form a knot. Put the cookies on a buttered cookie sheet, preferably nonstick, and refrigerate for at least 30 minutes, until firm, before baking. Repeat with the remaining dough.

6. Preheat the oven to 400°. Bake the cookies in the middle of the oven for 10 to 12 minutes, until slightly puffed and golden. Transfer to a rack and let cool before serving. (After baking, the cookies can be frozen for up to 3 months.)
—*Dorie Greenspan*

Deep-Fudge Brownies

Makes 3 Dozen

1½ sticks (6 ounces) unsalted
  butter
4 ounces Baker's unsweetened
  chocolate, cut into chunks
2 extra-large eggs
1 cup sugar
1 cup finely chopped walnuts
½ cup all-purpose flour
1 teaspoon very strong
  brewed coffee
1 teaspoon vanilla extract
A few drops of almond
  extract
36 perfect walnut halves

1. Preheat the oven to 325°. Butter and flour a 9-inch-square cake pan.

2. Melt the butter and chocolate together. Stir to blend thoroughly and let cool slightly.

3. In a large bowl, beat the eggs well. Gradually add the sugar and blend thoroughly. Add the cooled chocolate mixture and stir well. Stir in the walnuts. Sprinkle in the flour

by tablespoonfuls, stirring after each addition. Beat in the coffee and the vanilla and almond extracts.

4. Spoon the batter into the cake pan, beginning with the four corners. When the batter has settled in the pan to a perfectly smooth surface, place the walnut halves in even rows, six across and six down.

5. Bake for 25 to 30 minutes, or until the top has firmed.

6. Cut brownies while hot with a thin sharp knife. Brownies should be 1½ inches square, with a walnut in the center of each and quite soft. When cold, store in an airtight container, with wax paper between the layers. They will be at their best for about a week.

NOTE: If you'd like larger cakes, use 25 walnut halves in rows of five each way and cut 25 brownies instead of 36.
—F&W

Shortbread Petticoat Tails

Send a tin of this traditional shortbread to Scottish friends, and they'll be forever grateful. These Petticoat Tails can be stored in an airtight tin and refrigerated for up to one week, but they are best fresh from the oven.
Makes 8 Pieces

1 stick (4 ounces) unsalted
 butter, at room temperature
¼ cup plus 2½ teaspoons
 sugar
⅜ teaspoon salt
1¼ cups all-purpose flour

1. Preheat the oven to 275°. In a large bowl, cream the butter until pale and creamy, about 1 minute. Add the sugar and beat until well combined, about 1 minute.

2. Stir in the salt and the flour, ¼ cup at a time, until the mixture becomes smooth. Squeeze the dough into a smooth ball, flatten it into an even disk and place on a lightly buttered heavy cookie sheet.

3. Roll the dough into an even 8-inch circle, about ⅜-inch thick. Using the tines of a fork, prick the dough all over and decoratively mark the border of the shortbread by pressing halfway into the dough. Using a sharp long knife, score the shortbread into 8 wedges, cutting only halfway through the dough. *(The recipe can be prepared to this point up to 1 day ahead. Cover and refrigerate. Uncover and let return to room temperature for about 20 minutes before baking.)*

4. Bake the shortbread in the middle of the oven for 50 minutes, or until firm but still pale in color. Place the cookie sheet on a rack and let cool for 15 minutes. Cut the shortbread into wedges and let cool completely on the baking sheet, about 40 minutes longer. Store in an airtight tin.
—Diana Sturgis

Ginger-Fudge Nuggets

Rich, fudgy and gently spiced, these cakes are mixed in a saucepan and baked in miniature muffin tins. They may be stored in the refrigerator or freezer, but return them to room temperature before serving.
Makes 2 Dozen

2 teaspoons minced fresh
 ginger
1 teaspoon granulated sugar
¼ cup plus 2 tablespoons all-
 purpose flour
⅛ teaspoon ground ginger
Pinch of salt
4 tablespoons unsalted butter
2½ ounces bittersweet or
 semisweet chocolate, broken
 into pieces
⅓ cup (packed) brown sugar

¼ teaspoon vanilla extract
1 egg
4 ounces white chocolate,
 broken into pieces

1. In a small bowl, combine the minced fresh ginger and the granulated sugar; set aside for at least 30 minutes, stirring occasionally. In a medium bowl, combine the flour, ground ginger and salt.

2. Preheat the oven to 350°. Lightly butter 24 miniature muffin tins, approximately 1½ by ¾ inches.

3. In a heavy medium saucepan, melt the butter, bittersweet chocolate and brown sugar over low heat, stirring constantly, until smooth; remove from the heat.

4. One at a time, add the vanilla, the egg and the ginger-sugar mixture, stirring after each addition until incorporated. Add the flour mixture and mix until combined.

5. Spoon 1 teaspoon of the batter into each muffin cup; the cups should be only half filled. Bake for 9 minutes, or until the tops spring back when touched. Transfer to a rack to cool for about 15 minutes. Unmold and place on the rack until completely cool.

6. Melt the white chocolate in a double boiler over hot water, stirring until smooth. Dip the tops of the cakes into the melted chocolate, or frost the tops with the chocolate, if you wish, using a small spatula. Refrigerate to set the frosting.
—Dorie Greenspan

Gilded Chocolate Shortbread

The trick to baking a good shortbread with a tender, buttery bite is to use a minimal amount of flour—just enough to prevent the cookies from spreading while in the oven. Confectioners' sugar, rather than granulated, also helps them hold their shape. These shortbread cookies are shaped with crescent moon and star cutters. To really gild the lily, brush on powdered 24-karat gold dust before the cookies are baked.

Makes About 3 Dozen

2 sticks (8 ounces) unsalted
*   butter, softened*
1 cup confectioners' sugar
½ cup unsweetened Dutch-
*   process cocoa powder*
1 teaspoon vanilla extract
¼ teaspoon salt
2 cups all-purpose flour
24-karat gold dust (see Note)

1. In a large bowl using an electric mixer, beat the butter with ¾ cup of the confectioners' sugar and the cocoa, vanilla and salt on medium speed until just blended, about 30 seconds.

2. On low speed, mix in the flour in three parts until just incorporated, scraping the bowl after each addition. Refrigerate the dough, tightly wrapped, until well chilled, about 1 hour.

3. Preheat the oven to 325°. Sprinkle work surface with 2 tablespoons of the confectioners' sugar. Divide the dough in half; cover and refrigerate one piece. Roll the other piece into a 9½-inch square just under ½ inch thick. Using crescent moon and star cutters, stamp out cookies as close together as possible. Transfer to an unbuttered baking sheet. Combine the scraps and set aside. Repeat with the remaining

piece of dough, using the remaining confectioners' sugar, if necessary, to prevent the dough from sticking. Combine the scraps, roll out and cut until all the dough has been used.

4. Using a small, stiff paintbrush or a flat pastry brush, lightly paint the surface of each cookie with the gold dust. Bake the cookies for 15 minutes, or until firm and beginning to crisp on the bottom; do not overbake. Let the cookies cool on the baking sheet for 5 minutes, then transfer to a rack to cool completely.

NOTE: Gold dust, which is nontoxic, can be found at art-supply stores or at stores specializing in cake-decorating equipment.
—*Peggy Cullen*

Heavenly Puff Angels

These angels are made by cutting gingerbread girls out of puff pastry and then attaching homemade miniature palmiers (French puff pastry cookies) at the shoulder to form the wings. (See the photograph on page 236 to see what the finished cookie should look like.)

Since puff pastry is best when just baked, you can assemble the angels up to a week ahead and then freeze them unbaked. On Christmas morning, bake and serve them as a breakfast pastry with coffee.

Makes 9 Angels

1 package (1 pound) frozen,
*   all-butter puff pastry,*
*   thawed*
About 1 cup sugar

1. Line 2 heavy baking sheets with parchment paper and set aside. On a lightly sugared work surface, unfold the puff pastry and sprinkle ¼ cup of the sugar on each side. With a sharp knife, cut out an 8-by-6-inch rectangle.

2. Sprinkle each side of the rectangle with 1 to 1½ tablespoons of sugar. With one of the long sides toward you, fold in the top and bottom edges about ½ inch toward the center. Gently pat the folds flat, keeping the sides and the corners square and sprinkle with 1 tablespoon sugar. Fold in the top and the bottom edges again so that they meet in the center. Gently flatten and sprinkle with another tablespoon of sugar. Fold the bottom over the top and gently press the layers to adhere. Wrap tightly and refrigerate the folded dough until well chilled, about 20 minutes.

3. Using a 5-inch gingerbread-girl cutter, stamp out 9 cookies from the remaining puff pastry. Press the cutter down firmly and evenly, cutting as close together as possible, reversing the cookie cutter each time. Sprinkle generously with more sugar to prevent sticking. Arrange the cookies on the prepared baking sheets, leaving as much space as possible between them. Using a fork, prick each cookie in 6 places.

4. Preheat the oven to 425°. Cut the folded dough crosswise into eighteen ¼-inch slices (reserve any remaining dough and bake separately if desired). To form the wings, pinch the outer layer of dough on the rounded edge of each slice between your thumb and forefinger to flatten slightly. Use this flattened portion as a tab to tuck underneath the angle cookie at the shoulder; press firmly to attach the wing to the angel's body. *(The recipe can be prepared to this point and frozen, tightly wrapped, for up to 1 week. These go directly from the freezer to the oven.)*

5. Bake one sheet of cookies at a time in the middle of the oven until deep brown, puffed and crisp, about 15 minutes. Let the angels cool completely on the sheet, then gently peel off the paper; be careful to keep the wings intact.
—Peggy Cullen

Golden Almond Barquettes

A plate of these sweets and a cup of lemon tea is a guaranteed cure for sagging holiday spirits. You will need 12 barquette molds or 3-inch tartlet tins.

Makes 12 Barquettes

½ cup finely ground blanched almonds
¼ cup sugar
4 tablespoons unsalted butter, at room temperature
1 egg
½ teaspoon minced lemon zest
1 tablespoon fresh lemon juice
½ cup golden raisins
Pâte Brisée (p. 202)
¼ cup apricot preserves
1 tablespoon dark rum

1. In a small bowl, combine the ground almonds and the sugar. In a medium mixer bowl, beat the butter until light. Beat in half the almond mixture, the egg and then the remaining almond mixture, beating on high speed after each addition until incorporated. Stir in the lemon zest and juice and the raisins. Refrigerate for at least 1 hour. *(The recipe may be prepared ahead to this point and refrigerated for up to 1 week.)*

2. Lightly butter the barquette molds. On a lightly floured surface, roll out the Pâte Brisée about ⅛ inch thick. Invert a barquette mold on the pastry and cut out a piece ½ inch larger than the mold. Fit the piece of pastry into the mold and cut off the excess around the rim. Repeat with the remaining pastry. Freeze the filled molds for at least 20 minutes before baking.

3. Preheat the oven to 400°. Place the molds on a cookie sheet and bake for 10 minutes, or until slightly firm but not browned. Remove from the oven and let cool; leave the oven turned on.

4. Fill each shell with 1 tablespoon of the almond cream. Bake on the lowest rack of the oven until the tops are well browned, about 15 minutes. Cool the barquettes in the molds on a rack for 10 minutes, then unmold.

5. In a small heavy saucepan, melt the apricot preserves with the rum over low heat. Strain through a fine-mesh sieve and brush lightly over the barquettes.
—Dorie Greenspan

Mirlitons de Rouen

From Normandy come these wonderful, custardy tartlike cookies called *mirlitons*.

Makes About 2½ Dozen

1½ cups all-purpose flour
⅛ teaspoon salt
1½ sticks (6 ounces) cold unsalted butter, cut into small pieces

⅓ cup ice water
1 egg
¼ cup plus 2 tablespoons sugar
¼ cup plus 1 tablespoon heavy cream
¼ cup ground almonds
Pinch of freshly grated nutmeg

1. Sift the flour and salt into a large bowl. Cut in the butter until the mixture resembles coarse meal. Stir in the ice water to form a dough. On a floured surface, knead once or twice. Form into a ball, wrap and refrigerate for 10 minutes.

2. In a small bowl, beat together the egg, sugar, cream, almonds and nutmeg until blended to make a custard filling.

3. Preheat the oven to 350°. On a floured surface, roll the pastry out ⅛ inch thick. Cut 2½-inch circles with a crimped biscuit cutter. Press each round into a lightly oiled 1½-inch tartlet mold (or same size miniature muffin tin). Fill each shell two-thirds full with custard mixture and bake on a cookie sheet for 25 minutes, or until lightly browned.

4. Remove from the molds and cool on a rack.
—Monique Guillaume

Linzer Wreaths

This all-hazelnut version of linzer dough is formed into miniature tartlets. Once baked, these little gems can be stored in an airtight container for a week to 10 days. They also stand up well for shipping.

Makes 2 Dozen

1 cup hazelnuts (4½ ounces)
1½ cups plus 2 tablespoons all-purpose flour
¾ teaspoon baking powder
¼ teaspoon salt

¾ teaspoon cinnamon
1½ sticks (6 ounces) unsalted
  butter, softened
¾ cup sugar
½ teaspoon vanilla extract
1 egg, lightly beaten
⅓ cup raspberry jam

1. Preheat the oven to 350°. Place the hazelnuts in a large baking pan. Bake, stirring occasionally, until the skins are cracked and the centers begin to turn golden brown, about 15 minutes. Then transfer the hot nuts to a terrycloth towel and rub vigorously to remove most of the skins. Let cool completely.

2. In a food processor, combine the toasted hazelnuts with 2 tablespoons of the flour. Pulse until the nuts are finely ground but not oily and pasty.

3. In a small bowl, sift the remaining 1½ cups flour with the baking powder, salt and cinnamon. Set aside.

4. In a medium bowl, using an electric mixer, combine the butter with the sugar and vanilla and beat on high speed until light and fluffy, about 2 minutes. Beat in the ground nuts. Add the egg and continue beating until incorporated, scraping the bowl occasionally. Add the flour mixture to the butter mixture in two batches, beating on low speed just to incorporate. Refrigerate the dough, tightly wrapped, until cold, at least 2 hours or overnight.

5. Divide the dough in half. On a lightly floured work surface, roll out half of the dough about ¼ inch thick. Using a 2-inch round cookie cutter, stamp out circles. Center each circle inside ungreased ½-cup muffin tins. Repeat with the remaining dough scraps to fill all the muffin cups.

6. Divide the remaining dough into 24 equal pieces; roll each piece into a 6-inch log about ½ inch thick. Using a small knife, cut each log into 12 slices, each about ½-inch thick. Roll the slices between your palms to make small balls. Press 12 balls around the perimeter of each dough circle. The fit should not be too tight. Alternatively, roll the reserved dough into 24 logs about 5 inches long and place each log around the perimeter of each circle. Or let the dough soften and pipe it around the perimeter of each cookie using a pastry bag fitted with a ¼-inch plain tip.

7. Bake the tartlets for 17 minutes, or until lightly browned and firm. Unmold immediately onto a cooling rack. While still very hot, drop about ½ teaspoon of raspberry jam into the center of each wreath. Let cool completely before serving.
—Peggy Cullen

food gifts

Vanilla Sugar

For a really attractive gift, make the vanilla sugar in a decorative sugar sprinkler.

Makes 2 Cups

1 vanilla bean
2 cups granulated sugar

Place the vanilla bean in a small sugar canister or jar, if necessary folding it in half. Cover with the sugar. Cover the canister with plastic wrap, then screw on the lid. Let the sugar sit for several days to develop the flavor. Vanilla pods will last for months if kept covered with sugar in an airtight container.
—F&W

Quatre Epices

Quatre épices—which means, literally, "four spices"—is a traditional spice mixture used in French cooking to flavor marinades, pâtés, sausages and other preparations. Often, as here, more than the usual four spices are used for a more interesting result.

Makes About 6 Ounces

6 tablespoons freshly ground
  white pepper
2 teaspoons ground cloves
2 bay leaves, crushed fine
2 tablespoons ground ginger
2 tablespoons thyme

In a blender, food processor or spice mill, grind together the pepper, cloves, bay leaves, ginger and thyme. Pack the very fine powder into small jars with tight-fitting lids.
—F&W

Oriental Five-Spice Powder

For the people on your list whose cooking repertoires include Chinese dishes.

Makes About 4 ounces

2 tablespoons dried orange
  peel, ground to a powder
1 whole star anise*
2 tablespoons ground ginger
2 teaspoons ground cloves
3 tablespoons freshly ground
  white pepper
*Available at Asian markets

In a blender, food processor or coffee mill, grind together the orange peel, star anise, ginger, cloves and pepper to form a fine powder. Place in jars with tight-fitting lids.
—F&W

Sherry Ginger

Preserving fresh ginger in sherry has a beneficial side effect. Not only will it keep the ginger for use in cooking, but you can also use the ginger-spiked sherry. Whenever you use some of the sherry, just be sure to add some back to the bottle to keep the ginger covered. The amount of sherry you will need for the recipe below will depend on the size of the container you use to put the ginger in, so it would be wise to have twice as much as called for, just in case.

Makes About 2 Cups

One 3-inch piece of fresh
  ginger, unpeeled (see Note)
About 2 cups sherry

Place the ginger in a tall, narrow jar that has a wide enough mouth to accommodate the ginger. Pour in the sherry to cover the ginger. Cover the jar and set aside for at least 1 week to develop the flavors. Unless the gin-

ger is kept completely submerged, you should store this in the refrigerator to prevent spoilage.

NOTE: If you would prefer to peel the ginger first (although the peel is edible and really not objectionable), blanch it briefly in boiling water, rinse under cold running water and peel.
—F&W

Firewater

Firewater, also called hot vodka, is an unusual aperitif. The first sip shocks the palate awake, then, gradually, a feeling of warmth and appetite begins to pervade the senses.

Those who cannot take the heat can dilute firewater with straight vodka, but it should never be mixed with anything else.

Firewater made with fresh green chiles has a distinctly herbal flavor and a lovely, faintly flowery fragrance. The kind made from this recipe, with dried red peppers, is hotness pure and simple—an essence, a sensation instead of a taste. Use an inexpensive vodka for this brew since the hotness masks any subtleties of the more costly brands.

Makes 1 Bottle (750 ml)

3 small, dried hot red chiles
1 bottle (750 ml) 80-proof
  vodka

Add the peppers to the bottle of vodka, replace the cap and let macerate at least overnight. The firewater will get hotter and hotter for about 2 weeks, after which it will stabilize. Remove the peppers at any point or leave them in the bottle, as I do, for the duration. The flavor will be somewhat raw for the first month or so, although the firewater is perfectly drinkable from the moment of its creation. After it has aged for a

year, its heat will have rounded and mellowed. Aged firewater is more sophisticated and less aggressive but still gloriously hot.
—Leslie Land

Iced Cranberry Aquavit

This peach-colored aperitif is ideal for holiday toasting. The cranberries used to make this can be used in any cranberry relish recipe (see Note), but taste especially good in a relish flavored with caraway, to complement the flavors of the aquavit.

Makes 2 Bottles

2 packages (12 ounces each)
  cranberries
2 bottles (750 ml each)
  aquavit
2 tablespoons peppercorns

1. Divide the cranberries among three 1-quart jars. Pour in the aquavit to cover (rinse and reserve the aquavit bottles and caps). Add the peppercorns, dividing equally among the jars. Cover and let steep at room temperature for at least 3 days.

2. Strain through a sieve into a large pitcher; reserve the cranberries (see Note). Pour the aquavit back into the original bottles and store in the freezer.

NOTE: The cranberries can be used to make a flavorful sauce or relish. If you do decide to make cranberry sauce, here's a hint for removing the peppercorns from the cranberries: Place the drained cranberries in a large pot of water; the peppercorns will sink, so you can scoop the berries off the surface.
—Anne Disrude

Shallot-Celery Vinegar

You can make the vinegar with garlic instead of shallots

Makes 1 Quart

3 medium shallots (see Note),
  peeled
2 small inner ribs of celery
  with leaves
1 quart white wine vinegar

1. Thread the shallots onto a thin bamboo skewer; leave about 1½ inches of space between them.

2. Place the skewer and the whole celery ribs in a sterilized decanter, wine bottle or any other attractive bottle that will hold a little more than 1 quart. Add the vinegar. Close the top and let the vinegar sit for at least 1 week to develop the flavors.

NOTE: Be sure the shallots will fit through the mouth of the bottle you intend to store the vinegar in.
—F&W

Raspberry Vinegar

Brought back into the limelight by *nouvelle cuisine*, raspberry vinegar is actually a very old condiment. Traditionally served on salads, fruit salads and chilled melon, it may also be used to deglaze the pan for such sautéed foods as calf's or duck liver, chicken breasts or veal. Try this on vanilla ice cream for a memorable dessert.

Makes About 1 Quart

1½ pounds raspberries
½ cup sugar
About 1 quart red wine
  vinegar

1. Fill a clean, dry, large-mouthed quart jar with the berries and sugar, then fill up with vinegar.

2. Set the jar, uncovered, on a small rack (or other perforated support) in a large saucepan and pour enough water into the pan to come halfway up the sides of the jar. Bring the water in this bain-marie to a boil over medium heat. Lower the heat and simmer for 10 minutes.

3. Remove the jar from the water bath and let cool on a rack or folded towel. Close the jar with an airtight lid and shake well.

4. Refrigerate the mixture for 3 weeks, then strain the vinegar, pressing the berries lightly to extract juice. Discard the pulp. If the vinegar is too thick, add more wine vinegar.
—Monique Guillaume

Strawberry Vinegar

Ripe, juicy berries are a must when making fruit vinegar. It adds a nice change of flavor to a salad dressing. I like to hold on to the empty vinegar bottle and pour the strawberry vinegar into it when it is ready.

Makes About 1½ Cups

1 cup small ripe strawberries
  (about ½ pint), quartered
1 bottle (12 to 14 ounces)
  white wine vinegar (about 1
  pint)

1. Place the berries in a 2-cup glass jar and pour in the vinegar. Cover and set aside at room temperature for 3 days.

2. Strain the strawberry vinegar through a fine sieve. Pour into a clean bottle, using a funnel if necessary, cap tightly and store in a cool dark place.
—Diana Sturgis

Glace de Viande

Glace de viande, or meat glaze, adds an incredible depth of flavor to sauces, soups and stews, but making it is quite time-consuming. Because most people do not bother to make *glace de viande* for themselves, it makes a much-appreciated gift.

Makes 1 to 1½ Cups

6 pounds veal and beef bones,
  cut into 3- to 4-inch pieces
3 pounds chicken backs,
  wings and necks
1 large onion, unpeeled and
  cut in half
2 large garlic cloves, unpeeled
  and lightly bruised
2 large carrots, coarsely
  chopped or sliced
1 celery rib, coarsely chopped
½ teaspoon thyme

1. Preheat the oven to 425°. Place the ingredients in a large roasting pan and place in the oven for about 45 minutes or until well browned, turning the bones and vegetables twice.

2. Transfer all of the ingredients to a large kettle, leaving behind as much fat as possible. Pour off the fat from the roasting pan, then pour 3 cups of water into the pan. Bring to a boil over direct heat, scraping loose any browned bits. Add to kettle of bones and vegetables.

3. Pour into the kettle enough cold water to cover everything by 2 to 4 inches and bring to a boil. Boil over moderate heat for about 6 hours, skimming every hour or so to remove as much fat and scum as possible.

4. Strain the reduced liquid into a smaller pot. Cook over medium heat for about 2 hours, skimming often. Strain the liquid again, this time through a sieve lined with several thicknesses of cheesecloth. You should have 5 to 6 cups.

5. Reduce in a saucepan over medium heat until about 1½ cups remain, stirring often and reducing the heat to a simmer as the glaze thickens. When bubbles appear in the thickened dark-brown mixture, the *glace de viande* is ready. Turn it out into a small heatproof container and cool, uncovered. Label, cover and refrigerate. The extract should be refrigerated for storage (it will keep for weeks), or it may be frozen.
—*Michele Evans*

Basil Oil

You can use this infused oil in vinaigrettes, on its own tossed with pasta or rice, or drizzled over tomatoes and poached fish or fowl.

Makes About 1⅓ Cups

1 cup (tightly packed) fresh
  basil leaves
2 cups olive oil

1. In a large pan of boiling, salted water, blanch the basil leaves for 5 seconds. Drain and rinse with cold water.

2. In a food processor or blender, puree the blanched basil with ¼ cup of the oil. With the machine on, add the remaining 1¾ cups oil and process until well blended and smooth. Transfer to a glass jar, cover and let stand at room temperature for at least 24 hours.

3. Carefully pour off the clear green oil, leaving behind the thick basil puree. The strained oil can be refrigerated, covered, for up to 1 month.
—*Jean-Georges Vongerichten*

Ginger Oil

Makes About ¾ Cup

4 tablespoons ground ginger
1 cup grape-seed or safflower
  oil

1. In a medium bowl, whisk the ginger with 3 tablespoons water to form a paste. Gradually whisk in the oil. Pour into a jar and let stand at room temperature, covered, for at least 2 days.

2. Carefully pour the clear oil into a jar and discard the ginger sediment left behind. The oil can be kept covered in the refrigerator indefinitely.
—*Jean-Georges Vongerichten*

Curry Oil

Mix this oil with fresh lime juice and grated lime zest for a delicious vinaigrette-style sauce to go with shrimp, salmon or chicken.

Makes About ⅔ Cup

4 tablespoons curry powder
1 cup grape-seed or safflower
  oil

1. In a medium bowl, whisk the curry with 3 tablespoons of water to form a paste. Gradually whisk in the oil. Cover and let stand at room temperature for at least 2 days.

2. Carefully pour off the oil, leaving behind the curry sediment. The oil can be stored, refrigerated and covered, indefinitely.
—*Jean-Georges Vongerichten*

Chili-Orange Oil

Makes About 3 Cups

2 cups corn or peanut oil
¼ cup Oriental sesame oil
Zest of 3 large oranges (no
   white pith), well scrubbed
   (see Note) and finely minced
½ cup crushed hot red pepper
3 tablespoons Chinese salted
   black beans*
1 to 2 large garlic cloves,
   peeled and lightly smashed
*Available at Asian markets

1. In a heavy medium saucepan, combine the corn and sesame oils. Heat to 250°, or until hot enough to bubble up slowly around a pepper flake.

2. Add the orange zest, hot pepper, black beans and garlic. Remove from the heat, whisk gently to distribute the seasonings and set aside until cool.

3. Transfer the oil and seasonings to a glass jar and store in a cool, dark place. The oil keeps indefinitely.

NOTE: Oranges are frequently sprayed or subject to pollutants. To wash the peel, use an untreated abrasive pad, a gentle liquid soap and hot tap water, scrubbing lightly until the smell of the orange oil comes to the surface of the peel.
—*Barbara Tropp, China Moon Cafe, San Francisco*

Herbed Oil

This oil is a fine addition to salad dressings or oil-brushed breads such as focaccia.
   Makes About ½ Cup

1 teaspoon rosemary
½ teaspoon crushed hot red
   pepper
2 whole bay leaves, crushed
1 teaspoon thyme
½ cup olive oil

In a small container, combine the rosemary, hot pepper, bay leaves, thyme and oil. Cover and let stand at room temperature for at least 12 hours.
—*Diana Sturgis*

Oriental Chili Oil

If you prefer a very spicy oil, increase the amount of chile paste in this recipe.
   Makes ¼ Cup

¼ cup Oriental chile paste
   with garlic*
¼ cup Oriental sesame oil
*Available at Asian markets

In a small bowl, stir together the chile paste and sesame oil. Pour this mixture into a glass jar; cover and store in the refrigerator for up to 1 month. Bring the oil to room temperature before using.
—*Diana Sturgis*

Fennel-Garlic Olive Oil

Add this oil to salad dressings or toss with pasta for a quick holiday supper. Use regular olive oil or a fruity extra-virgin oil with a pretty green color for this recipe.
   Makes 1 Quart

2 bay leaves
2 to 3 dried fennel stalks
2 to 3 garlic cloves
1 quart olive oil

Put the bay leaves, fennel stalks and garlic into an attractive 1-quart glass bottle. Fill the bottle with the olive oil. Cap securely and store at room temperature for 2 to 3 days to develop the flavor.
—*Diana Sturgis*

Rosemary Oil with Red Chiles

You can substitute this oil in any dish calling for olive oil when you want to add an extra kick.
   Makes 1 Quart

5 large, thick branches of
   rosemary
2 dried hot red chiles
1 quart extra-virgin olive oil

Rub the rosemary branches between your fingers to bruise them. Using a knife, bruise the chiles, then put them and the rosemary in a jar with a tight-fitting lid. Pour the olive oil into the jar, seal and let stand at room temperature for 10 days. Strain the oil through a fine-mesh sieve and return to the jar. This oil will keep for up to 2 months.
—*Marcia Kiesel*

Roasted Peppers in Olive Oil

These roasted peppers are especially delicious when served on warm croutons of Italian bread. They can also be slivered and served, with a little of their oil, over spaghetti or room-temperature pasta salads. The peppers can be stored in their oil in the refrigerator for several weeks.

Makes About 1 Quart

12 red bell peppers
2 sprigs of rosemary or 2 bay
   leaves
2 garlic cloves, lightly crushed
2 strips of orange zest
2 to 3 cups olive oil

1. Preheat the broiler. Arrange the peppers in a single layer in a large baking tray. Broil, as close to the heat as possible, turning occasionally, until the peppers are blackened all over, 15 to 20 minutes.

2. Transfer the peppers to a large brown paper bag; close the top and let stand for about 10 minutes, until the skins loosen.

3. One at a time, hold the peppers under cold running water, rinse and gently pull away the charred skin; drain on paper towels.

4. Quarter each pepper and, using a paring knife, remove the stem, seeds and ribs. Place the peppers in a clean, dry 1-quart jar. Add the rosemary, garlic and orange zest.

5. Pour in the olive oil, adding enough to cover the peppers and fill the jar. Slide a clean blunt knife blade between the peppers to release any trapped air bubbles. Seal with a lid and store in the refrigerator.
—*Diana Sturgis*

Sherried Olives

The olives need to marinate for three to four days, so plan accordingly.
6 Servings

1 can (7½ ounces) pitted
   medium black olives
1 can (7½ ounces) pitted
   medium green olives
3 cups olive oil
1 cup dry sherry
1 cup sherry vinegar
1 small garlic clove, smashed
1 small red onion, cut into
   thin rings
1 tablespoon thyme

1. Drain the olives and discard the brine.

2. In a large jar with a tight lid, combine the olives with the remaining ingredients. Refrigerate, covered, for 3 or 4 days, shaking the jar from time to time.
—*W. Peter Prestcott*

Marinated Olives Le Cherche-Midi

Make a variation by marinating picholine or other brine-cured green olives in virgin olive oil with several broken dried fennel stalks and strips of lemon peel.
Makes About 1 Pint

½ pound Nyons or other dry-
   cured black olives
3 small dried hot red peppers
1 teaspoon herbes de
   Provence
2 garlic cloves, unpeeled and
   bruised
1 cup extra-virgin olive oil

In a 1-pint jar, combine the olives with the hot peppers. Add the *herbes de Provence*, garlic and oil and let marinate, loosely covered, in a cool place for 3 days.
—*Sally Scoville*

Mixed Pickled Vegetables

Makes About 4 Pints

1 quart distilled white vinegar
1½ cups sugar
1 tablespoon salt
1 blade of mace
1 bay leaf
½ pound carrots, quartered
   lengthwise and cut into 4-
   inch lengths
1 small head of cauliflower,
   cut into 1-inch florets
½ pound green beans
1 medium red onion, cut into
   ¼-inch rings
4 small, dried hot red chiles
   (optional)
1 teaspoon oregano

1. In a nonreactive saucepan, heat the vinegar, sugar, salt, mace, bay leaf and ½ cup of water to boiling. Reduce the heat and simmer for 15 minutes.

2. Meanwhile, cook the carrots in a medium saucepan of boiling water until crisp-tender, about 5 minutes; remove with a slotted spoon and drain. Add the cauliflower to the water and boil until crisp-tender, about 4 minutes; remove and drain. Boil the green beans until crisp-tender, about 4 minutes and drain. All the vegetables should remain crunchy.

3. Dividing the vegetables evenly, pack them into 4 hot pint canning jars, interspersing the cooked vegetables with onion rings. Add a dried chile pepper to each jar, if desired, and ¼ teaspoon of oregano.

4. Strain the hot vinegar to re-

move the herbs and return it to a boil. Pour the boiling vinegar over the vegetables in the jars to within ¼ inch of the rim. Cover with lids and tighten the screw bands to seal. Lower the jars onto a rack in a large pot of boiling water or into a water-bath canner; the tops should be covered by 1 to 2 inches of water. Return to a boil and process the jars for 15 minutes. Store on a cool, dark shelf.

—*F&W*

Pickled Red Cabbage

This pickled cabbage is best when stored for at least two months before eating.

Makes About 6 Pints

1 quart distilled white vinegar
1½ cups sugar
1 tablespoon salt
2 bay leaves
½ teaspoon whole black
    peppercorns
½ teaspoon whole cloves
2 large heads of red cabbage
    (about 3½ pounds each),
    finely shredded

1. Place the vinegar, sugar and salt in a large, nonreactive saucepan with 1 quart of water. Tie the bay leaves, peppercorns and cloves in a double thickness of cheesecloth and add to the pot. Bring to a boil over high heat, reduce the heat and simmer for 15 minutes.

2. Add half the cabbage and cook until just tender, about 2 minutes. Remove from the heat. Using a slotted spoon or tongs, remove the cabbage from the cooking liquid and tightly pack it into 3 hot pint canning jars. Fill each jar with about ½ cup of the cooking liquid to reach ¼ inch from the rim. Cover with lids and tighten the screw bands to seal.

3. Return the remaining liquid to a boil and repeat the cooking and filling with the remaining cabbage and another 3 hot pint jars.

4. Lower the jars onto a rack in a large pot of boiling water or into a water-bath canner; the tops should be covered by 1 to 2 inches of water. Return to a boil and process the jars for 15 minutes. Store on a cool, dark shelf for 1 week before serving.

—*F&W*

Giardinera

These Italian-style pickled vegetables are traditionally arranged in a large glass container, making them an especially attractive gift.

Makes About 1¾ Quarts

Pickling Solution:
2½ cups water
2½ cups distilled white
    vinegar
1½ cups sugar
1½ teaspoons salt
1 garlic clove, peeled
1 bay leaf, crumbled
¼ cup mixed pickling spices,
    tied in cheesecloth

Vegetables:
1 head of cauliflower,
    separated into small florets
1 bunch of broccoli, separated
    into florets (reserve stalks
    for another use)
8 tender celery ribs, cut on the
    diagonal into 1-inch pieces
3 large carrots, sliced
    diagonally
1 package frozen artichoke
    hearts, thawed
10 medium mushrooms

1. Make the pickling solution: In a large nonreactive pot, bring the water, vinegar, sugar, salt, garlic, bay leaf and pickling spices to a boil.

Reduce the heat, cover and simmer for 10 minutes.

2. Add all the vegetables, cover the pot, bring to a boil, stirring once or twice, then boil for 5 minutes.

3. Drain; reserve and cool the liquid. Discard the garlic and pickling spices. Place the vegetables on a large platter in a single layer and let cool. Slice the mushrooms.

4. In a 1½- to 2-quart glass apothecary jar or other attractive wide-mouthed glass jar, layer the vegetables in this order: artichoke hearts, carrots, broccoli, mushrooms, carrots, cauliflower and celery, repeating the pattern until all of the vegetables are used. In placing the vegetables, arrange them in rows around the jar, with the attractive parts against the glass; as you proceed, fill the center with the less attractive pieces. Pour the pickling liquid into the jar; it should cover the vegetables completely. (If it doesn't, make more solution in the same proportions of water, vinegar, sugar and salt; omit the spices. Cool, then add to the giardinera.) Cover the jar and refrigerate.

—*Michele Evans*

Curried Corn Relish

Makes About 4 Pints

2 cups finely chopped cabbage
    (8 ounces)
2 green bell peppers, seeded
    and finely chopped (1½
    cups)
2 red bell peppers, seeded and
    finely chopped (1½ cups)
1 medium onion, finely
    chopped (1 cup)
2 celery ribs, finely chopped
    (1 cup)
⅓ cup sugar
2 tablespoons curry powder
2 teaspoons dry mustard

1 tablespoon salt
½ teaspoon freshly ground
   white pepper
1½ cups cider vinegar
6 cups tender young corn
   kernels, fresh or frozen

1. Place all of the ingredients, except the corn, into a large saucepan. Add ½ cup of water. Bring to a boil, cover and cook over moderate heat for 10 minutes. Stir in the corn kernels. Return to a boil, cover and cook for 5 minutes longer.

2. Pack the relish tightly into 4 hot pint canning jars to within ¼ inch of the rim. Cover with lids and tighten the screw bands to seal. Lower the jars onto a rack in a large pot of boiling water or into a water-bath canner; the tops should be covered by 1 to 2 inches of water. Return to a boil and process the jars for 15 minutes. Store on a cool, dark shelf.
—F&W

Three-Pepper Relish

Makes About 3 Pints

3 cups finely chopped red bell
   peppers (about 3 pounds)
2 cups finely chopped green
   bell peppers (about 2
   pounds)
1 cup finely chopped Italian
   frying peppers (about 1
   pound)
1½ cups finely chopped
   onions (about 2 large)
1½ cups finely chopped celery
   (about 3 ribs)
1 cup granulated sugar
⅓ cup (firmly packed) light
   brown sugar
1 cup cider vinegar

1½ tablespoons mustard seed
2 teaspoons coarse (kosher)
   salt

1. In a large mixing bowl, combine the red and green bell peppers, the Italian frying peppers, onions and celery. Pour enough boiling water over the vegetables to barely cover them; let stand for 5 minutes.

2. Drain the vegetables and transfer to a large saucepan. Stir in the granulated sugar, brown sugar, vinegar, mustard seed and salt, stirring to mix well. Bring to a boil over high heat. Reduce the heat to moderately high and cook, uncovered, until the vegetables are tender but still slightly crunchy, about 5 minutes.

3. Using a slotted spoon, divide the relish among 3 hot pint canning jars. Fill each jar with enough of the cooking liquid (about ½ cup) to come to within ¼ inch of the rim. Cover with lids, and tighten the screw bands to seal.

4. Lower the jars onto a rack in a large pot of boiling water or into a water-bath canner; the tops should be covered by 1 to 2 inches of water. Return to the boil and process for 15 minutes. Store on a cool dark shelf for 2 weeks before using.
—F&W

Mango Chutney

This Indonesian-inspired chutney is as colorful as it is flavorful.
Makes About 5 Pints

6 large, firm-ripe mangoes,
   peeled and sliced into
   2½-by-½-inch strips
1 large yellow onion, thinly
   sliced
1 large red onion, thinly
   sliced
2 green bell peppers, thinly
   sliced

2 red bell peppers, thinly
   sliced
3 small or 2 large jalapeño
   peppers, sliced into thin
   rounds
¼ cup pickled hot peppers,
   sliced into thin rounds
1 cup (packed) brown sugar
¾ cup honey
2 teaspoons grated orange
   zest
¾ cup grapefruit juice
¾ cup cider vinegar
½ cup dried currants
½ cup golden raisins
2 tablespoons minced fresh
   ginger
1 teaspoon ground coriander
1 teaspoon mustard seed
¼ teaspoon freshly grated
   nutmeg

1. In a large saucepan, combine all the ingredients, tossing well to distribute the spices. Bring to a boil over moderately high heat. Reduce the heat to moderately low and simmer for 20 to 25 minutes, until the liquid thickens to the consistency of a light sugar syrup; remove from the heat.

2. Carefully ladle the hot chutney into 5 hot pint canning jars to within ¼ inch of the rims. Cover with lids and tighten the screw bands to seal. Lower the jars onto a rack in a large pot of boiling water or into a water-bath canner; the tops should be covered by 1 to 2 inches of water. Return to a boil and process the jars for 15 minutes. Store on a cool, dark shelf.
—F&W

Plum Porridge

This rich, spiced pottage, the ancestor of plum pudding, has a flavor reminiscent of old-fashioned mincemeat. It might be served in several ways. It does especially nicely as an accompaniment to cold sliced meat and poultry. It can also be served for dessert, topped with lightly sweetened whipped cream flavored with dark rum.

Makes About 2½ Quarts

6 cups beef stock
1¼ cups raisins
1¼ cups dried currants
1¼ cups pitted prunes,
   coarsely chopped
½ teaspoon freshly grated
   nutmeg
½ teaspoon ground cloves
½ teaspoon ground mace
½ teaspoon cinnamon
½ cup sherry
½ cup dry red wine,
   preferably Bordeaux
½ cup (packed) brown sugar
One 1-pound loaf firm-
   textured white bread, crusts
   removed

1. Place the stock, raisins, currants, prunes, nutmeg, cloves, mace and cinnamon in a large pan and simmer for 1 hour, or until the fruit is tender.

2. While the fruit is simmering, place the sherry, red wine and sugar in a small saucepan and simmer for 10 minutes to cook off the alcohol.

3. Cut the bread into 1-inch cubes and stir into the fruit mixture. Stir in wine syrup.

4. Refrigerate overnight to ripen the flavors. Heat the porridge carefully and serve. Pass additional sugar, if desired.
—*Philippa Pullar*

Dried Sour Cherries and Pineapple in Port

For a textural contrast, you can serve this with a hard cookie like biscotti. The fruit must marinate for at least 12 hours.

6 Servings

2 cups tawny port
¼ cup sugar
¼ teaspoon peppercorns
6 whole cloves
2 strips of lemon zest
½ cup dried sour cherries*
   (3 ounces)
1 whole small pineapple,
   about 1½ pounds, peeled
   and cut into 1-inch chunks
*Available at specialty food
   shops

1. In a small nonreactive saucepan, combine the port, sugar, peppercorns, cloves and lemon zest and bring to a simmer over moderate heat. Simmer for 5 minutes, stirring occasionally. Remove from the heat, stir in the dried cherries and let cool.

2. Place the pineapple chunks in a medium bowl. Pour the port mixture over the pineapple and refrigerate for at least 12 hours. Let come to room temperature; then spoon the fruit into 6 bowls and serve.
—*Lee Bailey*

Pears in White Rum

Makes About 3 Quarts

5 pounds firm-ripe, flavorful
   pears
¼ cup fresh lemon juice
4¼ cups sugar
4 cups white rum
6 whole cloves

1. Peel the pears, then quarter and core them, dropping them as you go into a large bowl of water with the lemon juice in it to prevent the pears from discoloring.

2. In a large, heavy saucepan, bring the sugar and 1 cup of water to a boil, stirring to dissolve the sugar. Drain the pears and add them. Bring to a full boil again, pushing the pears under the surface once or twice and remove from the heat. Let the pears cool in the syrup until just warm.

3. Meanwhile, place the canning jars in a pot of simmering water to cover. Boil them 10 minutes and reserve, off the heat, until needed.

4. Stir the rum into the pears and syrup. With a slotted spoon, pack the fruit carefully into three 1-quart hot canning jars, adding 2 cloves per jar. Pour in enough syrup to cover the fruit, leaving ¼ inch space below the jar's rim. Seal the jars with screwband tops and let stand in a cool, dark, dry place for at least 2 months before using. The pears will keep for about a year.
—*Monique Guillaume*

Three-Citrus Marmalade

Makes 6 to 7 Pints

2 lemons
2 oranges of a variety with
  seeds
2 grapefruits of a variety with
  seeds
About 10 cups sugar

1. Cut the lemons, oranges and grapefruits into paper-thin rounds, reserving all the seeds separately and place the slices in a bowl. Measure the volume of the slices—there should be about 2 quarts.

2. Measure out twice as much cold water as there is fruit and add the water to the bowl of fruit. Cover the bowl with plastic wrap and refrigerate overnight to soften the peel. Wrap the seeds in a 10-inch square of cheesecloth and tie it securely into a bag with kitchen string. Set aside.

3. Pour the fruit-and-water mixture into a large, nonreactive pan and add the bag of seeds (these help to set the marmalade). Bring the mixture to a boil and boil it gently, uncovered, for 1½ hours.

4. Allow the mixture to cool and then measure it—there should be about 10 cups. Return the fruit and liquid to the pan and add an equal amount of sugar. Stir to dissolve the sugar and bring the mixture to a boil. Boil it fairly rapidly again, uncovered, for about 30 minutes, stirring frequently.

5. Remove the pan from the heat to avoid overcooking the marmalade and test to see whether the marmalade will set: Place a teaspoon of the mixture on a cold plate and allow it to cool; the marmalade should now wrinkle when pushed with a finger. If it does not wrinkle, reboil and retest the marmalade at 5-minute intervals until a wrinkle is obtained. Be sure to remove the pan from the heat each time.

6. Remove and discard the bag of seeds and skim off any foam. Allow the peel to settle for about 5 minutes and then ladle the mixture into hot, sterile jelly glasses or straight-sided canning jars to within ¼ inch of their tops. Seal with melted paraffin or sterile two-piece lids if canning jars are used.
—*F&W*

Le Hameau's Confiture d'Oranges

Makes 5 to 6 Cups

6 oranges
3 lemons
4 cups sugar

1. Wash and dry the oranges and lemons. Thinly slice four of the oranges into rounds, removing and discarding any seeds. Place the slices in a large bowl and pour 1 quart cold water over them.

2. Using a sharp paring knife, carefully remove the zest from the two remaining oranges and the lemons. Cut the zest into narrow strips, wrap them in plastic and set them aside. Squeeze the juice from the two oranges and lemons from which you have removed the zest and add the juice to the bowl of orange slices. Cover the mixture with plastic wrap or a plate and allow the peels to soften in the water for 12 to 24 hours.

3. Pour the mixture into a large, nonreactive pan and stir in the sugar. Bring the mixture to a boil and then cook it at a steady simmer, stirring often, for 1½ hours. Stir in the reserved strips of zest and continue cooking for 5 more minutes.

4. Skim off and discard any foam that has risen to the surface and ladle the marmalade into hot, sterile jelly glasses or pint canning jars to within ¼ inch of the top. Seal with melted paraffin or with sterile two-piece lids if canning jars are used. When cool, store the marmalade in a cool, dark place.
—*F&W*

Mermellata of Orange and Onion

This Italian-style marmalade is an excellent accompaniment for cold meats, or it may be used as a glaze over a smoked ham before baking. Although the *mermellata* will not set firmly because of the lack of seeds and pith, it will thicken further when it has cooled thoroughly.

Makes About 1 Quart

4 large oranges—peeled,
  seeded and thinly sliced
  (3½ cups)
6 medium onions, thinly
  sliced (6 cups)
4 cups sugar
1 teaspoon cayenne pepper
1 cup distilled white vinegar

1. In a large, heavy pot, combine the oranges and onions with enough water to cover (about 5 cups). Bring the mixture to a boil and then simmer, uncovered, for 30 minutes.

2. Remove the pan from the heat and stir in the sugar. (If necessary, add enough hot water to cover the ingredients again.) Stir to dissolve the sugar and return the pan to the heat. Add the cayenne and vinegar and boil, stirring frequently, for about 40 minutes or until the *mermellata* is reduced to about 6 cups.

3. Cool the mixture and then refrigerate it in sterile, covered containers; it will keep for several weeks.
—*F&W*

Lime Curd

Tangy but not bitter, this flavorful spread is good on scones, toast or pound cake. It can also be used as a filling for cakes and small tarts. Lime curd will keep refrigerated for about one month. The same formula can be used for lemon curd, but there is no need to blanch the lemon zest.

Makes About 1 Cup

4 to 5 limes
1 whole egg
3 egg yolks
1 cup sugar
4 tablespoons unsalted butter,
  cut into pieces

1. Using a swivel-bladed vegetable peeler, remove the green zest from 2 of the limes. Scrape off any of the bitter white pith left on the zest. Place the zest in a small saucepan. Add enough boiling water to cover and blanch over high heat for 1 minute. Drain and pat dry on paper towels. Chop the zest finely. Halve and squeeze enough of the limes to produce ½ cup of lime juice.

2. In a small bowl, beat together the whole egg and egg yolks. In a small heavy saucepan, combine the lime juice and sugar; stir to partially dissolve. Add the beaten eggs, butter and the chopped zest. Cook over low heat, stirring, until the mixture thickens enough to coat the back of a spoon, about 20 minutes. (Do not let the mixture boil; it will thicken further as it cools.)

3. Strain the lime curd into a clean, dry heatproof jar, cover with a round of wax paper and let cool. Cover the jar and refrigerate until chilled before serving.
—Diana Sturgis

Raspberry Ketchup

This flavorful ketchup is delicious with hot or cold duck, turkey, chicken or pork, and it makes a tasty dip for broiled chicken wings or barbecued ribs.

Makes About 2 Cups

3½ cups raspberries (about 1
  pint)
½ cup sugar
1½ cups minced onions
  (about 2 large)
½ cup white wine vinegar
2 garlic cloves, minced
1½ teaspoons ground allspice

1. Place the raspberries in a medium nonreactive saucepan with 2 tablespoons of water and 1 tablespoon of the sugar. With a wooden spoon, mash the berries while bringing the mixture to a boil over moderate heat. Reduce the heat, cover and simmer for 5 minutes.

2. Press the mixture through a fine sieve to remove the seeds.

3. Return the sieved mixture to the saucepan and add the onions, vinegar, garlic, allspice and remaining sugar. Bring to a boil, reduce the heat to low and simmer uncovered, stirring occasionally, until the onions are tender and the mixture is reduced to 2 cups, 10 to 15 minutes. Puree in a food processor or pass through a food mill. Store in a covered jar in the refrigerator for up to 1 month.
—Diana Sturgis

Cider Honey

Makes a Scant ⅔ Cup

8 cups unfiltered,
  unpasteurized cider

1. In a large nonreactive saucepan, boil the cider over high heat until reduced by half, about 1 hour. As the cider boils down, use a wet pastry brush to dissolve and release any cider clinging to the sides of the pan.

2. Pour the reduced cider into a smaller saucepan and boil over high heat until it is reduced by half again, about 45 minutes. Pour the cider into yet a smaller saucepan and boil until it is reduced by half again (to about 1 cup), about 45 minutes longer.

3. From this point on you have to watch the cider carefully. Reduce the heat to very low and simmer the cider gently, constantly brushing down any cider that adheres to the sides of the pan. Don't let it get very dark or it will become bitter. When the cider is very thick, after about 30 minutes, pour it into a heatproof measuring cup to see how much is left. If you have more than ⅔ cup, return it to the pan and simmer until you have a scant ⅔ cup. Strain the cider honey through a fine metal sieve into a wide-mouthed glass jar. Stored at room temperature, the cider honey will have the consistency of pancake syrup; if you prefer it thicker, store in the refrigerator.
—Linda Merinoff

Chocolate Mint Sauce

For a real treat, spoon this sauce over vanilla or coffee ice cream and top with a dollop of freshly whipped cream. The sauce is best when served at room temperature.

Makes About 1½ Cups

6 ounces semisweet chocolate,
* broken into pieces*
½ cup milk
1 tablespoon unsalted butter
¼ cup crème de menthe
* liqueur*
1 teaspoon vanilla extract

1. In a heavy medium saucepan, combine the chocolate, milk and butter. Cook over low heat, stirring, until the sauce begins to simmer, about 5 minutes.

2. Immediately remove from the heat. Stir in the crème de menthe and vanilla. Pour the sauce into a clean, dry pint jar and let cool to room temperature. Cover and refrigerate.
—*Diana Sturgis*

Double-Scotch Butterscotch Ice Cream Sauce

This sauce will evoke memories of sweet old-fashioned sundaes. It can be warmed, but is best when served at room temperature and poured generously over vanilla ice cream. Stored in a tightly covered jar, the sauce will keep for up to two weeks in the refrigerator.

Makes About 1½ Cups

1 cup (packed) light brown
* sugar*
4 tablespoons unsalted butter,
* cut into pieces*
½ cup light corn syrup
½ cup heavy cream
2 tablespoons whiskey
½ teaspoon vanilla extract

1. In a heavy medium saucepan, place the brown sugar, butter, corn syrup and cream. Bring to a boil, stirring, over moderate heat. Reduce the heat to moderately low and boil, stirring, until reduced to 1½ cups, about 8 minutes.

2. Remove from the heat and let cool slightly, about 10 minutes. Stir the whiskey and vanilla into the sauce and let it cool to room temperature.

3. Pour the cooled sauce into a clean dry pint jar; cover and refrigerate. Let the sauce return to room temperature before using.
—*Diana Sturgis*

Pâte de Pommes

This traditional French confection, although mainly for children, was often served at dinner parties, after dessert and before coffee. An old custom was to serve a fruit paste with chocolates.

Makes About 100 Pieces

2 pounds McIntosh apples
1 tablespoon fresh lemon
* juice*
About 3 cups sugar
Walnut halves, for decoration

1. Peel, quarter and core the apples. Place them in a heavy saucepan with ½ cup of water and the lemon juice. Cover and bring to a boil. Lower the heat and simmer over low heat, stirring frequently with a wooden spoon, for 20 minutes, or until there is no liquid left. Remove from the heat.

2. In another saucepan, mix 2 cups of sugar with ½ cup of water. Without heating the mixture, stir occasionally for several minutes, or until the sugar has begun to dissolve. (The French use a silver spoon for this.)

3. Bring the sugar syrup slowly to a boil. Cook without stirring, but shake the pan frequently, until large bubbles appear. Add the apple mixture to the syrup and mix well.

4. Bring this mixture to a boil over medium heat. Lower the heat and simmer very slowly for about 30 minutes, stirring frequently with a wooden spoon. Crush any chunks of apple in the mixture against the side of the pan so the paste will have a uniform texture. After about 35 minutes, stir more frequently to prevent sticking or scorching. After about 50 minutes, the paste should detach itself from the sides of the pan. Watch the paste carefully, as the cooking time varies. Remove the pan from the heat when the consistency is as described.

5. Sprinkle one or two shallow square or rectangular pans with some of the remaining sugar, then pour in the paste, spreading to the desired thickness. Smooth the top, sprinkle it with some more sugar and let it stand at room temperature, uncovered, overnight.

6. Unmold the paste onto a cutting surface and cut it into squares or lozenges, using a sharp knife dipped into hot water. Dip each piece in more of the remaining sugar, coating all sides evenly. Press a walnut half into the top of each piece. Before serving, put the pieces into small paper candy cups.
—*Monique Guillaume*

Pepper Pretzels (p. 281), Blue Corn Pizzelle (p. 281),
Romano Leaf Wafers (p. 282) and Mediterranean Animal Crackers (p. 282).

Strawberry Vinegar (p. 259).

Raspberry Ketchup (p. 267).

Prunes in Red Wine (p. 151).

Quince Candy

The high pectin content of quinces makes them an ideal candidate for the typically French confection called *pâte de fruits*. Serve the candies with afterdinner coffee.

Makes About 100 Pieces

2 pounds quinces
1 tablespoon fresh lemon
    juice
About 3 cups sugar
Chopped almonds and/or
    diced candied fruit, for
    decoration

1. Because raw quinces are a bit difficult to peel and core, a preliminary step is helpful: Wash the quinces, put them into a saucepan and add water to cover. Simmer the fruit 10 to 12 minutes, or until a quince is soft when probed with a fork. Drain in a colander, then rinse under cold water.

2. Peel and core the quinces, then mash the flesh.

3. Place the mashed quince, with ½ cup of water and the lemon juice, in a heavy saucepan. Cover and bring to a boil. Lower the heat and simmer over low heat, stirring frequently with a wooden spoon, for 20 minutes, or until there is no liquid left. Remove from heat.

4. In another saucepan, mix 2 cups of sugar with ½ cup of water. Without heating the mixture, stir occasionally for several minutes, or until the sugar has begun to dissolve. (The French use a silver spoon for this.)

5. Bring the sugar syrup slowly to a boil. Cook without stirring, but shake the pan frequently, until large bubbles appear. Add the quince mixture to the syrup and mix well.

6. Bring this mixture to a boil over medium heat. Lower the heat and simmer very slowly for about 30 minutes, stirring frequently with a wooden spoon. Crush any chunks of quince in the mixture against the side of the pan so the paste will have a uniform texture. After about 35 minutes, stir more frequently to prevent sticking or scorching. After about 50 minutes, the paste should detach itself from the sides of the pan. Watch the paste carefully, as the cooking time varies. Remove the pan from the heat when the consistency is as described.

7. Sprinkle one or two shallow square or rectangular pans with some of the remaining sugar, then pour in the paste, spreading to the desired thickness. Smooth the top, sprinkle it with some more sugar and let it stand at room temperature, uncovered, overnight.

8. Unmold the paste onto a cutting surface and cut it into squares or lozenges, using a sharp knife dipped into hot water. Dip each piece in more of the remaining sugar, coating all sides evenly. Decorate the sugared pieces of finished paste with chopped almonds and/or diced candied fruit. Before serving, put the pieces into small paper candy cups.
—*Monique Guillaume*

Marzipan

Use this wonderful confection for stuffing figs or dates or for just making fanciful shapes to be visually appreciated and then later eaten. The marzipan can be flavored and tinted to provide you with a whole palette of colors and flavors (see Variations, below). Then you can shape the marzipan into balls, ovals, squares or logs and decorate them with candied cherries, candy coffee beans, lemon drops, candied mimosa, candied angelica, candied violets or candied mint leaves. Your creations do not need to be covered and will keep for a week or two.

Makes About 2½ Cups

1 pound confectioners' sugar,
    sifted
2 cans (8 ounces each)
    almond paste,* at room
    temperature
2 tablespoons light corn syrup
* Available at specialty food
    stores

1. Lightly sprinkle your work surface with some of the confectioners' sugar. Place the almond paste on the work surface and knead it to incorporate the confectioners' sugar. Continue to add the confectioners' sugar, working it in, until it has all been used and the mixture is smooth. If you have a heavy-duty electric mixer with a paddle, you can use it to speed up the kneading process.

2. Continuing to knead, gradually work in the corn syrup. When the marzipan is smooth, either use it immediately or wrap it tightly in plastic wrap (or place it in an airtight container) and store at room temperature for up to 3 days or in the refrigerator for up to 3 months.

3. When ready to use the marzipan, divide it into five equal portions and make the five variations below.

VARIATIONS

Crème de Cassis Marzipan: Knead a teaspoon of crème de cassis and 2 drops of red food coloring into one portion of the marzipan, kneading until the color is even. Use immediately or store as above.

Chocolate-Rum Marzipan: Pour 1 teaspoon dark rum over one portion of the marzipan; knead in 1 tablespoon cocoa powder until the color is even.

Coffee Marzipan: Dissolve 1 teaspoon instant coffee in 1 teaspoon boiling water; cool slightly. Knead the coffee essence into one portion of the marzipan and knead it until smooth.

Lemon Marzipan: Combine 1 teaspoon grated lemon zest with 1 teaspoon lemon juice and one or two drops yellow food coloring; pour the mixture over one portion of the marzipan and knead it until smooth.

Crème de Menthe Marzipan: Drizzle 1 teaspoon green crème de menthe liqueur over one portion of the marzipan and knead it until smooth.
—*Nicholas Malgieri*

White Chocolate Truffles with Praline Powder

Makes About 8 Dozen

1 pound sweet white
  chococolate
½ pint heavy cream
2 tablespoons dark rum
6 tablespoons praline powder
  (see Note) plus more for
  coating the truffles

1. Break or cut the chocolate into 1-inch pieces and place them in a heavy saucepan. Pour the cream over the chocolate and place the pan over moderate heat. Stirring constantly, cook the mixture only until it is warm and most of the chocolate has melted. Remove the pan from the heat and continue stirring until the chocolate has completely melted and the mixture is smooth.

2. Pour the ganache through a wire strainer into a bowl and let it cool to room temperature before using—it should not be warm to the touch.

3. Thoroughly mix the ganache before using; do not refrigerate or it will set. *(The ganache can be covered and kept at room temperature for 2 days.)*

4. In a mixing bowl, beat the ganache at high speed until it is at least as thick as heavily whipped cream. If this does not happen with the ganache at room temperature, place the bowl in the freezer for a minute and then whip it again. Make sure that you do not leave the ganache in the freezer too long or it will set.

5. Add the rum and praline powder and whip until the mixture is stiff.

6. To shape the mixture, half-fill a pastry bag fitted with a plain ¼-inch tip with ganache or use a teaspoon. On sheets of wax paper or parchment paper, squeeze out or shape the mixture into rounds that are about ½ to ¾ inch in diameter. When all the mixture has been used, refrigerate the truffles for several hours, preferably overnight, to allow the chocolate to set completely.

7. Pick up one truffle and, using the thumb and forefinger of both hands, push it together to form a ball (do not roll the mixture between your palms or it will soften too much). Place the ball in praline powder and roll it around briefly until it is well coated. As you complete them, set them aside on a plate and chill until serving time. Because ganache truffles soften easily, they should always be kept, covered, in the refrigerator.

NOTE: Make praline powder by pulverizing store-bought pralines in a food processor, or use Caramel Almond Confections (p. 277).
—*Nicholas Malgieri*

Coffee Cup Truffles

These free-form candies are easier to make than you might think, but be sure to use the best chocolate you can get your hands on.

Eat the truffles out of hand or drop into individual cups of hot coffee for a special holiday drink. Reserve any extra candies in the refrigerator or freezer until needed, as they tend to soften quickly.

Makes About 3½ Dozen Truffles

9 ounces bittersweet or
  semisweet chocolate, broken
  into pieces
⅔ cup heavy cream
⅓ vanilla bean
2 tablespoons unsalted butter
Pinch of cinnamon
3 tablespoons unsweetened
  cocoa powder
Pinch of salt
1 cup confectioners' sugar,
  sifted

1. Line the inside of an 8-by-4-inch loaf pan with wax paper. In the top of a double boiler over gently simmering water, melt the chocolate, stirring occasionally; remove from the heat and stir until smooth. Set aside. Alternatively, microwave the chocolate in a medium glass or plastic bowl at medium power for 60 seconds. Stir to redistribute and cook for 60 seconds more. Stir again; if the chocolate is not completely melted, repeat the microwave procedure for 30 seconds, just until the chocolate can be stirred smooth. Repeat again as necessary. (Take care not to burn the chocolate.)

2. In a small saucepan, warm the cream with the vanilla bean over low heat. Alternatively, place the cream in a glass measuring cup. Split the piece of vanilla bean, scrape it and add the bean and the scrapings to the

cream. Microwave on full power for 60 seconds.

3. Remove the cream from the heat and remove the vanilla bean. Gradually stir the cream into the melted chocolate until smooth. Add the butter, cinnamon, cocoa and salt; stir until incorporated. Scrape the chocolate mixture into the prepared pan and smooth the top. Cover and refrigerate. *(The truffles can be prepared to this point up to 3 days ahead.)*

4. To unmold, run a thin knife around the edges of the chocolate mixture and invert the pan onto a work surface. Trim the edges of the chocolate loaf, if necessary, with a long thin, very sharp knife. Then cut the chocolate crosswise into ¾-inch strips. Do not draw the knife out by pulling it toward you; pull it straight up after making a cut, holding down the chocolate.

5. Cut each strip crosswise into ¾-inch cubes and place on a baking sheet lined with wax paper. Cover with plastic wrap and freeze until ready to serve. *(The truffles can be made to this point and kept frozen up to 1 week.)*

6. Place the confectioners' sugar in a bag. Add the frozen chocolate cubes to the bag in batches; shake to coat them with the sugar. Place the truffles on a small decorative plate or in a sugar bowl and serve with freshly brewed coffee and a pitcher of warm milk.

—*Tracey Seaman*

Prune Truffles with Armagnac

These truffles make a sophisticated ending for an elegant dinner.
Makes 30 Truffles

¾ cup (4 ounces) pitted
  prunes, cut into eighths
¼ cup Armagnac
⅓ cup heavy cream
6 ounces bittersweet
  chocolate, such as Lindt or
  Tobler, broken into small
  pieces
1 tablespoon unsalted butter,
  at room temperature
½ cup (2 ounces) toasted
  pecans, finely chopped
Unsweetened cocoa powder,
  for coating

1. In a small bowl, combine the prunes and the Armagnac. Cover tightly and let macerate at room temperature for at least 1 hour.

2. In a small saucepan, bring the cream to a boil over moderately high heat. Add the chocolate and remove from the heat. Whisk until the chocolate is melted and the mixture smooth. Beat in the butter.

3. Drain the prunes, reserving 1 tablespoon of the Armagnac. Add the prunes, the reserved Armagnac and the pecans to the chocolate mixture, mixing until well combined. Transfer the mixture to a shallow bowl and refrigerate, uncovered, until firm, at least 3 hours.

4. Coat your palms with the cocoa. For each truffle, form about a teaspoonful of the cold truffle mixture into a ball, rolling it between your palms. Place the truffles on wax paper.

5. When the truffles are shaped, dredge them lightly in the cocoa, then toss gently from palm to palm to remove any excess. Place each truffle in a paper candy cup and re-

frigerate for at least 1 day to let the flavors mellow.
—*Dorie Greenspan*

Chocolate-Orange Truffles

These cocoa-dusted truffles make a rich and delicious nightcap.
Makes About 7 Dozen

Unsweetened cocoa powder,
  preferably Dutch processed
1 cup heavy cream
3 bars (3½ ounces each)
  bittersweet chocolate,
  broken into pieces
3 tablespoons unsalted butter
1 tablespoon minced orange
  zest
⅓ cup confectioners' sugar
2 tablespoons orange liqueur

1. Cover a tray with wax paper and dust lightly with cocoa powder. In a heavy medium saucepan, boil the cream over moderate heat until reduced to ½ cup, about 10 minutes. Remove from the heat.

2. Add the chocolate to the hot cream and stir until melted, about 5 minutes. Blend in the butter, orange zest, confectioners' sugar and orange liqueur. Cover and refrigerate until the mixture is firm enough to handle. *(The recipe can be prepared to this point up to 1 day ahead.)*

3. Shape the truffle mixture into 1-inch balls and place them on the prepared tray. Lightly dust the truffles with cocoa and chill for 20 minutes. Using a spoon, transfer the truffles to paper candy cups. Cover and refrigerate; return to room temperature before serving.
—*Diana Sturgis*

Pecan-Raisin Clusters

Dropped chocolates are the simplest of confections. Melted chocolate, tempered by a bit of stirring, is mixed with a roughly equal part of nuts and/or fruit and dropped like cookie dough, to form clusters. We particularly like this combination of pecans and golden raisins, but you can experiment with any mixture of coarsely chopped dried fruits and nuts.

Makes About 2½ Dozen

8 ounces semisweet or milk
  chocolate
1 cup (about 5 ounces)
  coarsely chopped pecans
½ cup golden raisins

1. Melt the chocolate and temper it by stirring or by working back and forth with a spatula, trowel or putty knife on a marble or Formica surface until the chocolate feels distinctly cool but is still semiliquid.

2. Toss the pecans and raisins in a medium bowl. Scrape the tempered chocolate into the bowl. Stir and fold with a rubber spatula to coat the fruit and nuts completely.

3. Drop heaping teaspoonfuls of the mixture onto wax paper. Allow the clusters to harden at room temperature until firm, about 1 hour, or refrigerate just until set. Store, tightly wrapped, at room temperature.
—F&W

Candied Grapefruit Peel

Makes About 120 Pieces

6 to 8 grapefruit, with skins
  free of blemishes
3 cups sugar
1 cup water

1. Cut each grapefruit in half and remove the fruit sections, or squeeze out the juice. Remove all the white pith from the yellow skin by inserting a knife or the tip of a spoon between the pith and the skin. Grasp the pith firmly and pull—the whole layer will come away.

2. Cut the peel into strips as uniform as possible, making them about ½ inch wide and 2 inches long.

3. Make a syrup by boiling 2 cups of the sugar with the water for a few minutes. Drop some of the strips of peel into the boiling syrup, making sure that all are covered (you will be cooking the peel in several batches). Place a large sieve over a bowl next to the pot. Cook the strips until they become completely transparent (30 to 45 minutes), then remove them to drain in the sieve. Repeat as necessary until all the peel is cooked, returning the drained-off syrup to the pan as you go. (If you run short of syrup, just boil more sugar and water together separately—2 parts of sugar to 1 part of water—and add it to the pan.)

4. When all the strips are drained and cool, roll them in the remaining cup of sugar until thoroughly coated. Lay the strips, outer surface down, on flat plates. (If laid sideways they will curl.) This delicious, moist confection will be at its best for only 4 or 5 days; kept longer, it will either dry out too much or become moldy. Store in an airtight container with wax paper separating the layers.
—F&W

Candied Orange Peel

I know that candied orange peel is sold in supermarkets and specialty stores, but it is simply not the same as homemade. Candied orange peel is not only a wonderful addition to chocolate or fruit cakes, but also a fine accompaniment to an after-dinner espresso. It will keep for up to three months in an airtight container at room temperature.

Makes About ¾ Cup

1 large navel orange
¼ cup plus 2 tablespoons
  granulated sugar
2 tablespoons crystal sugar
  (optional)

1. Preheat the oven to 250°. Cut the bottom and top off the orange and discard. Using a sharp knife, slit the skin of the orange into quarters from top to bottom; peel the orange. Stack the peels and cut them lengthwise into ⅛-inch-thick julienne strips.

2. In a small saucepan, place the orange peel and enough cold water to cover. Bring to a rolling boil over high heat and boil for 5 minutes. Drain, rinse under cold running water and repeat the procedure twice more.

3. Return the peels to the saucepan and add the granulated sugar and ¼ cup of water. Bring to a boil over moderate heat. Reduce the heat and simmer until the liquid evaporates and the sugar glazes the rinds, about 30 minutes. Drain on a rack set on a cookie sheet. Separate the peels.

4. Place the peels on the rack in the oven and bake until almost dry, about 20 minutes. Roll the rinds in the crystal sugar and store in an airtight container.
—Lydie Marshall

Caramel Almond Confections

These confections can be used for making the praline powder that is used to flavor the White Chocolate Truffles (p. 274) or you can just enjoy them as they are.

Makes About 2 Dozen

2 tablespoons unsalted butter, softened
2 cups sugar
2 tablespoons fresh lemon juice
1½ cups blanched, sliced almonds

1. Lightly grease two baking sheets with the softened butter.

2. Place the sugar and lemon juice in a heavy skillet and set it over moderate heat. Stirring constantly with a wooden spoon, cook the mixture just until the sugar melts and the caramel takes on a pale blond color, 8 to 10 minutes. To judge the color since the caramel will look darker in the pan than it really is, lift a spoonful out of the pan and allow it to run back into the pan in a ribbon. When the caramel approaches the correct color, wisps of smoke will appear. Do not cook too long or over too high a temperature or the caramel will foam and have to be discarded, for it will be bitter; if this should happen, start over.

3. Stir in the almonds and remove the pan from the heat. Working quickly, drop the mixture by tablespoonfuls, making sure that some almonds are in each spoonful, onto the buttered baking sheets. Let the confections cool to room temperature and then store in airtight containers.
—*Nicholas Malgieri*

Popcorn Candy

This nut, caramel and popcorn mixture makes a terrific holiday snack for kids and adults alike. It will keep in an airtight tin for up to three days, but chances are it won't last that long.

Makes About 10 Cups

3 cups sugar
½ cup light corn syrup
¼ cup vegetable oil
½ cup popping corn
1 cup pecans
1 cup almonds
½ cup walnuts
½ cup macadamia nuts

1. Preheat the oven to 350°. Place the sugar in a medium saucepan and drizzle the corn syrup over it. Cook over moderately low heat until the sugar melts and becomes golden, about 45 minutes.

2. Meanwhile, pour 3 tablespoons of the oil in a large saucepan. Add the popping corn, cover and cook over moderate heat, shaking constantly, until all the corn has popped; set aside.

3. Spread the pecans, almonds, walnuts and macadamia nuts on a large baking sheet. Bake for about 10 minutes, until lightly toasted. Let cool, then add to the popcorn.

4. Use the remaining 1 tablespoon oil to grease two 12-by-18-inch baking sheets. Divide the popcorn mixture into 2 batches and spread out on the prepared baking sheets.

5. Drizzle the hot caramel evenly over both batches of popcorn and nuts. When cool, place the candy on a flat surface and break into pieces; store in an airtight tin.
—*Diana Sturgis*

Sesame Seed Candy

Sesame seed candy is a customary holiday sweet for Middle Eastern Jews. This chewy version is studded with peanuts.

Makes 64 Candies

1½ cups raw unhulled sesame seeds* (about 8 ounces)
¾ cup dry-roasted unsalted peanuts, coarsely chopped
½ cup (packed) light brown sugar
¼ cup honey
Pinch of salt
2 tablespoons tahini* (sesame seed paste)
*Available at health food stores and many supermarkets

1. Grease a 9-inch-square metal baking pan and set aside. In a heatproof bowl, combine the sesame seeds and peanuts.

2. In a small heavy saucepan, using a metal spoon, stir together the brown sugar, honey, salt and 2 tablespoons of water. Bring to a rolling boil over moderate heat, stirring occasionally, and boil until a candy thermometer reaches 250°, about 4 minutes. Remove the syrup from the heat and stir in the tahini. Pour the mixture on top of the sesame seeds and peanuts and stir well.

3. Transfer the sesame mixture to the prepared pan and spread evenly with the back of a wet spoon. Using a sharp knife, cut the candies into 1-inch squares. Let the candy cool in the pan for 10 to 15 minutes before removing the pieces to wax paper with a metal spatula. The candies will continue to harden for about 1 more hour. Transfer to an airtight container and store at room temperature for up to 2 weeks.
—*Susan Shapiro Jaslove*

Pecan Buttercrunch

This buttercrunch also makes a great topping for ice cream.

Makes About 2¾ Cups

1¼ cups sugar
½ teaspoon fresh lemon juice
4 tablespoons unsalted butter
1½ cups pecan halves

1. Oil a large cookie sheet and a metal spatula. Place the sugar in a heavy medium saucepan. Add the lemon juice and rub it into the sugar until dispersed.

2. Add the butter and cook over moderately high heat, stirring until the sugar melts and becomes a deep amber color, about 10 minutes. Remove from the heat and stir in the pecans.

3. Immediately pour the mixture out onto the prepared cookie sheet. Using the oiled spatula, turn the sugar over onto itself until it stops spreading. Press the buttercrunch flat and set aside at room temperature to cool, about 15 minutes.

4. Chop the buttercrunch into 1-inch pieces. Place one-third of the buttercrunch in a food processor and chop coarsely into ½-inch pieces. Repeat with the remaining buttercrunch, adding it to the processor in 2 batches. (Any large pieces can be cut with a knife.)
—*Peggy Cullen*

Caramel-Pepper Nuts

These is Chinese "Cracker Jack," one of those tidbits that the Chinese classify as "foods to make the wine go down." White wine, red wine or beer are equally appropriate. The recipe belongs to Barton Levenson, a wonderfully imaginative Bay Area cook.

Makes About 2½ Cups

1 cup hazelnuts
1 cup raw skinned peanuts
½ cup sugar
1 tablespoon coarse (kosher) salt
1 tablespoon freshly ground black pepper
¼ teaspoon freshly ground cinnamon
1½ whole star anise pods* (equals 12 points)
6 whole cloves
2 teaspoons Szechuan peppercorns*
1½ teaspoons whole Java peppercorns (optional)
*Available at Asian markets and health food stores

1. Preheat the oven to 350°. Spread the hazelnuts and peanuts on separate baking sheets and toast, shaking the pans once or twice, until just beginning to brown, 10 to 15 minutes. Rub the hazelnuts in a kitchen towel to remove most of the skins.

2. In a small bowl, toss together the sugar, salt, ground black pepper and cinnamon to blend.

3. In a spice grinder, pulverize the star anise, cloves, Szechuan peppercorns and Java peppercorns. Strain through a fine-mesh sieve to eliminate husks. Add to the sugar mixture and toss to blend.

4. Heat a large heavy skillet, preferably cast iron, or a wok over high heat until hot enough to evaporate a bead of water on contact, about 1 minute. Add the nuts and toss for 1 minute, or until the nuts are hot and the nut oil has come to the surface; reduce the heat if necessary to prevent scorching.

5. Sprinkle the nuts with half the sugar seasoning mixture, then toss by shaking the pan vigorously until the sugar melts and turns a dark caramelized brown, about 1 minute. Add the remaining seasoning mixture and continue shaking the pan until the sugar again melts and coats the nuts, about 3 minutes. Use the handle of a wooden spoon to stir the nuts and break apart any globs of sugar.

6. Immediately turn the nuts onto a foil-lined baking sheet. As soon as they are cool enough to handle, separate with your fingers. Let cool completely. Store in a tightly sealed glass jar for up to 2 weeks.
—*Barbara Tropp, China Moon Cafe, San Francisco*

Curried Toasted Almonds

Makes About 1½ Cups

1 tablespoon unsalted butter
½ pound unblanched almonds
1½ tablespoons curry powder
½ teaspoon salt

In a large saucepan, melt the butter, add the almonds and sauté over moderately high heat, stirring frequently, until the skins begin to split, about 3 minutes. Sprinkle with the curry powder and salt and toss to coat the almonds well.
—*F&W*

Garlic-Toasted Almonds

6 to 8 Servings

½ cup coarse (kosher) salt
4 cups whole unblanched
   almonds
2 garlic cloves, crushed
   through a press
2 teaspoons vegetable oil

1. Preheat the oven to 325°. In a large bowl, dissolve the salt in 2 cups of hot water and add the almonds. Set aside to soak for 30 minutes; drain well.

2. Combine the garlic and oil and use the mixture to coat a baking sheet.

3. Scatter the almonds over the baking sheet and bake, stirring occasionally, until golden in color, about 20 minutes.

4. Remove the baking sheet from the oven and allow to cool for 20 minutes. Place the baking sheet in the still-warm oven and leave there overnight. Store the nuts tightly covered in the refrigerator.
—W. Peter Prestcott

Spicy Tamari Nuts with Rice Crackers

I've always loved the tamari-roasted nuts sold at health food stores. Here, hot sesame oil is added for a little zip, and the nuts are tossed with rice crackers for another kind of crunch.
Makes About 8 Cups

2 pounds mixed unroasted
   nuts, such as walnuts,
   pecans, almonds and
   cashews
¼ cup tamari sauce*
1 tablespoon hot sesame oil*

½ pound Oriental snack mix,
   such as assorted plain and
   seaweed-wrapped rice
   crackers and fried green
   peas*
*Available at Asian markets

1. Preheat the oven to 300°. Place the mixed nuts on a baking sheet in a single layer. Roast in the middle of the oven for 35 minutes, stirring once or twice.

2. Transfer the nuts to a large heatproof bowl and toss with the tamari sauce and sesame oil. Return the nuts to the baking sheet in a single layer and roast for 5 minutes, stirring occasionally, until glazed and dry.

3. Let the nuts cool completely, then toss them with the rice crackers and peas. (The mixture can be stored in an airtight container for up to 2 weeks.)
—Bob Chambers

Curried Pumpkin Seeds and Cornnuts

The subtle flavor of pumpkin seeds can be enhanced by any number of spices. Here, curry adds an Indian accent.
Makes About 4 Cups

2 tablespoons olive oil
1 tablespoon curry powder
1 pound shelled raw pumpkin
   seeds*
1 teaspoon salt
2 bags (3 ounces each)
   Cornnuts
*Available at health food
   stores

1. Preheat the oven to 350°. In a small skillet, combine the oil with the curry powder. Stir over moderately high heat until the oil just begins to smoke slightly, 2 to 3 minutes.

2. In a medium bowl, toss the pumpkin seeds with the hot curry oil. Sprinkle on the salt and toss until well distributed.

3. Spread the pumpkin seeds out on a jelly-roll pan and bake in the middle of the oven for 15 minutes, stirring occasionally, until lightly browned.

4. Return the pumpkin seeds to the bowl, add the Cornnuts and toss well to combine. Toss the mixture occasionally as it cools. (The mixture can be stored in an airtight container for up to 10 days.)
—Bob Chambers

Spiced Cashews

Makes About 2 Cups

1 egg white
2 cups (about 12 ounces) raw
   cashews
1½ teaspoons salt
1 teaspoon ground coriander
½ teaspoon cumin
½ teaspoon allspice
½ teaspoon cayenne pepper
"Available at health food
   stores and some specialty
   food shops

1. Preheat the oven to 300°. In a medium bowl, whisk the egg white with 1 tablespoon of water until the mixture is frothy and holds a soft shape. Add the cashews and fold until they are evenly coated.

2. In a small bowl, combine the salt, coriander, cumin, allspice and cayenne. Add the spices to the nuts and toss to mix well.

3. Line a baking sheet with aluminum foil and lightly butter the foil. Scatter the nuts on the sheet in a single layer and roast them in the oven for 30 minutes. Turn the nuts over with a spatula and roast for 30 minutes longer.

4. Cool the cashews completely and store in an airtight container.
—*Maria Piccolo & Rosalee Harris*

Spicy Cheddar Chive Rounds

These crackers get their kick from hot red pepper. Try them with apple wedges or as a crunchy nibble with anything from a cold beer to a Bloody Mary.

Makes About 100 Crackers

3 cups grated sharp Cheddar
   cheese (8 ounces)
1 cup freshly grated Parmesan
   cheese (4 ounces)
3 tablespoons dried chives
¾ to 1 teaspoon hot pepper
   flakes
½ teaspoon freshly ground
   black pepper
1½ cups all-purpose flour
6 tablespoons cold unsalted
   butter, cut into pieces
1 teaspoon salt
¾ cup buttermilk

1. In a large bowl, combine the Cheddar, Parmesan, chives, hot pepper flakes and black pepper. Toss well to blend.
2. In a food processor, combine the flour, butter and salt. Pulse until the mixture resembles cornmeal. Add the flour to the cheese mixture and toss until well combined. With a fork, stir in the buttermilk and mix just until the dough can be gathered into a ball.

3. Turn the dough out onto a lightly floured surface and knead it for 10 to 15 seconds. Divide the dough in half and roll each piece into a log 1 inch in diameter. Wrap the logs in wax paper and refrigerate until firm, 1 to 2 hours. *(At this point, the dough can be frozen for up to 2 months. Thaw before proceeding.)*
4. Preheat the oven to 325°. Slice the logs ⅛ inch thick and arrange the slices about ½ inch apart on 2 large baking sheets. Bake for 15 minutes, then switch the sheets and bake the crackers for 15 minutes longer, or until golden brown. Transfer to a wire rack to cool completely. *(The crackers can be stored in an airtight container for up to 10 days.)*
—*Bob Chambers*

Double-Oat Flatbread Crackers

Serve a piquant bean dip with this crunchy cracker. For a different-flavored cracker, just throw in a tablespoon of dried rosemary, marjoram or basil when you combine the dry ingredients.

Makes 4 Dozen

1 cup lukewarm water (105°
   to 115°)
¼ teaspoon sugar
1 envelope active dry yeast
1¼ cups old-fashioned rolled
   oats
1½ cups durum wheat flour*
½ cup oat bran
½ teaspoon salt
2 tablespoons extra-virgin
   olive oil
1 tablespoon honey
¼ cup poppy or sesame seeds
*Available at Italian or
   specialty food markets

1. In a small heatproof bowl, combine the warm water and sugar;

sprinkle the yeast on top. Set aside until frothy, 5 to 7 minutes.
2. In a food processor, process the rolled oats until finely ground. Add the flour, oat bran and salt; process to mix.
3. Add the olive oil, honey and yeast mixture to the processor. Blend well. Scrape down the sides of the bowl and process again to knead the dough until smooth and elastic, about 20 seconds. Rinse a medium bowl in hot water. Shape the dough into a disk, transfer to the warmed bowl and cover tightly with plastic wrap. Set aside in a warm place until doubled in bulk, about 1½ hours.
4. Transfer the dough to a lightly floured surface. Punch down and knead briefly, about 1 minute. Reshape the dough into a disk. Return it to the bowl, cover tightly and let rise until increased in bulk by about half, about 1 hour longer.
5. Preheat the oven to 450°. Sprinkle the poppy seeds on a lightly floured surface. Remove the dough from the bowl and cut into 4 pieces. Work with 1 piece at a time; wrap the other pieces in plastic wrap. Place the piece of dough on the poppy seeds and roll it out to a 6-by-12-inch rectangle. Using a serrated pastry wheel or small knife and a ruler as a guide, cut the dough crosswise into 12 strips, 1 inch wide. Transfer the strips to a large ungreased baking sheet. Repeat with the remaining dough.
6. Bake the crackers for 12 to 15 minutes, or until crisp and brown. Carefully transfer to a rack and let cool completely.
—*Tracey Seaman*

Blue Corn Pizzelle

This peppery cracker is formed in a traditional flat *pizzelle* iron. It can be served as is or folded over, taco style, and filled with guacamole, salsa and cheese.

Makes About 16

2 tablespoons minced green chiles
3 eggs
3 tablespoons sugar
1 stick (4 ounces) unsalted butter, melted
½ cup masa harina (cornmeal)*
2 teaspoons baking powder
¾ teaspoon salt
¼ teaspoon cayenne pepper
¼ teaspoon freshly ground black pepper
¼ teaspoon freshly ground white pepper
¼ teaspoon minced fresh thyme or ⅛ teaspoon crumbled dried
¼ cup plus 3 tablespoons blue cornmeal (atole)*
*Available at Latin American markets

1. Pat the chiles dry and, if using canned chiles, squeeze them between paper towels to remove any excess liquid.

2. Preheat the *pizzelle* iron on both sides. In a large bowl, beat the eggs with the sugar until thick and pale yellow in color, about 3 minutes. Beat in the melted butter.

3. In another bowl, mix together the masa harina, baking powder, salt, cayenne, and black and white peppers. Sift the mixture over the beaten eggs, add the chiles and the thyme and mix lightly. Fold in the blue cornmeal.

4. Grease the *pizzelle* iron only once, before making the first cracker.

Place one tablespoon of the batter in the middle of the heated iron and gently press down the other half of the iron. Using a knife, scrape off any excess batter and place the iron over the burner for 1 minute. Flip the iron and cook on the second side until browned, about 30 seconds. Transfer the *pizzelle* to a rack to cool and repeat with the remaining batter. *(The pizzelle can be prepared a few hours ahead, but should be crisped in a 350° oven for 1 to 2 minutes before serving.)*
—Nancy Christy and Laure Cantor Kimpton

Pepper Pretzels

Makes About 20

1 envelope active dry yeast
Pinch of sugar
1½ cups lukewarm water (105° to 115°)
¾ teaspoon finely minced garlic
1½ tablespoons olive oil
4 cups unbleached all-purpose flour
½ teaspoon thyme
½ teaspoon freshly cracked pepper
2 tablespoons plus 1 teaspoon table salt
2 tablespoons coarse (kosher) salt
2 tablespoons hulled sesame seeds

1. In a medium bowl, combine the yeast, sugar and 6 tablespoons of the warm water. Set aside until the mixture foams, about 10 minutes. Add the remaining warm water, the garlic and olive oil and mix well.

2. In a large bowl, stir together the flour, thyme, pepper and 1 teaspoon of the table salt. Form a well in the flour mixture and pour in the yeast mixture. Gradually stir until the dough masses together.

3. Turn the dough out onto a floured work surface and knead until smooth, about 10 minutes. If the dough is still sticky, knead in a little additional flour. Place the dough in a clean bowl and cover with plastic wrap. Set aside in a warm place until doubled in size, about 30 minutes. *(The recipe can be prepared to this point up to 3 days ahead. Cover the dough and store in the refrigerator.)*

4. Turn the dough out onto a floured surface and knead for 15 minutes. Roll the dough into a 12-by-6-inch rectangle and cut it into about 20 strips. Roll each strip into a smooth 16-inch-long rope and form into a pretzel shape; secure the knots with a dab of water. Place the finished pretzels on baking sheets lined with parchment paper; set aside to rise for 10 minutes.

5. Preheat the oven to 425°. In a large saucepan, combine the remaining 2 tablespoons table salt and 3 quarts of water and bring to a boil.

6. Drop the pretzels, about 6 at a time, into the boiling water and cook until they rise to the surface. Using a slotted spoon, return the pretzels to the baking sheets. Sprinkle each pretzel with a pinch each of coarse salt and sesame seeds. Repeat with the remaining pretzels.

7. Spray the bottom and sides of the oven with water to create steam and bake the pretzels until evenly browned, about 30 minutes.
—Nancy Christy and Laure Cantor Kimpton

Mediterranean Animal Crackers

These spicy crackers are studded with crunchy sesame seeds and flavored with garlic and thyme.

Makes About 100 Crackers

¼ cup hulled sesame seeds
1½ teaspoons salt
1½ cups all-purpose flour, sifted
1¼ cups whole wheat flour, sifted
1 teaspoon freshly cracked pepper
2 garlic cloves
¾ teaspoon thyme
6 cups vegetable oil
½ cup olive oil

1. In a small skillet, toast the sesame seeds over moderate heat, stirring constantly, until lightly and evenly browned, about 2 minutes.

2. In a large bowl, combine the salt, sesame seeds, all-purpose and whole wheat flours and pepper.

3. Using a garlic press, mash the garlic into 1 cup of water and add the thyme.

4. Using a wooden spoon, stir the water mixture into the dry ingredients until thoroughly combined.

5. Turn the dough out onto a well floured surface or pastry cloth. Sprinkle the dough with flour and divide it in half. Roll each piece into a 20-inch round about 1/16 inch thick. (Lift the dough occasionally and flour underneath to prevent it from sticking.)

6. Using 3- to 5-inch animal-shape cookie cutters, stamp out the crackers. Roll out any scraps of dough and cut out more crackers.

7. In a very large deep skillet or electric frying pan, heat the vegetable and olive oils to 425° on a deep-fat frying thermometer.

8. Fry the crackers, a few at a time, turning once, until crisp, lightly browned and puffy, 1 to 2 minutes on each side. Using a slotted spoon, remove the crackers from the skillet and place on paper towels to drain. Dab off any excess oil. Sprinkle lightly with salt and let cool.
—*Nancy Christy and Laure Cantor Kimpton*

Romano Leaf Wafers

These wafers are formed by spreading a soft dough across a stenciled leaf pattern. Metal leaf stencils come in large and small leaf patterns, but we recommend the large size for this cracker. Stencils are available in kitchenware stores for a couple of dollars each.

Makes About 27 Leaf Wafers

2 tablespoons hulled sesame seeds
2½ tablespoons unsalted butter, softened
1 teaspoon sugar
2 egg whites, lightly beaten
½ cup freshly grated Romano cheese
¼ teaspoon salt
½ teaspoon freshly ground pepper
½ cup all-purpose flour

1. Preheat the oven to 325°. Line a large cookie sheet with parchment paper.

2. Put the sesame seeds in a small skillet and cook over moderate heat, stirring constantly, until lightly toasted, about 1 minute; set aside.

3. In a medium bowl, cream the butter with the sugar. Gradually beat in the egg whites, beating for 1 minute. Beat in the cheese, salt and pepper. Fold in the flour.

4. Place the leaf stencil on the parchment paper. Using a large metal spatula, press 2 teaspoons of the dough evenly and smoothly through the stencil, scraping off any excess. Carefully lift the stencil straight up, leaving the leaf imprint on the paper. Wipe the underside of the stencil to prevent sticking. Repeat with the remaining dough.

5. Bake the crackers in the middle of the oven for 8 to 10 minutes or until firm. Using a spatula, flip the crackers and bake for about 2 minutes longer, or until lightly golden. Cool on a rack.
—*Nancy Christy & Laure Cantor Kimpton*

Grace Stuck's Applesauce Fruitcakes

The grandmother of a dear friend made this recipe each year for her family's Minnesota Christmas celebration. Dark and moist, the applesauce-and-molasses-based fruitcake is filled with a tangy assortment of dried—not candied—fruit. The fruitcakes will keep up to three months, making these a perfect do-ahead gift for the holidays. If you make them in advance, brush the cake periodically with more brandy. Chilling them will make slicing easier.

Makes 10 Small Loaves

3 cups unsweetened applesauce, preferably homemade
2 sticks (8 ounces) unsalted butter, cut into chunks
1¼ cups sugar
½ cup dark molasses
⅓ cup honey

1 box (15 ounces) golden
  raisins
1 box (15 ounces) dark raisins
1 cup dried currants
1 cup dried sour cherries, *
  coarsely chopped, or
  substitute more currants
1 cup dried apricots, coarsely
  chopped
2 cups walnuts, coarsely
  chopped (about 8 ounces)
2 cups pecans, coarsely
  chopped (about 8 ounces)
4½ cups all-purpose flour
1 tablespoon plus 1 teaspoon
  baking soda
2 teaspoons cinnamon
1 teaspoon freshly grated
  nutmeg
1 teaspoon allspice
1 teaspoon salt
½ teaspoon ground cloves
Walnut and pecan halves, for
  garnish
½ cup brandy
*Available at specialty food
  shops

1. In a medium nonreactive saucepan, heat the applesauce over moderate heat. Add the butter, a few pieces at a time, and stir until the butter is melted and the applesauce is hot and bubbling, 4 to 5 minutes. Add the sugar, molasses and honey and cook, stirring, until the sugar dissolves, about 1 minute. Let the applesauce cool to room temperature.

2. Preheat the oven to 275°. Butter and flour ten 5-by-3-by-2-inch loaf pans (available in disposable foil). In a large bowl, combine the golden and dark raisins, the currants, cherries, apricots, walnuts and pecans with the applesauce.

3. In a medium bowl, sift together the flour, baking soda, cinnamon, nutmeg, allspice, salt and cloves. Fold into the applesauce-fruit mixture until just blended. Quickly di-

vide the batter among the pans and smooth the tops with a rubber spatula dipped in water. Press walnut and pecan halves into the tops to decorate.

4. Bake the fruitcakes for 60 to 70 minutes, or until a knife inserted in the center comes out clean. Let the cakes cool in the pans for 1 hour. Unmold them onto a rack and let cool to room temperature. Brush the brandy all over the fruitcakes. Wrap tightly first in plastic wrap, then in aluminum foil. Store in a cool, dry place for at least 1 week and up to 3 months before serving.
—Bob Chambers

Scotch Hogmanay Fruitcake

Makes One 9-Inch Ring Cake

Cake:
2½ cups all-purpose flour
¾ cup candied cherries, half
  of them halved
½ cup mixed candied peel or
  mixed candied fruit, in small
  pieces
2½ cups golden raisins
1¼ cups dried currants or
  dark raisins
6 tablespoons ground
  blanched almonds
¼ cup ground walnuts
1 cup granulated sugar
1 tablespoon baking powder,
  sifted
¼ cup honey
7 eggs, lightly beaten
1 cup Scotch whiskey plus
  additional for moistening
  the cake

Decoration:
1¾ cups confectioners' sugar,
  sifted
2 tablespoons orange juice
2 tablespoons Scotch whiskey
½ cup mixed candied fruit, in
  small pieces
20 candied cherries
2 tablespoons ground
  almonds

1. Make the cake: Preheat the oven to 300°. Butter and flour a 9-inch tube pan, preferably the springform type.

2. Sift the flour into a large mixing bowl. Add the cherries, candied peel, golden raisins, currants, almonds and walnuts. Mix thoroughly, using your hands, until there is no loose flour.

3. Beat in the granulated sugar and baking powder. Beat in the honey, eggs and whiskey, beating well after each addition.

4. Pour the batter into the prepared pan and bake for 1 hour. Lower the temperature to 200° and bake for 1 hour longer. Loosely cover the cake with foil and bake for 35 minutes longer, or until a cake tester emerges dry from the center. Let the cake cool in the turned-off oven with the door open.

5. Take the cake out of the oven and let stand overnight, then unmold. This cake is at its best after at least one week's storage—if possible store it longer, in a cake box or wrapped in foil. Sprinkle it from time to time with a little additional Scotch whiskey.

6. Decorate the cake: In a small bowl, blend the confectioners' sugar, orange juice and whiskey. Frost the top of the cake and let dry for 30 minutes. Then decorate with the candied fruit, cherries and almonds.
—Monique Guillaume

1 cup plus 2 tablespoons
  superfine sugar
4 eggs
2 teaspoons grated lemon zest
1 tablespoon heavy cream

1. Preheat the oven to 350°. Butter and flour two 8½-by-4½-by-2¾-inch metal loaf pans.

2. In a small bowl, cover the currants with the sherry and let macerate for 15 minutes.

3. In a medium bowl, sift the cake flour, cardamom, baking powder and salt.

4. In a large mixer bowl, beat the butter until light and fluffy. Gradually beat in 1 cup of the sugar. Add the eggs, one at a time, beating well after each addition. Beat in the lemon zest. With the mixer on low speed, gradually beat in the flour mixture, 1 cup at a time; beat until well blended. Fold in the sherry with the currants.

5. Scrape the batter into the prepared pans and smooth the tops evenly. Drizzle the cream over the loaves and sprinkle with the remaining 2 tablespoons sugar. Bake for 50 minutes, or until the cakes are golden brown and a toothpick inserted in the center comes out clean.
—*Mimi Ruth Brodeur*

Lemon-Lime Pound Cake

Makes 1 Loaf Cake

2 sticks (8 ounces) unsalted
  butter, softened
2 cups sugar
5 eggs, at room temperature
1 tablespoon grated lemon
  zest
1 tablespoon grated
  lime zest
2 cups sifted all-purpose flour
½ teaspoon salt
¼ teaspoon baking powder
1½ tablespoons fresh
  lemon juice
1½ tablespoons fresh
  lime juice

1. Preheat the oven to 325°. Butter and flour a 9-by-5-by-3-inch loaf pan.

2. In a large mixer bowl, cream the butter until smooth, about 1 minute. Gradually add 1½ cups of the sugar and beat until light and fluffy, 4 to 5 minutes. Add the eggs, one at a time, beating well after each addition; beat in the grated lemon and lime zests.

3. Sift together the flour, salt and baking powder onto a sheet of wax paper. Gradually add the dry ingredients to the butter mixture in 4 to 5 additions, beating on low speed until just blended after each addition.

4. Spoon the batter into the prepared pan. Bake the cake for 1 hour and 15 minutes, or until a cake tester inserted into the center comes out clean and the edges of the cake begin to pull away from the sides of the pan. Cool the cake in the pan on a rack for 5 minutes.

5. Meanwhile, in a small nonreactive saucepan, combine the remaining ½ cup of sugar, the lemon juice and the lime juice. Cook over moderate heat, stirring until the sugar dissolves, 1 to 2 minutes. Do not boil. Remove the citrus glaze from the heat.

6. Invert the pan to unmold the cake. Set it on a rack over a sheet of wax paper. While the cake is still warm, brush all over with the hot citrus glaze. Let cool completely. Wrap in plastic wrap and then overwrap with aluminum foil. Let the cake stand in a cool place for at least 1 day before slicing. The cake will improve overnight and will keep, tightly wrapped, for up to 1 week.
—*Janet Fletcher*

Butter Pecan Loaf

Makes 1 Loaf Cake

1 stick (4 ounces) unsalted
  butter
¾ cup pecans
2 cups all-purpose flour
1½ teaspoons baking powder
¼ teaspoon salt
4 eggs
1¼ cups sugar
⅔ cup heavy cream
6 tablespoons Cognac or
  other brandy

1. Preheat the oven to 325°. Butter a 9-by-5-by-3-inch loaf pan. Line the bottom of the pan with wax paper. Butter the paper, then dust the sides and the bottom of the pan with flour; tap out any excess.

2. In a large skillet, melt the butter over moderately low heat. Add the pecans and cook, stirring, until the nuts are a rich brown, about 5 minutes.

3. Drain the nuts in a strainer placed over a measuring cup to catch the butter. Toss to remove as much butter as possible. (There should be ½ cup of melted butter in the cup; if there isn't, add enough melted butter to measure ½ cup.) Let the butter cool to room temperature and reserve. Coarsely chop the toasted pecans and reserve.

4. In a medium bowl, sift together the flour, baking powder and salt.

5. In a large mixer bowl, beat the eggs on medium speed to break them up. Gradually add the sugar on medium-high speed and beat until light and fluffy, about 6 minutes. Add the cream and beat to blend.

6. Reduce the speed to low, add the flour mixture and beat until just blended; do not overmix. Scrape down the sides of the bowl. Add the Cognac and the chopped pecans and stir to blend. Fold in the reserved melted butter until there are no streaks.

7. Pour the batter into the prepared pan. Bake for 1½ hours, or until a cake tester inserted into the center comes out clean. Let the cake cool in the pan for 10 minutes, then unmold and finish cooling on a wire rack. When completely cooled, wrap in plastic wrap and overwrap with aluminum foil. Let the cake stand in a cool place for at least 1 day before slicing. The cake will keep, tightly wrapped, for up to 1 week.
—*Janet Fletcher*

Chocolate Brownies Loaf

This fudgy cake is studded with walnuts and subtly flavored with coffee. For best results, use Dutch-process cocoa; it is darker and more mellow than other cocoa powders.

Makes 1 Loaf Cake

1¼ cups all-purpose flour
1¼ cups sugar
6 tablespoons Dutch-process cocoa powder
1 tablespoon instant coffee granules
1 teaspoon baking soda
¾ teaspoon salt
1 cup toasted walnuts, coarsely chopped
1½ cups sour cream
1 egg
1½ teaspoons vanilla extract
4 tablespoons unsalted butter, melted and cooled

1. Preheat the oven to 350°. Butter a 9-by-5-by-3-inch loaf pan. Line the bottom of the pan with wax paper. Butter the paper, then dust the bottom and sides of the pan with flour; tap out any excess.

2. In a medium bowl, stir together the flour, sugar, cocoa, coffee, baking soda and salt until well blended. Stir in the nuts.

3. In a large bowl, whisk together the sour cream, egg, vanilla and melted butter. Add the dry ingredients to the liquid ingredients and stir with a rubber spatula until just blended. Pour the batter into the prepared pan and spread evenly.

4. Bake the cake for 1 hour and 10 minutes, or until a cake tester inserted into the center comes out clean. Leave the cake in the pan and allow it to cool on a rack for 10 minutes, then unmold and finish cooling on the rack. Wrap carefully in plastic wrap, then overwrap with aluminum foil. Let the cake stand in a cool place for at least 1 day before slicing. The cake will keep, tightly wrapped, for up to 10 days.
—*Janet Fletcher*

index

contributors

Jean Anderson is a food writer and the author of 17 cookbooks, including most recently *Jean Anderson's Sin-Free Desserts* (Doubleday) and the upcoming *German Cooking Today* (HarperCollins).

Lee Bailey is a designer and cookbook author currently working on several books: *Cooking for Friends, Lee Bailey's Tomatoes, Lee Bailey's New Orleans* and *Lee Bailey's Corn*.

Melanie Barnard is a restaurant critic, food writer and co-author (with Brooke Dojny) of *Parties!* (HarperCollins).

Julia Child, renowned cookbook author, television personality and co-founder of The American Institute of Wine and Food, will be writing a *Food & Wine* column called "Julia's Favorite."

Peggy Cullen is a baker, candymaker and food writer.

Marion Cunningham is a cookbook author, columnist and cooking teacher.

Janet Fletcher is a food and wine writer and the author of *More Vegetables, Please* (Harlow & Ratner).

Jim Fobel is a food writer and the author of numerous books, including *The Whole Chicken Cookbook* (Ballantine) and *Diet Feasts* (Doubleday).

Camille Glenn is a food columnist and the author of *The Heritage of Southern Cooking* (Workman).

Joyce Goldstein is chef/owner of Square One in San Francisco and the author of *The Mediterranean Kitchen* and *Back to Square One: Old World Food in a New World Kitchen* (both from Morrow).

Doric Greenspan is a food writer and the author of *Sweet Times, Simple Desserts for Every Occasion* and a work in progress tentatively titled *Chocolate Through and Through* (both from Morrow).

Ken Haedrich is a food writer and the author of *Home for the Holidays* and *Ken Haedrich's Country Baking* (both from Bantam).

Ken Hom is a cooking teacher and cookbook author.

Quinith Janssen is a food writer.

Susan Shapiro Jaslove is a food writer and recipe developer.

Nancy Harmon Jenkins is a food historian and writer currently working on a history of American ethnic groups and their foods, to be published by Bantam Books in 1993.

Ann Kischner is the owner and pastry chef at The Shoalwater in Seaview, Washington.

Leslie Land is a food writer living in Maine.

Susan Herrmann Loomis is a journalist and the author of *The Great American Seafood Cookbook* and *Farmhouse Cookbook* (both from Workman). She is currently working on a book entitled *Seafood Celebrations* due out in 1993.

Sheila Lukins is the food editor for *Parade Magazine* and the author of *The New Basics, The Silver Palate Cookbook* and an upcoming international cookbook (all from Workman).

Nick Malgieri is the director of the baking program at Peter Kump's New York Cooking School and is the author of *Great Italian Desserts* (Little, Brown) and *Nick Malgieri's Perfect Pastry*. He is currently working on a complete guide to baking to be published by HarperCollins in 1993.

Lydie Marshall is a food writer, cooking teacher (A La Bonne Cocotte, New York City) and the author of *Cooking with Lydie Marshall* (Knopf) and *A Passion for Potatoes* (HarperCollins).

Elin McCoy and **John Frederick Walker** are contributing wines and spirits editors for *Food & Wine* and the authors of *Thinking About Wine* (Simon and Schuster).

Michael McLaughlin is a food writer and the author of *Back of the Box Gourmet* (Simon and Schuster), (as co-author) *The El Paso Chile Company's Texas Border Cookbook* (Morrow) and the upcoming *52 Meat Loaves* (Simon and Schuster). He is currently working on *Wild About Mushrooms* (Chronicle) and *The Secret Ingredient: More Recipes from the Back of the Box Gourmet* (Simon and Schuster).

Linda Merinoff is a cooking teacher and the author of *Gingerbread* (Fireside).

Joan Nathan is a food writer and the author of *An American Folklife Cookbook, The Jewish Holiday Kitchen* (both from Schocken Books). She is currently working on *Jewish Food in America* for Knopf.

Jacques Pépin is a cooking teacher, newspaper columnist and the author of ten cookbooks, the most recent of which are *Cuisine Economique* and *The Short-Cut Cook* (both from Morrow); and *Today's*

Gourmet and *Today's Gourmet II* (KQED, Inc.), the companion books to the first two seasons of his current PBS series of the same name. He willl also be contributing a regular column to *Food & Wine* entitled "Jacques' Favorite."

Philippa Pullar is a food writer and cookbook author who lives in London.

Stephan Pyles is chef and co-owner of Routh Street Cafe in Dallas. He is also the author of the upcoming *The New Texas Cuisine* due from Doubleday in 1993.

Richard Sax is a food writer and cookbook author. He is currently working on a book called *Old-Fashioned Desserts*.

Gordon A. Sinclair is the owner of Gordon restaurant in Chicago.

Barbara Tropp is chef/owner of China Moon Cafe in San Francisco and the author of *The Modern Art of Chinese Cooking* (Morrow) and *The China Moon Cookbook* (Workman).

Jean-Georges Vongerichten is the chef and co-owner of JoJo in New York City and the author of *Simple Cuisine* (Prentice-Hall).

Patricia Wells is the restaurant critic for *The International Herald Tribune* in Paris and the author of *Simply French* (Morrow), *Bistro Cooking, The Food Lover's Guide to France* and *The Food Lover's Guide to Paris* (all from Workman). She is currently working on a book for Morrow called *Trattoria Cooking*.

We would also like to thank the following individuals and restaurants for their contributions to *Food & Wine* and to this book:

Nancy Christy; Michele Evans; Pearl Byrd Foster; The Four Seasons (New York City); **Fraunces Tavern** (New York City); **Monique Guillaume; Michael James; Laure Cantor Kimpton; Silvio Pinto; Joanna Pruess; Sally Scoville; Martha Stewart.**

And the members of the *Food & Wine* staff, past and present:

Mimi Ruth Brodeur; Jim Brown; Bob Chambers; Anne Disrude; Cathy Fredman; Marcia Kiesel; John Robert Massie; Maria Piccolo; Warren Picower; W. Peter Prestcott; Tracey Seaman; Diana Sturgis; Jessica Weber; Elizabeth Woodson; Susan Wyler; Tina Ujlaki.

PHOTO CREDITS

Cover: Dennis Galante. **Pages 33-36:** Jerry Simpson. **Pages 53-56 and 73-76:** Mark Thomas. **Pages 93-96:** Jerry Simpson. **Pages 113-115:** Karen Capucilli. **Page 116:** Michael Weiss. **Pages 133-136:** Michael Skott. **Pages 153-156:** Dennis Galante. **Pages 173-176: Dennis Gottlieb. Pages 193-196:** Maria Robledo. **Pages 213-216:** Mark Thomas. **Pages 233-236:** Elizabeth Watt. **Pages 269-271:** Steven Mark Needham. **Page 272:** Jerry Simpson.